PONTIFICAL INSTITUTE OF MEDIAEVAL STUDIES

STUDIES AND TEXTS

22

LAND AND PEOPLE
IN
HOLYWELL-CUM-NEEDINGWORTH

STRUCTURES OF TENURE AND PATTERNS OF SOCIAL ORGANIZATION
IN AN EAST MIDLANDS VILLAGE
1252-1457

BY

EDWIN BREZETTE DEWINDT

TORONTO

PONTIFICAL INSTITUTE OF MEDIAEVAL STUDIES

1972

ISBN O-88844-022-7

PRINTED BY UNIVERSA — WETTEREN (BELGIUM)

For Anne

Who knows the reason why

TABLE OF CONTENTS

PREFACE

The path of success for modern science has been to probe ever more deeply the secrets of cellular life. While the day has hopefully long passed where it is necessary to warn scholars of the danger of confusing methodologies from the natural with those of the 'human' sciences, the dynamics of the former is such that there is still to be found a certain analogical value in the comparative use of concepts and terms. So social historians still speak of the family as the basic cell of society. And, the area of interest here, scholars speak of the village as the fundamental grouping of peasant civilizations. To traditional mediaeval historiography it will come as a surprise that the village could be a vital source of civilizations. And, it must be admitted, the case is still *sub judice*. However, the place of village studies looms so large in modern social history and social science, and first probings have established possibilities for the mediaeval historian too, such that further investigation is urgently required.

The past generation has witnessed beginnings of the application of methods developed by studies of primitive communities of the non-western world to the surviving historical communities of the west. The pioneer study of the Irish villager in the late 1930's has been succeeded by studies of French, Greek, Turkish and Welsh villagers over the 1960's. Not surprisingly, this new current of research has excited the historian to consider the possibilities for fresh scientific investigation into the village and small community. It still remains to be established whether the historical village can be studied in anything like that intimacy possible to the anthropological and sociological investigation of the contemporary village.

A number of recent articles on the court rolls of mediaeval English villages have probed the possibility for a more immediate if not more intimate investigation of village life. This is the first volume of a series of monographs to be published on English villagers in the fourteenth and fifteenth centuries. Since the vitality of village life can only be properly studied by the fullest possible recognition of an involved community structure and the detail of individual action, this analysis of villagers imposes its own form on the style of the historiographer. Furthermore, as it is the first volume of the series, descriptions of methods and findings have been deliberately discursive, and with no space available to edit texts, the variety to be found in original spellings and texts has not been fully normalized.

Selected as an experiment rather than a model, Holywell-cum-Needing-worth did not in the final analysis offer information on villagers as fully coherent as may be found in records for other villages now under investigation. Nevertheless, the study does perform an invaluable transitional task on two points : first, by indicating the different perspective obtainable on traditional problems of survival and wealth as experiences of specific villagers rather than impersonal groups ; and secondly, by distilling data for further exploitation by the student of the family and smaller community.

J. A. RAFTIS.

ACKNOWLEDGEMENTS

IN the course of researching and writing this study of Holywell-cum-Needingworth, I have received the help of many persons and institutions. Among the latter, I am especially indebted to the British Museum and the Public Record Office, London, for permission to make extensive use of the account and court rolls of Ramsey Abbey upon which the bulk of this work is based ; to the Northampton Record Office and the Norwich Public Library, for the use of additional Ramsey materials on deposit in their collections; to the Huntingdonshire Record Office, and especially Mr. P. G. M. Dickinson; and to the University of Detroit.

Unfortunately, it is impossible to thank all the persons — teachers, colleagues and friends — who have helped over the years to bring this study to fruition, but there are some whose contributions have been so valuable that they must be recorded. Foremost is Professor J. Ambrose Raftis, C.S.B., of the Pontifical Institute of Mediaeval Studies, Toronto, a man of rare insights, a remarkable teacher who has the special gift of opening doors that students seldom dreamed existed. It is he who originally conceived the idea for this study and whose constant direction, suggestions and criticisms made it a reality, although, naturally, the responsibility for errors or shortcomings is mine alone.

I am indebted also to my parents, Joseph and Edwina DeWindt, for their confidence and understanding during four intensive years of work, as well as for their gift to me of the love of history; to Dr. Stuart F. C. Niermeier, of the University of Toronto, for being a sounding-board for ideas in fruition; to Mr. Henry A. Schankula, of the University of Kentucky, for invaluable assistance in preparing statistical materials; to Professor Michael M. Sheehan, C.S.B., of the Pontifical Institute, for his encouragement; to Miss Mary Patricia Hogan, of St. Francis Xavier University, Antigonish, Nova Scotia, and Miss Ellen Wedemeyer, of Loyola University, Montreal, for their ready willingness to share with me findings from their own research into the mediaeval village. I would also like to thank Fr. James P. Morro, C.S.B., Director of Publications of the Pontifical Institute, who helped make the final transition from typescript to printed page seem easier than it was, and Miss Beryl Wells, who, together with Professor Raftis, double-checked my proofreading and thereby saved me from several disasters.

One person remains, to whom I am especially indebted: my wife, Anne, who, during the final stages of getting the manuscript ready for the press and the correcting of proofs, shrewdly refused to have anything to do with preparing the Index, and who sustained me throughout with her good humour and a continuous supply of cheese sandwiches.

29 September
The Feast of St. Michael,
University of Detroit.

LIST OF TABLES AND APPENDICES

I

TABLES

II

APPENDICES

LIST OF ABBREVIATIONS

(Tables and Appendices)

Agricultural

a	=	acre
c	=	cotland
cr	=	croft
m	=	messuage
pl	=	placea
r	=	rod
sel	=	selion
v	=	virgate

Monetary

d	=	pence
ob	=	half-penny
s	=	shilling
q	=	farthing

Titular

AK	=	akerman
BD	=	beadle
BF	=	bailiff
C. Aut	=	Custos Autumpni
C. Camp	=	Custos Camporum
CN	=	constable
CR	=	collector redditus
HY	=	hayward
J	=	juror
P. Aut	=	prepositus autumpni
R	=	reeve
T	=	taster

Actions

ale	=	brewing infraction
ast	=	assault
cl	=	claim
deflt	=	default
extra	=	off the manor
f. cl	=	false claim
defam	=	defamation
h & c	=	hue and cry
hamsok	=	breaking and entering
insult	=	defamation through insult
l.c.	=	license of concord
non hab	=	failure to appear or present
non op	=	failure to work
prop	=	property case
s.l.	=	*sine licentia*, either marriage or off the manor without license
sang	=	assault to the drawing of blood
tr	=	trespass
resc	=	rescue: the recovery of distrained items from an official

INTRODUCTION

Descriptions or studies of mediaeval English rural society have long been devoted to detailed examinations of manorial institutions and economy or to the legal disabilities of servile peasants considered as a class. Much attention has consequently been given to questions of manorial administration, agricultural practices and productivity[1] and the limitations or resstrictions of villeinage.[2] Within the past 30 years, however, increasing attention has been paid to the mediaeval English village as more than an adjunct to a manor or manorial complex and to its peasant population as more than economic units or legal types. Often associated with the pioneering study of Professor G. C. Homans,[3] it is a historiography that has advanced — largely through the efforts of W. O. Ault, G. Duby and J. A. Raftis — to embrace comparative studies of village and peasant institutions — both public and private — and has contributed heavily to the present awareness and understanding of the human dimensions of village life in the Middle Ages.[4] Both approaches are extremely important

---

[1] For example, in terms of estate complexes or regional studies, See M. Chibnall (Morgan), *The English Lands of the Abbey of Bec* (Oxford, 1946); N. Denholm-Young, *Seignorial Administration in England* (London, 1937); E. A. Kosminsky, *Studies in the Agrarian History of England in the Thirteenth Century* (Oxford, 1956); F. M. Stenton, *Types of Manorial Structure in the Northern Danelaw* (Oxford, 1910); A. E. Levett, *Studies in Manorial History* (Oxford, 1938); R. H. Hilton, *The Economic Development of Some Leicestershire Estates in the Fourteenth and Fifteenth Centuries* (Oxford, 1957); J. A. Raftis, *The Estates of Ramsey Abbey* (Toronto, 1957). Local studies have included: N.S.B. and C. C. Gras, *The Economic and Social History of an English Village* (Cambridge, Mass. 1930); F. J. Davenport, *The Economic Development of a Norfolk Manor* (Cambridge, 1906); A. E. Levett, *The Black Death on the Estates of the Bishopric of Winchester* (Oxford, 1916); F. W. Maitland, "History of a Cambridgeshire Manor", *Collected Papers*, II (Cambridge, 1911); W. G. Hoskins, *The Midland Peasant* (London, 1957); P. D. A. Harvey, *A Medieval Oxfordshire Village: Cuxham, 1240 to 1400* (Oxford, 1965).

[2] See, for example: D. C. Douglas, *The Social Structure of Medieval East Anglia* (Oxford, 1927); F. W. Maitland, *Domesday Book and Beyond* (Cambridge, 1897); Paul Vinogradoff, *Villainage in England* (Oxford, 1892); *English Society in the Eleventh Century* (Oxford, 1908); *The Growth of the Manor*, 2nd. rev. ed. (London, 1911); and A. J. Poole, *Obligations of Society in the XII and XIII Centuries* (Oxford, 1946).

[3] See G. C. Homans, *English Villagers of the Thirteenth Century* (Boston, 1941).

[4] Professor W. O. Ault has devoted many years to examining the institution of the village by-law in mediaeval England, the results of a lifetime of study having recently appeared in *Open-Field Husbandry and the Village Community* (Philadelphia, 1965). Georges Duby, following in the footsteps of Marc Bloch — and dealing with the Continent as well as England — combines

and valuable in extending knowledge of mediaeval rural England, and especially of the mediaeval English peasant, but each differs widely in its basic attitude towards the peasant. Whereas the former tends to reveal him in relationship to the manor, or, more precisely, to the demesne economy of the manor as well as to the King's court and is less immediately concerned with his personal identity, the latter reveals him primarily in relationship to his social community, to his family and to his neighbors, and must, in consequence, take greater cognizance of his personal identity. There is, of course, a continuing need for studies of the administration of individual manors, estate complexes and local agrarian economies as well as of problems of legal status in mediaeval England. There is also a continuing need for further comparative studies of more personal and village-oriented institutions. But, even more, there is now a very real need — indeed, even a very real demand — to carry the village-directed historiography one step further and to investigate, as much as sources allow, the social structures, human relationships and individual peasants of one specific locality, in order that the variety, diversity and personal individuality of peasant society may be realized in a way prohibited by more broadly-based and general comparative studies of village institutions. Such local studies are already well familiar to students of anthropology and sociology in contemporary societies, where the individual "village study" has become almost a commonplace.[5] Nor is there now any serious question that such a study of a *mediaeval* community is within the realm of possibility, although only a generation ago it would have been considered a matter of extreme doubt. Specifically, the methodology of the economic,

a thorough mastery of economics and agrarian problems with a sensitivity for the sociological and anthropological aspects of peasant society in *L'economie rurale: la vie des campagnes dans l'occident medieval*, 2 vols. (Paris, 1962). J. A. Raftis, drawing upon extant court rolls for several Ramsey Abbey villages from the late thirteenth to the early fifteenth century, has provided an exhaustive and provocative study of many aspects of peasant and village institutions — from inheritance customs to local administrative and governmental practices — in *Tenure and Mobility* (Toronto, 1964), and has further examined other aspects of village society in three recent comparative studies — "Social Structures in Five East Midland Villages", *Economic History Review*, 2nd. series, Vol. XVIII (No. 1, 1965), pp. 83-100; "The Concentration of Responsibility in Five Villages", *Mediaeval Studies*, Vol. XXVIII (1966), pp. 92-118; "Peasant Mobility and Freedom in Mediaeval England," *Report of the Canadian Historical Association* (1965), pp. 117-30 — and one local study: "Changes in an English Village after the Black Death," *Mediaeval Studies*, XXIX (1967), pp. 158-77.

[5] See, for example: Isabell Emmett, *A North Wales Village* (London, 1964); James Littlejohn, *Westrigg: The Sociology of a Cheviot Parish* (London, 1963); W. Williams, *A West Country Village Ashworthy: Family, Kinship and Land* (London, 1963); and Margaret Stacey, *Tradition and Change: A Study of Bambury* (Oxford, 1960).

administrative and legal historian of rural England has traditionally
— and quite properly — involved the amassing, tabulation and analysis
of vast quantities of minute local details. The staggering investigations
of a Thorold Rodgers, for example, into wages and prices depended on
the availability of hundreds of such items being recorded in manorial
account rolls, while the Beveridge studies of corn yields were similarly
founded on a veritable mountain of statistics gathered from the same
sources. As recently as 30 years ago, the student of the mediaeval peasantry,
on the other hand, was fortunate if his manorial accounts or other administrative documents even gave him the names of the tenants of a manor.
When the time came for making statements about the inner workings
of peasant society, about village life, he could do little more than reach
for his well-thumbed copy of Chaucer or Langland and present the peasant
as seen through the eyes of poetic genius. If he followed the former, the
resulting picture was at least guaranteed of being entertaining. If he
followed the latter, it was certain of being as curious and enigmatic as
if painted by Hieronymus Bosch. But in either case, the search for a means
of letting the peasant speak directly for himself had to be abandoned and
reliance placed on outside witnesses. Today, of course, the direct voice
of the mediaeval English peasant has still not been found. No discoveries
have been made of hitherto unknown collections of peasant "Paston
Letters", and no regiment of village Margery Kempes has suddenly come
to light. Nevertheless, the student today is perhaps better equipped to
come closer to the individual peasant than at any previous time, primarily
because of the recent development of techniques for the exploitation of
the information contained in manor court rolls.[6] No longer must the
investigator despair of obtaining detailed information on his subject and
envy the economist his account rolls. Through patient — and often
wearisome hours — with his court rolls, he can amass a body of details
on the activities of individual peasants in a variety of relationships and
contexts. Thus, in this present study, aggregative analysis of 53 court
rolls from the late thirteenth to the middle of the fifteenth century results,
first, in an index of over 1000 separate cards, each containing data on
individual peasants ranging in number from one to over 50 items for
specific persons. The process whereby such information is obtained involves
the notation of every time a specific peasant name occurs in the court

---

[6] The realization of the potential of court rolls is largely the result of the labours of Professor
J. A. Raftis and also Professor W. O. Ault both of whom have been able to base major studies
of village life and institutions on court roll evidence alone. See Raftis, *Tenure and Mobility*, and
Ault, *Open-Field Husbandry and the Village Community*.

rolls, together with the context of the entry. As a result, the individual peasant can be seen in a wide variety of situations: as tenant, parent, child, husband or wife, official, pledge, craftsman or transgressor. To give a practical example, the Bercar'/Shepperd family of Needingworth shall be cited. Between 1288 and 1457, the names of 14 members of the family are supplied by local court rolls. About two of them, only one bit of information is found : Galfridus Bercar' was reported as having been engaged to the villager Sarra Beneyt in 1288 without license, and Alice Shepperd was fined twopence for trespassing in the woods in 1375. For others, however, there is more variety. Thus, for Walter Bercar' the following details are known from court rolls:

> 1288: 12 d. fine for assaulting and insulting Radulph, son of Henry Prepositus.
> — Out of tithing, fined 6 d. and threatened with banishment from the village unless he put himself in tithing.
> — Subject of a hue and cry raised by Radulph Prepositus, for which he was fined 6 d.
> — Leased a small parcel of land from the villager Roysea le Franklyn.
> — Fathered a child — out of wedlock — by Katerina Franklyn, daughter of Roysea (above).
> 1294: Subject of a hue and cry — with his wife — raised by John Clerk.
> — Fined 6 d. for failure to prosecute a charge against Walter Gray.
> — Failed to be prosecuted by Walter Gray.

To cite another family — the Lawemans — the following details are found on just one member alone, William Laweman:

> 1307: Noted as butcher for village.
> 1318: Pledge for Matilda Colyn. Owed a debt by Nicholas Scot.
> 1322: Juror for the view of frankpledge.
> — Fails to be presented in court by Robert Gerold, his pledge in an earlier case.
> — Raises the hue and cry on William Palmere.
> — Fails to be presented in court by William le Eyr.
> — Trepasses in the demesne.
> — Pledge for Nicholas Godfrey.
> 1326: Juror for the view of frankpledge.
> — Ale-taster for Needingworth.
> 1328: Pledge for Matilda Bundeleg.
> — Unresolved license of concord with William Bundeleg.
> — Juror for the view.
> 1332: Juror for the view.
> — Juror for the *curia*.

Admittedly, such information does not, when drawn together, constitute a full biography of the peasant in question, but it provides detailed record of some of his activities in the village. In the case of William Laweman, for example, he can be seen in several contexts, performing different functions: as a butcher, as a personal pledge, as a lender of money, and as an official. It tells the student something about William Laweman as an individual — and, with like information on over 800 other persons, it distinguishes him from his neighbors; in short, secures his own identity. Such details certainly tell the investigator more about his peasants as persons than does a simple list of tenants, or, for that matter, Geoffrey Chaucer. In addition, once the results of the process of aggregative analysis have been gathered together and indexed, they may be put into a broader context, reconstituted in terms of village structures, institutions and networks of relationships in ways that shall be evident from a reading of this present study, especially Chapters III and IV, which are essentially the products of first, aggregative, and then the reconstitutive analysis of local court rolls. Here simple tabulation plays a major role. In examining such a question as the exercise of juror responsibility, for example, by referring to the card index on individual peasants, the names of all persons known to have served as jurors are first obtained. Their names are totalled for the number of men serving as jurors over the years, while, by directing attention to the individual surnames, the number of family groups thereby represented is also obtained. Then, by adding up the times an individual served as a juror — as well as the number of times each member of a separate family group served — a total is obtained of the number of men in a specific family who served as jurors, as well as how frequent and consistent the actual service was — both for the man and the family. It is a short step from there to compare families with one another, and, after the process has been repeated for every known person and family group in the village, to assess the relative degree of involvement in such an activity of individuals and families. To further explore this point then, the relationship of the exercise of juror responsibility to questions of residence and status can be weighed. Regarding the former, jury families can be compared to lists made of long-term and short-term resident families — a list compiled by taking a particular surname clearly representing a family group and noting the first year it appeared in the records and the last, thereby giving a rough estimate of the number of years a family remained settled. Finally, since account rolls from the late fourteenth century further supply tenurial information, including the names of local land-holders and their tenements, it is possible to discover, first, if specific jurors and juror families were involved in the customary structure of the manor, and, secondly, if so, to what extent they were involved. Admittedly a perhaps obvious method, nevertheless it is by just such a process of extensive tabulation, of the laborious counting of names and entries,

cross-indexing and comparisons, that the student is able to assess questions
of official responsibility, family settlement, suretyship relations and the
climate of non-conformity (e.g. by the simple counting of the number
of trespasses, assaults, etc. in the court rolls, noting the parties involved
and, again, by comparing the persons thus named with lists of known
officials, tenants and residents, and by comparing the number of such
acts from decade to decade or half-century to half-century) prevailing
in the village. If an arduous method, it is nevertheless a workable and
fruitful one, as shall be seen from the studies contained in Chapters III
and IV.

Consequently, because of the demand for a truly local and intensive
study of peasant society in mediaeval England, and because of the practi-
cability of actually conducting such a study through the exploitation
of local sources — and primarily of court rolls — for detailed and statistical
information, the present investigation has been undertaken, in an attempt
to disclose and examine the peasant population of one local community
from the latter thirteenth to the middle of the fifteenth century in terms
of the peasants' relationships to their manor, their village and to each
other. Moreover, since the veritable heartland of early manorial studies
was the English midlands, and especially the sprawling estate complex of
Ramsey abbey, it is fitting to return to that region and to that lordship
for the object of this initial investigation. It was here that the foundations
were laid for the scholarship of the "classic" or "typical" manorial unit
— in those days before the works of Kosminsky, Postan and Hilton demonstrated and confirmed that there really was no such thing. It is here also
that the coincidence of the manor and village was most often found, where
the two institutions formed — in Harvey's words — "a single and complete
economic unit and social community"[7] — and where, consequently, the
object of study is readily delimited and confined.

The community chosen for the present study is the Ramsey manor and
village of Holywell-cum-Needingworth. Surviving to the present day,
it is located some 10 miles south of Ramsey and two and a half miles east
of St. Ives at the south-eastern corner of Huntingdonshire in the old Hur-
stingstone Hundred and is separated from the Cambridgeshire border
by the waters of the river Ouse, which forms both its southern and eastern
boundaries. The mediaeval community — as does the modern parish —
consisted of two settlements forming one administrative, economic and
social unit: Holywell, situated on the river bank proper, and Needingworth,

---

[7] *A Medieval Oxfordshire Village: Cuxham, 1240 to 1400*, p. 9. Hereafter cited "Cuxham".

a little to the north and separated from the former only by the common fields lying between them. The soil upon which it rests is made up of Oxford and Ampthill clays, with admixtures of alluvium peat and valley gravel.[8] Up through the second half of the eighteenth century much of its territory was still occupied by fen — the entire eastern half, for example — while its south-western corner, lapped by the waters of the Ouse, was meadow,[9] with the arable fields being confined to the central, western and north-western sections of the region. The two settlements were joined — and still are — by a road running north and south through the centre of the common field, named the "Mill Road" (at least from the eighteenth century) for the windmill — mentioned as early as 1279 — situated almost at the mid-point of the length of the road. Holywell itself derived its name from the well and spring found in the churchyard near the eastern end of the village, at the point where the land steeply drops and becomes meadow.[10] Needingworth seems to have been derived from "enclosure of Hnydda's people".[11] The locality itself appears to have experienced early settlement — possibly prehistoric but most certainly by the Roman era.[12] Both Holywell and Needingworth were acquired by the newly — founded abbey of Ramsey in the late tenth century, surely prior to the year 1000.[13]

---

[8] *The Victoria History of the Counties of England: Huntingdonshire.* Ed. William Page, Granville Proby (London, 1926), I, pp. 6-7, 13-16; II, pp. 175-88. Hereafter cited "VCH. Hunts."

[9] This information is largely based on a map of Holywell-cum-Needingworth drawn up for the Duke of Manchester in 1764 and now preserved in the Huntingdon County Record Office. I am deeply grateful to Mr. P. G. M. Dickinson, County Archivist, for making a photographic reproduction of this map available to me.

Because of financial limitations, it has been found impossible to include a reproduction of this — or any other — map in the present study.

[10] *VCH. Hunts.* II, p. 178. See also A. Mawer and F. M. Stenton, *The Place-Names of Bedfordshire and Huntingdonshire* (Cambridge, 1926), pp. 209-10. The name was variously spelled: "Haliwell, Haliwelle, Halywell, Halliwell, Hallywelle." Another Ramsey manor of the same name — consistently spelled "Hollewell" — is located in Bedfordshire and is not to be confused with the Hunts. Holywell-cum-Needingworth.

[11] See Mawer and Stenton, pp. 209-10. The name was variously spelled "Neddingewurda, Niddingworth, Nidingwrth, Niddyngworthe" in the Middle Ages.

[12] See *VCH. Hunts.* I, p. 217, 222; pp. 254-55; p. 266.

[13] There still remains some confusion as to the original grants to the abbey. Holywell was first mentioned in the late tenth century, when it belonged to a certain Athelstan Mannessone. He was a contemporary of the foundation of the abbey (*ca.* 970 — See J. A. Raftis, *The Estates of Ramsey Abbey: A Study in Economic Growth and Organization*, p. 1. Hereafter cited "Raftis, *Estates*" or "*Estates*".) and is remembered as one of its early benefactors in the years immediately following the initial endowments to the monastery through gift, exchange or purchase by St. Oswald and Aethelwin the Ealdorman (*Ibid.*, pp. 1-2; 6-9). That Holywell was one of his holdings is learned from a Latin version of an original Anglo-Saxon narrative preserved in the Ramsey *Chronicon*

By 1086, the manor itself was described in the Domesday Survey as
being assessed at nine hides, with two ploughs actually on the demesne

(i.e. *Chronicon Abbatiae Rameseiensis, a saeculo x. usque ad annum circiter 1200.* Ed. W. Dunn Macray.
Rolls Series, 83. London, 1886. Pp. 59-61. Hereafter cited "Chronicon"), in which it is described
"quomodo Aethelstanus Mannessone in vita sua de possessionibus suis et terris disposuit, et hoc
Ailwyno Aldermanno et caeteris amicis suis notum fecit, et quod post ejus obitum exinde factum
sit." (*Ibid.*, p. 59). According to this account, Athelstan, motivated by concern for his salvation,
granted Chatteris and Wold to the abbey. To his wife he gave four other holdings, including
Ellesworth, to be hers until her death, at which time they too were to pass to the monastery.
He also gave her Over and Holywell, to do with whatever she wished (*Ibid.*, pp. 59-60). Apparently,
however, someone in the Mannessone household was not especially pleased with these arrangements, because after his death it was related that his widow, on the advice of relatives ("parentum
inducta suggestione") and claiming a prior *viva voce* agreement with her husband, demanded
that the abbey permit her to freely possess Ellesworth and dispose of it as she wished (*Ibid.*, p. 60).
This the monks allowed, but with the provision that Slepe fall into their hands after the death
of her daughter, Alfwenna (*Ibid.*, p. 61). To this the widow agreed, and peace was made between
the two parties (*Ibid.*).
    From this narrative of Athelstan Mannessone's donations, the condition of Holywell seems
to be relatively clear. It was his, and he gave it to his wife, not the abbey. But a post-Conquest
list of Ramsey military fees and conventual manors, preserved in the Ramsey Cartulary, states
that the abbot held two plough-lands in Holywell in demesne "ex collatione Athelstani Mannesone."
(*Cartularium Monasterii de Rameseia*. Ed. W. H. Hart and Ponsonby A. Lyons. Rolls Series, 79.
London, 1884. Vol. I, p. 271. Hereafter cited "Carts") Since the *Chronicon* — or "Liber Bene-
factorum" as it was sometimes called — was a veritable *apologia* for Ramsey's holdings and did
not record any such bequest by Athelstan Mannessone himself to the abbey, and since the post-
Conquest list referred to the plough-lands as coming "ex collatione Aethelstani," it is possible
that they had been granted to the abbey by his widow, who had Holywell to dispose of as she
wished, or — more likely — as there was no record of such a donation, she may have passed
the property on to the woman called Alfwara, who died in 1007 and was buried at Ramsey (*Carts.*
III, p. 167). She it was, described in the *Chronicon* as "genere nobilis sed fidei devotione nobilior,"
who bestowed many precious gifts upon the abbey and "terram de Haliwelle et ecclesiam de
Ellesworth, cujus erat advocata, cum quadam ejusdem manerii portione" (*Chronicon*, p. 84).
Whatever the final answer, however, Holywell was, by *ca.* 1000, in the possession of Ramsey
abbey, and shortly thereafter the monastery received the church of the vill in a bequest from
the presbyter Gode (*Ibid.*, p. 85: "Gode praeterea quidam, presbyter de Haliwelle, totam terram
quam tenuit simul cum ecclesia sua post dies suas Ramesensi coenobio assignavit.")
    The early disposition of Needingworth is likewise obscure. It was purchased from King Edgar
by St. Oswald for the price of two gold and relic-encrusted crucifixes in the early days of the
abbey's foundation, and it was described in the *Chronicon*'s account of the transaction as a "villa"
(p. 48). The transaction, however, has been the subject of some discussion. According to the
VCH (*Hunts.* II, p. 176) it was subsequently exchanged by St. Oswald for Kingston or Wistow
"and may have been part of the lands in Slepe bestowed on the abbey by Aethelstan Manneson
and confirmed by Edgar in 974, and may have been the 9 (sic) carucates of land in Holywell
which later are said to have been given to the abbey by Aethelstan Manneson." However, a
close examination of the language of the *Chronicon* tends to dispel this picture. To be sure, Oswald
did purchase Needingworth from the king for two crucifixes. It is also probable that he exchanged
it for Wistow (*Ibid.*, p. 49: "Pro qua itidem villam de Wystowe, quia ecclesiae Ramesensi vicinior

and supporting 26 *villani*.[14]

The manor and village complex survived the Norman Conquest relatively intact,[15] and by the early twelfth century, as a result of Abbot Reginald's

accesu magis competens erat et recessu, a memorato rege in escambiam accepit, acceptam Deo et Sancto Benedicto in perpetuam solemniter traddidit haereditatem.") But it appears that Oswald then took steps to regain Needingworth. The chronicler praises, in general terms, his wisdom in that he redeemed Needingworth for the church and three hides of Gomechester, assigning it to the monastery. ("Provida autem antecessorum nostrorum sagacitas, suspecta prudenter praecavens pericula, praedictam villam de Nidingworthe pro commutatione memoratae ecclesiae et trium hidarum de Gumecestria, ecclesiae Ramesensi in funicularem haereditatis perpetuae sortem redemit." *Chronicon*, p. 49.) Granted that the Latin of the text may not be the clearest, still the subject of "redemit" is more likely Oswald than King Edgar, since Oswald's actions were those which governed the sentences preceding this passage. Consequently, despite the misgivings of the compilers of the VCH, it seems best to let the *Chronicon* account stand, and consider Needingworth as having entered into the Ramsey complex in the late tenth century, primarily through the actions of St. Oswald.

[14] The Domesday of Huntingdonshire, edited by F. M. Stenton, may be found in *VCH. Hunts*. I, with the survey of Holywell on page 343.

"M. *In Haliewelle* the abbey of Ramsey has 9 hides (assessed) to the geld. There is land for 9 ploughs, and (the abbey has) land for 9 ploughs in demesne apart from the aforesaid hides. There are now 2 ploughs on the demesne, and (there are) 26 villeins and 3 bordars with 6 ploughs. There is a church and a priest, and (there are) 30 acres of meadow . Woodland for pannage 1 league in length and 1 in breadth. T.R.E. it was worth 8 li. and (it is worth the same) now. Aluuold has 1 hide of this land of the abbot, and has 1 plough and 3 bordars. It is worth 10 s."

For discussion of the probable fiscal character of hidage figures employed throughout the survey, see Stenton, *VCH. Hunts*. I, pp. 322-33. See also, R. Weldon-Finn, *Introduction to Domesday Book* (London, 1963), pp. 104-15.

There is no mention anywhere in the Huntingdonshire Domesday of Needingworth, but the fact that when, in the 1252 extent for the manor in which Needingworth is clearly included (*Carts*. I, p. 295 *et seq*.), the assessment for the vill was eight hides (one-half having been ceded to the Priory of St. Ives, 1102-7: *Carts*. II, pp. 214-15), it is not unlikely that Needingworth was contained in the Domesday description of Holywell.

H. C. Darby overlooks this omission of Needingworth altogether in his study of the geography of Huntingdonshire as based upon the Domesday information. See *The Domesday Geography of Eastern England* (Cambridge, 1952), pp. 315-21.

[15] Following the Conquest, Ramsey estates were not entirely free from encroachment by the invaders, but the Normans did not, as elsewhere, descend upon them like a pack of hungry wolves. (See Raftis, *Estates*, p. 23). The abbey was subject to the imposition of knights' fees, however, and although the assessment was only four knights, the abbey had more than that number on its estates by the early twelfth century. (See H. M. Chew, *The English Ecclesiastical Tenants-in-Chief and Knight Service* (Oxford, 1932), pp. 3-5, and supplemented by H. G. Richardson and G. O. Sayles, *The Governance of Mediaeval England* (Edinburgh, 1963), p. 66. See also *Carts*: I, p. 271; III, pp. 218-25; and Raftis, *Estates*, p. 25 *et seq*.) Holywell itself, however, appears to have escaped the full extent of alienations that could follow in the wake of such a policy. Indeed, its most serious period of alienation — involving the conversion of villeinage to freehold — occurred long after the Conquest, in the early thirteenth century. See *Infra*, Chapter I, pp. 32-37.

(1114-30) *divisio* of monastic properties,[16] it had assumed the status of a *conventus* manor, charged with the obligation of contributing regularly to the food supply of the monastery,[17] and it remained such until the abandonment of the food rent system after the Black Death.[18] Lastly, the period between the early twelfth century and the middle of the thirteenth century was generally one of final adjustments in the extent of territory and the confirmation of abbatial titles to properties in Holywell-cum-Needingworth.[19] By 1252 — the date of the first surviving integral extent for the manor[20] and the point of departure for the present study — the manor had reached a point of firm definition: neither its disposition nor size would undergo any radical or major changes for the remainder of the Middle Ages, with its lordship remaining intact until the Dissolution and its territorial extent remaining virtually unaltered to the present day.[21]

Holywell-cum-Needingworth was, then, by the middle of the thirteenth century a village of ancient origin coterminous with a manor whose lordship had been continuous from the eleventh century. Situated at what was a popular fording spot of the river Ouse and only a little over two miles

[16] For a discussion of the *divisio* policy of Abbot Reginald, whereby certain manors were reserved for fulfiling the material needs of the monastic community and others set aside to allow the abbot to acquit his feudal obligations, see Raftis, *Estates*, pp. 33-37.

[17] Holywell was charged with the obligation of a half-farm and was normally included in the returns with the full-farm manor of Slepe. For details on the nature of the system of food farms, see *Carts*. III, pp. 160-69; also Raftis, *Estates*, Chapter III (pp. 61-96) and Appendix B, pp. 309-13.

[18] See Raftis, *Estates*, p. 253.

[19] Since the subject of the present study is essentially the village society of Holywell-cum-Needingworth from the late thirteenth to the middle of the fifteenth century, and not the territorial growth of the manor, no attempt has been made here to detail the process between 1100 and 1250 whereby the abbey gained a virgate here or a tenement there in Holywell or Needingworth. The relevant materials — charters and confirmations of grants to Ramsey — can be found in the Cartulary, but in the last analysis they tell very little of peasant society but are rather of more concern to the student of the growth of Ramsey's lordship or of the purely territorial development of the estates.

[20] An earlier extent for Holywell, which can be dated *ca.* 1160 (See Raftis, *Estates*, Appendix A, pp. 305-8) and is found printed in the Ramsey Cartulary (Vol. III, pp. 281-85), has been shown by Reginald Lennard to belong only partially to Holywell, the bulk of the extent being a description of the manor of Lawshall in Suffolk. See "An Unidentified Twelfth-Century Customal of Lawshall (Suffolk). *English Historical Review*, Vol. 51 (1936), pp. 104-7.

[21] The acreage of the parish in 1926 — the date of the VCH description — was given as 2, 911, which included vast expanses of territory previously occupied by fen (i.e. at least through 1764). For further amplification of this point, see *infra*, Chapter I, pp. 28-33 and especially p. 32, note ♯ 42.

to the east of the market town of St. Ives, it was by no means a community living outside the ebb and flow of mediaeval civilization — if, indeed, any village was — and it provides a good example of what was probably the more common type of mediaeval English experience: namely, a self-contained, local community with an agricultural orientation and submitted to the authority of a feudal lord. As such, it is worthy of study for extending historical understanding of English peasant society in the late Middle Ages.

However, there is yet another reason for investigating aspects of the social organization of Holywell-cum-Needingworth in the late Middle Ages, and it is essentially a matter of sources. It is surely a commonplace to state that the nature and scope of any historical investigation is dependent on and largely determined by the kind and amount of source material available to the student, but it nevertheless bears repetition. Thus, questions of manorial administration can only be studied if administrative records have survived. So too with aspects of demesne economy, lordship, territorial expansion, village and private institutions. If there are no records, there can be no investigation. In addition, the survival of relevant materials alone does not guarantee fruitful study, but rather the degree to which they have survived. The inner-workings of demesne economy, for example, cannot be examined if only a handful of demesne-oriented records has come down and then in no connected series but rather from isolated years scattered over a century or more. In short, the dependence of the student on his records is both very real and very heavy. They will determine what he can most profitably examine, the depth of his examination, and even the period in time to which he can direct his attention. In the case of Holywell-cum-Needingworth, the student is faced with a manor and village complex for which the overall survival of records — manorial, administrative, demesne, village and private — is by no means suffocating. For the manor, the number and quality of records of local administration and demesne production are anything but large and exhaustive. For village institutions and the social relationships obtaining within the community, the supply of records — primarily in the form of court rolls — is also far from ideal, but a sufficient number has come down from the late thirteenth through the middle of the fifteenth century to permit at least a tentative examination of selected aspects of local society, especially when supplemented by information contained in the few administrative and demesne sources surviving from the same period. In short, if not supplied with an ideal body of local materials, the student is at least provided with a workable one. A closer examination of such sources themselves will clarify this further.

The major sources for any meaningful study of Holywell-cum-Needing-worth are the account rolls and court rolls of the manor. None of the former has survived prior to the first decade of the fourteenth century, while the earliest court roll preserved is from 1288. These two bodies of material — coupled with a handful of private charters and copies of charters preserved either in the Public Record Office, the British Museum or the un-edited Ramsey Register kept at the Norwich Public Library and another unedited body of Ramsey-related materials at the North-amptonshire Record Office — provide the basis for knowledge of the structure and operation of the manor and the inhabitants and workings of the village in the late thirteenth century, and fourteenth century up to the 1390's. From the 1390's, the survival of an extensive body of cellarers' rolls from the Ramsey central administration together with the *gersuma* list of the abbey — or "Court Book" — covering the years 1397 to 1468 and both preserved in the British Museum, provide information on the local land transactions of Holywell residents for the first half of the fifteenth century and consequently serve as a supplement to account rolls and court rolls of the same period. In addition, the first truly detailed description of the manor, including the number and size of its tenements, the names of its major tenants and their obligations, is an extent of 5 February, 1252, which is found printed in the Cartulary of the abbey,[22] while a second — though less specific — description of the manor is afforded by the Hundred Roll survey of 1279, two versions of which are in existence: one edited by the Record Commission,[23] the other — in a fifteenth-century hand — unedited and found in the Public Record Office.[24] In short, it is only between the middle of the thirteenth and fifteenth centuries that the amount and type of source material for Holywell-cum-Needing-worth has survived to permit a workable local investigation of its village society and peasant inhabitants. Prior to the middle of the thirteenth century, Holywell materials are sparse and disjointed, ranging from a tentative survey of the manor in the Domesday of 1086 and a fragmented extent of *ca.* 1160[25] to scattered donations of properties to the abbey and confirmations of the same, and a few records of the central administration concerned with the food rent and conventual systems which mention the manor obliquely. Similarly, after the 1450's there have survived only

---

[22] *Carts.* I, pp. 293-305.

[23] *Rotuli Hundredorum tempore Henrici III et Edwardi I.* Ed. W. Illingworth, J. Caley. Record Commission: London, 1818. Vol. II, pp. 602-3.

[24] PRO SC 12-8-56.

[25] See *supra*, p. 10, note # 20.

five account rolls from the period 1451 to 1500, all clustered around the nine years from 1473 to 1482,[26] and only four court rolls from the period 1460-1500.[27] As a result, the most fruitful period for investigation is that from the latter thirteenth century to the middle of the fifteenth century, when the supply of local sources is extensive and varied enough to permit some study of the innerworkings of the community, and where extents, surveys, accounts, court rolls, *gersumae* lists, cellarers' rolls and private charters can be used as complements and supplements to each other in forming a picture of the identities, resources and activities of the inhabitants of Holywell-cum-Needingworth.

Despite the improved availability of sources for Holywell-cum-Needingworth between 1252 and 1457, however, the improvement is largely a relative one. Compared with the number and type of records preserved for the eleventh and twelfth centuries and for the fifteenth century after 1457, the student of Holywell from the 1250's to the 1450's is better equipped to examine the community than at any other time, but compared with the bulk of sources — especially demesne sources — that have survived for other manors and villages in the fourteenth century alone, he is far from being smothered beneath piles of information.[28] This can first be seen in the number of account rolls that have come down for mediaeval Holywell.

The first Holywell account roll is dated 1307/8.[29] It is preserved in the Public Record Office, London, as are all the known account rolls for the manor. Unfortunately, the roll does not form part of a surviving connected series. The next roll to come down intact is for the years 1323/24,[30] followed by a third from 1346/47.[31] There then follows a 10-year gap, with an account roll for 1355/56.[32] The next is six years later — 1362/63[33] — followed by a roll for 1370/1371.[34] There is then a period

---

[26] 1473/74: PRO SC 6-878/8; 1475/76: PRO SC 6-878/9; 1478/79: PRO SC 6-878/10; 1479/80: PRO SC 6-878/11; 1481/82: PRO SC 6-878/12.

[27] 1467: PRO SC 2-179/71; 1483: PRO SC 2-179/72; 1487: PRO SC 2-179/73; 1493: PRO SC 2-179/74.

[28] See, for example, Harvey, *Cuxham*, p. 9 *et seq.* A. E. Levett, *The Black Death on the Estates of the Bishopric of Winchester.* (Oxford, 1916) For Ramsey manors, that of Warboys is served by an abudance of account and court rolls beginning in the late thirteenth century.

[29] PRO SC 6-877/15.

[30] PRO SC 6-877/17.

[31] PRO SC 6-877/18.

[32] PRO SC 6-877/19.

[33] PRO SC 6-877/20.

[34] PRO SC 6-877/21.

of 20 years unrepresented by account rolls, the next surviving roll being dated 1391/92.[35] Only a fragmented account survives from 1396/97,[36] and in 1399 begins the first and only period of survival of reasonably close and connected accounts. Thus, there is a roll for 1399/1400,[37] 1400/1401,[38] 1401/1402,[39] 1403/1404,[40] 1404/1405,[41] 1408/1409,[42] 1409,[43] 1412/13,[44] 1413/14,[45] 1415/16,[46] and 1417/18.[47] The series then breaks off again, this time for 32 years, resuming with an account for 1449[48] and followed by a roll for 1451.[49] There are no further surviving accounts after that date until 1473/74.[50]

As can be seen, there are serious gaps in the account roll series for the fourteenth and early fifteenth centuries. Consequently, any attempt to examine the year-by-year workings of the manor — its administration, agricultural programs and the productivity of its demesne — is out of the question. This is further intensified by the content of the surviving rolls themselves. With but one exception (1391/92), no fourteenth century roll supplies any information as to the utilization of demesne fields, the sowing practices in those fields or even their yields. Only in the accounts for 1391/92, 1399/1400, 1400/1401 and 1401/1402 is detail given as to what strips were sown, how many acres in the strips, and what, in fact, was sown in them, and although this reveals the employment of a three-field rotation involving the sowing of wheat, rye, beans, peas and oats, without a longer — and closer — series of rolls, it is pointless to attempt to analyze the practice. Indeed, it is this lack of continuity to the account

---

[35] PRO SC 6-877/22.
[36] PRO SC 6-877/23. Specifically, only the first membrane of the roll has survived, listing customary tenants and their properties.
[37] PRO SC 6-877/24.
[38] PRO SC 6-877/26.
[39] PRO SC 6-877/27.
[40] PRO SC 6-877/28.
[41] PRO SC 6-877/29.
[42] PRO SC 6-877/30.
[43] PRO SC 6-878/1.
[44] PRO SC 6-878/2.
[45] PRO SC 6-878/3.
[46] PRO SC 6-878/4.
[47] PRO SC 6-878/5.
[48] PRO SC 6-878/6.
[49] PRO SC 6-878/7.
[50] It should be noted that the account rolls for Holywell-cum-Needingworth preserved in the Public Record Office — composed of long membranes sewn together at the ends — are examples of final accounts, not drafts of preliminary accounts drawn up before the final audit.

roll series that most powerfully prevents examination of Holywell's manorial economy. The profits from sales of wheat, rye, oats, beans and dredge as contained in the surviving accounts could, for example, be tabulated, together with the expenses of the reeve for repairs to manorial buildings and for tools, but it is virtually impossible to attach any meaning to the figures thereby obtained.

If the Holywell account rolls for the fourteenth century and first half of the fifteenth century are not numerous enough, therefore, to permit a study of the economic development of the manor and its demesne, they can at least be employed for examining the proprietary and manorial commitments and obligations of individual Holywell peasants — especially after the middle of the fourteenth century. Beginning with the year 1362/63, the rolls began to regularly record the names of the manor's tenants, starting at first with peasants leasing properties in the demesne — a practice whose development the few rolls themselves allow to be traced — together with the yearly rents owed by such tenants.[51] By 1370/71, the accounts were not only listing demesne tenants by name but also renters of fen properties and the customary tenants of the manor, along with their tenements, and information as to the nature of the tenure itself.[52] Consequently, from at least the year 1370 it is possible for the student to know the identities of at least Holywell's direct manorial tenants, as well as the size of their properties and the nature and extent of their obligations arising from their tenures. In addition, since the accounts of 1307/8, 1323/24, 1346/47, 1362/63, 1370/71, 1391/92, 1399/1400, 1400/1401, 1401/1402, 1403/1404, 1404/1405 and 1408/1409 supply details on the disposition of work obligations owed by customary tenants of the manor as a whole, it is possible to obtain an impression of the actual extent of such obligations in specific years, while the accounts further distinguish between tenures *ad opus* and *ad censum*, thereby making it possible to trace the process of commutation on the manor over the fourteenth and early fifteenth centuries. Furthermore, despite the failure of the five surviving account rolls prior to 1370 to name customary tenants, the fact that the 1252 extent had named the tenants at that time permits an assessment of familial continuity in tenure from the mid-thirteenth to the third quarter of the fourteenth century simply by the comparison of tenants' surnames.

---

[51] A tentative move towards demesne leasing had been made in the 1330's, and a few names of peasants taking up such properties had been inscribed in the rolls for 1346/47 and 1355/56.

[52] Customary tenants ceased to be specifically recorded in account rolls beginning with the roll for 1399/1400, although tenants of demesne continued to be listed and were throughout the remainder of the fifteenth century.

In short, what the few surviving account rolls of the fourteenth century and first half of the fifteenth century, coupled with the 1252 extent and even supplemented by the 1279 Hundred Roll survey of the manor, afford the student primarily is information on land, particularly the tenements and properties held directly from the lord of the manor, together with their size, their obligations, and, in 1252 but especially after 1370, the names of the tenants themselves. As a result, a general index is provided to the proprietary resources and manorial commitments of specific Holywell peasants and peasant families, so that their relationship to the manor — indeed, their very place in the manorial structure — can be judged. Further, given such information, it even becomes possible to determine — by comparison — which peasants were deeply involved in the life of the manor and which were not, as well as the general duration of their involvement.

Manorial accounts and extents in themselves, however — even when abundant — are not totally sufficient guides to the tenurial involvements of individual peasants, since they present a picture of land-holding that is both demesne-centred and static and frozen in time. But land opportunities for mediaeval English peasants were not rigidly confined to the perpetual holding of villein tenements directly from a lord. Fortunately for the student of Holywell's peasantry, evidence of this fact — of both the extent of land involvements and the fluidity of the turn-over in lands — exists, although here again the sources are not as numerous or extensive as could be wished. Nevertheless, there have survived some 30 charters or copies of charters concerning the acquisition or conveyance of free lands by Holywell people between the middle of the thirteenth century and the middle of the fifteenth century, with the majority belonging to the period 1300 to 1350 and found preserved in the Ancient Deeds collection of the Public Record Office, the British Museum and also in a collection of Ramsey materials in the Northamptonshire Record Office and the Ramsey Register at the Norwich Public Library.[53] As for inter-peasant conveyances, although the Holywell court rolls for the first half of the fourteenth century contain record of 21 instances of purchases, leases or sales of lands between peasants, the major source for this activity — and involving the transfers

---

[53] The Public Record Office charters have been conveniently calendared in *A Descriptive Catalogue of Ancient Deeds in the Public Record Office* (London, 1890-1902), 4 vols. The remaining charters or copies thereof are unedited and uncalendared and may be found in British Museum Additional Charter 33767 and the Ramsey Register. The documents at Northampton are part of a collection of records relevant to the le Moigne family — a knightly family holding extensive property in Needingworth and Holywell as well as in other Ramsey estates in the thirteenth century.

of customary or demesne lands — is the one surviving *gersuma* list of the
abbey, containing accounts of the customary property transactions of
peasants on 29 Ramsey estates and preserved as a record of entry fines,
but covering only the years 1397 to 1468. Sometimes referred to as the
Ramsey "Fifteenth-century Court Book"[54], it is found in the British Museum
as Harleian Manuscript 445. Composed of 256 folios, it includes 149
entries — presumably drawn from local court rolls — directly concerned
with Holywell-cum-Needingworth alone, the first from the year 1399
and the last from 1457. As such, it is an extremely valuable source of
information on the property involvements of Holywell peasants in the
first half of the fifteenth century, and it can be used for assessing the degree
of inter-peasant land transactions, familial retention of property, the
turn-over rate in land during the period covered, as well as for providing
additional details on the property commitments of individual villagers
at specific points in time and not found in either surviving account rolls
or court rolls. In addition, it can be supplemented with information
of a similar nature from another contemporary source: an extensive body
of records of the Ramsey central administration preserved in the British
Museum under the general heading of "Ramsey Papers", whose third
and fourth volumes contain records of generally small property transactions
involving Ramsey estates' peasants and the abbey cellarer, and among
which are found some 68 Holywell entries from 1392 to 1482, with 63
occurring between 1392 and 1452.[55]

All the above sources, then, when taken together, can provide, if not
a complete picture, at least a general index to tenants in Holywell-cum-
Needingworth between 1252 and 1457: their proprietary resources, their
relative place in the tenurial structure of the manor and the degree to
which their land interests involved them in tenurial relationships within
their own families and with their neighbors. It is even possible to attempt a tentative assessment of the extent of individual peasants' tenurial
obligations, whether in terms of services or rents.

But land, and peasants' relationships to land, far from exhaust investigation of a mediaeval English rural society. To describe the place occupied

---

[54] See Raftis, *Estates*, Appendix I, pp. 321-23, for a discussion of this important manuscript.
The present writer is now engaged in preparing an edition of this source.

[55] BM.Add.Mss 33445, 33446, 33447, 33448, etc. Volumes I and II (33445 and 33446) are
primarily rent or receipt books from 1350 through 1362, containing the returns to the central
camera of rentals on various Ramsey manors and including such Holywell items as the fen rentals
and reeve's arrears of 1351, 1352, 1353, 1354, 1355, 1356, 1357, 1362 and 1363. Volumes III
and IV (33447 and 33448) cover the years 1389 to 1508.

by individual peasants on a manor is but a first step in describing the village life of such a society, since the village experience transcends the manor. It is here that the importance of the local court rolls must be emphasized, since a wide variety of inter-peasant relationships, individual activities and social institutions are to be found mirrored in the records of local court sessions — and especially in the records of the views of frankpledge, which were charged not only with enforcing manorial discipline and obligations but with general peace-keeping and the regulation of national assizes as well. In the use the peasant made of his court to register private contracts, redress private injuries and even enforce village discipline through the promulgation of by-laws, the importance of the court to the maintenance of village life cannot be ignored,[56] while their extreme value as a means for examining aspects of village social life has been recently — and conclusively — established.[57] Indeed, one of the most important uses to be made of court rolls is as a tool for examining the nature and dimensions of a peasant economy (as distinct from the manorial economy), where court roll records of debts, contracts and incidental information on individual pastoral or craft pursuits can afford a rough index to village and inter-peasant economic activities not arising from the customary structure of the manor.

Fortunately for the student of Holywell's peasantry, a reasonably good series of court rolls has been preserved. They are to be found on deposit in either the Public Record Office or the British Museum. Specifically, rolls for 53 court sessions have survived between 1288 — the earliest preserved roll — and 1457,[58] accounting for 47 individual years. Thirty-nine of the sessions were views of frankpledge, the remaining 14 being the records of *curiae*. The condition of the individual rolls varies from excellent to badly damaged or faded, but only one — the roll for the *visus* of 1307[59] — is seriously incomplete, the first half being missing, while the roll for the *visus* of 1292 is alone so damaged, torn and faded as to be all but illegible.[60] All told, the 53 sessions supply a total of some 2500 separate and legible entries concerning Holywell peasants and involving a variety of business from the election of village and manorial officials to violations of national assizes of ale or local by-laws, pleas of

---

[56] For amplification of these points, see *infra*, Chapter III, p. 162 *et seq.*

[57] In the work of J. A. Raftis in particular. See *supra*, p, 1, note ♯ 4.

[58] There are four additional court rolls for the years 1467, 1483, 1487 and 1493, of which the last three were *curiae*.

[59] PRO SC 2-179/15.

[60] BM.Add.Roll 34337.

debt to assault and battery, personal trespasses to work derelictions, surety-ship relationships to land transactions. In addition, the court rolls provide such information on some 830 named peasants, including residents, transients and outsiders, or approximately three times as many persons named as tenants in either surveys, account rolls, "Court Book" or miscellaneous central administrative records between the 1250's and the 1450's. Consequently, it is possible for the student to investigate questions of inter-personal relationships in the village, patterns of settlement and residence, the exercise of official responsibility at the community level, and, given the tenurial information for individual peasants found in accounts and related sources, to assess the degree to which manorial commitments and land-holding influenced a peasant's place and role in the village. Further-more, it is even possible — due to the survival of two subsidy rolls for the taxes on personal movables of 1327 and 1332[61] in addition to the tenurial information already cited and the evidence of roles in village administration provided by court records — to form a rough picture of the different levels of wealth and general economic prosperity existing in the community in the first and second halves of the fourteenth century and even the first half of the fifteenth century.

Such, then, are the nature, number and concentration of surviving records for Holywell-cum-Needingworth that the student, if not permitted to investigate the economic and administrative history of the manor in any striking detail, is nevertheless able to examine aspects of its village society: its members, their economic resources, their place and role in the community and their relationships with each other. As a result, the present study has been divided into four chapters, each concerned with a major aspect of the peasant experience in Holywell-cum-Needingworth from the mid-thirteenth to the mid-fifteenth century—itself a two-hundred year period of deep and powerful changes and crises in the economic and social history of rural England, beginning at the sunset of a great age of agricultural and demographic growth and expansion and continuing through years of increasing manorial stagnation, sharp population decline, plague and peasant restlessness. However, as much as the student might desire to explore all the many facets of development and change in the period in terms of his chosen locality, he must confine his labours to questions best illustrated by his own particular sources. Thus, in the following study, Chapters I and II are primarily devoted to a presentation and examination of the patterns of tenurial relationships obtaining in

[61] PRO E. 179/122-4.

late mediaeval Holywell-cum-Needingworth between its peasants, the manor and their neighbors. The major sources of information upon which the two chapters are based, although drawing upon all surviving documentation including court rolls, miscellaneous central administrative records and private charters, are the extent of 1252, the Hundred Roll of 1279, the few surviving account rolls from 1307 to 1451, and the so-called "Fifteenth-century Court Book" (BM. Harl. MS. 445). Naturally, one reason for the emphasis on tenurial patterns in Chapters I and II lies in the fact that the earliest documentation to survive for Holywell to any appreciable degree — extents, surveys, accounts and Court Book — is in itself tenurially oriented, but it should also be pointed out that this fact is an illustration of the very major role played in mediaeval English society by land and questions of individual relationships to land.[62] Therefore, although the nature of the sources themselves contributes to a stress on tenurial patterns, the generally recognized importance of land to the peasant and to his way of life — to his personal prosperity or lack thereof, his position in both manorial and village structures and even his legal actions, both public and private — also demands extensive consideration of the problem. Needless to say, major aspects of Holywell's manorial history — as distinct from its village history — from the mid-thirteenth to the mid-fifteenth century must be left uninvestigated, since, as already noted, the few surviving records are not adequate for any detailed study of demesne production or overall manorial economic developments. Indeed, what in fact can be said of the manorial economy of mediaeval Holywell-cum-Needingworth has already been exhausted by Professor Raftis in his analysis of the Ramsey estates, and the student of Holywell can add nothing new to that study.[63]

[62] For the general significance of this point in peasant history, as well as for the importance of a peasant and village economy, see Robert Redfield, *The Little Community* (Chicago, 1960), Chapter II; and for an analysis in the context of contemporary peasant life, see E. R. Leach, *Pul Eliya, A Village in Ceylon: A Study of Land Tenure and Kinship* (Cambridge, 1961), especially pp. 296-306. Finally, for the Middle Ages and England, F. R. H. DuBoulay, *The Lordship of Canterbury* (New York, 1965), Chapter I provides useful observations on the same point.

[63] See *Estates, passim*. Professor Raftis even had the fuller advantage of dealing with the surviving Holywell material in the context of the estates of the abbey as a whole.

Finally, it should be added that the present study is not even able to contribute to the continuing inquiry into local mediaeval English field systems, their arrangement or use. As mentioned above, only four account rolls from 1392 to 1402 bothered to even name demesne strips and their sowings, while, further, there are no surviving mediaeval maps of Holywell-cum-Needingworth to indicate the location of separate fields or divisions within them. Not even the earliest known map — that of 1764 — gives such information, being content to simply label the stretch of property

Whereas Chapters I and II, drawing extensively upon surveys, accounts and the Court Book, are essentially concerned with the relationships of Holywell peasants to land and to the manor, Chapters III and IV, relying heavily on the surviving local court rolls, are primarily directed to the peasants of Holywell-cum-Needingworth as members of a village community. Here the student is entering into largely uncharted waters, since the investigation of the mediaeval English village community and peasant culture is still at an early stage of development. The strongest precedents for his studies are the works of Homans, Ault and Raftis, and it cannot be claimed that all the possible areas of research have been neatly and firmly defined. Given the great mass of individual and personal detail to be found in local court rolls, the student can be presented with a wide variety of questions to investigate. He can, for example, embark on the reconstruction of separate peasant family histories, in terms of place in village administration, tenure or occupations. He can explore and examine the phenomenon of groups in the village — groups of families, officials, tenants, artisans, tradesmen, servants, transients — and attempt to judge their composition, behavior and role in the social structure. He can also, if his particular set of sources are complete and detailed enough, borrow questions from the social scientist — in particular, the social anthropologist — and, to quote Redfield, study his locality as "a whole", "an ecological system", "a community within communities" or "a combination of opposites".[64] He can further study his village and villagers in isolation or as compared and contrasted with other villages and other villagers. There is, in short, no hard-and-fast rule he must follow, no definite historiography as yet to govern his investigations. As such, the student frequently finds himself in the role of an experimenter, and what control there is over his selection of questions for study is primarily a control exercised by the number, content and extent of local sources, which suggest areas of research most capable of fruitful development. Thus, in Chapter III, because of the clear evidence of separate family groups and the large number of personal names — approximately 1000 — of individuals in the village at varying times between 1250 and 1450, investigation is made into the general demographic and settlement patterns obtaining in the village through the fourteenth and first half of the fifteenth

between the settlements of Holywell and Needingworth "Common Field". As a result, although the student has the names of individual demesne strips from both the 1252 extent and fifteenth-century account rolls (see *infra*, Chapter I, p. 28, note # 19), he cannot indicate where they were located, except with a vague "somewhere between the two settlements."

[64] *The Little Community, passim.*

centuries, including consideration of the number of families known to be in residence at given periods, their lengths of stay, their replacement patterns and, indeed, their very survival. This last has also led to attention being given to questions of family relationships to land as well as to the broader question of peasant subsistence as it applied in mediaeval Holywell.

Following consideration of demographic trends, study has been made of the roles assumed by specific groups of peasant families and individuals in the overall administrative life of the manor and village; in short, of the degree to which locals assumed and exercised positions of official responsibility in the community. Such an inquiry is itself made possible by the close connection existing between local administrative and governmental institutions and the court as well as by the abundance of officials — jurors, tasters, beadles, constables, for example — actually named in the court rolls in the course of the fourteenth and early fifteenth centuries. This study, further, has led to a classification of specific persons and families in terms of major, lesser and minor roles of official activity, with an attempt also being made to determine the general economic and social conditions prevalent in the groups thereby classified.

Finally, having investigated demographic patterns and different "service roles" of local groups of peasants in late mediaeval Holywell-cum-Needingworth in Chapter III, Chapter IV, because of the substantial evidence of interpersonal surety relationships and contracts as well as the clear assignation of responsibility for violations of peace and local regulations, directs itself to examining the degree of cohesion and inter-peasant cooperation and intra-village harmony obtaining in the community from the end of the thirteenth century to the middle of the fifteenth century. Here stress is placed on exploring the role of interpersonal and inter-group relationships in contributing to a united and inter-dependent village community in the early fourteenth century, as well as to indicating what their absence or modification over the course of years after 1350 meant in terms of the social organization of the village community. Admittedly, there remain other questions of local village society that could be subjected to investigation, but the nature and extent of the surviving Holywell court rolls prohibit their development. For example, although the institution of the personal pledge, or court-related surety relationship, as well as inter-peasant contracts, are examined in the broad context of intra-village cooperation, both could be studied separately and in themselves. The same may be posited of local manufacturing (e.g. the brewing of ale) or trades and skills as being essential village services and as elements in a village economy, while the place and role of servants, transients and outsiders in the village could also form an individual study. Even local criminal disturbances could be examined both as an index to the degree of violence in the community and in terms of village discipline and social control.[65] Unfortunately, the number alone of Holywell court rolls surviving from the late thirteenth century to the mid-fifteenth century is too limited to allow proper investigation of such questions without risk of resorting to dangerous and ultimately fruitless speculation.[66] Consequently, it has been thought best to concentrate major attention on the activities and roles of groups, whether familial, occupational or economic, within the village, together with a consideration of the nature and place of inter-group relationships in serving the needs and maintaining the organization of the local society. In this way, at least the extent of peasant activities, relationships and commitments is demonstrated to have been broader and deeper than demesne and tenure-oriented manorial sources tend to indicate, while such an investigation further emphasizes, in terms of identifiable members of one local community, the essential vitality, resourcefulness, resilience and adaptability of the mediaeval English peasant. It is not a complete or exhaustive analysis of peasant experience in the late Middle Ages; because of source limitations, it cannot even be claimed

[65] For a summary of these and other aspects of village society capable of study through court rolls, see J. A. Raftis, "Peasant Mobility and Freedom in Mediaeval England." *Report of the Canadian Historical Association* (1965), p. 129.

Note should also be made of another aspect of local society which cannot be satisfactorily examined at present: the local church. That Holywell had a parish church is known; the Church of St. John the Baptist, standing today and whose structure dates — in some parts — from the thirteenth century, while the fact of a church was mentioned as early as the late tenth century, when it was granted to the abbey by the presbyter Gode (see *supra*, note ♯ 13). It was under the jurisdiction of the bishop of Lincoln, and appointments of its rectors in the thirteenth and fourteenth centuries can be found throughout the several volumes of the editions of the Lincoln registers printed by both the Canterbury and York society and the Oxford press, as well as in volumes of the calendars of the Patent Rolls of the English kings of the fourteenth century. (For a convenient list of known Holywell rectors, see Rev. A. G. Pearce Higgins, *A Short History of the Parish Church of Holywell-cum-Needingworth*. Ridley Press, Cambridge and St. Ives, 1955, Appendix II.) In addition, the property endowments of the church — together with its tithe rights — can be found in the 1252 extent (*Carts*. I, pp. 293-94). However, little more can be said of the church or of the life of the parish in the Middle Ages, at least at the present time. It would be highly instructive to be able to weigh the strength of the relationship between Holywell peasants and their church, but this cannot be attempted until it has been determined whether or not records of the ecclesiastical courts of the Lincoln diocese and including the Huntingdon deanery have been preserved, and, if so, to what extent.

[66] For example, whereas records for 53 court sessions from the late thirteenth to the mid-fifteenth century have survived for Holywell-cum-Needingworth, for the same general period there have come down 60 court rolls for the Ramsey village of Houghton, 84 rolls for Broughton, 83 rolls for Upwood, 78 rolls for Warboys and 91 rolls for Wistow.

to be a complete or exhaustive analysis of the peasant experience of Holy-well-cum-Needingworth. But it is hoped that the present study can be accepted as at least a modest and beginning step down the still dimly-lighted and only partially cleared road leading to the eventual supplying of a voice to the one mediaeval figure who has been silent and treated as either an economic unit or a legal problem for too many years.

CHAPTER I

STRUCTURES AND PATTERNS OF TENURE, 1252-1370

In attempting to understand any social group in mediaeval England, it is impossible for the modern student to ignore land and questions of land tenure.[1] Whether the object of study be kings, barons, knights, bishops, monks or burgesses, land, and the relationship to land, will be found to play a major role in defining group or individual interests, wealth and power, and rights and obligations.[2] With the exception of religion, land was the one element common to all groups in society, and perhaps nowhere was the importance of land and its tenure more overt than among that great mass of mediaeval English men and women called "the peasantry".[3] To understand this peasant society, therefore — indeed, to understand a single group within it — it is necessary to devote attention to its relationship to land and to attempt to discover the place occupied by land in questions of village life, peasant obligations, prosperity and even survival. These last are questions as alive and real for students today as they were for F. W. Maitland and Paul Vinogradoff,[4] and although no student of one village community from the late thirteenth century to the middle of the fifteenth century can hope to discover definitive answers to them that will hold true for mediaeval England as a whole, still he can attempt

[1] See, for example, F. Pollock and F. W. Maitland, *History of English Law before the Time of Edward I* (2nd ed., Cambridge, 1898), I, esp. pp. 232-34.

[2] See, for example, G. A. Holmes, *The Estates of the Higher Nobility in the Fourteenth Century* (Cambridge, 1957); R. S. Hoyt, *The Royal Demesne in English Constitutional History* (New York, 1950); F. R. H. DuBoulay, *The Lordship of Canterbury* (New York, 1966); A. Ballard, *The Domesday Boroughs* (Oxford, 1904), and *The English Borough in the Twelfth Century* (Cambridge, 1914).

[3] J. A. Raftis, "Peasant Mobility and Freedom in Mediaeval England," *Report of the Canadian Historical Association* (1965), pp. 117-30, has drawn striking attention to the sheer size of the peasant population of mediaeval England: "But there still remains the main body of mediaeval life, called variously villagers, serfdom, peasantry — that 90% of mediaeval men and women who were small people on the land ..." (p. 120).

[4] See Maitland, *Domesday Book and Beyond*; Vinogradoff, *Villainage in England, The Growth of the Manor*. Among more recent studies, E. A. Kosminsky's *Studies in the Agrarian History of England in the Thirteenth Century* (esp. Chapters IV, V and VI of that book), R. H. Hilton's *A Mediaeval Society* (London, 1967), DuBoulay's *The Lordship of Canterbury* (esp. Chapter IV) and J. A. Raftis', *Tenure and Mobility* bear witness to the still pressing need to define economic, legal and social conditions prevailing in rural England in the Middle Ages.

to shed some light on the questions by examining them as fully as his sources allow on the local level, to see if and how his locality corresponded to the country at large. Consequently, in this and in the next chapter, attention shall be directed to the peasants of Holywell-cum-Needingworth primarily as tenants from the years of high farming of the mid-thirteenth century to those of demesne strangulation and agrarian decline of the early fifteenth century. In the process, attempts shall be made to examine questions of the land-hunger of the latter 1200's, the nature and place of customary and free tenure in the community, the commutation trends of the fourteenth century, the effect of plague and the degree of stratification within the peasantry along tenurial lines, and to assess — as much as possible — the impact of such phenomena on the lives of Holywell peasants. To accomplish this, the present investigation has been divided into two chapters, corresponding to the two major periods in late mediaeval Holywell's manorial and tenurial history: from 1252 — the date of the first and only integral extent for the manor — through the 1360's, a period of essential continuity in tenurial practice and manorial administration; and from 1370 through the 1450's, a time of profound administrative changes, of the gradual abandonment of direct demesne farming and the eventual replacement of old forms of customary tenure by life lease. Throughout both periods, however, the position of the peasant — indeed, his relationship to the manorial institution itself as reflected in his tenurial commitments — shall be the primary object of the present investigation. It is not the place of the peasant in Holywell's manorial operation that is of chief concern here; rather, it is the place of the manor in the life of the peasant.

The survival of detailed manorial and private records for Holywell beginning only in the middle of the thirteenth century prevents investigation into peasant landholding conditions prior to the 1250's. Neither the Domesday Inquest of 1086 nor the mid-twelfth-century extent (c. 1160) for the manor provides anything approaching comprehensive tenurial or even personal material. The former states only that in 1086 there were 26 villeins and three bordars holding from the abbot of Ramsey, while one hide (of a total assessment of nine hides) was held by a certain Aluuold, who in turn had three tenants of his own.[5] In short, all that can safely be said of the eleventh century is that in 1086 there were at least 33 persons holding property in Holywell, and that 26 — or, more probably, 29 — were in some sense customary tenants of the abbey. As for the twelfth

---

[5] Domesday Survey in *VCH.Hunts.* I, p. 343. See *supra*, p. 9, note ♯ 14 for full entry.

century, the truncated extent dated c. 1160[6] records that in the time of King Henry I there were 26 virgates in the manor, but that by the time of the extent (*nunc*) only 15 of these virgates were held for works, eight having been put *ad censum*. In addition, there is record of 14 cotlands. As for tenants, however, the extent lists the names only of the *censuarii*: seven men holding eight virgates and one cotland, and three men holding each a croft. The record, therefore, is infuriatingly incomplete, having neglected to account for possibly 74 per cent. of the tenants at that time.[7] Only from the middle of the thirteenth century does the state of records for Holywell begin to improve. However, it is an improvement more of quantity than of quality. The extent of 1252[8] is valuable in that it provides a list of the major tenants on the manor in the mid-thirteenth century and enumerates the conditions under which they hold their individual properties. Like all such comprehensive manorial surveys, however, it does not cut beneath the surface of the tenurial structure to reveal the place of sub-tenants on the manor. Nevertheless, despite its shortcomings, it does at least give information on the number of basic customary and free land units in 1252, their holders and the terms of tenure. This is a happier situation than that found in the Hundred Roll survey of 1279,[9] which provides a rather extensive breakdown of the free tenurial structure but seriously neglects the customary tenants. On the other hand, the five surviving account rolls from the 55 years between 1308 and 1363 are dismally imprecise. Three of them (1307/8,[10] 1323/24,[11] 1355/56[12]) mention neither the number of customary units nor their tenants, while the remaining two (1346/47,[13] 1362/63[14]) record only the number of such units, but also neglect tenants. Fortunately, there has also survived from the period 1252-1370 a handful of scattered land charters from Holywell in addition

---

[6] *Carts.* III, p. 281 *et seq.* See *supra*, p. 10, note ♯ 20.

[7] The percentage is only an estimate based on the assumption of one tenant for each of the 15 virgates and 13 cotlands. That there may have been less than 38 actual tenants in Holywell in the 1160's is admitted: the possibility of one man holding more than one piece of land immediately comes to mind. On the other hand, there could just as easily have been more than 38: the possibility of fragmented units — e.g. half-virgates — cannot be ruled out.

It should be noted further that the existence of 26 virgates in 1160 and the records of 26 *villani* in 1086 indicates that the villeins of Domesday were in all probability virgaters.

[8] *Carts.* I, p. 293 *et seq.*

[9] *Rotuli Hundredorum*, II, pp. 602-3. (Hereafter: RH) PRO SC 12-8-56.

[10] PRO SC 6-877/15.

[11] PRO SC 6-877/17.

[12] PRO SC 6-877/19.

[13] PRO SC 6-877/18.

[14] PRO SC 6-877/20.

to a few notices of land transactions in the manorial court rolls, primarily from the early fourteenth century. What all this means for the student is that he cannot probe very deeply into tenure between 1250 and 1370. A broad outline of the tenurial structure is possible, but an exhaustive description of its parts is frustrated. Nevertheless, given the supplementary evidence of subsidy rolls for 1327 and 1332, inheritance customs and village status as reflected in the sessions of the local court, the student may still try to make some observations about land and land tenure in Holywell from the mid-thirteenth century through the mid-fourteenth century.

Holywell-cum-Needingworth in the Middle Ages may best be described as belonging to the category of manors termed "medium" sized by Kosminsky.[15] To discuss tenurial structure, therefore, it is necessary to first determine the amount of arable obtaining in the thirteenth and fourteenth centuries. Unfortunately, none of the surviving records gives an exact figure in terms of acres. Nevertheless, there is reason to set the total at between 1100 and 1200 acres. To begin with, there is the question of the demesne. According to the Domesday of 1086, the abbey at that time had two ploughlands actually in demesne.[16] Taking a ploughland to be about 120 acres, the demesne of the late eleventh century was minimally 240 acres. The twelfth-century survey gives no information on the demesne, while the 1252 extent lists the strips in the demesne for a total of 30 "culturae" but declares the acreage to be unknown.[17] The Hundred Roll of 1279, however, still lists two ploughlands in demesne,[18] while evidence from the early fifteenth century indicates a rough continuity between the demesne area of the 1200's and the 1400's. Specifically, in 1252 the demesne had been divided among some 30 strips. From 1400, records in the account rolls of demesne leasing and sowing practices provide names for 28 strips.[19] Again, from the same early fifteenth-century sources,

---

[15] *Studies in the Agrarian History of England in the Thirteenth Century*, p. 96. (Hereafter, *Studies*).

[16] *VCH.Hunts*. I, p. 343.

[17] *Carts*. I, p. 294. "Dominicum hujus manerii consistit in pluribus culturis, sed nescitur quantae acrae in eisdem continentur."

[18] RH. II, p. 602. PRO SC 12-8-56.

[19] The names in the 1252 extent were as follows (*Carts*. I, p. 294) :

Ourelitlehoue	Edriches leuge
Nethrelitlehoue	Guren
Estlange	Trichiacre
un-named ("cultura adjacens januae de Haliwelle")	Tuxhounegeren
Redehalfacre	Hunderlunde
Blakerode	Smethes

the acreage of the demesne can be approximated. Thus, in 1400, 167 acres were sown and some 104 acres were leased — a total of 271 acres.[20] The following year, some 148 acres were sown and 104 acres leased, or 252 acres.[21] By 1413, when the entire demesne had been let out, the total was 311½ acres.[22] Consequently, if the demesne in Holywell c. 1400 amounted to a little over 300 acres scattered through 28 strips, it is not unlikely that the demesne of the thirteenth century, described at times as two ploughlands and scattered through 30 strips, was roughly the same. It would be tempting, of course, to suggest that the Holywell demesne had grown from 240 to over 300 acres between 1252 and 1400,[23] but it would also be unwise. The demesne had remained stable at two ploughlands from 1086 through 1279. It had apparently not increased during the boom conditions in the thirteenth century. If it had not done so then,

Blakehille	Sinfuldole
Middefurlonge	Sypenefurlange
Presteslade	Nethrebradewey
Berimers	Overebradewey
Estlanges in Brericroft	Mannesbrigge
Netherde in Brerecroft	Seven Aker
Stonidole extra Crucem	Gorem
le Brache	Waddone
Wolnotheslenge	Benehille

Those from the early fifteenth century were as follows (PRO SC 6-877/24, 26, 27, 28, 29):

Benehill	Mechilhowe
Brache (le)	Bradeweye
Buryhegge	Crowchedole
Middilfurlong	Estlonge
Overebrerecroft	Hegfurlong
Oxhowe	Sevenacre
Schepenfurlong	Thirtyacre
Le Smethe	Wodebrok
Stonydole	Cotedole
Nethbrerecroft	Waddon
Prestlade	Fyve Incheslade
Mereweye	Brerecroft
Redhalfacre	Mannsbrigge.
Lytelhowe	

[20] PRO SC 6-877/24.
[21] PRO SC 6-877/26.
[22] PRO SC 6-878/2.
[23] As occurred at Cuxham, where the demesne apparently added some 15 acres from 1300 to the middle of the fourteenth century. See Harvey, *Cuxham*, p. 46.

it is unlikely that it did between 1300 and 1400 — during the critical years of agricultural stagnation and demographic decline.[24]

For the sake of convenience, then — and allowing for possible but minor fluctuations over the years — the demesne in Holywell in the thirteenth and fourteenth centuries may be described as comprising some 300 acres of land. In addition, its area probably underwent no major changes from the 1250's to the 1400's; indeed, it had probably remained relatively stable from the eleventh century, even during the years of intensive colonization characteristic of English agrarian life in the late twelfth and thirteenth centuries.

The demesne in mediaeval Holywell-cum-Needingworth did not comprise all the available arable, however. By the 1250's there were both freemen and villeins holding land of the abbey, and the land in turn was divided into free and customary units, broken down into virgates, cotlands, crofts and other parcels. The questions to be asked are, first, what were the land units in Holywell and how much land did they cover, and, secondly, how many units were there at given points in Holywell's mediaeval history ?

Like most other manors in the mediaeval Midlands, arable in Holywell-cum-Needingworth was primarily parcelled out in terms of virgates, cotlands and crofts. Unlike most other manors, however, the Holywell virgates and cotlands were, respectively, smaller and larger than in other localities. The virgate, or yardland, is generally understood to have comprised some 30 acres of arable,[25] although it was far from being a rigidly standardized unit of measurement and could therefore differ from manor to manor or even within a manor.[26] On Ramsey estates alone, the size varied from 15 acres to 40 acres.[27] Nevertheless, even within the Ramsey

---

[24] See M. M. Postan, "Mediaeval Agrarian Society in its Prime: England." *Cambridge Economic History of Europe*, I (2nd. ed. Cambridge, 1966), pp. 548-52; p. 585 *et seq.* (Hereafter cited: CEH, I.) for agrarian conditions in both the thirteenth and fourteenth centuries, and J. A. Raftis, *Estates*, Chapter VIII, Section I (p. 222 *et seq.*) for the slump in production on Ramsey estates beginning near the end of the thirteenth century.

[25] See G. C. Homans, *English Villagers of the Thirteenth Century*, p. 73; H. S. Bennett, *Life on the English Manor* (Cambridge, 1937), p. 339; Kosminsky, *Studies*, p. 35; Hilton, *A Mediaeval Society*, p. 115; L. C. Latham, "The Manor and the Village," in *Social Life in Early England* (Oxford, 1960), p. 37.

[26] Kosminsky, p. 35; Hilton, *A Medieval Society*, p. 115, where the virgate, or yardland, is noted as being anywhere from 25 to 30 acres or more, depending on the locality.

[27] From extents compiled in the middle of the thirteenth century, for example, it is learned that a virgate in Hemmingford Abbots comprised 15 to 18 acres (*Carts.* I, p. 380); in St. Ives, 16 acres (*Ibid.*, p. 284); in Houghton, 18 acres (*Ibid.*, p. 364); in Abbots Ripton, 20 acres (*Ibid.*, p. 321); in Raveley, 20 acres (*Ibid.*, p. 354); in Stukeley, Elton and King's Ripton, 24 acres (*Ibid.*, pp. 392, 490 and 398); in Barton, 23 to 28 acres (*Ibid.*, p. 475); in Girton, Chatteris, Warboys,

complex, out of 17 manors represented by mid-thirteenth-century extents, 13 boasted 20 acres or more to the virgate. Four had virgates of less than 20 acres, of which Holywell was one. There a virgate was described as averaging 18 acres of land.[28] In short, the Holywell virgate of approximately 18 acres was from forty to thirty per cent. smaller than the average mediaeval English virgate holding.[29]

Besides the virgate, there were two further divisions of land in mediaeval Holywell: the cotland and the croft. The former presents a problem of identification for the student. Generally, the mediaeval English "cottar" was a smallholder, with "only an acre or two",[30] and his small plot was variously described as a "cote", "cotland", or "cotsetland" or even a fardel.[31] However, as with the virgate, so too the cotland was not a rigidly uniform parcel. Kosminsky noted that, whereas in Cambridgeshire the cottar's tenement could be as small as an acre, in Oxfordshire and War-wickshire cotlands could be found "of twenty-four or even thirty-four acres".[32] The Holywell cotland — whose tenant was the *cotmannus* — was somewhere between both extremes: probably about 10 acres. The extent itself does not give the acreage, but its description of the *opera* and heriot due from a customary cotland is identical to that demanded of a half-virgate.[33] In addition, the tenants of the Ramsey manor in Girton, also described as "cottemanni" in the mid-thirteenth century, held parcels of land which owed one-half the services due from a virgate and which comprised 10 acres.[34]

Upwood and Wistow, 30 acres (*Carts.* I., pp. 492, 429, 308, 343, 354); in Broughton, 32 acres (*Ibid.*, p. 337) and in Cranfield possibly as high as 40 acres (*Ibid.*, p. 438).

[28] *Carts.* I, p. 295: "Octodecim acrae, alicubi et amplius, faciunt virgatam." The three other Ramsey manors with virgates of less than 20 acres were Houghton, Hemmingford Abbots and St. Ives.

[29] 40 % if the figure of 18 acres is contrasted to the 30 acre virgate; 30 % if the Holywell virgate is expanded to 20 acres — allowing for the extent's "alicubi et amplius". However, the 1279 Hundred Roll description of the Holywell virgate as 16 acres probably indicates that the figure of 20 acres was seldom reached (RH. II, p. 602; PRO SC 12-8-56).

[30] Bennett, p. 36.

[31] Vinogradoff, *Villainage in England*, p. 256.

[32] *Studies*, p. 36.

[33] *Carts.* I, p. 301: "uxores cujuslibet habentis dimidiam virgatam dabunt ad herietum duos solidos, sex denarios." The cotlander's widow "dabit ad herietum duos solidos, sex denarios." (*Ibid.*, p. 303). Similarly, the *censum*, or commutation, rate for a full Holywell virgate in the fourteenth century was 15 s. per annum, that for a cotland 7 s. 6 d., or one-half the virgate rate. For the cotland's labour services, see *infra*, p. 75.

[34] *Ibid.*, p. 495. Also, in Houghton a "cotagium" was accounted as a half-virgate (*Ibid.*, p. 368). For a more traditional cotland, see the entry for the "cotlandarii" in Abbots Ripton (*Ibid.*, p. 325). Week-work, for example, there involved but one day.

The Holywell virgate, then, was smaller than the traditional, or average, virgate, and the cotland larger. The only land unit that did in fact correspond to others of the same designation in England was the croft. Again, the extent gives no acreage content for the croft, but it was most likely between one and five acres,[35] and probably closer to one acre, even though the Holywell customary croft imposed the obligation of Monday week-work[36] — the tenement of the *lundinarius*[37] — and, from the early fourteenth century, bore a *censum* rate of three shillings and more: almost half the rate of the cotland.[38]

With at least approximate acreage figures for the three main land units in mediaeval Holywell, an attempt can be made to estimate the over-all amount of arable for the late Middle Ages — especially as the number of units underwent no major changes during the two centuries between the 1250's and the 1450's.[39] According to the list of tenements in the 1252 extent, there were at that time, "praeter dominicum", some 88 units of land, consisting of: one hide, one-half hide, 26 virgates, one-half virgate, 18 cotlands, 25 crofts and 16 smaller holdings.[40] Using the figure of 90 acres to the hide — based on the extent's definition of five virgates equalling a hide[41] — the Holywell virgate of 18 acres, a cotland of 10 acres and one acre to the croft, the arable was approximately 829 acres. This, added to the demesne estimate of 300 acres, gives a total of some 1129 acres of arable in the latter thirteenth century.[42] That Holywell

---

[35] See, for example, Vinogradoff, *Villainage in England*, p. 256; Bennett, p. 63.

[36] See *infra*, p. 75 *et seq.*

[37] For the *lundinarii*, see Vinogradoff, *Villainage in England*, p. 256; Bennett, p. 64, note ♯ 1.

[38] This in itself is not an argument that can be pushed too far, since a *censum* rate bore more directly on the amount and value of the *opera* being commuted than on the actual acreage of a tenement.

[39] See *infra*, p. 38 *et seq.*

[40] *Carts*. I, p. 295 *et seq.* An additional virgate pertaining to the church has been excluded from this figure (*Ibid.*, p. 293). The hide and 11 crofts were held by Berengarius le Moigne, a knight, the half-hide, a half-virgate and six strips of arable — once part of the demesne — by the prior of St. Ives.

[41] *Carts*. I, p. 295. "Et quinque virgatae terrae faciunt hydam."

[42] It should be mentioned here that the term "acre" is itself vague and cannot be precisely defined for mediaeval England. However, it seems clear that the "acre" in Holywell corresponded to the modern statute acre rather than to the nebulous "customary acre" of the Middle Ages. For the former, see Kosminsky, p. 35, and Vinogradoff, *Villainage in England*, p. 241 *et seq.* For the latter, see *infra*, p. 40, note ♯ 80.

It should also be noted that the estimated total of 1129 acres is relatively close to the sum of the demesne and the hidage figure of 8½ (*Carts*. I, p. 295). Taking the hide at 90 acres, the total is 1065 acres. However, this cannot be pressed too far because of the acutely uncertain nature of the term "hide". It too, like "virgate" and "acre", is an often imprecise label, and,

had not undergone any major expansion since the eleventh century seems likely, although it cannot be proved due to the nature of Domesday terminology. In 1086 the manor had been assessed at nine hides and was said to have nine ploughlands in demesne — although two ploughlands were actually being worked. In addition, there had been 26 villeins on the manor at that time. Now, assuming, for the moment — itself highly questionable — that the 26 villeins were all virgaters at 18 acres and that the ploughland was 120 acres, an arable figure of 1568 acres is obtained. If, on the other hand, a ploughland figure of 90 acres is used, the result is 1270 acres. Clearly, however, this cannot be pressed too far, given the problematic character of Domesday figures and terms. Perhaps the safest course, then, is to simply observe that there exists no positive evidence that the arable in Holywell had increased to any major degree by the thirteenth century from what it had *probably* been in the eleventh century.

But if the approximate amount of available arable in Holywell had not significantly changed between the late eleventh century and the middle of the thirteenth century, its distribution had. In 1086, the Domesday Book had recorded the presence of 26 villeins and one freeman as well as six *bordarii*.[43] Whether there were more free tenants in Holywell in 1086 is not certain, nor, for that matter, is it certain how many sub-tenants may have been concealed behind the 26 *villani*. Nevertheless, with a demesne capable of accomodating nine ploughs but using land for only two,[44] it seems likely that the tenant population was not large and that seven ploughlands, or over 500 acres of land, were still unexploited. In addition, if the 26 *villani* were virgaters or near-virgaters,[45] the balance

---

as in its use in Domesday, may bear little or no relation to concrete reality. That it was clearly not uniform — even on Ramsey estates — can be seen from extents for nine other villages in the mid-thirteenth century. In Warboys, the hide equalled four virgates, or 120 acres; in St. Ives, five virgates (80 acres); in Abbots Ripton, four virgates (80 acres); in Broughton, six and a half virgates, or 208 acres !; in Upwood and Wistow, four virgates (120 acres); in Houghton, six virgates (108 acres); in Hemmingford Abbots, six virgates (90-108 acres), and in Stukeley, four virgates (96 acres). See *Carts*. I, pp. 308, 284, 321, 333, 343, 354, 364, 380 and 392.

[43] *VCH.Hunts*. I, p. 343. Although Aluuold was not actually designated "liber", the fact that he held one hide — possibly the same hide later held by the le Moignes — and was mentioned at the end of the survey strongly suggests free status.

[44] This is based on the Domesday statement that the abbot "has land for 9 ploughs in demesne apart from the aforesaid hides. There are now two ploughs on the demesne ..." (*Ibid.*).

[45] This seems highly probable, since the extent of *ca*. 1160 refers to there having been 23 virgaters *ad opus* in the time of Henry I (*Carts*. III, p. 281). As there were also 14 cotlands at that time, in addition to the virgaters, the probability is strengthened even more, while the coincidence of the 26 *villani* of 1086 with the 26 virgates in 1160 cannot be ignored.

between customary and freehold tenure was decidely tipped in favour
of the former.

By 1252, however, a quite different picture presents itself. Outside
of demesne, there were at least 88 units of land. Actually, there were
even more. Out of 26½ virgates accounted for, three were further divided
into half-virgate tenements. In addition, the Hundred Roll of 1279 indicates
that Berengarius le Moigne — the knightly holder of one hide in 1252
— had at least 12 tenants: three virgaters and nine croft-holders;[46] while
the Prior of St. Ives had three tenants, all virgaters. In short, the Holywell
arable in 1252 "praeter dominicum" was split-up into some 105 parcels
of land. Even more important, the balance between customary (villein)
and freehold land was different from what it had been two centuries earlier.
Approximately 442 acres were held in villeinage in 1252, dispersed into
from 47 to 53 units,[47] and some 376 acres, divided into 52 parcels, were
held freely. Percentagewise, out of a total estimated arable of 1129 acres
in 1252, 27% was retained in demesne, 39% was held in villeinage, and
34% was freehold. In this respect, Holywell was typical of other Midland
manors in the thirteenth century, for, according to Kosminsky's calculations
based on the Hundred Rolls, in the late thirteenth century freehold generally
comprised about 30% of the total arable and villeinage about 40%.[48]

That Holywell did not deviate from the late thirteenth-century Midland
pattern of the disposition of free and villein land is perhaps comforting
to the student, but more important is the question of how this situation
was achieved. Clearly freehold had increased and villein land had decreased
from as recently as the 1160's, when there were still 23 virgates and 14
cotlands in villeinage.[49] By 1252, there were still 14 cotlands, but the
virgates had shrunk to 16. (See Table I) What, it remains to be asked,
had happened since the eleventh and twelfth centuries to bring about
the conditions prevailing in 1252? The over-all amount of arable in
Holywell does not seem to have grown radically between c. 1100 and 1252,
nor had the demesne. Yet freehold apparently had advanced and villein
land retreated. Where did the former come from, and where did the
latter go?

The answers to these questions are not as readily forthcoming as might

---

[46] Specifically, "coterelli" — cottars. RH. II, p. 603; PRO SC 12-8-56.

[47] There were 47 units of land in terms of virgates, cotlands, half-virgates and crofts. There
were, in addition, six small parcels of less than an acre — mostly carved out of the demesne —
held for money rent but listed among the holdings of the "consuetudinarii". Carts. I, pp. 304-5.

[48] *Studies*, pp. 203-4.

[49] *Carts*. III, p. 281.

at first be expected. For one, although the surviving records for Holywell give the impression of intensified freehold activity in the thirteenth century, it cannot be definitely stated that freehold prior to the 1200's had been negligible. There is evidence of the one hide held by Aluuold in 1086, for example.[50] In addition, there may have been alienation in the wake of the Conquest.[51] In any event, an early twelfth-century survey of knights' fees and manors pertaining to the abbey makes specific reference to the existence of free tenants in Holywell: "Abbas Rameseyae tenet ... apud

TABLE I

CUSTOMARY TENEMENTS IN HOLYWELL-CUM-NEEDINGWORTH, 1252-1370

	1252				1306/7				
	Op.	Cens.	Man.	Total	Op.	Cens.	Man.	Off.	Total
Virgates	16	0	0	16	9	8	0	0	17
Cotlands	14	0	0	14	6	6	0	3	15
Crofts	11	2	1	14	13	0	0	0	13

	1323/24					1346/47			
	Op.	Cens.	Man.	Off.	Total	Op.	Cens.	Man.	Off.	Total
Virgates	9	8	0	0	17	12	5	0	0	17
Cotlands	6	6	0	3	15	6	6	0	3	15
Crofts	13	0	0	0	13	9	4	0	0	13

	1355/56					1362/63			
	Op.	Cens.*	Man.	Off.	Total	Op.	Cens.	Man.	Off.	Total
Virgates	12	5	0	0	17	11½	5	0	½	17
Cotlands	6	6	0	3	15	6	6	0	3	15
Crofts	0	10	3	0	13	0	13	0	0	13

	1370/71				
	Op.	Cens.*	Man.	Off.	Total
Virgates	15	2	0	0	17
Cotlands	10	2	0	3	15
Crofts	0	13	0	0	13

* = includes *arentatum* as well as *censum*.

[50] *VCH.Hunts.* I, p. 343.

[51] For the problem of knights' fees and alienation on Ramsey properties in general in the late eleventh and early twelfth centuries, see H. M. Chew, *The English Ecclesiastical Tenants-in-Chief and Knight Service* (Oxford, 1932), pp. 3-5; Richardson and Sayles, *The Governance of Mediaeval England*, p. 66; and Raftis, *Estates*, p. 25 *et seq.*

Halywelle novem hidas, quas liberi et custumarii tenent ..."[52] Furthermore, donations by Abbot Aldwin (1107-13) and a certain Sewin (1102-7) "aucipitrarius" accounted for the half-hide and three virgates held in free alms by the Prior of St. Ives.[53] Since the demesne throughout this period was still two ploughlands,[54] it is likely that much of the free land was coming from the seven extra ploughlands that had been in demesne — at least potentially, but uncultivated — in 1086.[55]

But the demesne — or, more precisely, this "potential" demesne — was not the only source of free lands. Although reclamation projects and assarting were common to Ramsey estates in the twelfth and early thirteenth centuries[56] — as throughout England[57] — they did not loom large in fen-nudged Holywell. Rather, from the early thirteenth century it was the villeinage that was nibbled away for the creation of additional freeholds. Seven virgates most certainly disappeared from the customary framework between c. 1160 and 1252. In the former time, there had been 23 virgates in villeinage — eight of which were then *ad censum* — while only 16 remained by 1252. (See Table I) That many were to be found among the free virgates of that year is strongly implied by the extent. For example, out of 11 freemen holding properties of various sizes in 1252, seven held five virgates and four cotlands all of which had some servile obligations attached to them in addition to money rent. Aspelon of Holywell held two virgates for which he owed ploughing services,[58] John Gere a cotland and a half owing forensic service,[59] Radulph de Hamptone a cotland which was expressly described as once having been "in villenagio",[60] Robert Morel a cotland and half owing "servitia servilia"

---

[52] *Carts.* I, p. 271.

[53] *Carts.* II, p. 214.

[54] *Carts.* I, p. 271.

[55] *VCH.Hunts.* I, p. 343. The releasing and alienation of demesne properties in the twelfth century was, further, a consistent feature of the policy of Abbot Walter (1133-61), contributed to in large measure by the disruptions of the Civil War. See Raftis, *Estates*, Chapter III, Section III, and esp. p. 86.

[56] See Raftis, *Estates*, p. 105.

[57] See Postan, CEH, I, p. 549 *et seq.*

[58] *Carts.* I, p. 296. "Aspelon de Halywelle tenet mansum suum, et duas virgatas terrae, pro quibus facit homagium Abbati, et sectam curiae de Broucthone, et dat per annum sex solidos ...; et arabit etiam per annum, scilicet ad semen frumenti unam acram, ad semen hordei unam acram, et tempore warrecti unam acram."

[59] *Ibid.*, "Johannes Gere tenet ... unam cotlandam et dimidiam, pro quibus dat octodecim denarios ... Facit forinsecum servitium cum villata."

[60] *Ibid.*, p. 297.

in addition to money rent,[61] Robert Freman a virgate owing weekly ploughing service as well as liabilities to merchet, pannage, tallage and *gersuma*,[62] Richard Forestarius a virgate for the same services as Robert Freman,[63] and Cristina of Houghton a virgate, which was declared to have been given over previously to one Simon Fikebert by Abbot Hugh (1216-31) "sine assensu conventus".[64] Interestingly, if the four free cotlands mentioned above are understood as corresponding to half-virgates,[65] then the seven free tenants listed held a total of seven virgates — the exact number subtracted from the customary framework since the late twelfth century.

It cannot be strictly determined when this alienation from the villeinage occurred, but it was probably during the time of Abbot Hugh Foliot (1216-31), who had gained a somewhat dubious reputation for alienating the customary lands on abbey properties.[66] Certainly a note found appended to the 1252 extent relative to Richard de Hamptone's cotland suggests that the alienation to freehold in that case had not occurred prior to 1200, for not only had Richard's father, Robert, held the cotland before him from Abbot Robert Triainel in villeinage, but he had also held a virgate "quae antiquitus fuit ad opus" in addition to a half-hide and two more virgates.[67]

Clearly, then, the freehold properties in Holywell had increased and the customary lands had decreased between 1160 and 1252. Furthermore, the former had increased at the expense of the latter, and this had most probably occurred between 1200 and 1231. However, by 1252 the juggling of free and customary land was virtually over. There would be no further major incursion into villein land after that date. With but one slight readjustment remaining, customary land in Holywell had reached a plateau by 1252, and it would hold it for the next two centuries. As regards freehold, here the student is victim to the absence of sufficient records. The extent of 1252 is the only source to provide adequate information on the amount of land held freely in mediaeval Holywell. The Hundred Roll of 1279 is, in turn, the only source to allow a glimpse of the network

---

[61] *Carts*, I, p. 297.

[62] *Ibid.*, p. 298. "Arabit etiam qualibet septimana per annum, praeter Natale et autumnum, super terram domini ... Dabit etiam pro filia sua maritanda, gersumam, talliagum, et pannagium cum villata." He further owed precarial service as well as customary rents, with the exception of heusyre (*Ibid.*).

[63] *Ibid.*

[64] *Ibid.* See *infra*, p. 50, note 135.

[65] See *supra*, p. 31, note ⌗ 33.

[66] See Raftis, *Estates*, p. 106.

[67] *Carts.* I, p. 297, note ⌗ 1.

of tenurial relationships within the freehold structure. Thereafter, the surviving manorial account rolls beginning in the early fourteenth century concern themselves only with the demesne and customary lands, while even information from charters or court rolls — themselves not in over-whelming abundance[68] — peters out after 1350. That freehold was an important side to the practice of tenure in fourteenth and fifteenth-century Holywell is more than probable. Despite occasional evidence of the sale of some free tenements to the abbey after 1252,[69] there is no indication anywhere that the abbey succeeded in buying up almost 400 acres of land. The problem, then, is a simple one: for reasons not known, records of free tenure in Holywell-cum-Needingworth from the middle of the fourteenth century are not available. The student of Holywell, therefore, is faced with the opposite of the situation that confronted W. G. Hoskins in his study of Wigston Magna,[70] and he must consequently abandon the question. To attempt to speculate on free tenure in the fourteenth and fifteenth centuries would be not only sterile; it would be extremely unwise.

But if Clio, in one of her frequent capricious moods, slams the door to the freehold structure on the investigator, she leaves ajar the door leading to the customary structure. As already indicated, customary, or villein, land in Holywell had reached a plateau by 1252. In that year there were 16 virgates, 14 cotlands and 14 crofts in villeinage, accounting for a probable 442 acres of land, and broken down into at least 47 units of 13 full virgates, six half-virgates, 14 full cotlands and 14 crofts. This disposition of units appears to have remained unchanged through 1279, the time of the Hundred Roll survey.[71]

---

[68] See *infra*, p. 43 *et seq.*

[69] *Ibid.*

[70] *The Midland Peasant: The Economic and Social History of a Leicestershire Village* (London, 1957). Hoskins found considerable information on freemen and free land in the village but little or no information on customary tenants and holdings. See Chapter III, and esp. p. 55.

[71] The Hundred Roll itself declares that there were 26½ virgates in villeinage ("Item dicunt quod abbas Ram' habet in dictis villatis xxvj virgatas terre et dimidiam in villenagio." RH. II, p. 602; PRO SC 12-8-56), but Professor Kosminsky was quick to point out that this was a probable scribal error of writing "xxvj" for "xvj" (*Studies*, p. 28, note ♯ 2). On the other hand, it could be possible that the figure is not a mistake, but rather a combined total. The survey overlooks, for example, the 14 cotlands in Holywell — a point overlooked as well by Kosminsky, who mistook the 14 "coterelli" for the cotlanders and who consequently believed the crofts had been omitted, although the *opera* described as due from the "coterelli" were those for crofts, not cotlands (*Studies*, p. 30, note ♯ 1) — and refers to three virgates obtained from Berengarius le Moigne ("Item Abbas habet tres virgatas terre in villenagio de dicto Berengario" RH. II, p. 603; PRO SC 12-8-56). If the 14 cotlands are understood as equalling half-virgates and the three "new" virgates are included in calculation, the result is 26 virgates. Whatever the case, whether the scribe meant

By the first decade of the fourteenth century, however, a final readjustment in the number of customary units had taken place. The account rolls for 1307-8,[72] and 1323-24[73] give no numbers for customary tenements, but the roll for 1346-47[74] sets the number at 17 virgates, 15 cotlands and 13 crofts.[75] However, when the customary rent payments of 1307-8 and 1323-24 are broken down, they too are found to have come — in most cases — from 17 virgates, 15 cotlands and 13 crofts.[76]

to write "xxvj" or "xvj", where the extra one-half virgate came from is a mystery, although it could represent a part of the freehold falling back into villeinage. Such a case would not be impossible — an identical process was occurring on the Oxfordshire manor of Cuxham (See Harvey, p. 115, where six villein tenements increased to eight at the expense of freehold between 1277 and 1279) — especially in view of strong efforts by Ramsey abbots from Ranulph (1231-53) through Robert of Nassington (1342-49) to regain alienated properties and buy-out freeholds on abbey estates (See Raftis, *Estates*, pp. 109, 112, esp. note # 60).

It should also be noted that if, in fact, the virgate figure of 26½ is a scribal error for "xvj", and if cotlands were not taken into account at all, then the three "new" virgates from the le Moigne family did not remain in villeinage for long but — with one possible exception — disappeared by the 1340's.

Finally, it is also possible that the figure of 26½ was correct but represented the result of dividing 16 (the RH. virgate figure) into 428 acres — the sum of virgates and cotlands in 1252 — which produces a result of 26 and 3/4.

[72] PRO SC 6-877/15. "Compotus Nicholi prepositi de halywell a festo sancti Michaelis Anno domini J abbatis xxii usque ad eundum festum Anno revoluto."

[73] PRO SC 6-877/17. "Compotus Rogeri de Cranfeld prepositi de halywell de omnibus receptis et expensis suis a festo sancti michaelis Anno domini S. abbatis. viii. usque ad idem festum Anno revoluto." The Public Record Office has mistakenly dated this roll "1325".

[74] PRO SC 6-877/18. "Compotus Johannis Bigge prepositi ibidem a festo sancti Michaelis anno domini R. abbatis, v^to usque ad idem festum anno revoluto." The Public Record Office has dated this roll as either "1348" — the time of Abbot Robert of Nassington (1342-49) — or "1354" — the time of Abbot Richard of Sheryngton (1349-78). However, "Ric" was normally used to designate the abbacy of Richard, and "R" commonly referred to Robert. Therefore, the earlier date is the correct one. Furthermore, as Robert became abbot on 22 January, 1342, the fifth and sixth years of his rule were 1346 and 1347 — not "1348".

[75] The statement is first made in the account roll's rendering of the customary rent payment of heusyre: "Et de viij s. v d. de hewshire de xvij virgatis et xij cotmannis et ix croftis in opere et censu ... Et desunt x d. de bedello et ij akermannis cotmannis et iiij d. de iiij croftis dismissis ad firmam." PRO SC 6-877/18.

[76] In 1307/8, at the St. Andrew term, 8 s. 9 d. q. were paid as heusyre. According to figures supplied in the extent, a virgate paid 12 d. annually, or 4 d. a term; a cotland paid 6 d. or 2 d. a term; and crofts paid 1 d. (*Carts.* I, p. 298, 302, 303). Excused from payment in 1307/8 were three cotlands *in officio* — one to the beadle, and two to the ploughmen. Seventeen virgates (at 4 d. each) and 12 cotlands (at 2 d. each) would account for 7 s. 8 d. of the total, leaving 13 d, q., 13 d. of which would come from 13 crofts (at 1 d. each). At the Annunciation term, 7 s. 8 d. were paid as heusyre — or the total from 17 virgates and 12 cotlands. At the St. Benedict term, 8 s. were paid , accounting for 17 virgates and 12 cotlands, with 4 d. left over — which may have come from one of the free virgates owing customary rents. If the same calculations are repeated

There had been a change in the number of customary units from the mid-thirteenth century, to be sure, but it was by no means a radical one. Virgates and cotlands had each increased by one since 1252. Crofts, on the other hand, had been reduced by one. More important, however, is the fact that the figures of 17, 15 and 13 obtaining by the early fourteenth century would remain fixed thereafter — well into the fifteenth century; and therefore it is possible to speak of a very real continuity to customary land from the middle of the thirteenth century, the only shift being the addition of some 28 acres and the loss of about an acre between the 1270's and the first decade of the fourteenth century. Whether the seventeenth virgate and fifteenth cotland were the result of freehold falling back into villeinage — as was not uncommon in England at this time[77] — or simply part of the le Moigne tenement which had been released to the abbey by 1279[78] cannot be established. But what is of concern here is that, as did the demesne, so too the customary land in Holywell-cum-Needingworth displayed continuity and underwent no significant changes from the late thirteenth century to the fifteenth century.[79] Furthermore, if the total amount of arable in villeinage remained primarily stable during the fourteenth and into the fifteenth century, so too did the number of units into which that land was divided. This is not just a question of virgates and cotlands;[80] it is a question of subdivisions within those larger units.

for the heusyre payments of 1323/24, the total is again 17 virgates, 15 cotlands (12 paying) and 13 crofts.

Similarly, the payments for maltsilver, heringsilver and brewsilver and the *argentum vinee* may be employed. In 1307/8, the maltsilver figure of 21 s. 9 d. is the total from 17 virgates, 12 cotlands (three excused) and 12 crofts. In 1323/24, the sum is again 21 s. 9 d. Heringsilver rendered 14 d. ob. in 1307/8 — a total from 19 virgates, but again two could have been free virgates owing some customary rents. In 1323/24, it yielded 13 d. ob., or a total from 18 virgates. *Argentum vinee* in 1323/24 was paid by nine virgates and 13 cotlands — eight virgates *ad censum* and two cotlands *in officio* being excused.

[77] See *supra*, p. 38, note # 71.

[78] The tenement of Berengarius le Moigne — rated at one hide and several small properties in 1252 — had been granted to the abbey at some point between 1267 and 1279, for the Hundred Roll speaks of a carucate, three virgates and nine "coterelli" held by the abbey "de dono domini Berengarii le Moyne" (RH. II, p. 603; PRO SC 12-8-56). The charter of the transaction has been preserved in the Cartulary (II. pp. 345-46). The grant was part of a wide bestowal on the abbey of properties in Holywell, Needingworth, Woodhurst and Walton and cost the abbey 500 pounds. (*Ibid.*, p. 346).

[79] For this reason — i.e. continuity in demesne and villeinage — it may be supposed that the undocumented free land in Holywell also underwent no major alterations in size during the same period.

[80] It may also be observed that the amount of arable did not change significantly after the fifteenth century either. A map of Holywell-cum-Needingworth preserved in the Hunts. Record

Subdivision, or fragmentation, of tenements was a not uncommon feature of the late thirteenth-century and early fourteenth-century English rural landscape.[81] The pressures of an expanding population are normally cited as a reason for the widespread division and further subdivision of tenements in English villages at this time,[82] and extensive splitting-up of virgates into half and even quarter units is not infrequently encountered.[83] It was a time of real land-hunger,[84] and, in addition to fragmentation of properties, the smallholder and the landless peasant loomed large in almost every locality. Indeed, Kosminsky has estimated that for the region covered by the Hundred Rolls in 1279 (the Midlands and East Anglia), some 29% of the peasantry was inadequately supplied with land — i.e. having less than 5 acres — while a further 36% were but half-virgaters, holding between 10 and 20 acres.[85] M. M. Postan, on the other hand, from evidence of 104 manors on the estates of the bishops of Winchester and Worcester, Glastonbury Abbey and East Anglian Lancastrian estates at the end of the thirteenth century, has concluded that some 50% of the peasantry was insufficiently supplied with land — that is, by Postan's calculations, holding 10 acres or less.[86] The problem

Office and drawn up in the year 1764 gives the total acreage — excluding the vast and yet undrained fens — at that time as just over 1228 acres, most of which was being used for pasture by the late eighteenth century. In addition, an enclosure map — of 1810 — and of which photographic copies are preserved in the Cambridge University Library, shows the extent of individual holdings in the village at the early nineteenth century, the acreage figure then — including properties reclaimed from the fens — being at a little over 2500 acres. Since over a thousand of these acres were located in parts that were still fen up through 1764, the actual acreage — in terms of arable (or possible arable, given the predominance of pastoral activity) had not altered significantly from the Middle Ages. (This is further confirmed by the statement that of the 2911 acres comprising the parish in the 1920's — VCH.Hunts. I, p. 175 — just a little over half is arable or heathland, the rest being meadow and pasture.)

Not only does this point to a continuity of acreage, however. It also points to the close approximation of the Holywell acre to the modern understanding of the term, so that the student of Holywell is not afflicted with the problem often presented by the "customary acre" of the Middle Ages, whose actual size could vary widely. See G. Turner, "Introduction" to the *Calender of the Feet of Fines Relating to the County of Huntingdon* (Cambridge, 1913), and H. L. Gray, *English Field Systems* (Cambridge, Mass. 1913).

[81] See Kosminsky, p. 216; Postan, CEH, I, p. 563; Hilton, *The Economic Development of some Leicestershire Estates in the XIV and XV Centuries*, p. 100; *A Medieval Society*, pp. 114-15; and F. R. H. DuBoulay, *The Lordship of Canterbury*, pp. 134-35.

[82] See Postan, CEH, I, p. 563.

[83] The heavy occurrence of the half-virgater, for example, has been noted by Kosminsky (p. 216), as well as by Hilton (*A Medieval Soceity*, p. 121) and Postan (CEH, I, p. 618).

[84] See Postan, CEH, I, p. 552 et seq.

[85] *Studies*, p. 216.

[86] CEH, I, p. 622.

is complex, involving consideration of both the fragmentation of land parcels on the one hand and the amount of land held by individual peasants on the other. In general, it may be said that fragmentation was common throughout England, that it is agreed that the representative peasant, who is alleged to have maintained himself at a subsistence level, was the half-virgater, with between 10 and 20 acres of land — or, more probably, between 12 and 15 acres[87] — and that anywhere from a third to a half of the peasantry was supplied with 10 acres of land or less.

Holywell, at least on the surface, both conformed to and differed from this pattern. It differed in that although there is evidence of fragmentation of tenements in the second half of the thirteenth and first half of the fourteenth centuries, the fragmentation was not excessive, especially within the customary structure. Specifically, in 1252 the extent recorded the existence of 47 units of customary land: 13 full virgates, six half-virgates, 14 full cotlands and 14 crofts. The Hundred Roll failed to yield any such breakdown of customary units, nor did the account rolls of 1307-8, 1323-24, 1346-47, 1355-56,[88] and 1362-63.[89] However, the account roll of 1370-71,[90] in its list of customary tenants on the manor, reveals 51 units of land: 13 full virgates, seven half-virgates, two quarter-virgates, 14 full cotlands, two half-cotlands and 13 crofts (see Appendix II). In short, in over one hundred years, from the 1250's to the beginning of the 1370's, customary land units in Holywell had been fragmented only to the degree that their total number had increased by four. In addition, this had occurred only in the cases of one virgate — which had been split in half, one half then being further divided into two quarters — and one cotland, which had been halved. Furthermore, since both the virgate and the cotland subjected to this last fragmentation were held *ad censum* in 1370-71,[91] it may be wondered if the fragmentation itself had not occurred only around or shortly after 1300 — when *censum* policies reappeared on the manor after an absence of a century.[92] This is a strong probability since it would perhaps have been easier to arrange for the disposition of a quarter virgate *ad censum* than of one *ad opus*.[93]

---

[87] CEH, I, pp. 618-22; and see Hilton, *A Medieval Society*, pp. 114-15; 121-23.

[88] PRO SC 6-877/19.

[89] PRO SC 6-877/20.

[90] PRO SC 6-877/21.

[91] See *infra*, p. 95 *et seq.*

[92] *Ibid.*

[93] It is not impossible, of course — to believe so would be to underestimate the sometimes incredible ingenuity of the abbey's administrators.

On the surface, therefore, excessive fragmentation of customary tenements does not appear to have played a major role in Holywell's tenurial history in the latter thirteenth and early fourteenth centuries. But it must be admitted that this could, in fact, be erroneous. It has been generally recognized that entries in extents, surveys or accounts do not always reflect tenurial realities with great precision,[94] for, especially as regarded customary land, the primary concern was with fixing responsibility for work or rents due from a tenement and not necessarily with the exact number of persons having an interest in the tenement.[95] As a result, one man might easily be recorded in an extent as holding a virgate — meaning he was responsible for its services — while, in reality, he may have split that virgate into two, three, four or even more parts and sub-let them to his neighbors.[96] Thus, as R. H. Hilton and others have observed, fragmentation and subdivisions of tenements in response to acute land-hunger would escape notice in formal manorial records but would in fact exist in the context of the peasant land market.[97]

Fortunately, the existence of this peasant land market in mediaeval England is not merely a matter of scholarly speculation but is in fact substantially documented. It is beyond dispute that it was flourishing

[94] See, for example, Hilton, *A Medieval Society*, p. 161 ("... the picture of a tenant population evenly divided between these categories is ... quite false. Formal differences in the size of holdings ... were both exaggerated and minimized by the working of the peasant land market ...") and also p. 163. Much the same warning has been voiced by Postan, who has noted, with reference to the estates of St. Peter's, Gloucester, that "manorial sources conceal from our view large numbers of tenants' sub-tenants." (CEH, I, p. 622.)

[95] This "depersonalization" of *opera*, as it may be called, has been particularly stressed by Professor Raftis in *Tenure and Mobility*, pp. 15-16. Indeed, one of the few cases in which the manorial administration would pay special attention to the land dealings of its villein tenants involved the private sub-letting of a customary tenement by a villein to a freeman — with the eventual possibility of alienation. Hence, no doubt, the reason for the nullification of just such an act in Holywell by the villager John de Upwode, who attempted to sub-let his customary properties to two freemen (i.e. one free man and one free woman) in 1318:

"Et dicunt quod Johannes de Upwode nativus tenens de domino dimidiam virgatam terre servilis et de celarario unam virgatam terre servilis praeterquam unam croftam dimisit inde Johanni de Herynggs' libero duas acras et dimidiam ad terminum trium annorum, et Johanne le Clerk duas acras ad eundum terminum. Et totum residuum dicte terre praeterquam tres acras quas retinet penes se dimisit eisdem Johanni et Johanne ad servandum hoc anno pro medietate vesture inde proveniente. Ideo preceptum est quod tota predicta terra capiatur in manus domini, et de exitibus inde provenientibus domino respondeatur." (PRO SC 2-179/18).

[96] An excellent example of this is given by Raftis, *Tenure and Mobility*, pp. 175 and 239, from the Ramsey village of Shillington (1313), where John Hamond sub-let his half-virgate "per percellas aliis diversis."

[97] See Hilton, *A Medieval Society*, p. 161; Postan, CEH, I, p. 626.

in the thirteenth and fourteenth centuries,[98] and, as M. M. Postan has indicated, there is even reason to suspect its existence as early as 1200[99]. That it was not absent from Holywell can also be documented. In addition, in Holywell — as in other localities — it was a market engaging the activities of both freemen and villeins and predominately concerned with small parcels of land, whether free or customary.[100]

The earliest surviving comprehensive evidence of the land market in mediaeval Holywell — the Hundred Roll of 1279 — shows less its actual operation than it does the result of that operation, and it does so further exclusively with respect to freemen. It reveals, in effect, a network of tenurial relationships barely hinted at by the rigid descriptions of the extent some twenty-seven years earlier. The latter had recorded the presence of 11 freemen as tenants on the manor in 1252, from a knight and a cleric to free peasants, holding properties ranging in size from a hide to a pythel.[101] Together, they had held some 376 acres of free land and 10 acres of customary land: one hide, one-half hide and a half-virgate, 10 full virgates, five full cotlands — one of which was a customary cotland — 11 crofts, three manses, six strips and one pythel. By 1279, the one hide — previously held by Sir Berengarius le Moigne — had been sold to the abbey, but there were still 10 virgates, the half-hide (of the Prior of St. Ives, who also held three virgates overlooked by the extent)[102] and a little over 30 acres of free land held freely by a total of 14 persons, one of whom — Robert Morel — had been a tenant in 1252. What is most revealing about the Hundred Roll survey, however, is the tenurial network

---

[98] Professor Raftis, for example, in *Tenure and Mobility*, pp. 63-93, has produced one of the most recent and most comprehensive studies of the peasant land market as it existed on Ramsey manors in the late thirteenth and fourteenth centuries. See also: Homans, *English Villagers of the Thirteenth Century*, p. 19, p. 201 *et seq.*; Kosminsky, *Studies*, p. 38; and Hilton, *The Economic Development of some Leicestershire Estates*, pp. 98-99, for earlier appraisals of the thirteenth and fourteenth-century land market, and the *Carte Nativorum* (Ed. C. N. Brooke and M. M. Postan) for peasant charters from both centuries. In addition, a forthcoming study of the Ramsey village of King's Ripton presently being conducted by Anne Reiber DeWindt (University of Toronto) promises to examine the extent of this early fourteenth-century land market in the context of a single community.

[99] See *Carte Nativorum*, "Introduction", esp. p. xxxix.

[100] The involvement of both freemen and villeins in land leasing and selling in thirteenth and fourteenth-century England has been ably demonstrated most recently by Raftis, *Tenure and Mobility*, pp. 63-93, and Postan, *Carte Nativorum*, "Introduction", pp. xxviii-xxix especially. The smallhold predominance in such transactions is emphasized by the texts in both of the above works and has further been stressed by Homans, *English Villagers of the Thirteenth Century*, p. 201 *et seq.*

[101] See Appendix I.

[102] *Carts.* II, p. 214.

obtaining in the free structure. Thus, the 10 virgates, which were assigned to six persons in 1252 — of which one was a quadruple virgater (Aspelon of Holywell), one a double virgater (Robert Morel) and the remaining four single virgaters (William le ELyr, Robert Freman, Richard Forestarius and Cristina of Houghton)[103] — were still held by six persons in 1279 — of which two men held four and a half virgates jointly (William Hildegar and John But), one held two virgates (Rannulph de Clarvall), one held a virgate and a half (Richard le ELyr) and two held one virgate each (Adam le ELyr and Robert le Frankelein). However, whereas all 10 virgates had been held directly of the abbot in 1252, only eight were so held in 1279. In the latter year, Rannulph de Clarvall held two virgates from Robert Morel, who himself was described as holding only a messuage of one rod, two acres of land and a half-acre of meadow, although, in addition to the two virgates he was apparently sub-letting to Rannulph de Clarvall, he was lessor to William Hildegar of four acres, one rod of land and to Helyas le Hunderd of two acres, one rod.[104] It may be supposed that if an extent had been made of the manor in 1279, Robert Morel would have been set down as holding two virgates and more from the abbot — as he was in 1252[105] — although, in actual fact, he was not retaining the bulk of his property in his own hands.[106]

Robert Morel was not the only freeman in Holywell to have sub-tenants in 1279, however. William Hildegar, who, with John But, held four and a half virgates from the abbot and who, alone, held four acres, one rod from Robert Morel, had a tenant himself: Reginald de Newton, who held a small messuage from him.[107] Reginald de Newton, in addition, was the tenant of Robert Gere for a messuage with a croft of an acre and a half.[108] Finally, William of Houghton (de Houtan'), who may or may not have held from the abbot, had three tenants in 1279: Robert Pollard, holding a messuage and croft of three acres, Adam le ELyr — himself a free virgater of the abbot — holding two acres, and Michael of Holywell — a smallholder of the abbot[109] — holding one acre.[110]

---

[103] See Appendix I.

[104] See PRO SC 12-8-56.

[105] *Carts*. I, p. 297.

[106] It may be further supposed that if such an extent had been drawn up in 1279, Ranulph of Clarvall and Helyas le Hunderd would have been omitted altogether, since they held of Robert Morel, not the abbot.

[107] RH. II, p. 603; PRO SC 12-8-56.

[108] *Ibid*. Robert held 10 acres of land, a messuage of a rod and four acres of meadow from the abbot.

[109] *Ibid*., he held one acre.

[110] *Ibid*.

As admitted, however, the Hundred Roll gives a picture of tenures in Holywell that is both lop-sided and static. It reveals evidence only of free inter-peasant land transactions and further presents them as frozen. But the land market in mediaeval Holywell from the late thirteenth century was neither so narrowly confined nor so rigid. It was a fluid market and one that engaged both free and villein. These facts are emphasized by the few surviving personal charters and court roll entries relative to land conveyance within the village. Although they are not enough in number nor full enough in content to permit a satisfactory description of inter-personal tenurial relationships within the community, they nevertheless bear witness to the real vitality and variety of the land market itself.

In 1281, for example — two years after the Hundred Roll survey — Michael of Holywell, who had held two acres of land from the abbot and William of Houghton in 1279 — received from Abbot William two messuages of customary land in the village, containing over six selions of arable which he and his wife were to hold all the days of their life in return for an annual payment of 10 shillings.[111] About the same year, William of Houghton granted a half-acre of free land in the fields of Holywell

---

[111] Ramsey materials preserved in the Northamptonshire Record Office: (Delapre Abbey, f. 3ᵛ):

" Die Annunciationis beate marie Anno regni regis Edwardi filii regis Henrici octavo, convenit ita inter venerabilem priorem Dominum Willelmum dei gratia Abbatem de Rames' ex una parte et Michaelem de haliwell et Margeriam uxorem eius ex altera videlicet quod predictus abbas concessit et dimisit Michaele et Margerie illud mesuagium in haliwell quod iacet iuxta aquam inter mesuagium Henrici filii Ricardi et mesuagium Walteri Pollard una cum illo mesuagio quod Domina Roysea le moyne quondam tenuit nomine dotis in eadem villa cum crofta adiacente in qua continentur sex seliones terre arabilis, Tenenda et habenda dicta duo mesuagia cum crofta de predicto abbate et successoribus suis dictis michaele et margerie omnibus diebus vite eorum, Reddendo inde annuatim dicto Abbati et successoribus suis dicti Michaelis et margeria (...) decem solidos ad duos terminos anni, videlicet ad pascham quinque solidos, et ad festum sancti michaelis quinque solidos, pro omnibus serviciis consuetudinibus et demandis. Post decessum vero dictorum michaelis et margerie revertantur dicta duo mesuagia cum crofta ad predictum abbatem et successores suos integre et pacifice cum omnibus edificiis et aliis pertinenciis suis sine contradictione alicuius subsequentis. Pro hac autem concessione et dimissione dederunt dicti michaelis et margeria predicto abbati dimidiam marcam sterlingorum in gersumam. In cuius rei testimonium alter alterius scripto sigillum suum apposuit /4ʳ/ Hiis testibus Willelmo Hildegar, Willelmo de Stowe, Ranulpho de Clervaus, Roberto Morel, Johanne de Bradenach, Johanne folyot, Roberto de hale clerico et aliis."

The customary nature of the land is emphasized by the 10 shilling payment in lieu of "servitia, consuetudines et demanda", the restrictions on alienation ("revertantur dicta duo mesuagia cum crofta ... integre et pacifice cum omnibus edificiis ...") and the payment of a half-mark in gersuma.

and Needingworth to Radulph de Vernun.[112] Indeed, between the 1280's and the 1340's, evidence has been preserved of 33 individual transfers — or attempted transfers — of property by sale, lease or grant and between freemen, villeins and the abbey.

In 1288, Roysea le Franklyn attempted to lease one and a half acres of land and a half-acre of meadow to the villager Walter Bercar', and two and a half acres of land to Robert Russell.[113] In the same year, the villager Robert Sky attempted to lease one acre of land to Nicholas Faber and one acre of land to a Henry Dyke.[114] In each case, the lease was nullified by the court and the land ordered seized. The reason is not given, but it was certainly not a prohibition of sub-letting between freemen and villeins. As Professor Raftis clearly demonstrated in his study of peasant land conveyances on Ramsey manors in the thirteenth and four-

---

[112] Ramsey materials, Northants, f. 3ʳ. "Sciant presentes et futuri quod ego Willelmus de houcton' dedi et concessi et hac presenti carta mea confirmavi Radulpho de Vernun pro servicio suo unam dimidiam acram terre cum pertinenciis in campis de haliwelle et de Nidingworth abutantem super iter infra haliwelle et Nidingworth iacentum inter terram Ade le heyr et terram Ade filii Gilberti, habendam et tenendam de me et heredibus meis sibi et heredibus suis et cuicumque dare vel assignare vendere vel assignare voluerit libere quiete bene et in pace et integre cum omnibus libertatibus dicte terre pertinencibus, Reddendo inde annuatim michi et heredibus meis ille et heredes sui vel sui assignati unam par (....) pro (....) seculari servicio exactione et demanda et (....). Et ego Willelmus de houcton et heredes mei predictam acram cum pertinenciis predicto Radulpho et heredibus suis vel assignatis contra omnes gentes warentizabimus acquietabimus et defendemus in perpetuum. pro hac autum donatione et concessione et carte (et) mee confirmatione dedit michi dictus Radulphus viginti solidos sterlingorum in gersumam /3ᵛ/ et ut hec mea donacio et concessio et carte mee confirmationis perpetuam habeat potestatem huic presenti scripto sigillum meum apposui. Hiis testibus Domino Berengario le Moyne, Willelmo hildegar, Johanne Gere, Willelmo le heyr, Roberto Morel, Ricardo de hampton', Ricardo le messager, Johanne filio Roberti et aliis."

It may be noted that both John Gere and William le ELyr acted as witnesses to this transaction in 1280 or 1281. Both were free tenants of the abbot in 1252, yet both were omitted in the Hundred Roll survey of 1279. The former had held freely a cotland and a half in 1252, the latter a virgate. Since, in 1279, a Robert Gere held some half-dozen acres of land and Richard le ELyr and Adam le ELyr each held virgates, this may be interpreted as examples of the conveyance of land within a family before death — a not uncommon practice. (See Raftis, *Tenure and Molility*, pp. 42-46, for Ramsey villages, and also M. M. Postan and J. Titow, "Heriots and Prices on Winchester Manors." *Economic History Review*, 2nd series. XI (1958-59), pp. 392-417, for the practice on Winchester estates.)

[113] PR SC 2-179/5. "Roysea le Franklyn locavit unam acram terre et dimidiam et dimidiam acram prati ad duas vesturas Waltero Bercar'. Ideo capiatur etc."

"Et dicunt quod eadem Roysea locavit Roberto Russell duas acras terre et dimidiam. Ideo preceptum est etc."

[114] *Ibid.* "Et dicunt quod Robertus Sky locavit unam acram terre Nicholo Faber ad ij vesturas, et unam acram terre Henrico Dyke ad eundum terminum. Ideo capiatur etc."

teenth centuries, there were very few restrictions on a villein leasing customary land to a freeman, or on a freeman leasing free land to a villein.
The only hard and fast rule seems to have been a general prohibition
on the conveyance of villein lands — especially to freemen — without
the consent or knowledge of the lord.[115] Since Robert Sky was undoubtedly
a Holywell villein,[116] and at least one of the two men to whom he leased
land was free — Henry Dyke[117] — the nullification of his arrangement
could have been based on his having acted without seigniorial permission.
The same may also apply to the case of Roysea le Franklyn, whose legal
status, despite her surname normally being associated with the free,[118]
is not at all certain, who may have been leasing the parcels to her two
fellow villagers without first obtaining permission.[119]

Whatever the reason for the nullification of the 1288 transactions, they
were exceptions to the general pattern of unrestricted conveyance. The
only other recorded case of the court nullifying a transaction was the
1318 instance of John de Upwode, a villein, who had tried to sublet all
but three acres of his customary tenement of a virgate and a half to two
free villagers.[120] Remaining examples of conveyance were carried out
without any difficulty. Thus, in 1301, John Bercar' purchased one rod
of land from Mariota Seman and was ordered only to produce his charter
in the court.[121]

From the year 1308 survives the first in a handful of charters concerned
with the land transactions of the Needingworth villein Richard le Eyr.

---

[115] See *Tenure and Mobility*, pp. 82 and 84 *et seq*; 90-91.

[116] Robert had been reeve of either Holywell or Slepe in 1279. A cellarer's roll for that year,
involving receipts from both vills, without distinction, refers to "Robertus Sky Prepositus." (BM.
Add.Ch. 39736.)

[117] It is not stated in the court roll that Henry was a freeman, but it is probable, especially
as he never again appeared in the village. Nicholas Faber, who served as an ale-taster for Needingworth in 1301, was probably a villein.

[118] See Homans, pp. 248-49.

[119] Walter Bercar' was most probably a villein — other members of the family certainly were
and continued to be long after the middle of the fourteenth century, when the family name had
been anglicized to "Shepperd". Robert Russell, who was village butcher in 1311 and 1313
and a court juror in 1313, may have been personally free, but it is unlikely. Richard Russell
— a tenant in 1252 — had been a villein, and later members of the family gave no sign of being
free.

[120] See *supra*, p. 43, note ♯ 95, for text.

[121] PRO SC 2-179/11. The amount paid for the land was not indicated. Apparently the
actual purchase had been made a year earlier, in 1300, for in the 1301 entry John was ordered
to find a new pledge for producing his charter, and consequently Nicholas Faber replaced Robert
Franklyn as John's guarantor.

That Richard was a villein is documented in three sources. Charters of 6 and 8 March, 1317, described him as "nativus",[122] while six years earlier, in 1311, he was fined sixpence in the manor court for falsely claiming free status.[123] That there was cause for some confusion in the matter of Richard's legal status arose from two situations. First, the Eyr family had been free at an earlier date — they were among the freeholders in both 1252 and 1279[124] — but had obviously given up their freedom, or at least one line of the family had done so, sometime before 1300. Secondly, Richard, although a villein, was openly engaged in the holding of free lands and was even a suitor at the honour court of Broughton.[125]

On 4 October, 1308, Richard le Eyr granted to Geoffrey of Holywell, his wife Beatrix and their daughter Emma free lands located, not in Holywell or Needingworth, but in St. Ives, in return for an annual token gillyflower.[126] It was not an outright grant, however, but rather a twenty-year lease, for two years later, on 22 September, 1310, Geoffrey and Beatrix turned over the St. Ives properties to Robert de Swayefeld and his wife Emma (presumably their daughter, now married to Robert), and the charter recording the transfer referred to the tenure as the "residue of a term of twenty years in 5 acres, $3\frac{1}{2}$ roods of land in St. Ives which they (i.e. Geoffrey and Beatrix) held of Richard le Eyr of Nyddyngworth."[127]

In 1315, Richard le Eyr was again letting-out land, this time in Needingworth, to Joan, daughter of Ralph of Needingworth, for a term of seven years from the date of the charter (29 September, 1315).[128] The following year, between 29 September and 18 October, 1316, he released free land and meadow parcels to William and Mariota le Eyr. The first grant (29 September) was for a *placea* "with the house built thereon, and other land in Needingworth, for a certain sum of money which they gave him in

---

[122] *A Descriptive Catalogue of Ancient Deeds in the Public Record Office* (London, 1890), Vol. I, ♯ A 1210 (p. 148) and ♯ A 1308 (p. 148). Further references to volumes in this series will be cited "Ancient Deeds".

[123] PRO SC 2-179/16.

[124] See Appendix I. The name was variously spelled "Eyr, le Eyr, Leyr, le Heyr, Heyr, Heredis, Heres".

[125] Richard was noted for default at the Broughton court of 1351 (BM.Add. Ch. 39471).

[126] *Ancient Deeds*, I, ♯ B 1559 (p. 365). The land — described as five acres two years later — may have formed part of the original tenement of a free half-virgate in St. Ives granted to William le Eyr by Adam the son of Richard of Needingworth in 1247 (Ramsey materials, Northamptonshire Record Office, f. 1ᵛ) and which William was still holding in 1251 (*Carts.* I, p. 287).

[127] *Ibid.*, I, ♯ A 1214 (p. 137). In 1317, Robert and Emma in turn released the land to the abbey and received them back from the abbot for the term of their lives for five shillings' annual rent. (*Ibid.*, ♯ A 140, A 1309).

[128] *Ibid.*, ♯ A 1307 (p. 147).

his need"[129] — in other words, the grant was apparently Richard's way
of repaying a loan. The second grant, dated 18 October, was for "land
in Niddingworth meadow, in a place called 'le Fordole'".[130] That the
land was indeed free land is confirmed by a charter of 8 March, 1317,
in which William le Eyr released to Simon, abbot of Ramsey, "all his title
to a certain portion of a messuage and land in Niddingworth, which
he held by demise of Richard le Eyr, 'nativus' of the said abbey".[131]

The final recorded episode in Richard le Eyr's varied dealings in land
is found in the court roll for 1328, where he obtained one messuage of
a half-virgate of free land from the fee of the lord:

> "Et dicunt quod Ricardus le Eyr perquisivit unum mesuagium
> dimidie virgatae terre libere de feodo domini. Et venit in plena
> curia et ostendit cartam suam et fecit fidelitatem."[132]

Other villagers besides Richard le Eyr were dealing in land in Holywell
during the first half of the fourteenth century, however. William of Houghton, who had three tenants in 1279, sold a *pecia* of one messuage to the
freeman Egidius of Holywell in 1306,[133] and in the same year he bought
a *pecia* of a messuage from Robert Pollard — who had been one of his
tenants in 1279.[134] Robert Pollard, in addition to selling the aforesaid
pecia to William, also sold a messuage to Simon le Botwryte in 1306.[135]

---

[129] *Ancient Deeds*, I, *Ibid.*, ♯ A 1310 (p. 148).

[130] *Ibid.*, ♯ A 1300 (p. 147).

[131] *Ibid.*, ♯ A 1308 (p. 148).

[132] PRO SC 2-179/25.

[133] PRO SC 2-179/12. "Et dicunt quod Egidius de halywelle emit de Willelmo hokyton unam
peciam de mesuagio suo ad quantitatem viginti perticarum in longitudine et in latitudine quatuor
perticarum. Ideo distringatur ad ostendendam cartam suam."

[134] PRO SC 2-179/12. "De Michaele de halywell plegio Willelmo de hokyton quia non habuit
dictum Willelmum ad ostendendam cartam suam de una pecia mesuagii quam emit de Roberto
Pollard. vj.d. plegius Willelmus le Eyr. Et preceptum est quod dictus Willelmus distringatur
ad ostendendam cartam suam etc."

Since William already had a pledge for producing his charter in 1306, it may be inferred that
the purchase from Pollard had taken place the previous year. It may even further be suggested
that the *pecia* of a messuage bought by William was the same one he sold to Egidius of Holywell
in 1306.

[135] *Ibid.* "Adhuc preceptum est distringere Simonem le Botwryte ad ostendendam cartam suam
de uno mesuagio quod emit de Roberto Pollard de halywell. Et testatum est quod distringatur
per unam astam et non iustificiat se. Ideo tenatur dicta districtione, et plus capiatur donec etc.".

According to the court roll of 1318 (PRO SC 2-179/18), Robert Pollard still had at least one
messuage in that year.

It may further be noted that Robert Pollard's relationship to William of Houghton — noted
in 1279 — appears to have been terminated in or before 1304. In that year, William — whose
surname was "Fykeberd" and who was the son of Simon Fikeberd and Cristina of Houghton

Yet another Hundred Roll tenant was active in the early fourteenth century: Ranulph de Clervaux (de Clarvall, de Claris Vallibus, de Clersuay). In 1311, he sold eight acres of land to a Thomas de Warewyke and 10 acres of land to John Baroun.[136] The following year (1312), the same John Baroun received a messuage, a virgate (i.e. 18 acres of land) and two acres of meadow from Ranulph's widow, Cristiana.[137]

Nor did it stop at that. Sometime after 1312, John received from Cristiana what appears to have been the bulk of the remainder of her late husband's properties: two messuages, another virgate (i.e. 18 acres of land) and two more acres of meadow.[138]

John Baroun and the Clervaux were not the only people busy in land affairs in 1311, however. In that year, Michael of Holywell was active again, selling a half-acre and rod of land to the widow of John Thomeys.[139]

(the latter tenant of a free virgate in 1252) — released his properties to the abbey. "Universis Christi fidelibus presens scriptum visuri vel audituri Willelmus filius quondam Simonis Fykeberd de Houcton salutem in domino sempiternam. Noveritis me concessisse, remisse et omnino pro me et heredibus meis quietum clamasse Imperpetuum Domino Johanni, dei gratia Abbati Rameseiensi et eiusdem loci conventui et eorum successoribus totum jus et clamum quod habui vel aliquo modo habere potui ... et in una dimidia marca annui redditus quam anuatim recipere consuevi de quodam tenemento Roberti Pollard in villa de haliwell ..." BM.Add.Ch. 33742.

[136] PRO SC 2-179/16. "Et dicunt quod Johannes Baroun perquisivit de Ranulpho de Clerevaus x acras terre qui venit et ostendit cartam suam etc. et fecit fidelitatem in curia de Broughton.

"Et dicunt quod Thomas de Warewyke perquisivit de eodem Ranulpho viij acras terre. Ideo distringatur ad ostendendam cartam suam etc."

[137] *Ramsey Register*, 41ʳ. "Johannes Baroun venit in plena curia et fecit domino fidelitatem pro uno messuagio, xviij acris terre et ij acris prati que perquisivit de Cristiana que fuit uxor Rannulphi de Claris Vallibus in Niddyngworth et halywell et habet diem ad cognoscendum per que servitia etc. usque ad Natalem domini."

[138] *Ramsey Register*, 5ᵛ. "Johannes Baroun venit in plena curia et fecit domino fidelitatem pro duo messuagiis, xviij acris terre et duabus acris prati que perquisivit de Xpiana que fuit uxor Ranulphi de Clarisvallibus in Nidingworth et halywell et habet diem ad cognescendum per que servitia etc. usque ad Natalem domini."

Ranulph had held a messuage, two virgates and 10 acres of meadow from Robert Morel in 1279 (RH. II, p. 603; PRO SC 12-8-56). Obviously, at some time between 1279 and 1311, Ranulph had acquired full title to them. That Robert would have so relinquished them is not improbable, especially as the last members of his family appear briefly in the Holywell court roll of 1294: all women — Alice, Elena and Isabella Morel — and all described as Robert's daughters. (BM. Add.Ch.39597.)

It may further he added that John Baroun rounded off his dealings with the Clervaux family in 1322. In that year, he acquired a croft in Ramsey from Radulph de Clervaus — Ranulph's son (BM.Add.Ch. 33767). In 1325, he apparently disposed of it, for in that year he granted a messuage in Ramsey to Roger and Matilda of Houghton (*Ancient Deeds*, II, p. 357).

[139] PRO SC 2-179/16. "Et dicunt quod (...) relicta Johanni(s) Thomeys perquisivit dimidiam acram terre et unam rodam de Michaele de haliwell (...) Et compertum est quod tenetur de domino et fecit fidelitatem."

In the same year, Matilda Clericus, widow of John Clericus of St. Ives, inherited an acre and a half of free land her husband had bought in Holywell from John and Thomas of the village of Bernewell.[140] In subsequent years, the villein Henry Tyffayne received a half-acre of land from a Margaret Godale in 1318,[141] and in 1321 a John le Fischer granted an unspecified amount of land in the Needingworth field called "Schortbene-hill" to Adam Wyoth,[142] while Roysea le Clerk received an acre of free land from the Vicar of St. Ives.[143] In 1341, the Feet of Fines for Hunting-donshire recorded a dispute over two messuages, four acres of land and an acre of meadow in Needingworth between John Gavelok and William and Matilda Smyth of that vill.[144] In 1336, agreement was reached between Roger de Cranfeld of Needingworth and Thomas and Matilda Filers of Fenystanton over a messuage and rood of land in Needingworth,[145] and in 1345 there was a dispute between Abbot Robert Nassington and Robert le Somenour and his wife Johanna of St. Ives over a half-acre of land and five messuages in St. Ives and Holywell.[146] Lastly, there were not only land transactions between villagers in the early fourteenth century. Between 1317 and 1349, at least five sales of property to the abbey itself were made by persons holding free lands within Holywell and Needing-worth and either residing in or outside the village.[147]

---

[140] PRO SC 2-179/16. "Preceptum est seisire in manus domini unam acram terre libere salvo iure cuilibet quam Johannes Clericus liber qui mortuus est emit de Johanne de Bernewell et di-midiam acram terre quam idem Johannes emit de Thoma de Bernewell quousque heredes dicti Johannis venerint et fecerint domino ea que facere debent pro predicta terra. Et postea compertum est quod Matilda vidua dicti Johannis que adhuc superstes est coniungitur cum uno suo et osten-dit cartas que hoc testantur."

[141] PRO SC 2-179/18. "Willelmus le Palmere est plegius Henrici Tyffayn ad ostendendam cartam suam de dimidia acra terre quam adquisivit de Margareta Godhole ad proximam."

[142] Ancient Deeds, II, ♯ A 1206 (p. 137). John granted land again to the same Adam Wyoth in 1332. (Ibid., I, ♯ A 1367, p. 154).

[143] PRO SC 2-179/21. "Et dicunt quod Roysea le Clerk adquisivit unam acram terre libere de vicario de Sancto Ivone. Ideo distringatur ad ostendendam cartam suam ad proximam. Postea venit et ostendit cartam suam et fecit fidelitatem."

[144] A Calendar of the Feet of Fines Relating to the County of Huntingdon levied in the King's Court from the fifth year of Richard I to the end of the reign of Elizabeth, 1194-1603. Ed. G. J. Turner. Cambridge Antiquarian Society, Octavo Publications, No. XXXVII, 1913, p. 71. Unfortunately, the Feet of Fines give no indication as to the final resolution of a dispute, but they are never-theless helpfull in documenting rival claims to pieces of free land in the village.

[145] Ibid., p. 68.

[146] Ibid., p. 73.

[147] In 1317, a William de Cortone and a Richard de Spalding were granted a license of mort-main to grant properties in Needingworth to the abbey (Carts. II, p. 112). In 1325 and 1327, Robert Swayefeld and William de Eyr, respectively, released lands to the abbot, and in 1329

The examples given above of land transfers through sale, grant or lease in Holywell-cum-Needingworth from the late thirteenth to the middle of the fourteenth century are evidence not only of a very real land market in the village, but also confirmation of the fact that in Holywell, as elsewhere in England, individual tenements were not necessarily as uniform and rigid in reality as they were in the descriptions of extents, surveys and account rolls. Admittedly, the majority of the cases cited involved freemen, but this must be ascribed to the accidental survival of records, for, as shown, the land market was not restricted to the *liberi tenentes*. The example of Richard le Eyr, *nativus*, is striking proof of that fact alone. In addition, Richard le Eyr serves also as a good example of a villein dealing in the free land market. However, if it was true that both freemen and villeins engaged in the buying, selling and leasing of free and customary land in the village, and that consequently labels such as "virgater, cotlander and crofter" cannot always be assumed to rigidly define the total number of acres held by an individual villager, still it may be wondered if the land market produced radical alterations in the composition of individual holdings. For one, with the exceptions of John de Upwode, Thomas Gere and John Baroun, the majority of the land transactions cited concerned small parcels of land, seldom exceeding an acre or two. This, coupled with the implication of a frequently rapid

a William de Nauntone and his wife Joan surrendered "all their rights in the manors" of Holywell and Needingworth (*Ancient Deeds*, IV, ♯ A 7258, p. 140). Finally, between 1343 and 1349, Thomas Gere, a Holywell freeman, sold half his tenement to the abbey for just over 33 pounds (*Chronicon*, p. 355).

Thomas Gere is himself an example of activity in land. The son of a Roger Gere, he was nevertheless the heir of Robert — holder of a cotland and a half in 1252 and still a tenant in 1279. In 1297, upon attaining the age of 21, Thomas was put in possession of his inheritance, described as two messuages and 17 and a half acres of land, for which he was to render 18 d. a year, two suits at the Broughton court and forensic service: *Ramsey Register*, 31ʳ — "Inquisitio facta per bonos et legales homines in plena curia (i.e. de Broughton) de etate Thome filii Rogerii de halywell et heredis Roberti Gere qui dicunt per sacramentum suum quod habet etatem viginti unius anni et amplius et quod dictus Robertus tenuit die qua obiit in eadem duo messuagia et xvij acras terre et dimidiam cum pertinentiis. Et fecit fidelitatem coram senescallo et recognovit quod debet domino pro dicta terra octodecim denarios ad tres anni terminos et faciet duas sectas ad istam curiam et faciet forinsecum servitium."

Since the holding was probably former villein land, this may be an example of Robert Gere — himself a freeman but perhaps married to a *nativa* — arranging to have his freehold taken up by a free heir, thereby frustrating its possible resumption into villeinage. With the exception of Thomas, all other Geres in fourteenth-century Holywell were *nativi*.

In 1311, Thomas purchased a free virgate (i.e. 18 acres of land) in Holywell from Ivo of Hurst (PRO SC 2-179/16), and in 1332 he sold one acre "de feodo domini" to John, the son of Egidius of Holywell (PRO SC 2-179/26).

turn-over in such holdings — for example, Richard le Eyr's grants to William le Eyr and their regranting to the abbey within two years, the quick transfer of one *pecia* from Robert Pollard to William of Houghton to Egidius of Holywell within one year, and the evidence of leases for specific short terms of two crops — raises the suspicion that the land market may have been utilized less for creating permanent additions to total acreage than to meet immediate and temporary needs or for quick gain.[148]

In general, then, although it must be admitted that the availability of the land market offered opportunities for very real variety in the actual sizes of individual holdings at any one time, it may also be tentatively concluded that, given the markedly smallhold nature of the land market, the variations in tenements would most likely be in terms of a few acres rather than in terms of massive blocs of virgates, semi-virgates or whole cotlands.[149]   That there were more tenants, more actual landholders in the village than indicated by an extent is readily granted, for this would be a result of the workings of the land market. However, if the number of actual landholders in the village is to be increased beyond that given

---

[148] It is extremely difficult to advance solid supports or proofs for this suspicion from the surviving records, but it is a question that may bear further study than has already been given. Postan, for example, has stressed the predominance in land dealings of the "wealthier villagers", who possibly acquired extra lands for the purpose of subletting them for profit (CEH, I, pp. 625-26). Unfortunately, for Holywell, not enough examples of land transfers have survived to permit a quantitative assessment of individual involvements. What has survived neither confirms nor denies Postan's suggestion, since, although a Richard le Eyr would have stood among the top level of villagers — at least from the standpoint of tenure (the Eyrs had been virgaters throughout the second half of the thirteenth century) — and the family itself was represented more than once on court juries, there is no way to determine confidently how active or inactive some villagers who appeared as lessors, buyers or sellers but once or twice really were. (The Bercars, for example, were represented twice — by Walter and John — but the family itself did not assume a definitely major role in the village until after the middle of the fourteenth century.) Despite these difficulties, however, the question of the exploitational nature of the land market in the early fourteenth century still remains, and perhaps it is tentatively supported not only by the more readily recognizable exploitational quality of land dealings after the middle of the century (See *infra*, Chapter II), but also by a reappraisal of the importance and varied uses of the small parcel in village economy. For some suggestions as to the important place of smallholds in the mediaeval village, see G. Duby, *L'économie rurale*, pp. 59-62, 166 *et seq.*, 191-192 and 377-79 for European society in general, and Raftis, *Tenure and Mobility*, pp. 91-92, for the English Midlands in particular.

[149] The exception in Holywell would of course be John de Upwode, who tried to sublet his virgate and a half in 1318. But it may be wondered if John was not indeed an exception, at least in Holywell. In such a village, where the normal virgate averaged only 18 acres, it may be questioned how many single virgaters would have been willing or able to regularly dispose of a half or more of their tenements.

in a "frozen" and demesne-oriented source, it should probably be increased in terms of the small and intermediate tenants, rather than of large landholders.

This having been stated, attention can now turn to the very question of the proportion of large, intermediate and smallholders in Holywell-cum-Needingworth in the latter thirteenth century and first half of the fourteenth century. Specifically, consideration shall be given first to the concentration of tenants classified in terms of virgates, semi-virgates, cotlands, crofts and other parcels, and, secondly, in terms of probable estimated acreage. An attempt shall then be made to determine how the Holywell pattern corresponded to that generally posited for mediaeval England at the time.

Using the extent as a guide for 1252 — but mindful that the actual total number of landholding persons in the village was probably not given — there were at least 56 peasants (both free and villein) holding land in Holywell-cum-Needingworth in that year[150]. Of these 56 peasants, nine were freemen and 47 were villeins or *consuetudinarii*. Of the freemen, there were six virgaters, two of whom were multiple virgaters.[151] Two other men held cotlands.[152] In addition, a double virgater — Robert Morel — also held a cotland and a half besides his virgates. The remaining freeman was a smallholder at one pythel.[153] Among the 47 villeins, 13 persons held a virgate apiece, six men were half-virgaters, 13 were cotlanders, 13 — four of them women and all widows — held crofts, and two persons held even smaller parcels. There were no villeins recorded as holding two virgates or more, but there were at least five multiple tenants: one virgater also holding a forera, a cotlander also holding one rod, and three croftholders who also held a forera each. (See Appendix I) Calculating on the basis of land units alone, then, out of 56 peasants named as tenants in 1252, two men — or 4 % — held two virgates or more of land. Seventeen persons — or 30 % — held virgates; six — 11 % — held half-virgates; 15 — 27 % — held cotlands;[154] 13 — 23 % — held crofts; and three persons — or 5 % — held other small parcels. Or, compressing the figures into larger blocs: of the 56 peasant tenants in 1252, 30 % were virgaters, 38 % were semi-virgaters (considering the cotland as a semi-virgate) and 28 %

---

[150] Berengarius le Moigne, holding a hide, and the Prior of St. Ives, holding a half-hide and three virgates, have been omitted as exceptional cases in Holywell's tenurial structure.

[151] See Appendix I.

[152] See Appendix I.

[153] See Appendix I.

[154] See Appendix I.

were smallholders. An additional 4 % held two virgates or more. Viewed in this manner — from the standpoint of land units — Holywell was not unlike the majority of midland villages in the second half of the thirteenth century, for, according to Professor Kosminsky's calculations, of the manors studied in 1279, 36% of the tenants were half-virgaters and 29% were smallholders.[155]

However, as already pointed out, the Holywell virgate and cotland differed in acreage from the mediaeval English "norm". Consequently, it is necessary to further break-down the peasant tenants of 1252 according to probable acreage. Taking the virgate as 18 acres, the cotland as 10 acres and the croft as averaging an acre, it appears that of the 56 peasants in the mid-thirteenth century, three — or 5 % — held each over 20 acres of land;[156] 17 — or 30% — held 18 acres of land; 20 — or 36% — held about 10 acres; and 16 — or 29% — held an acre or a little more. Compressing these figures, it may be observed that in 1252, out of 56 peasant tenants in Holywell, 20 — or 35.7 % — held 18 acres of land or more, and 36 — or 64.3 % — held about 10 acres of land or less.

This, however, is only a rough calculation based on known tenants listed in the extent, and, as repeatedly pointed out, the extent did not necessarily account for all persons holding land, in one way or another, in the village. A more accurate picture of the disposition of land in Holywell in 1252 would require the consideration of two other factors: first, the land market, and, secondly, the population. Regarding the former, it has been observed above that the land market was very real and reasonably fluid. It was also largely a smallhold market, and it may therefore be suggested that in all probability many of the persons actually holding land in the village but not mentioned in the extent would be smallholders and thus increase the number of tenants at 10 acres or less. As for population, here the student is forced to resort to a rough speculation. There are no population figures for Holywell for any period in the Middle Ages. What is certain about 1252 is that there were at least 56 peasant landholders in the village, representing some 49 distinct family groups.[157] That these were not all the families in Holywell in the 1250's may be supposed from conditions in the early fourteenth century. In 1300, for example, there is convincing evidence for the presence in the village of approximately 66 family groups.

---

[155] *Studies*, p. 216.

[156] Aspelon of Holywell, *ca.* 72-80 acres (four virgates); John Gere, *ca.* 25 acres (two and a half cotlands); and Robert Morel, *ca.* 51-55 acres (two virgates, one and a half cotlands).

[157] This last statement is based on the number of individual surnames among the tenants.

Since, by the early 1300's, a demographic decline in England was already in motion,[158] whereas population was, in general, heavy in the middle of the thirteenth century,[159] it may be suggested that the number of families in the village in the 1250's was probably at least equal to the number in 1300, and possibly even larger. Even if it were the same — 66 families — the extent would have failed to supply information on some 26% of village families. If, further, out of the 49 known tenant families, 31 — or 63% — were represented as holding only 10 acres of land or less, a corrected estimate of the total number of families in the village holding 10 acres or less — and including the landless — is 48, or 73%.[160] It is a high figure, to be sure, but, given the emphasis of recent scholarship on the great mass of the smallholding population in mediaeval England in the thirteenth century,[161] it should not come as a surprise.

If, however, it is accepted that 63% (based on the number of definitely-known tenant families) to 73% (based on an estimate of the probable total number of families) of the families in Holywell were engaged in holding 10 acres or less of land in the 1250's, it may be asked if any evidence exists for a similar disposition in subsequent years. Unfortunately, because of the absence of adequate lists of tenants in the Hundred Roll of 1279 and the account rolls between 1307/8 and 1362/63, that is a question that cannot be satisfactorily answered. There is not a useable list of tenants in Holywell after 1252 until the account roll for 1370/71. Nevertheless, on the basis of information supplied in that late source, out of 52 known village tenants,[162] two held more than one virgate,[163] 11 held a virgate (26%), seven held half-virgates or a little more, three held more than one cotland (19%), nine held cotlands (17%), and 20 held other — and smaller — parcels (39%). In terms of acres, however — not of units — four men held more than 20 acres of land, or 8% of the known 52 tenants.

---

[158] See *infra*, Chapter III, p. 166 *et seq.*

[159] *Ibid.*

[160] As already indicated, this is a highly speculative estimate. The figure of 48 is the result of adding 31 known 10-acre or less tenant families to 17 additional probable families, that in turn is based on a probable 66 families in the village in the 1250's. That the 17 "shadow" families were in the 10-acre or less bracket is itself another probability, based essentially on the fact that the land market was largely a smallhold market.

[161] See, for example, Postan, CEH, I, p. 622, who does not shrink from suggesting a minimal figure of 50% as the result of investigation of conditions on some 104 Midland manors.

[162] There were some 96 persons holding property altogether in Holywell in 1370/71, but 44 were non-residents, holding, in addition, fen parcels but little, if any, arable.

[163] See Appendix II. The two men held from a virgate and a quarter to a virgate and a cotland. There were no double virgaters listed as such.

Twelve held between 18 and 20 acres, or 23 %; nine held from 11 to 17
acres, or 17 %; six held from six to 10 acres, or 12 %; and 21 held five
acres of land or less, or 40 %. Compressing these figures, out of 52 named
tenants, 31 % held 18 acres of land or more, 17 % held between 11 and
17 acres, and 52 % held 10 acres or less. In terms of families, out of 39
village families known to be tenants in 1370/71, 16, or 41 %, held 18 acres
of land or more; five, or 13 %, held between 11 and 17 acres; and 18,
or 46 %, held 10 acres or less.[164] However, as there were a probable 53
families in the village in 1370,[165] — and again assuming that these 14
"shadow" families were smallholders (if tenants at all) — a corrected
estimate of the landholding of families would be: 30 % at 18 acres or more;
10 % at 11 to 17 acres; and 60 % at 10 acres or less. That this is a different
proportion from the one suggested for 1252 is immediately recognizable.
Nevertheless, it must further be admitted that it is not radically different.
The persons and families holding 18 acres of land or more still remained
in, or near, the 30-percentile range, and again in 1370/71 as in 1252,
the majority of these were bunched around 18 acres. The real readjustment
between 1252 and 1370 was in the percentage of persons and families
holding 10 acres or less. Whereas in 1252, 64.3 % of the known tenants
had held 10 acres or less, in 1370 the figure had dropped to 52 %. Similarly
in terms of families: 63 % to 73 % of the village families (both known and
estimated) had held 10 acres or less; in 1370, 46 % to 60 % held in that
range. The reduction can be explained by the appearance of the category
of villagers holding over 10 acres of land but less than full virgates. They
accounted for some 17 % of the tenants listed in 1370, and, in terms of families, from 10 % to 13 %. Their appearance comes as no surprise. Considering
the factors of demographic decline in the village in the fourteenth century
and the increased utilization of leases and rental policies by the abbey,
especially after the middle of the century,[166] it is to be expected that Holywell
would experience a general increase in the amount of land held by individuals or families, particularly as this seems to have been common to most of
England at the time.[167] What the student would like to know is when

---

[164] More specifically: 20 acres or more — 10, or 26 %;
                          18-20 acres   — 6, or 15 %;
                          11-17 acres   — 5, or 13 %;
                          10 acres or less   — 18, or 46 %.

[165] See *infra*, Chapter III, p. 167.

[166] See *infra*, Chapters II and III, p. 144 *et seq.*, and 166 *et seq.*

[167] See Postan, CEH, I, p. 565, where attention is drawn to the gradual decline in the number
of wholly landless men from the early fourteenth century, for example, while, writing of the
late fourteenth century, it is noted that there occurred a further reduction in the number of village
smallholders, who "declined ... by promotion into the groups above them ..." (p. 630).

this shift began to take place in Holywell, and in this the silence of the few account rolls from the first half of the fourteenth century frustrates his finding an answer. Court roll entries for the period, in their notices of individual work derelictions, are a small aid in providing names of some — but not all — customary tenants on the manor (i.e. holders of virgates, cotlands and crofts), but they do not indicate the nature of the tenement held by the person being fined for non or poor perfomance of work. Thus, between 1311 and 1318, the names of at least 15 customary tenants can be learned in this way.[168] These 15 persons — men and women — in turn represented 13 individual families,[169] and of these families, six were still actively present in 1370.[170] In addition, in 1370 these six families were all at least semi-virgaters. Indeed, one was a semi-virgate family (Moke), three were single virgate families (Asplond, Gray, Palmere), and two held more than a virgate (Hunne and Scot). Since, further, at least three of the families had been present in 1252 (Gray, Hunne, Scot), at which time one (Gray) was a cotland family and the remaining two virgaters, they would not seem to have suffered any diminution of their properties during the intervening 118 years.[171] This in itself is not surprising, especially in view of the customary blood right to property obtaining in the Midland villages, including Holywell.[172] But it does

[168] PRO SC 2-179/16, 17 and 18. From 1311: William Moke and Alexander Brun, both fined for not working. From 1313: William Palmere, Stephan Colyn, Radulph Gray, Robert Gray, Adam de Ripton, Simon Laweman, John le May and Matthew ad Portam — all failing to work. From 1318: Robert Asplon, Reginald Clericus and John Hunne — for working poorly — and Robert Scot and Katerina Brun, for ploughing badly.

[169] Moke, Brun, Palmere, Colyn, Gray, Ripton, Laweman, May, Portam, Asplon, Clericus, Hunne and Scot.

[170] Asplon, Gray, Hunne, Moke, Palmere and Scot.

[171] One — the Gray family — had even come up, from a cotland in 1252 to a virgate in 1370.

[172] For the most recent and comprehensive study of the blood right on Ramsey estates, see Raftis, *Tenure and Mobility*, Chapter Two, pp. 33-63; and for an earlier, but still valid, discussion of impartible inheritance practices in the Midlands, see Homans, Chapter VIII-X. As an example of its working in Holywell, the following entry from the 1294 court roll can be cited (BM.Add. Ch. 39597):

"Sampson filius Ade Gilbert de Nyddingworth per plegium Johannis Medici de sancto Ivone dat domino. xij d. pro inquisitionem curie habenda utrum ipse magis ius habeat in illo messuagio et virgata terre quondam patris sui sicut petit quam Maycusa soror eius sicut tenet, quam quidam Maycusa cum dictis messuagio et virgata terre de domino J. abbate gersumavit ad opus Roberti filii sui propter absentiam dicti Sampsonis. Et inquisitio venit et dicit quod dictus Sampson secundum consuetudinem ville magis ius habuit in predicta terra post mortem matris sue quam dicta Maycusa soror sua ..." See *Court Rolls of the Abbey of Ramsey and of the Honor of Clare*, ed. W. O. Ault (New Haven, 1928), p. 225 for the remainder of the text, and Raftis, *Tenure and Moblity*, p. 50, for the full text in translation.

imply a continuity to tenure within the three families, and it is not unlikely
that in the cases of the remaining three families involved in customary
tenure from the second decade of the fourteenth century through 1370,
continuity was also characteristic of their tenurial history.

This only means, however, that their commitment to land had not
decreased during the first half of the fourteenth century. It casts no real
light on that mass of the tenant population who were not virgaters or
semi-virgaters but were rather smallholders. Nor does it help to clarify
the emergence of the intermediate group of landholders who stood between
the semi-virgater and the virgater. About both these groups it may only
be suggested — given the scarcity and reticence of the sources — that the
increase in the number of acres in individual and family holdings, although
doubtlessly owing something to a reduction in population — the number
of customary tenants holding more than one unit confirms this (See Appendix
II) — and the normal workings of the village land market, was probably
given real momentum from the 1350's, when the manor's demesne became
more and more available to the villagers on leasehold terms.[173] The list
of tenants in 1370 at least implies this, for of 21 persons holding five acres
of land or less, 10 held demesne lands.[174] In addition, of the nine men
holding between 11 and 17 acres of land, three were exclusively demesne
lessees,[175] while even among 16 persons holding 18 acres or more, three
held both customary and demesne lands.[176]

But the holding of arable land in Holywell was only one side of the
picture of tenure by 1370. The account roll for 1370/71 also provided
names for 52 persons holding land described as meadow (*pratum*). All
told, over 100 acres of grass land was held in 1370, the bulk of which
was fen.[177] However, of the 52 tenants, only 13 were Holywell and Need-

---

[173] See *infra*, Chapter II, p. 144 *et seq.*

[174] Thomas Asplond (1 a), Thomas Bernewell (1 a), Adam Hroff (1 a), John Hunne (1 a),
William Machyng (2 a), John Pope (1 a), William Raven (1 a), Nicholas and William Scharp
(2 a), John Shepperd (1 a).

[175] John Essex (12 a), Nicholas Godefrey (12 a), and William Raven (11 a). A fourth, John
Hamond, held a half-virgate and rented an acre of demesne, and a fifth, William Reve, held
a cotland and leased an acre of demesne.

[176] John Hemyngton held about 22 acres (including two cotlands and one croft), of which
one acre was demesne (5%); Robert Houghton held some 26 acres (1/2v, 1/2c), of which 11
acres — 42% — were demesne lands; Nicholas in the Lane, who held approximately 23 acres
of arable (1¼v) rented only one acre of demesne, or 4 % of his total.

[177] PRO SC 6-877/21. Six meadow regions were involved: Drihirst, Eestlang, Flegholm,
Merslake, Middilfurlong and Dichfurlong. Of these, all but Drihirst were described as "fen".
The acreage of Drihirst — which was held entirely by one tenant, Cristina de Cranfeld, for 15 s.

ingworth residents — accounting for Drihirst meadow, Flegholm marsh and approximately 20 additional acres of meadow or fen. The remaining 39 persons were villagers of neighboring communities — Slepe, Wodehurst, Caldecote and even Broughton.[178] Of the 13 Holywell people, six were not recorded as holding any arable — either customary or demesne.

The reason for this sudden burst of activity in grass land is not clear. Indeed, it is not even certain that it was sudden. The importance of meadow for pasture to the mediaeval English peasant is a commonplace,[179] and Holywell-cum-Needingworth, bordering on the fens as it did, certainly had its share of grass land, a fact that had deserved special mention as early as 1086.[180] At that time there had been 30 acres of meadow and additional pasture land ("woodland for pannage") one league by one league.[181] Exactly what the acreage figure for meadow was by 1300 is not known, but attacks upon the fens for pasture purposes had most certainly been carried out by that date.[182] But why the intense interest in the fens by the 1370's? Was there in fact a "pasture hunger" in the second

---

per annum — and of Flegholm — which was shared by the villagers Nicholas in the Lane, John Nicholas and others (un-named) for 75 s. — were not given, but out of Eestlang, 28 acres were released; 23 acres were released from Merslake, 10 acres from Middilfurlong and over 32 acres from Dichfurlong, for a total of over 93 acres. The total revenue from the rental (described as a "sale" — venditio — in 1370/71) was over 23 pounds (£23. 11 s. 1 d.), while in the last decade of the fourteenth century and first of the fifteenth century, £21. 6 s. 7 d. was the revenue from a little over 128 acres of fen.

[178] See, for example, PRO SC 6-877/24 and 26.

[179] See, for example, Hilton, A Medieval Society, p. 116 who points out quite succinctly that "A holding consisting only of arable was not viable under medieval conditions."

[180] Raftis, Estates, p. 152 has already brought attention to the fact that "In Domesday the marsh appurtenant to Holywell (one league by one league) and Warboys (one league by one-half league) manors had alone received mention, though even these were not evaluated."

[181] VCH.Hunts. I, p. 343.

[182] The Hundred Roll gives the meadow at 20 acres, with an additional 10 acres from Berengarius le Moigne. This, however, is meadow in demesne. A further meadow — "pratum pertinente ad manerium suum" — was credited to the abbot, containing 100 acres (RH. II, p. 603; PRO SC-12-8-56). Among the free tenants alone — including the Prior of St. Ives — some 39 ½ acres of meadow were held in 1279. If the meadow is taken at 130 acres in the late thirteenth century, it comprised about 10 % of the land in use on the manor — which is the average given by Hilton, based on his studies of West Midland manors (A Medieval Society, p. 117).

As regards fen reclamation, Raftis has observed that a movement "to exploit the fen for pasture" was in evidence in the twelfth and thirteenth centuries (Estates, pp. 152-53), and although there have survived no records actually documenting this for Holywell-cum-Needingworth, the evidence of eight "mowable meadows" (prata falcabilia) and a marsh (mariscus) to be mowed twice a year by 1252 (Carts. I, p. 295), and the ability of the manor to accomodate up to 500 sheep by the 1350's (Estates, p. 147, Table XXXI: a flock of 540 in 1356) indicates a relative degree of success in making use of the rich fen properties.

half of the fourteenth century in Holywell ? — as has been in fact proposed
by M. M. Postan for rural England in the thirteenth century.[183] Unfortunately, there is no real answer to this question. The Holywell peasant
had long enjoyed definite pasture rights and rights of common on the
manor. In fact, in the thirteenth century Holywell and Needingworth
had been a common pasturing ground for other communities, from as
close as St. Ives[184] to tenants of the bishop of Ely.[185] However, it is possible
that under such doubtlessly crowded conditions, pasture and grass land
was frequently not in overflowing abundance. This may explain the
frequent inclusion of meadow land (*pratum*) in many of the tenements
described in the Hundred Roll. Nevertheless, the abbey itself does not
appear to have entered into a sweeping program of fen rentals or sales
in Holywell until the 1370's, although, given the fact that this was also the
date when a wide-scale relinquishing of direct management of the desmene
came into evidence, it cannot be stated with certainty that the fen policy
was not itself complementary. In any event, the few surviving central
administrative records of the abbey do not record any startling revenues
coming from meadow and fen sales prior to 1370. In 1351, for example,
the receipts of the abbot's *camera* included only 40 shillings from such
sales.[186] In 1352, 50 shillings were received.[187] In 1353, 60 shillings;[188]
in 1354, 7 were collected "de feno ibidem vendito";[189] in 1355, 30 shillings
and in 1356, 40 shillings.[190] This certainly does not compare with the
£23 of 1370/71, or the £21 of subsequent years.[191]

But, as already stated, the reason for this keen — and apparently intensified — interest in grass land escapes precise detection. Possibly it
reflected an emphasis on sheep-raising by villagers, although this cannot

---

[183] CEH, I, p. 554.

[184] *Carts.* I, p. 295. "Et in praedictis pratis, post fenum asportatum, communicabunt omnes,
tam de Sancto Ivone quam de Haliwelle et Nidyngworthe, cum omnibus averiis suis ..."

[185] *Ibid.*, p. 216. In an agreement between the abbot of Ramsey and the Bishop of Ely of 24
April, 1294, "Concessum est ... quod lada, quae ducit de Nydyngworthe usque magnam ripam,
non fiat ita profunda quin bestiae episcopi et hominum suorum et aliorum communicantium
possint transire ad pasturam suam versus Haliwelle, et inde redire sine nocumento et gravamine."

Holywell people, in turn, shared pasture rights with villagers of St. Ives, Woldhurst, Woodhurst
and the bishop of Ely in the woods around St. Ives (*Ibid.*, p. 283).

[186] BM.Add.Ch. 33445 (Ramsey Papers, Vol. I. Ramsey Abbey Rent Book), 3ᵛ.

[187] *Ibid.*, 22ʳ. "De prato ibidem vendito hoc anno, L s."

[188] *Ibid.*, 40ʳ.

[189] *Ibid.*, 75ᵛ.

[190] *Ibid.*, 92ᵛ.

[191] See PRO SC 6-877/24 and 26.

be proved. If land statistics for Holywell people prior to 1370 are not easy to find, livestock figures are non-existent. That the abbey used Holywell for sheep-raising in the fourteenth century has been documented elsewhere.[192] That the villagers did likewise may be suspected, especially as the court rolls from the second half of the century — and into the fifteenth century — carry frequent references to trespasses by local people "cum bidentibus". Nevertheless, on the basis of such imprecise evidence, it would be unwise to assume that Holywell, at least in 1370, was a village predominantly of sheep-raisers, although it may be suspected that pastoral interests were intensifying.[193]

This apparent digression on meadow and fen properties has not been totally without purpose, however. If it does not admit of a ready explanation nor essentially alter the primary observation on the extent of individual landholding in the village — only rarely, for example, is a villager encountered holding more than two or three acres of meadow or fen — it does emphasize another and apparently increasing dimension to tenure in the village by 1370. Whereas prior to that date land information — including the evidence of the smallhold market — had been largely concerned with arable (*terra*), after 1370 the conjunction of land and meadow (*terra et pratum*) becomes more frequent, until, by the fifteenth century, the two will have become virtually inseparable. Prior to 1370, the Holywell tenant — when, in fact, he appeared — did so mostly as a man concerned with picking up bits of arable. By 1370, although the interest in arable was still very much alive and, indeed, a slight upward trend in the content of individual tenements was discernible, the Holywell tenant also began to appear as a man interested in picking up bits and pieces of meadow and fen as well. In some cases, in fact, this interest in grass land outweighed the involvement in arable land. Cristina de Cranfeld, for example, holding Drihirst meadow, appeared to have no arable in 1370, while John Nicholas, a virgater, together with his associates ("cum sociis suis"), was willing to take up — at 75 shillings — 40 *peciae* of Flegholm marsh.[194] In such cases, it is fair to assume that the individual's primary economic orientation was either pastoral or directed to deriving income from consequent subletting of pasture.

---

[192] See Raftis, *Estates*, pp. 144-46, and p. 147, Table XXXI. The flocks in Holywell numbered 421 in 1307/8, 540 in 1355/56, 264 in 1362/63, 119 in 1370/71, 431 in 1391/92, and 500 in 1399/1400. (*Ibid.*).

[193] The notation "transgressionem fecit cum bidentibus", for example is admittedly frequent, but it is not overwhelmingly more frequent than the familiar "transgressionem fecit cum averiis" or "cum porcis".

[194] PRO SC 6-877/21.

By the second half of the fourteenth century, therefore, changes were
beginning to appear in Holywell-cum-Needingworth's tenurial picture.
Grass land had begun to assume a not inconsiderable place in tenants'
properties, and a new group of intermediate landholders began to emerge,
holding either newly-leased demesne land or combinations of customary
units.[195] Indeed, more striking than the interest in fen or meadow was
the place being assumed by demesne land by 1370, and the number of
men holding multiples of customary tenements (eight men, or 21% of
38 customary tenants). The former can be initially explained by the
abbey's policy of gradually abandoning direct management of sections
of the demesne from the middle of the century, but the second trend —
multiplicity of tenements — as well as the reasons behind demesne leasing
are not so easy to pinpoint. Given the absence of precise documentation,
the best course is to ascribe the leasing of the demesne to a decline in
agrarian profits felt on Ramsey manors over the first half of the fourteenth
century,[196] and to associate the increasing multiplicity of tenements with
the general decline in population common throughout England in the
fourteenth century. That the latter — population decline — was a real
issue in Holywell can be reasonably documented. Whereas there were
some 65 families in the village in 1320, the number had dropped to 61
by 1330 and to 53 by 1360.[197]

It is not the purpose of this study to enter into the still-lively debate
over the possible reasons for agrarian and demographic recessions in
fourteenth-century England. The evidence for Holywell surviving from
the period is too sparse and disjointed to cast any new or significant light
on the questions involved. Even the place of plague cannot be adequately
assessed for the village. The Black Death struck Holywell in the winter
and spring of 1349, but no worthwhile documentation of its effects has
been preserved. That it may have claimed some half-dozen families
as immediate victims and left an equal number badly maimed or dying
— or, in short, that it killed or mortally wounded a little less than a quarter
of the families in the village — is a possibility,[198] but that its visitation

---

[195] The AtteWelle family, for example: John — 1½c; Robert — 1/2v, 1/4v.

[196] For a careful study of the decline in agrarian production on Ramsey manors from as early
as the latter thirteenth century, see Raftis, *Estates*, Chapter VIII, p. 217 *et seq.* In Holywell alone,
customary lands released *ad censum* had been in evidence as early as 1307/8, additional *opera*
were being commuted — or "sold" — also in that year, and in 1346/47 11 acres of demesne
were already let-out to villagers and had been since 1339.

[197] See *infra*, Chapter III, p. 167.

[198] *Ibid.*

had played havoc with the village and manorial life can be neither proved nor even assumed. It is true that from the years immediately following the first onslaught of the plague the reeves and beadles for the manor of Holywell began to experience difficulties in balancing their accounts and repeatedly fell into debt,[199] but although it is possible that a state of insolvency may reflect serious upset in the manor as a result of the plague, the connection cannot be insisted upon or pressed too far due to the lack of detailed information. Similarly, there is no striking sign of any serious vacancy problem in Holywell in the years following the Black Death. Indeed, there seems to have been no serious vacancy problem in Holywell at all until after the beginning of the fifteenth century. Thus, in 1356 — the year of the first post-plague account roll — there were only three vacancies recorded — all crofts. By 1363, there were none, and there was only one in 1370/71 — a croft.[200] This lack of serious vacancy problems, coupled with the fact that the balance between *ad opus* and *ad censum* tenures — a balance favoring the former and first observable in 1307/8 — remained substantially unaltered until 1370, at a time when large-scale *censum* and *arentatum* programs were being employed on other Ramsey manors to encourage tenure,[201] further suggest that whatever effects the plague may have had on Holywell, they were not immediately catastrophic. This does not mean that the plague made no impression on life in the village — it's real impact was felt, for example, but probably not until after 1370[202] — but only that its immediate results are not observable, and what is observable is a mild and minor dislocation of manorial operation, not a dramatic upheaval.

---

[199] Whereas prior to 1350 there is no record of consistent indebtedness by Holywell reeves and beadles, in 1351 Richard de Cranfeld, reeve, was 33 s. 4 d. in arrears (BM.Add.Ch. 33445, 3ᵛ). In the following year, Thomas of Houghton owed 60 s. 3 d. q. (BM.Add.Ch. 34484). By 1358, arrears in excess of seven pounds were still owed (BM.Add.Ch. 34486), and over 16 pounds in 1359/60 (BM.Add.Ch. 34487). A look at other surviving cellarer's receipts from the 1360's reveals a similar condition: arrears amounted to 73 s. 4 d. in 1363 (BM.Add.Ch. 33446, 48ᵛ). For further discussion of this question of solvency as regards the Ramsey estate complex as a whole, see Raftis, *Estates*, pp. 254-56 and p. 259.

[200] PRO SC 6-877/19, 20 and 21.

[201] See Raftis, *Estates*, Chapter IX, esp. p. 251 *et seq*. There was a change in the balance between *ad opus* and *ad censum* and *arentatum* tenures in Holywell between 1347 and 1356, but it was a moderate one and concerned only the crofts, the customary unit carrying the least work services. There is no indication that the heavier-obligated virgates or cotlands were rearranged in this period. Indeed, in 1346/47, out of 17 virgates, 12 were *ad opus*, and out of 15 cotlands, six were also *ad opus*. In 1356, the proportion was the same: 12 virgates and six cotlands *ad opus*. The first real alteration in this balance occurred in 1370/71, when three virgates and four cotlands were taken out of commutation and returned *ad opus*.

[202] See *infra*, Chapter II, p. 107 *et passim*.

To summarize briefly at this point: if one word were to be used to describe tenurial practices and policies in Holywell-cum-Needingworth from 1252 to 1370, it would be continuity. Continuity was characteristic not only of the amount of land available over the almost one-hundred and twenty-year period but also of the number of customary units into which the land was divided. Similarly with regard to the concentration and dispersal of tenements in individual hands, a basic continuity prevailed: over half the Holywell tenants from the mid-thirteenth century past the middle of the fourteenth century were smallholders, and roughly a third were large landholders in the sense of virgaters. In addition, familial continuity to tenure also remained a vital factor. For example, out of six families present in the latter 1200's and still present in 1370, four had undergone no alteration in the composition of their tenements in 118 years.[203] Finally, even despite the existence of a fluid village land market as early as the 1200's, it is not until 1370 that evidence begins to appear of a regular mul-tiplicity of tenements — especially of customary lands — with respect to individual peasants. By 1370, however, this many-faceted continuity was at death's door. Subsequent years were to witness a change in the amount of land available to peasants — through an ever-increasing dispersal of the manorial demesne — while the pressures of demographic decline helped contribute to a steady weakening of those commitments to land that were characteristically familial and perpetual. Even the conditions under which land was held were to undergo alteration — by restriction — until, by the second decade of the fifteenth century, the holding of land would be based almost exclusively on the ability to pay for it — in rent — in hard cash.

But such changes, although hinted at through the presence of tentative demesne leases and sporadic multiple tenements, were still largely in Holywell's future in 1370. In that year, a period in the village's tenurial history was coming to an end, but few probably sensed it. The machinery and component parts of tenure were still pretty much what they had been for over a century, and the Holywell peasants could still be classified

[203] The families were:

	1252	1370
Godfrey	v	v
Godrich	c	cr
Gray	c	v
Lane	v	v
Hunne	v	v
Scot	v, c	v, c

in terms of large, intermediate and smallholders. It is necessary, therefore, to go beneath the surface of this tenurial superstructure and investigate — in so far as the sources permit — what it meant to the Holywell peasant. It is not enough to merely list the number of virgates, cotlands and crofts on the manor between 1252 and 1370; an attempt must be made to evaluate their relationship to the peasant's work and rent obligations. What responsibilities or burdens did land-holding place on the Holywell peasant in the late thirteenth and first half of the fourteenth century? What was, in short, the nature of his commitment to the manor as a result of his being a tenant?

As indicated above, there were two major categories of land — exclusive of demesne — in mediaeval Holywell: free land and customary land.[204] Both could be — and were — held by men regardless of their personal legal status. Thus, free land could be held by villeins and customary land by freemen. On a crudely practical basis, the difference between the two types of tenure lay in their required services. A free tenement often involved the payment of an annual money or token rent and suit to the lord's honour court (at Broughton). The customary — or villein — tenement, held at the will of the lord and subject to manorial custom, involved especially the liability to render a regular quota of weekly work services on the demesne as well as an annual payment of fixed rents in money and kind (customary rents) and incidental payments of *gersuma, heriot* and *merchet*. These are well-known conditions of tenure, of course, but although they were common throughout mediaeval England, they were not necessarily uniform or identical in every county, shire or even bloc of estates. There were even variations within individual manors. In this, Holywell was no exception, neither with respect to free nor customary tenures.

Concerning Holywell free tenures, money rent was their most characteristic feature. In 1252, out of 16 peasant free properties, 14 rendered a combined total annual rent of 32s. 9d. There was no special uniformity to the rents. In one case, a free virgate paid two shillings a year; in another, free virgates owed four shillings. But there was a general stability. Thus, in 1279, again out of 16 free tenements or tenement blocs, 13 owed rents amounting to 34s. 4d. Further, as in 1252, so too in 1279 the amount of rent owed by a tenement was not necessarily directly related to the size of the tenement: some virgates owed two shillings, some messuages

---

204 The literature on the distinctions between free and customary land and tenures is extremely large and still growing. A still serviceable introduction to the problems involved may be found in Pollock and Maitland, I, p. 239 *et seq.*

owed from one penny to 10 shillings. One feature stands out, however: Holywell free tenements generally corresponded to the pattern observed for such tenures by recent scholars,[205] in that they were characterized by a money rent, which money rent, in turn, was frequently so low as to be little more than a token.[206]

It is generally recognized, however, that free tenements in mediaeval England were not always held for money rent and money rent only.[207] Many were also liable to render some non-monetary service, either honorary or even base. Here, too, Holywell was no exception. In addition to the regular obligation of suit at the honour court at Broughton, several Holywell free tenements by the mid-thirteenth century owed the performance of some servile labour. As indicated earlier, this was probably a reflection of the customary origins of some of the tenements prior to the 1250's, but whatever the precise reason, the fact remained that the peasant holding certain free properties in Holywell — whether he himself was free or villein made no difference — was obliged to render not only his annual money rent but labour service as well. Consequently, two virgates (out of a total of four) held by Aspelon of Holywell in 1252 owed, in addition to six shillings' rent, ploughing service.[208] John Gere, for a cotland and a half, paid eighteen pence and performed forensic service "cum villata".[209] William le ELyr held a virgate, owed two shillings and forensic service,[210] as did Robert Morel for two virgates;[211] Robert Freeman, for one virgate,[212] paid two shillings and also had to plough every week (*qualibet septimana*) — Christmas and autumn excepted — as well as being liable to such villein dues as merchet, tallage, pannage, customary rents, carrying service and *precariae*.[213] The same obligations were owed by Richard Forestarius, a virgater, and Cristina of Houghton, also a virgater,[214] while a certain Mauricius, for a "pythel", paid fifteen pence but was also required to

---

[205] See Kosminsky, *Studies*; R. H. Hilton, *A Medieval Society*, p. 123.

[206] See *supra*, p. 49 *et seq.*, for other free properties rendering a gillyflower or a pound of cumin or pepper. See also Hilton, *A Medieval Society*, p. 144.

[207] *Ibid.*, pp. 129-31.

[208] *Carts.* I, p. 296. "Et arabit etiam per annum, scilicet ad semen frumenti unam acram, ad semen hordei unam acram, et tempore warrecti unam acram."

[209] *Ibid.*

[210] *Ibid.*, p. 297.

[211] *Ibid.* Robert Morel also held a cotland and a half which required the full complement of villein works — i.e. the *opera* of a half-virgate.

[212] *Ibid.*, pp. 297-98.

[213] *Ibid.*, p. 298.

[214] *Ibid.* Both Richard and Cristina owed larger rents for their virgates: four shillings a year.

find one man for the autumn *precaria*.[215] On an individual basis, therefore, it can be seen that out of nine free peasants holding free property in Holywell in the mid-thirteenth century, although all owed money rent for their tenements, eight were also responsible for labour services, ranging from light to heavy. In addition, of the nine, one — John Gere — also held a cotland in villeinage, with the result that he was further obligated to render the *opera* incumbent upon that tenement: weekly ploughing, three days' work a week from 1 August to 29 September, "a mane usque ad vesperam", and precarial service.[216]

Finally, the terms governing free tenures in Holywell in the 1250's were not unique to that decade. They appear to have remained in force through the remainder of the thirteenth century, and probably even past 1300. Thus, in 1279 examples can be found in the Hundred Roll of free tenements still owing labour services — from *precariae* to ploughing[217] — while in 1297, when Thomas Gere entered into his inheritance he still owed forensic service.[218]

Free tenure was only one side of the land structure in Holywell-cum-Needingworth in the thirteenth and fourteenth centuries, however. The other side centred on customary land, comprising over 400 acres of arable and involving over 50% of the village tenants at any one time.

From the middle of the thirteenth century to 1370, customary tenures in Holywell were unevenly divided into holdings *ad opus* and *ad censum*. The former applied to tenure in return for specific work services on the demesne by the tenant; the latter arrangement was a commutation for a money payment of all or part of the *opera* normally required throughout the year. At no time between 1252 and 1370 did tenures *ad censum* outnumber *ad opus* tenures, but by the middle of the fourteenth century the commutation of services had advanced far beyond its narrow limits in the late 1200's.

---

[215] Carts. I, p. 298.

[216] *Ibid.*, pp. 296-297. The full complement of *opera* required from a cotland may have been reduced in John's case, but it is not certain. The duties mentioned above were set down for him in the extent's description of his "complete" holdings, and as such they are a reduction of the total work load for the cotland. However, later in the extent, John Gere is again included among the "customarii" holding cotlands *ad opus*, and his work is indicated to be the full amount due (*Carts.* I, p. 303). The problem is not easily resolved, but it is likely that John Gere did indeed owe the full complement of works for his villein cotlands, since works were not usually readjusted to suit the legal status of the tenant.

[217] RH.II, p. 603; PRO SC-12-8-56. For example, Henry the son of Richard, for a messuage, owed two shillings and two *precariae*. William Hildegar and John But, for four and a half virgates, owed ploughing services.

[218] See *supra*, p. 52, note # 147.

Specifically, in 1252, out of 44 customary units of land — virgates, cotlands and crofts — 41, or 93% of the total, were *ad opus*. Only two crofts were held *ad censum*; the heavier-obligated virgates and cotlands had not been commuted.

This predominance of *ad opus* tenures in the mid-thirteenth century was not uncommon to the English countryside of the time. Although the twelfth century, with its conditions of instability resulting from civil war and political confusion, had witnessed wide-scale commutation on manorial estates throughout England[219] — including even Holywell where some 12 villein tenements (eight virgates, one cotland and three crofts) had been released from labour services[220] — the first half of the thirteenth century had been the occasion of an agricultural boom, a period of "high farming", with the result that labour services had once again assumed their importance as landlords returned to intensive cultivation of previously neglected demesnes in an attempt to profit from the increased demand for agricultural produce and favourable market conditions.[221] Consequently, the commutation process in evidence in the twelfth century was, in the thirteenth century, "arrested on some estates and even reversed on others".[222] Such had clearly been the case in Holywell, where commutation was at a new low by 1252 and where, by 1279, the balance had not changed.[223]

But the agrarian boom of the first half of the thirteenth century began to take on the aspect of a thud by the late 1200's.[224] Whether or not the result of English agriculture having overextended itself,[225] retrenchment in production became more common from the early fourteenth century. On Ramsey estates, this set-back — marked by a "constriction of demesne cultivation"[226] — had begun as early as the last two decades of the thirteenth century. In Holywell alone, the food farm owed to the convent

---

[219] See Postan, CEH, I, p. 606 *et seq*; also p. 585 *et seq*.

[220] *Carts*. III, pp. 281-82.

[221] See Postan, CEH, I, p. 607, 581 *et seq*. for the general picture in England at the time. For the Ramsey estates in particular, which were undergoing a process of reorganization described as "a reaction towards the previous high in demesne cultivation" (Raftis, *Estates*, p. 118) and characterized by attempts to recover alienated freehold and a lessening of commutation programs, see Raftis, *Estates*, Chapter IV, pp. 97-128.

[222] Postan, CEH, I, p. 607.

[223] According to the Hundred Roll, all customary land was *ad opus* in 1279. However, the survey neglects crofts, and consequently it is possible that there had been no change since the 1250's. See RH.II, pp. 602-3; PRO SC-12-8-56.

[224] See Postan, CEH, I, p. 587.

[225] *Ibid.*, pp. 548-59.

[226] Raftis, *Estates*, p. 222 *et seq*.

had begun to fail, while the corn livery to the cellarer had not met its quota from as early as 1284.[227] Whether a consequence of low yields, a new method of crop rotation, a development of pasture lands at the expense of arable, adverse weather conditions, or a combination of all or some of these, production had slipped and, by the early 1300's, cultivation was being cut back.[228]

The earliest reflection in Holywell's customary structure of this slump in production is found in 1307, when the balance between *ad opus* and *ad censum* tenures is revealed to have been readjusted. Exactly when the readjustment had taken place is not known, but by 1307, out of 45 customary holdings of virgates, cotlands and crofts, only 28, or 62%, were *ad opus*. Eight virgates out of 17 were at that time *ad censum*, and of 15 cotlands, six were *ad censum* while three had been released to manorial officials as partial payment for their services.[229] This arrangement continued through 1324, but by 1346 another alteration had occurred. Of the 45 customary units, 27, or 60%, were then *ad opus*. Five virgates (a reduction of three from 1307 and 1324) and six cotlands were *ad censum*, three more cotlands were still *in officio*, and of 13 crofts, four had been dismissed "ad firmam". (See Table I).

Then came the Black Death, and although its immediate effects were not dramatically catastrophic, it may have contributed to yet another readjustment of the *ad opus/ad censum* balance, for by 1356 only 21 — out of 45 — customary tenements were *ad opus*, or 47%. The change had been made, however, with the crofts. Virgates and cotlands remained frozen at their 1346 level: five virgates *ad censum*, 12 *ad opus*; six cotlands *ad censum*, three *in officio* and six *ad opus*. The 13 crofts, on the other hand, had all been commuted: eight were *ad censum* and five had been placed in the newly-introduced category of the *arentatum*.[230]

This new balance remained through 1363,[231] but by 1370 yet another

---

[227] *Estates*, p. 217 and Table XXXVIII — Chapter VI, Section III, p. 180.

[228] For a discussion in depth of this problem as it concerned the Ramsey manors, see Raftis, *Estates*, p. 217 *et seq.*

[229] PRO SC 6-877/15. At the terms of the Annunciation and the Nativity of the Blessed Virgin, the account roll notes that 40 shillings were received "de viij virgatis terre ad censa." It is further stated that payment is omitted from the *argentum vinee* "de vj cotmannis ad censa, Bedello et ij akermannis."

[230] PRO SC 6-877/18. From the heusyre payments of the Andrew term, four pence are excused "de iiij croftis dimissis ad firmam", while 30 shillings are paid "de v virgatis et vj cotmannis ad censa."

[231] The introduction of the *arentatum*, however, did not prevent three of the crofts from being vacant in 1356. (PRO SC 6-877/19.)

shift had occurred — to the detriment of the commutation trend. Whereas *ad opus* tenure had been losing ground from the early fourteenth century — beginning at a high of 93 % in 1252, dropping to 62 % in 1307, 60 % in 1346 and 47 % by the 1350's — by 1370 it was entering into a new period of emphasis as the Ramsey administration itself underwent re-organization and efforts were made to revive demesne production.[232] In that year, out of 45 customary units, 25, or 56%, were *ad opus*. Thirteen crofts were still distributed between *ad censum* and *arentatum* tenures,[233] three cotlands were *in officio*, but only two virgates and two cotlands more had been commuted.

Despite shifts in the proportion of *ad opus* tenures in Holywell over the thirteenth and fourteenth centuries — shifts essentially connected to the policies of the abbey relative to demesne cultivation — the customary tenure *ad opus* was an integral part of the manorial organization, and it would remain so until the early fifteenth century. Thus, the *ad opus* tenure, as a guarantee of readily available and comparatively cheap labour for the demesne, was of key importance to the manorial operation, but it was also important to the Holywell peasant. Over half the available land between the 1250's and 1370 was customary land, and as the balance between *ad opus* and *ad censum* tenures tipped in definite favour of the latter at only one period — the 1350's — the resident, settled Holywell villein had to recognize the *ad opus* tenure as a regular part of his manorial life. Consequently, what demands it placed on him must now be considered.[234]

There were three units of customary land in mediaeval Holywell-cum-Needingworth that required labour services: the virgate, comprising approximately 18 acres of arable; the cotland, of some 10 acres; and the croft, a tenement most likely about an acre in size. In return for holding one virgate *ad opus*, the Holywell tenant was required to perform week-work. That is, he was expected to work on the demesne a specified number

---

[232] PRO SC 6-877/20. There was only one minor adjustment: a half-virgate was given over to the reeve as payment for his services.

[233] See Raftis, *Estates*, p. 259 and esp. p. 261 *et seq.*

[234] There are only two competent sources of information for the *opera* required of customary tenants in Holywell in the thirteenth and fourteenth centuries: the extent of 1252 and the Hundred Roll of 1279. The former is the more detailed, in so far as it provides numerous examples of the works that could be demanded. On the other hand, it can, at first glance, be misleading, since the individual works so minutely described were not necessarily required in any one work season. For this reason, the rough outline of services (for that is what it is) in the Hundred Roll is a less confusing and more fundamental guide to *opera*. For the purposes of this investigation, the two sources have been used in conjuction with each other.

of days each week. This number varied with the agricultural work seasons. Between the feast of St. Michael the Archangel (29 September) and the Gules of August (1 August) — a period covering the two work seasons of Winter and Summer — he was to work two days each week. Although neither the extent nor the Hundred Roll indicates which days these were, the account rolls from the late fourteenth and early fifteenth century declare them to have been Monday and Wednesday. On these two days, both the extent and Hundred Roll agree that the virgater will work at whatever the lord will require of him.[235] On a third day — Friday — he must be ready to do ploughing services.

From 1 August through the duration of the "Autumn" work season (roughly one month, or until early September)[236] was the heaviest work period — the harvest season. At that time the virgater was required to work four days a week (Monday through Thursday).[237] For the remaining three or four weeks of the "Post Autumn" season, his obligations were cut back — still four days, Monday through Thursday, but less work was exacted each day.[238]

The virgater was also required to supply additional labourers for the Autumn and Post Autumn periods as well as for the irregular *precariae*, or "boon works" of the Autumn season. Provision was made in the 1252 extent for three such *precariae*,[239] although the Hundred Roll did not attempt to number them,[240] and no more than two in one year were recorded

---

[235] *Carts.* I, p. 299. "quodcunque opus sibi fuerit injunctum." RH.II, p. 603; PRO SC 12-8-56: "ad quod opus dominus voluerit."

[236] 1355/56 is a typical example (PRO SC 6-877/19). The autumn season extended from 1 August to 5 September ("a Gula Augusti usque quintem diem Septembris per v septimanas."

[237] The Hundred Roll gives five days as the work schedule during autumn ("Et a gula augusti dum autumpnus durat operatur qualibet septimana per v dies." RH.II, pp. 602-3; PRO SC-12-8-56). The extent does not specify at all. However, the post-1350 account rolls speak only of four days, with two *opera* required each day (PRO SC 6-877/19, 20, 21, 22, etc.), and it is not unlikely that this had been the practice from the thirteenth century.

[238] According to the later (post-1350) account rolls, only one *opus* a day was owed.

[239] Food was provided by the lord at these *precariae. Carts.* I, p. 300: "Veniet etiam ad primam precariam in autumno cum quatuor hominibus et habebunt panem, servisiam, potagium, carnem et caseum; et duo homines habebunt tres panes, ita quod quantitas panis unius duobus ad prandium sufficiat; et panis erit de frumento et siligine, ita quod major pars sit frumentum. Et inveniet unum hominem in crastinum, ad reddendum cibum diei praecedentis.

"Veniet autem ad secundam precariam, sicut ad primam, quae erit ad panem, potagium, aquam, allecia, et caseum; et erit panis ut supra.

"Ad tertiam autem precariam veniet sicuti ad primam, si dominus voluerit, ad quam habebunt in omnibus sicut ad primam."

[240] The Hundred Roll only notes tersely: "Et faciet precariam." RH.II, p. 603; PRO SC-12-8-56.

in the later account rolls.[241] As to the number of men to be supplied at the *precariae* and during the Autumn and Post Autumn seasons, the virgater was to provide four men at each *precaria*, two men for the Autumn season, and one man for the Post Autumn period.[242]

In addition to the regular week-work, however, further obligations were incumbent upon the Holywell virgater. Most were financial. He was expected to pay *merchet* on the marriage of his daughter, pannage,[243] the *gersuma* fine upon entry to property, and he was subject to tallage — this last being assessed at 16d. a year in 1279.[244] This did not exhaust his financial obligations, however, for there remained the various annual customary rent payments.

The customary rents, apparently representing commutations of former payments in kind to the lord,[245] were paid at fixed intervals during the year. For *heusyre* — seemingly a form of "house rent" — a virgater owed 12d. a year, payable in three equal installments of fourpence each.[246] He also owed one penny a year in *argentum vinee*, one-half penny and a farthing for *heringsilver*, and ninepence for maltsilver.[247] The rates of the customary rents were fixed by the time of the extent in 1252, and they were exacted annually — from *censuarii* as well as *operarii* — up into the early fifteenth century.[248]

---

[241] In 1356, there was one *precaria*. (PRO SC 6-877/19). There were two in 1363 (PRO SC 6-877/20), one in 1371 (PRO SC 6-877/21), one in 1392 (PRO SC 6-877/2), one in 1400 (PRO SC 6-877/24), none in 1401 (PRO SC 6-877/26: "nullus hoc anno") and one in 1402 (PRO SC 6-877/27). That a third *precaria* was exceptional is indicated in the extent itself, where the gastronomic reward is of better quality than for the second, being identical with the food for the first. (See *supra*, p. 73, note # 239.)

[242] *Carts.* I, p. 299. "a Gula Augustii ... quamdiu messis durabit, inveniet duos homines." RH.II, p. 603; PRO SC-12-8-56: "et a gula augusti dum autumpnus durat operatur ... cum duobus hominibus ... Et post autumpnum usque ad festum sancti Michaelis operatur ... cum uno homine." For the *precariae*, see *supra*, notes # 239 and 240. The Hundred Roll does not mention the number of labourers for *precariae*.

[243] Pannage rates were set down in the extent at 1d . for a pig over one year, and 1/2 d. for a pig of a half-year ("pro porco super annum unum denarium pro porco bienno obolum." *Carts.* I, p. 298.) For a sow, nothing was owed.

[244] RH.II, p. 603; PRO SC-12-8-56:" Et dat ad tallagium per annum xvj d."

[245] See Nellie Neilson, *Customary Rents* (Oxford, 1910).

[246] The three terms were: the feast of St. Andrew (30 November), the feast of the Annunciation (25 March) and the feast of the translation of St. Benedict (11 July).

[247] In addition to money rents, the virgater also paid in kind: two hens at Christmas and eight eggs at Easter (*Carts.* I, p. 299). The Hundred Roll gives 16 eggs at Easter and a ring of oats for *fodercorn* (RH.II, p. 603; PRO SC-12-8-56.

[248] The *opera* just described were the obligations normally imposed on a Holywell customary virgater holding from the abbot of Ramsey. Within the village itself, however, in the latter

After the virgaters in Holywell came the cotlanders. As already indicated,[249] the Holywell cotland was probably 10 acres of arable and was consequently the equivalent of a half-virgate. It bore the same *opera*, heriot and — eventually — commutation or *censum* value as a semi- or half-virgate.[250]

As stated, the *opera* due from a cotland were one-half the services owed by a virgate. Instead of two days' work from 29 September to 1 August, one day (Monday) was owed, with the additional ploughing service on Friday. During the Autumn season, four days' work was required (Monday through Thursday), but only one *opus* each day,[251] and for the remainder of the work year — the Post Autumn period — two days' work (Monday and Wednesday) each week was owed. In addition, the cotlander also paid the various rents, but at lesser rates: sixpence for *heusyre*, sixpence for maltsilver, one-half penny for brewsilver, one penny for *argentum vinee*; and he was subject to carrying services, *precariae* and keeping the watch at the St. Ives' fair.[252]

The croft was the smallest land unit held for labour services, and con-

thirteenth century, there were exceptions, specifically among the tenants of the Prior of St. Ives and Berengarius le Moigne. Even when the latter's lands were sold to the abbey, the power of custom was strong enough to maintain the variant terms of tenure intact. This was evidenced in the Hundred Roll survey, where three customary virgates received from le Moigne imposed lighter labour services on their tenants. Each owed two day's work a week from Michaelmas to 1 August, but during the heavy autumn season the tenant was required to work, not four, but three days, supplying two labourers as well. During the final, post autumn period, his work obligations were cut back to two days' each week, with ploughing on a third (RH.II, p. 603; PRO SC-12-8-56). In addition, he owed the usual incidental rents, five shillings to the *redditus assisus*, and he was subject to the regular carrying and *precariae* services.

The tenants of the Prior of St. Ives were even less burdened by *opera*. One of his virgaters, Robert Brain, "operatur per ij dies in septimana per annum ad quod opus dominus voluerit excepta septimana festivalis. Et tercio die arrabit. Et faciet precariam et averagium ad voluntatem domini et dat vij gallinas per annum. Et dat redempcionem, gersumam, leyrwit, pannagium et heusyre. Ceteri duo sui pares faciunt eosdem consuetudines et servicia sicut Robertus Brain facit uterque per se qui tantum tenementum tenet et hii tres dant dicto priore dimidiam marcam per annum." (RH.II, p. 603; PRO SC-12-8-56).

[249] See *supra*, p. 31 *et seq.*

[250] See *infra*, Chapter II, p. 144.

[251] This was specified in the late fourteenth-century accounts. For example, in 1362/63, a cotland worked Monday, Tuesday, Wednesday and Thursday in Autumn but rendered only four *opera*, whereas a virgate worked the same days but gave eight *opera*. (PRO SC 6-877/20.)

[252] The extent makes no mention of how many labourers the cotlander was to provide in autumn, but as he was expected to supply the same number — four — at *precariae* as a virgater (*Carts. I*, p. 303), it is possible that he was, like the virgater, also responsible for two men in autumn and one man in post autumn.

sequently the *opera* it owed were light. From Michaelmas to 1 August, one day week-work was required, and no mention was made of ploughing. From 1 August to Michaelmas, two days' week-work was owed.[253]

Some customary rents also applied to crofts, but again the amounts were less than those from a cotland or virgate: one penny for *heusyre*, threepence for maltsilver. In addition, there were the usual liabilities to tallage, pannage, merchet, carrying services, *precariae* and duties at the St. Ives' fair.[254]

Such, then, were the basic work obligations required of a Holywell customary tenant *ad opus*. It may be wondered, however, just how representative they were. Was, in short, the Holywell customary tenant more or less burdened than villeins on other manors in neighboring and distant parts of the country? No absolute answer to such a question can really be given, but a few statistics may at least be presented for the purpose of comparison.

Within the Ramsey estate complex, there was no rigid uniformity to week-work required of virgates, semi-virgates or cotlands and crofts on different manors. Out of nine manors, besides Holywell, whose extents supply information on *opera*, three were characterized by virgates comparable to the size of the Holywell virgate: Abbots Ripton, with a virgate of 20 acres; Houghton, with a virgate of 18 acres; and Hemmingford Abbots, with a virgate of 15 to 18 acres. On only one of these — Hemmingford Abbots — was week-work in the winter and summer identical to Holywell (two days'). On Abbots Ripton and Houghton, the virgater had to work *three* days a week. As for the load during the heavy Autumn season, again only one — Abbots Ripton — demanded the same amount of work — four days' — as Holywell. The other two required three days' work. (See

---

[253] What days of the week were worked by crofts is not known. By the time of the later account rolls in the second half of the fourteenth century, all Holywell crofts were held in commutation.

[254] It is not stated if the croftholder was to supply labourers in autumn. However, for the *precariae* he was to provide one man (*Carts.* I, p. 304): "ad quamlibet precariam autumni inveniet unum hominem." Also, it would seem he had to be present himself (PRO SC-12-8-56: "Et faciet precariam et averabium cum corpore." The Record Commission edition of the Hundred Roll is incomplete at this point.)

It should also be noted that, as with the virgater, so too the croftholder's terms of tenure varied depending on original ties of lordship. The tenants of the former le Moigne crofts in 1279 owed services different from those of the abbot's tenants. Seven worked the same schedule of one day in winter and summer and two days in autumn, but two — Alexander AteGate and Matilda, daughter of William — worked four days in summer and four days in autumn. There is no mention of either winter work or *precariae* service for them. (PRO SC-12-8-56. The Record Commission — RH.II, p. 603 — gives three days' work in summer for Alexander and Matilda.)

Table II). Regarding semi-virgates or cotlands, whereas Abbots Ripton and Houghton required one day's week-work in Winter and Summer — as in Holywell — the Holywell semi-virgater or cotlander had to work more in Autum (four days) than at Abbots Ripton (one day) or Houghton (three days). Finally, a Holywell croftholder had to work more in Autumn (two days) than at Hemmingford Abbots (one day) or even Warboys and Broughton. (See Table II).

Furthermore, on those Ramsey manors where the virgate was substantially larger than at Holywell (i.e. from 24 to 32 acres), the obligation to week-work was equally variable. Thus, a Holywell virgater holding 18 acres and required to work four full days in Autumn worked more than the 30-acre virgater at Warboys (three days) or the 24-acre virgater of King's Ripton (three days). In addition, he worked on an equal footing with the 32-acre virgater of Upwood, but less than the 32-acre virgater of Broughton (five days) or the 24-acre virgater of Stukeley (five days). (See Table II). In effect, the obligations to week-work of the Holywell virgater represented the average for eight other Ramsey manors (Warboys, Abbots Ripton, Broughton, Upwood, Houghton, Hemmingford Abbots, Stukeley, King's Ripton), but they were manors where the virgate itself averaged 22 acres, with a spread from 18 acres to 32 acres.

Outside the Ramsey estates, the semi-virgater (at 12 acres) of Cuxham (Oxfordshire) was required to work two days a week in Winter and Summer — against the Holywell semi-virgater's (or cotlander's) one day — but only three days in Autumn, as contrasted to the Holywell demand of four days. (See Table II).[255] On the other hand, a virgater (with 36 acres) at Buckland (Gloucs.) was required to work four days every other week in Winter and Summer — compared to the Holywell 18-acre virgater's two days every week — and five days during Autumn. In addition, the Buckland virgater had to provide only two men for *precariae*, whereas in Holywell four men were required. (See Table II).[256] The point to be made, then, is that, compared with 10 other manors both within and outside the Ramsey complex, the Holywell customary virgater or semi-virgater — whose tenement was, in most cases, smaller than on other manors — was generally required to work less in Winter and Summer but as much — or more — in Autumn than in the other localities.

But having indicated how many days each week in a season a Holywell virgater, cotlander or croftholder was expected to work for the lord, it

---

[255] See Harvey, *Cuxham*, p. 119.
[256] See Hilton, *A Medieval Society*, pp. 133-34.

TABLE II

WEEK-WORK ON RAMSEY AND OTHER MANORS

	HOLYWELL			WARBOYS			ABBOTS RIPTON			BROUGHTON			UPWOOD		
	V	C/1/2V	CR	V	C/1/2V	CR	VL	C/1/2V	CR	V	C/1/2V	CR	V	C/1/2V	CR
WINTER & SUMMER	2	1	1	3	3	1	3	1	?	3	?	1	3	?	2
AUTUMN	4	4	2	3	2	1	4	1	?	5	?	1	4	?	2
POST AUTUMN	4	2	2	3	2	1	4	1	?	5	?	1	4	?	2
PRECARIAE	4	4	1	4	?	1	?	?	?	3	?	?	?	?	?

	HOUGHTON			HEMMINGFORD			STUKELEY			KINGS RIPTON			CUXHAM		
	V	C/1/2V	CR	V	C/1/2V	CR	V	C/1/2V	CR	V	C/1/2V	CR	V	C/1/2V	CR
WINTER & SUMMER	3	1	?	2	?	1	2	?	?	1	?	?	?	2	?
AUTUMN	2	3	?	3	?	1	5	?	?	3	?	?	?	3	6
POST AUTUMN	2	3	?	3	?	1	5	?	?	3	?	?	?	3	6
PRECARIAE	?	?	?	?	?	?	?	?	?	?	?	?	?	?	?

	BUCKLAND (Gloucs.)		
	V	C/1/2V	CR
WINTER & SUMMER	4	?	?
AUTUMN	5	?	?
POST AUTUMN	?	?	?
PRECARIAE	2	?	?

may be asked just what this obligation to work meant. What actual work was required of a tenant? What kind and how much work was he expected to perform in a work day? This is not an idle question. It is related to gauging the degree to which tenure was — or could be — a burden to the peasant, and an investigation of it first involves consideration of what was meant by the term "work" (*opus*).

The 1252 extent is the only source that provides a comprehensive catalogue of specific *opera* that could be demanded of a Holywell tenant. At first glance, it is a formidable body of minutely detailed services, from mowing to threshing, winnowing to digging — including even the measurements of corn to be threshed or the length, breadth and depth of trenches to be dug.[257] The same detail is exhibited in the description of carrying services, even to specifying when the expenses for journies were to be borne by the tenant and when by the lord.[258]

However, the *opera* described, and the broader question of week-work, must be approached cautiously. In the first place, each of the services so minutely set down in the extent constituted one work unit, or one *opus*,[259] and the general rule was that only one *opus* — or one work unit — was required each work day in the Winter, Summer and Post Autumn seasons. Only in the heavy Autumn period were two *opera* required each work day, and then only of virgaters.[260] Furthermore, one such *opus* did not

---

[257] See *Carts.* I, pp. 299-300.

[258] *Ibid.*, p. 300. "Faciet averagium apud Rameseiam, et in comitatu Huntedoniae de blado manerii vel blado aliter emendo, sumptibus propriis quotiens dominus voluerit.

"Et si extra comitatum facerit averagium, et ipse et unus virgatarius sibi conjunctus, inveniet unum equum sumptibus domini."

[259] For example, *Carts.* I, p. 299: "si fossare debeat in plana terra, faciat unam perticam fossati pro uno opere, habentis profunditatem duorum spadegraf, et latitudinem in summitate quinque pedum et in fundo unius pedis." P. 300: "et portabit ad curiam unum bussellum boni et puri frumenti, et allocabitur ei pro opere unius diei ... Et si nuces fuerint abundantes in bosco Abbatis, colliget unam calligam mediocris quantitatis, plenam nucibus bene mundatis, pro opere unius diei."

[260] Practical examples of these and subsequent statements can be drawn from the second half of the fourteenth century and early years of the fifteenth century, when work statistics for Holywell were recorded in detail. There is, however, no evidence for believing that the policies governing work after 1350 were not the same as governed work prior to 1350.

Thus, the account roll of 1363/63 (PRO SC 6-877/20) states, under the heading of "Winter Works (*Opera Hiemalia*)": "De xj virgatis dimidia in opere a festo sancti michaelis usque vigiliam pentecosti (xx die maii) ... per xxxiij septimanas et iij dies non operabiles de virgata per septimanam ij opera diebus lune et mercurii ... De vj cotmannis in opere per idem tempus de quolibet per septimanam j opus die lune."; and under "Autumn Works": "De predictis xj virgatis dimidia in opere a gula Augusti usque iiij^{tum} diem Septembris per v septimanas viij opera diebus lune, mercredi, mercurii et jovis qualibet die ij opera ..."

necessarily take a full day to perform. As Bennett has already observed, one *opus* was "only something like half a day's actual work".[261] The Holywell extent itself confirms this, for it specifically indicates when work was to occupy a full day,[262] and several of the *opera* described in the extent could readily be performed in half a day. On the other hand, it was only in the Autumn season when two *opera* each work day were required, and this was normally the one season when a full day's work was expected on other Ramsey manors.[263] Consequently, although agricultural labour itself is heavy and time-consuming — and was even more so in the non-mechanized Middle Ages — it cannot be assumed that in a week requiring two *opera* from, for example, a virgater, two full days of work on his land were lost to the tenant.

But if a work day frequently involved only half a day's work, there were even further reductions and relaxations of the work load in Holywell. For one, works were sometimes excused. If a virgater were called to keep the watch at St. Ives and his appointed time fell on a work day, or if he were to perform carrying services, his domestic *opus* was excused.[264] For a cotlander, the payment of the customary rents of *heusyre* and *argentum vinee* counted as one work.[265] More importantly, works were excused in the event of illness. For a virgater this was expressed in two ways. If he were so ill that he could not leave his house at any time before the Autumn period, he was quit of *heusyre* and all work, with the exception of ploughing.[266] If he were ill during the Autumn period, he was excused one-half his work, and this relaxation of his obligations continued as long as the illness endured, up to a year and a day. If, however, he were yet ill after that time, or if he fell ill again, the work was to be performed.[267]

---

[261] *Life on the English Manor*, p. 104.

[262] *Carts.* I, p. 299 "et carriabit fenum domini cum socio sibi adjuncto per totum diem pro uno opere." P. 303: "Seminabit tota die, qua non herciat."

[263] For example, Warboys: "A Gula Augusti operabitur qualibet hebdomada per unum diem a mane usque ad vesperam, usque ad festum Sancti Michaelis." (*Ibid.*, p. 315.) Or Broughton: "a Gula Augusti usque ad festum Sancti Michaelis, qualibet septimana, per omnes dies praeter sabbatum operabitur a mane usque ad vesperam ..." (*Ibid.*, p. 336.)

[264] *Ibid.*, p. 301.

[265] *Ibid.*, p. 302.

[266] *Carts.* I, p. 300. "Et si infirmetur, ita quod non exeat domum propriam, ab omni opere et heusyre ante autumnum erit quietus, praeter aruram."

[267] *Ibid.*, p. 301. "In autumno vero a medietate operis sui ob infirmitatem erit quietus, et habebit istum relaxationem toto tempore quo aegrotaverit, usque ad exitum unius anni et unius diei.

"Et si post annum et diem duret ejus infirmitas, vel aliter aegrotaverit, deinceps faciet omnia opera, quae ad tenuram suam pertinet."

The same provisions were extended to cotlanders and croftholders as well.[268]

Works were further excused in the event of religious festivities. The eight days of Christmas constituted one such period.[269] Individual holydays were another, although exactly how strictly this was followed is open to question.[270] The extent seems to indicate that a day excused for a holyday had to be made up at a later date.[271] However, this was apparently not insisted upon, for by 1279 a holyday seems to have cancelled a work day with no provision for its being satisfied later.[272] This was clearly the practice by the late fourteenth century, when account rolls survive listing the actual holydays cancelling work.[273] There was, nevertheless, a reluctance — perhaps even a refusal — to credit a full complement of holydays in the year, for, in the second half of the fourteenth century, the greatest

---

[268] *Carts.* I, pp. 302, 304. That excuses for illness were not just theoretical is demonstrated in account rolls from the second half of the fourteenth century and the early fifteenth century. In 1371, Richard Gray was excused 16 works for illness lasting eight weeks in summer ("et in allocatione Ricardi Gray languentis ad mortem per viij septimanas xvj opera." PRO SC 6-877/21). In the summer of 1392, 10 *opera* of Walter Beaumeys were excused ("Et in allocatione Walteri Beaumeys virgatarii egrotantis per v septimanas confessus et communicatus x opera." PRO SC 6-877/22). In 1401, eight of John Palmere's works were excused by illness in autumn ("Et in allocatione operum Johannis Palmere virgatarii egrotantis per j septimanam confessus et communicatus viij opera." PRO SC 6-877/26). In 1402, eight opera of John Sande were excused for eight weeks' illness in winter (PRO SC 6-877/27). In 1404, 12 works of Thomas Nicholas, virgater, were excused for six weeks' illness in winter and six works each of John Hunne and Richard Reve were excused in summer (PRO SC 6-877/28).

[269] According to the extent of 1252, the ploughing service remitted at that time had to be made up in the following week by a full day's work. *Carts.* I, pp. 299-300.

[270] This question of holydays still awaits detailed investigation. Homans in his description of the "Husbandman's Year" (*English Villagers of the Thirteenth Century*, Chapter XXIII, pp. 353-80) does not attempt to evaluate their effect on the work schedule of mediaeval manors. Bennett (*Life on the English Manor*, pp. 115-18) is skeptical, doubting that anything like the 40 or 50 actual holydays was allowed in the Middle Ages. For Holywell, the extent is of little help, mentioning only the eight days of Christmas. Nor do the extents of other Ramsey manors clarify the problem, as none goes into the matter in any consistent detail (Upwood — *Carts.* I, p. 344 — mentions the Christmas and Easter seasons, for example, but nothing else). The present investigator hopes to conduct a more extensive study of this question in the near future.

[271] *Carts.* I, p. 302. "Et sciendum quod si dies festus evenerit aliquo die operabilis, non allocabitur eis, sed operabuntur alio die pro eodem."

[272] PRO SC-12-8-56; RH.II, p. 603: "et a gula augusti dum autumnus durat operatur qualibet septimana per v dies cum duobus hominibus nisi festum impediat."

[273] PRO SC 6-877/20, 1362/63, is a good example. Under the heading "opera autumnalia", the following is recorded: "Inde allocantur predictis xj virgatis dimidia pro diebus sancto Laurentio (Jovis), Assumptione Beate Marie (marcredi) et sancto Bartholomeo (Jovis) — lxix opera. Et predictis vj cotmannis in opere pro eisdem diebus festivalis xviij opera."

known number of holydays allowed was five — in 1363.[274] One was recorced in 1371, one in 1392, four in 1400, three in 1401, three in 1402, one in 1404 and three in 1405.[275] On the other hand, in 1356, when all six holydays normally excusing work from the 1360's on,[276] fell on work days, only three were allowed.[277]

Even though the number of holydays cancelling work may not have been staggering — nor even comparable to the number that perhaps should have been allowed — their effect was not altogether negligible. It is not unlikely that the holydays recognized in the latter fourteenth century were also credited in the early 1300's, and it is worth noting that they all fell within the heaviest work seasons: Autumn and Post Autumn.[278] The results — in years for which detailed account rolls have been preserved — were as follows. In 1356, 54 of 664 Autumn works were excused, or

---

[274] PRO SC 6-877/20. Saint Laurence — Thursday, 10 August,
    Assumption — Tuesday, 15 August,
    St. Bartholomew — Thursday, 24 August,
    Exaltation of the Cross — Thursday, 14 September,
    Saint Mathew — Thursday, 21 September.

[275] *1371:* Assumption — Thursday, 15 August: PRO SC 6-877/21.
    1392: Assumption — Thursday, 15 August: PRO SC 6-877/22.
    1400: Saint Laurence — Tuesday, 10 August: PRO SC 6-877/24,
        Saint Bartholemew — Tuesday, 24 August,
        Nativity of the Virgin — Wednesday, 8 September,
        Saint Mathew — Tuesday, 21 September.
    1401: St. Bartholomew — Wednesday, 24 August: PRO SC 6-877/26,
        Nativity of the Virgin — Thursday, 8 September.
    1402: Assumption — Tuesday, 15 August: PRO SC 6-877/27,
        St. Bartholomew — Thursday, 24 August,
        St. Mathew — Thursday, 21 September.
    1404: Nativity of the Virgin — Monday, 8 September: PRO SC 6-877/28.
    1405: Nativity of the Virgin — Tuesday, 8 September: PRO SC 6-877/29,
        St. Mathew — Monday, 21 September.

[276] Saint Laurence   : 10 August,
    Assumption   : 15 August,
    St. Bartholomew : 24 August,
    Nativity of the
              Virgin : 8 September,
    Exaltation of the
              Cross : 14 September,
    St. Mathew   : 21 September.

[277] PRO SC 6-877/19. The feasts excused are not named. Just the number — three — is given.

[278] It will be recalled that the Autumn and Post Autumn periods extended from 1 August to 29 September.

TABLE III

THE EFFECT OF HOLYDAYS ON *OPERA* OWED (AUTUMN & POST AUTUMN) PER
VIRGATE AND COTLAND, 1363-1405

Year	Owed		Excused		% Excused	
	V	C	V	C	V	C
1363	65	33	8	5	12	15
1371	59	29	2	1	3	3
1392	54	27	2	1	4	4
1400	59	29	6	4	10	14
1401	70	35	5	3	7	8
1402	53	26	7	4	13	15
1404	58	29	1	1	2	3
1405	45	23	4	2	9	9

8 %.[279] In 1363, 87 *opera* were excused in the Autumn season out of 805
assessed, or 11 %. In the Post Autumn period, 23 out of 214 *opera* were
excused, or, again, 11 %.[280] In 1371, 40 *opera* were cancelled in Autumn
by the feast of the Assumption, only 5 % of 824 assessed works.[281] In 1392,
5 % again were excused in Autumn, or 38 out of 743 *opera*.[282] In 1400,
of the Autumn *opera*, 73 out of 882, or 8 %, were excused, but 14 %, or
39 out of 286 Post Autumn *opera* were cancelled.[283] In 1401, 9 % of the
Autumn works, or 80 out of 984, and 22 % — or 27½ out of 126 — of the
Post Autumn works were excused.[284] In 1402, 10 % of the Autumn works,
or 14 out of 214 were excused.[285] In 1404, 10 %, or 25 out of 240 Post
Autumn *opera* were cancelled,[286] and in 1405, 9 %, or 80 out of 904 Autumn
works were excused by holydays.[287] The effect of holydays on the work
obligations of individual virgates and cotlands for the same years can be
seen from Table III, where the overall average of the years involved was
7.5 % for virgates and 9 % for cotlands. Although the absence of competent
accounts for the first half of the fourteenth century makes any statistical

[279] PRO SC 6-877/19.
[280] PRO SC 6-877/20.
[281] PRO SC 6-877/21.
[282] PRO SC 6-877/22.
[283] PRO SC 6-877/24.
[284] PRO SC 6-877/26.
[285] PRO SC 6-877/27.
[286] PRO SC 6-877/28.
[287] PRO SC 6-877/29.

knowledge impossible, it is probable that the effect of holydays on works prior to 1350 was of a comparable nature.[288]

It may, of course, be wondered if more feast days were in fact allowed than the records indicate. For example, both the early and late account rolls — and even the 1252 extent — mention specific days singled out for the payment of customary or other rents and as key dates for the agricultural cycle. Thus, the following festive dates consistently stand out: Michaelmas (29 September), the feast of St. Andrew (30 November), the Annunciation (25 March), the Translation of St. Benedict (11 July), Hokeday (the second Tuesday after Easter) and the Gules of August (1 August, or Lammas day). Even though it cannot be proved that these were days when there was no work, still it is likely. Especially is this so with respect to the first four saints' days, since they were traditional "rent-paying" dates, and even though it is possible that the reeve may have gone about the village and fields searching out individual tenants to collect the installments due, it is improbable. On the other land, it is equally possible that, if work was not done on the demesne on those specific days, the actual settling of accounts to the lord through the reeve may have been considered an *opus*, and therefore, technically, the day would not have been "free". For example, the payment of *heusyre* by a cotlander was, according to the extent, considered *unum opus*.[289]

Nevertheless, whatever was the actual disposition of the days mentioned above, it must be admitted that the Holywell customary tenant was not

---

[288] It should further be noted that although the occurrence of holydays could cancel out anywhere from 5% to 10% of autumn or post autumn works, the percentage of the *total* annual *opera* obligation excused by holydays was much less, for the holydays allowed, as already pointed out, fell exclusively between 1 August and 29 September. Thus, in 1355/56, the total assessment for the year was 2456 *opera*, of which only 54, or 2%, were excused by the three allowed holydays. For subsequent years, the results were as follows:

Year	Assessment	Excused	%
1362/63	2431	110	5
1370/71	3179	40	1
1391/92	2977	38	1
1399/1400	3352	112	3
1400/1401	3546	111½	3
1401/1402	3318	94	3
1403/1404	3424	25	7
1404/1405	3326	80	2

[289] *Carts.* I, p. 302. "... dat ad tres terminos anni sex denarios ad heusyre ..., ad luminare obolum, magistro vineae unum denarium; et allocabitur ei pro uno opere."

flooded the year 'round with cancelled works for festive reasons. Even the sessions of the local court were, in the majority of instances, scheduled on days when there could be no conflict between it and the work on the demesne. Thus, out of 29 dated sessions between 1288 and 1398, none was scheduled during the heavy harvest season, and only nine were held on work days — either a Monday or a Wednesday — in either the Winter or Summer seasons. However, despite the fact that festive days cancelling work obligations for the Holywell peasant were not abundant, it must still be acknowledged that some feast days were allowed, and that the majority — possibly even all — occurred during the harvest months, when the work load of the peasant was its heaviest.

Finally, week-work was not only excused by occasional special services, illnesses and some religious feasts. Sometimes the full quota of *opera* was not required, and the work units not strictly needed were commuted for money payments, or — in the more practical language of the account rolls — "sold". It was, of course, a common practice throughout England in the thirteenth and fourteenth centuries, and provisions were generally made for the policy in advance by assigning a fixed monetary value to seasonal work units.[290]   In Holywell, from the early fourteenth century and throughout the remainder of the Middle Ages, one winter work (*opus hiemale*) was valued at one-half penny, one summer work (*opus estivale*) at one penny, one autumn work (*opus autumnale*) at twopence, and one post autumn work (*opus post autumnale*) at one penny.[291]   The number commuted or sold in a year varied according to need. With regard to Holywell, it is not certain when the sale of works became a regular practice, but the policy itself had assumed prominence on most Ramsey estates in the 1290's, when a retrenchment in production became discernable. In any event, the Holywell account roll for 1307/8 recorded 976 winter works sold.[292] In 1323/24, 405 works were sold: 240 winter works, 94½ summer works, 29 autumn works and 41½ post autumn works.[293]   In 1346/47, 288 works were sold: 158 winter works, 5 summer works and 125 post autumn works.[294] In 1355/56, there was no evidence of works having been sold, and only a fraction — 29½ winter works — were

---

[290] For examples of this policy in the West Midlands at the end of the thirteenth century, see Hilton, *A Medieval Society*, pp. 132-36. For the Ramsey estates, where the sale of works became pronounced from the 1290's, see Raftis, *Estates*, p. 222 *et seq.* See also Kosminsky, p. 164 *et seq.*

[291] The rates were first recorded in full in the account roll for 1323/24 (PRO SC 6-877/17).

[292] PRO SC 6-877/15.

[293] PRO SC 6-877/17.

[294] PRO SC 6-877/18.

sold in 1362/63, out of a total assessment of 2431 *opera*.[295] In 1370/71, however, the trend took on an upward curve once more: 498 works were sold: 161 winter works, 72 summer works, 88 autumn works and 177 post autumn works.[296] In 1391/92, 965 *opera* were sold: 492 in winter, 147 in summer, 162 in autumn and 164 in post autumn.[297] By 1399/1400, a new high was reached: 1015½ *opera* were sold, or about 30% of a total assessment of 3352 *opera*,[298] and it continued to mount in subsequent years. Thus, in 1400/1401, 1149½ *opera* — out of a total 3546 — were sold.[299] In 1401/1402, 1250½ were sold of 3318 assessed, or 39%,[300] and 1460 out of 3424 were sold in 1403/1404.[301] Finally, in 1404/1405, 1409 works were sold — out of a total of 3326[302] — and, although account rolls are missing for the next three years, the process continued until 1409, when *ad opus* tenures were eliminated in Holywell,[303] for in winter of that year 471 *opera* out of 1408 assessed were sold.[304]

The sale of works was a regular feature of manorial administration in Holywell throughout the fourteenth century and into the first decade of the fifteenth century. As already indicated, however, its effect was not uniform from year to year. Thus in 1370/71, 16 % of the total work assessment was commuted, for the full complement of *opera* projected for that year was 3179. In 1391/92, the 965 *opera* sold were 32 % of the 2977 total. As noted, 30% were sold in 1399/1400, and 32% were sold in 1400/1401. In 1401/1402, 39 % were sold, 42% were sold in 1403/1404, and 42 % again were sold in 1404/1405. On the other hand, in 1362/63, only 1 % had been sold — which is not surprising, considering the probable need for labour in the 1350's and 1360's following the plague. As for the early fourteenth century, here speculation must be called into play, since the three surviving account rolls between 1300 and 1350 provide no break-down of work figures. However, using a rough average of 140 *opera* per year for a virgate and 70 *opera* a year for a cotland in 1307/8 and 1323/24 and 146 *opera* per virgate and 73 *opera* per cotland in 1346/

[295] PRO SC 6-877/20.

[296] PRO SC 6-877/21.

[297] PRO SC 6-877/22.

[298] PRO SC 6-877/24. The break-down was as follows: 559 winter works, 13½ summer works, 206 autumn works and 119 post autumn works sold.

[299] PRO SC 6-877/26. Winter: 741; Summer: 233; Autumn: 171; Post Autumn: 4½.

[300] PRO SC 6-877/27. Winter: 723½; Summer: 188½; Autumn: 202; Post Autumn: 136½.

[301] PRO SC 6-877/28. Winter: 839; Summer: 257; Autumn: 240; Post Autumn: 124.

[302] PRO SC 6-877/29. Winter: 937; Summer: 234; Autumn: 238; Post Autumn: 0.

[303] See *infra*, Chapter II.

[304] PRO SC 6-877/30.

47,[305] and an estimated 60 *opera* a year for a croft,[306] and taking into consideration the number of units *ad opus* at the time of the three account rolls, the following projections are obtained: 1307/8 and 1323/24: 2460 *opera*; 1346/47: 2739 *opera*. Using these figures, then, the effect of *venditio operum* in 1307/8 would have been 39% sold; in 1323/24, 16% sold; and in 1346/47, only 11% sold — again not a surprising figure, since it was in that year that the abbey was apparently engaged in a reintensification of demesne cultivation since three virgates had been returned *ad opus* at that time.

So far, however, attention has been directed to the effect of work sales on the overall, yearly work obligation. What of its effect by *season*? For 1323/24, its effect may be estimated to have been as follows: *Winter works* — 22%; *Summer* — 18%; *Autumn* — 5%; *Post Autumn* — 19%.[307] In 1346/47, the result was probably as follows: *Winter* — 15%; *Summer* — 8%; *Autumn* — 15%. In subsequent years, account rolls survive giving precise work figures, and the percentage of works sold by season can be more exactly presented, as may be seen from Table III.

[305] These figures are based on projecting the number of *opera* owed per unit per season. The length of the season has been estimated from calendars in Cheney's *Handbook of Dates for Students of English History*, Tables 5, 11, 24, 25, 26. The length of the seasons is projected as follows: *1307/8* — Winter: 30; Summer: 14; Autumn: 5; Post Autumn: 3. The same holds for 1323/24. For 1346/47: Winter: 27; Summer: 16; Autumn: 6; Post Autumn: 3.

In years for which actual figures have survived, the obligations were as follows:

YEAR	VIRGATE	COTLAND
1355/56	206	93
1362/63	176	89
1370/71	171	85
1391/92	166	83
1399/1400	171	85
1400/1401	186	94
1401/1402	167	83
1403/1404	170	85
1404/1405	164	83

[306] No crofts were *ad opus* after 1350, but assuming one *opus* a week for approximately 10 months, and two *opera* a week for two months, the result is 60 *opera* a year. (Based on obligations outlined in the 1252 extent.)

[307] This is based on the fact that the winter season normally extended from 29 September to Hokeday (the second Tuesday after Easter and usually the beginning of the "summer" season), which, in 1307/8, comprised some 30 weeks. Using the extent figures of two *opera* a week per virgate in winter, and one *opus* a week for each cotland and croft, and, further, multiplying these figures by the number of units *ad opus* (nine virgates, six cotlands and 13 crofts), the total winter work projection is 1110 *opera*.

TABLE III

SALE OF *OPERA* BY SEASON IN HOLYWELL, 1362-1405

(W = Winter; S = Summer; A = Autumn; PA = Post Autumn)

	1362/63			1370/71			1391/92			1399/1400		
	Assessed	Sold	%	Assessed	Sold	%	Assessed	Sold	%	Assessed	Sold	%
W	1047	29½	2	1640	161	10	1510	492	33	1794	559	31
S	365½	0	0	400	72	18	418	147	35	390	131½	34
A	805	0	0	824	88	11	743	162	22	882	206	23
PA	214	0	0	315	177	56	306	164	54	286	119	42

	1400/1401			1401/1402			1403/1404			1404/1405		
	Assessed	Sold	%	Assessed	Sold	%	Assessed	Sold	%	Assessed	Sold	%
W	1620½	741	41	1680	723½	37	1720	839	49	1840	937	52
S	615½	233	38	600	188½	31	520	257	49	546	234	43
A	984	171	17	824	202	22	944	240	25	904	238	26
PA	126	4½	4	216	136½	64	240	124	52	26	0	0

The fact that *opera* were sold with regularity from the early fourteenth century in Holywell does not mean that the peasant was relieved of works with no strings attached. As is obvious from the phrase *Venditio operum* itself, there was a string attached: a monetary one, and, consequently, if the peasant's work was not required in its entirety, he had to pay to make up the difference. The cost of these commutations to the Holywell customary tenant *ad opus* has been set down in Table IV, arranged by season. Although it is not possible to determine the cost to each peasant individually, it can be seen that the financial demand on the *ad opus* group collectively could range from a little over a shilling in one year (1362/63) to over five pounds in another (1403/4). Consequently, unlike holydays, which cancelled a work obligation outright, the sale of works only eliminated the need to perform or supply manual labour but imposed on the peasant the task of paying the lord the cash value of the work being waived. The peasants may have benefited from the extra time thereby alloted them, but it was time that they bought and paid for, sometimes at a not inconsiderable price.

The customary *ad opus* tenant in Holywell, therefore, although obligated to the performance of *opera* for his land, could find his yearly work quota relaxed from various causes. Either his work did not occupy a full day, or works could be cancelled by illness, commuted for money, or — in the heaviest work season — reduced by the occurrence of holydays. In addition, there was another element to be reckoned with: the disposition or inclination of the individual to work. At times, he did not bother to appear at his appointed task, preferring instead to pay a fine to the lord in the court for his absenteeism.[308] The court rolls for the manor record such causes. In 1288, Robert Pye was fined sixpence because "non venit ad berciam domini".[309] In 1307, Robert Aleyn was fined sixpence for not working, and Richard Gray and Richard le Frankeleyn were fined ninepence each for failing to perform carrying services.[310] In 1311, William Moke and Alexander Brun paid sixpence each for not working,[311] and in 1313 a total of nine villagers was fined for failing to work: William Palmere, sixpence and threepence (for two derelictions), Stephan Colyn sixpence, Radulph Gray sixpence, Adam de Ripton sixpence, William Moke sixpence on one occasion and threepence on another, Robert Gray

---

[308] I have not been able to establish any direct correlation between court fines imposed and the value of the work unperformed. The fines themselves tended to be standardized.

[309] PRO SC 2-179/5.

[310] PRO SC 2-179/15.

[311] PRO SC 2-179/16.

TABLE IV

VALUE OF COMMUTED (I.E. "SOLD") *OPERA* IN HOLYWELL, 1307-1405

	1307/8	1323/24	1346/47	1362/63	1370/71	1391/92
WINTER	40s.	10s.	6s.7d.	14d.ob.q.	6s.8d.ob.	20s.6d.
SUMMER	0	7s.10d.ob.	5d.	0	6s.	11s.5d.
AUTUMN	0	4s.10d.	0	0	14s.8d.	27s.
POST AUTUMN	0	3s. 5d.ob.	20s.10d.	0	14s.9d.	13s.8d.
TOTAL	40s.	26s. 7d.	27s.10d.	14d.ob.q.	42s.1d.ob.	72s.7d.

	1399/1400	1400/1401	1401/1402	1403/1404	1404/1405
WINTER	23s. 3d.ob.	30s.10d.ob.	30s. 1d.ob.q.	34s.11d.ob.	19s.ob.
SUMMER	10s.11d.ob.	19s. 5d.	15s. 8d.ob.	21s. 5d.	19s.6d.
AUTUMN	34s. 4d.	28s. 6d.	33s. 8d.	40s.	30s.8d.
POST AUTUMN	9s.11d.	4d.ob.	11s. 4d.ob.	10s. 4d.	0
TOTAL	78s. 5d.	82s.10d.	90s.10d.ob.q.	106s. 8d.ob.	98s.2d.ob.

sixpence, Simon Laweman sixpence, John le May threepence, and Matthew ad Portam threepence.[312] Again in 1318, William Moke was fined three pence for not working[313] — which seems to have become a minor habit with him — while in 1328 William Bundeleg and John Wodereve were fined threepence each for failure to work.[314] In 1339, William Gray and a member of the Franklyn family paid sixpence and threepence, respectively, as penalty for not working.[315]

By the 1350's, an intensification of work derelictions was in evidence, and failures to work became an almost regular item in court rolls up into the first decade of the fifteenth century. Thus, out of 19 court sessions whose records have survived from 1288 to 1339, only 21 failures to work were reported. On the other hand, between 1353 and 1403 — and, again, from 19 surviving court sessions — 191 failures to work were reported. Although this startling increase in work dereliction in the second half of the fourteenth century was no doubt aggravated by the mortality inflicted on the village by the plague and by a steadily decreasing population through the remainder of the century, it was very likely also a product of the gradual break-down of smooth village organization discernible in those post plague decades.[316] But whatever the explanation, its incidence was high and — at least in the context of Holywell's previous experience — unprecedented, reaching as much as 25 derelictions in one year (1353), (see Table V) and involving as many as 26 persons at one time (1386).[317] Clearly, then, there were times when the Holywell peasant simply failed to work, and the abbey made allowances for the possibility by the provision of a system of fines.

There is one final dimension to the question of *ad opus* tenures and the fulfilment of their work obligations which remains to be considered: the use of hired or substitute labour by a tenant. Due to the frequent fragmentary nature of the sources, no statistics can be produced for Holywell. Nevertheless, there is evidence of the existence of a labour force that

---

[312] PRO SC 2-179/17.

[313] PRO SC 2-179/18.

[314] PRO SC 2-179/25.

[315] PRO SC 2-179/30.

[316] For an example of this "break-down of the social community" in the Ramsey village of Upwood in the generation after the Black Death — a break-down characterized by increased violence within the village and the neglect of properties — see Raftis, "Changes in an English Village after the Black Death." *Mediaeval Studies*, XXIX (1967), pp. 164-65. For the extent of this phenomenon in Holywell itself, see *infra*, Chapter IV, p. 259 ff.

[317] By comparison, the greatest number of derelictions and persons in one year prior to 1350 was in 1313, when nine persons were guilty of 11 failures to work. See PRO SC 2-179/17.

TABLE V

FAILURES TO WORK IN HOLYWELL, 1288-1398

Year	Non op'	No. of Persons
1288	1	1
1294	1	1
1307	3	3
1311	2	2
1313	11	9
1318	1	1
1328	2	2
1339	2	2
1353	25	22
1354	4	4
1359	10	10
1364	6	5
1372	7	6
1375	7	7
1378	24	23
1386	29	26
1389	7	7
1391	16	16
1394	14	14
1396	12	10
1398	5	5

could be tapped by both lord and tenant for the performance of work. It is first indicated in the extent, under the regulations for *precariae*. The virgater was to be responsible for securing the services of four men. So too was the cotlander, while the croftholder had to supply one man. The virgater — and, presumably, the cotlander as well — was also to provide two men for the Autumn work season. Furthermore, it was stated that when such men were found, the personal attendance of the tenant at the work was not required.[318] Moreover, the excuse of works due to illness indicates substitute labour. The virgater, if he were so ill that he could not leave his house, was free of all work, except ploughing, and if he were ill during the harvest, he was excused half his work. It does not seem plausible

---

[318] *Carts.* I, p. 300. "Et sciendum, quod quotiens invenit quatuor homines, bene licet ei domui remanere si voluerit." Although this provision specifically referred to virgaters, it was likely applicable to cotlanders as well, and possibly also to croftholders, although this last is uncertain due to the Hundred Roll stipulation that the croftholder worked "cum corpore." (PRO SC-12-8-56; RH.II, p. 603.)

that if a man were as ill as allowed in the extent he would be expected to appear in the fields behind a plough. Rather the implication is clearly that personal *service* is not the real issue in the scheme of *opera*, but personal *responsibility* for securing the means necessary to perform works.[319] In short: labourers.

Now, that labourers were in fact an important element on mediaeval English manors in the thirteenth and fourteenth centuries has been frequently, and comprehensively, established.[320] Therefore, it is nothing unusual to posit for Holywell the possibility of hired labourers. But it is more than merely a possibility. For one, the court rolls speak of persons employed by villagers as household servants. More importantly, the 1307/8 account roll recorded the number of workers at the autumn *precaria* of 1308: 112 in addition to the manorial *famuli*.[321] It was not the full quota that could be expected according to the guidelines set down in the extent — which, if each virgater and cotlander had supplied four men and each croftholder one man, would have amounted to 141 — but it is a figure in excess of the number of probable customary tenants.[322]

Who these labourers were cannot be precisely determined, but some possibilities suggest themselves. For one, it is likely that, at least in the early fourteenth century, they mostly came from within the village. If not long-established residents, they were most likely at least residing there temporarily. The account roll of 1307/8 seems to imply this by referring to the 112 *precaria* workers as "custumarii". As to what villagers, it is not unlikely that a tenant called upon his own family as one source of labour — sons, daughters, even his wife.[323] Not only were they available, but they would involve no heavy expense to him. However, this source

---

[319] This emphasis on responsibility for work rather than personal performance — what has been termed a "depersonalization of *opera*" — has recently been stressed by Professor Raftis, *Tenure and Mobility*, pp. 15-16.

[320] See, for example, M. M. Postan, "The Famulus". *Supplement to the Economic History Review* (No. 2, 1950) for the place of the regular "hired worker" on the manorial demesne. More generally, see Kosminsky, who has contributed greatly to an understanding of the place of labourers on English manors (Chapter VI, esp. p. 292 *et seq.*), while, most recently, R. H. Hilton has drawn attention to the use of hired labour in the West Midlands (*A Medieval Society*, pp. 136-37).

[321] PRO SC 6-877/15. "Idem computavit in expensis pro magna precaria autumpni videlicet pro v^{xx} xii custumariis, fabro, molendinario et famulis domus."

[322] Although the number for the early fourteenth century is not certain, there were probably no more than 50 customary tenants. There were, for example, only 45 full customary tenements, and even if it is assumed that each virgate was halved — which, in fact, cannot be assumed — the number of tenants would then have been only 72: still 40 less than the 112 workers at the *precaria*.

[323] See Bennett, p. 103.

cannot be pressed too far, for it would require evidence of generally large families — five members or more — which, in Holywell, were not in overwhelming abundance.[324] Consequently, another source of labour should be sought, and one can be found in Holywell — among the peasants who held little land or who were, in fact, landless. Kosminsky has stressed the importance of these people — the "coterelli" of the Hundred Rolls, or the croftholders and the smallholders in general — as a supply of labour.[325] That there was a considerable number of such persons in Holywell in the fourteenth century — and even the latter thirteenth century — is beyond question. It will be recalled, for example, that an estimated 73 % of village families in the 1250's held less than 10 acres of land or no land at all, while 60 % were in the same position by 1370.[326] Furthermore, as there were, in the fourteenth century, only 45 full customary tenements, while evidence exists of over 100 adults in the village known *by name* at any period between 1300 and 1350,[327] there were clearly many persons — and even entire families — not holding adequate parcels of customary land, or any land. For them, their income would have to have been derived from working in the village — posssibly as craftsmen — or by working for their neighbors. Even the croftholder would most likely have found himself a part of this labour pool, since the croft, being about an acre, was hardly calculated to support a family comfortably.

There was, then, a supply of labour in the village, but it must be admitted that the tenants who would primarily benefit from it were the virgaters, semi-virgaters and cotlanders. The remaining tenants — the croftholders and even lesser tenants — and the non-tenants were the means whereby the virgater and cotlander could reduce and, at the same time, meet his personal work obligation, while upon these lesser holders would fall the bulk of the day-to-day burdens of physical labour. Their position was surely not an enviable one, and one can readily appreciate the dual pressure that weighed upon the croftholder: required to work for the lord in return for his croft and also dependent upon his neighbors for employment to supplement his rudimentary income to effectively support his family and meet the customary rents and other incidental dues incumbent upon him. True, he benefited from holydays, as did the virgater and the cotlander, and the extent even recognized that he could get sick, just like everybody else. But he was probably the most heavily-burdened

---

[324] See *infra*, Chapter III, p. 186 *et seq.*
[325] See *Studies*, p. 292 *et seq.*
[326] See *supra*, p. 36 *et seq.*
[327] See *infra*, Chapter III, p. 169.

tenant in the customary structure, and the closest to a very real and very grim poverty.[328]

Such, then, was the composition of *ad opus* tenure in Holywell-cum-Needingworth from the late thirteenth through the fourteenth centuries. For all practical purposes, it underwent no major alteration throughout the entire period.[329] For the tenant himself, a customary tenement *ad opus* imposed two unchanging sets of obligations. First, he was called upon to render annually the customary rent payments. For a virgater, this amounted to roughly two shillings (22d.ob.q.). The cotlander paid approximately a shilling (13d.ob.), and the croftholder fourpence. These were constant from year to year. The second set of obligations concerned the work, and here variation played a part. The amount of work in a year could fluctuate, affected by seasonal needs of the demesne, weather conditions, supply of labourers, manorial administrative programs, individual illnesses and holydays. What did not change was the tenant's responsibility for having the required work performed.

Customary tenures, although traditionally founded on obligations to perform work, could be — and were — established in return for money rent commuting all or part of the *opera* normally demanded. This was the customary tenure *ad censum*. Whereas attention has already been drawn to the commutation of some *opera* at specific seasons of the year, the *ad censum* tenure differed in that the commutation of all — or most — *opera* was arranged prior to the occurrance of the work seasons. By the middle of the thirteenth century, it was already an old practice, and it could be found in Holywell records as early as the 1160's.[330] It was not, however, intrinsically a permanent condition: lands released *ad censum* could be recalled and have their work services reimposed if necessary. This had happened in Holywell between the second half of the twelfth century and the middle of the thirteenth century — as, indeed, it had happened throughout rural England — when the thirteenth-century agrarian boom had occasioned a greater concentration on demesne cultivation and profit farming.[331] Consequently, by 1252 no virgates or cotlands were to be

---

[328] For amplification of the plight of the "cottar" in mediaeval England, see Kosminsky, p. 301 *et seq.*, and for the most recent summary of the conditions of the smallholder and his role as a labourer, see Postan, CEH, I, pp. 622-24.

[329] The only changes were in the numbers of units *ad opus*. The conditions of tenure remained the same.

[330] *Carts.* III, p. 281.

[331] See *supra*, p. 70 *et seq.*

found *ad censum* in Holywell.[332] As indicated previously,[333] no alteration in this arrangement was visible until the first decade of the fourteenth century. By then, the constriction of demesne production dating from at least the 1290's resulted in a return to releasing customary tenements *ad censum*. In both 1307/8 and 1323/24, eight virgates and nine cotlands had been taken out of *opus* — three of the latter having been dismissed to the beadle and two ploughmen in return for their services — or 38 % of the total of 45 customary units.[334] By 1346, although only five virgates were *ad censum*, nine cotlands (including three *in officio*) were still released from work services, as well as four of 13 crofts, or 40% of the total. In less than 70 years from the date of the Hundred Roll — when there was no evidence of any *ad censum* customary tenures — the holding of land for commuted services in Holywell had grown from 0% to 40%. Clearly, then, the *ad censum* customary tenure had been making a strong advance over the first half of the fourteenth century. It continued to do so into the 1350's. By 1355, although the disposition of virgates and cotlands had not changed since 1346/47, that of crofts had. Despite three vacant crofts in that year, all 13 had been freed of *opera*, eight having been put *ad censum* and five having been converted into holdings *in arentata*. As a result, by 1355, 60% of the villein land in Holywell had been taken out of the *ad opus* category, and this distribution remained in force through 1363.[335] Then came the 1370's, and the beginning of a renewed interest in demesne cultivation on Ramsey manors. By 1370, the commutation trend in customary tenures had been arrested and even reversed: only two virgates and two cotlands were *ad censum*, three cotlands were still *in officio*, and the 13 crofts remained undisturbed: eight *ad censum*, five *in arentata*. In short, by 1370 the commutation level had been returned to what it had been 50 years earlier, in the 1320's — to 38 %.

As already mentioned, *ad censum* could represent a commutation of

---

[332] It must be noted, however, that the change was not as striking as would first appear. In 1160 there had been 23 virgates and 14 cotlands in villeinage, of which 15 virgates were *ad opus* and, probably, 13 cotlands. By 1252, seven of the virgates had been lost to freehold, so that in that year there were 16 virgates and 14 cotlands *ad opus*. Consequently, although *ad censum* tenure played no part in the virgate or cotland structure of 1252, the number of such units in that year represented but a slight increase (by one) over the number *ad opus* in the 1160's.

[333] See *supra*, p. 71.

[334] The three cotlands *in officio* were not, strictly speaking, *ad censum*, as they were quit of all *opera*, customary rents and *censum* payments. The only obligation they may have imposed was the provision of labour at *precariae*.

[335] There was only one minor change by 1362/63: one-half virgate had been released to the reeve, *in officio*, leaving 11½ *ad opus*. PRO SC 6-877/20.

all or part of the labour services incumbent upon a specific tenement. In fourteenth-century Holywell, it appears to have been a commutation of all week-work. Not commuted were the responsibility for *precariae* and the payment of customary rents, although this latter was even waived in the case of crofts *in arentata*.[336]

The commutation rates themselves were fixed and were first clearly enunciated in account rolls of the second half of the fourteenth century. A virgate rendered 15 shillings *censum* annually, a cotland paid 7s.6d., and a croft *ad censum* was normally valued at 3s.4d. Those *in arentata* varied from three to five shillings.[337]

These rates were not arbitrary assessments, however, but were directly related to the "selling price" of the *opera* being commuted. Not that the *censum* was always an exact equivalent of works commuted. In some years the value of the *opera* was less than the *censum*, in other years more.[338] But the *censum* was, nevertheless, an attempt to approximate the annual work value.[339]

---

[336] Of the customary rents for virgates and cotlands, only the one penny *argentum vinee* was waived. That the other rents were owed is indicated in the account rolls, where reference is consistently made to the payment of rents from lands both *in opere* and *ad censum*. The relaxation of all week work is confirmed by accounts of the second half of the century, for *opera* were assessed only on tenements actually *ad opus*. Finally, whether or not the *censum* also commuted ploughing service is not indicated, but probably it did not, since this had not been released in the 1160's, nor were even the free tenements of customary origin rid of them in the latter 1200's (See *supra*, p. 36). See Raftis, *Estates*, p. 225, where it is noted that at Broughton, 1314/15, the *censum* appeared to have commuted heusyre and maltsilver customary rent payments for virgates.

[337] The rates 15 s. and 7 s. 6 d. are first found expressly stated in the account roll for 1362/63 (PRO SC 6-877/20). The rate for crofts (3 s. 4 d.) was initially encountered in 1346/47 among the crofts "ad firmam". That the rates 15 s. and 7 s. 6 d. were in effect in the first half of the fourteenth century can be demonstrated by the payment of the *censum* in 1346/47 by 15 virgates and six cotlands of 30 shillings at each of the four terms, with a virgate paying 3 s. 9 d. and a cotland 22 d. ob. a term (4×3 s. 9 d. = 15 s.; 4×22 d. ob. = 7 s. 6 d.; 5×15 s. = 75 s.; 6×7 s. 6 d. = 45 s.; 75×45 s. = 120 s.; 120 s. ÷ 4 = 30 s.)

Note should be made of the increase in *censum* rates from the twelfth century. In the 1160's, the average *censum* for eight virgates was 3 s. 2 d.

[338] In 1355/56, a virgate's total assessed *opera* came to 15 s. 10 d., those of a cotland 7 s. 7 d. ob. (PRO SC 6-877/19.) In 1362/63, the value of a virgate's *opera* was 15 s. 3 d., a cotland's 7 s. 7 d. (PRO SC 6-877/20.) In 1370/71, a virgate was assessed works in value of 13 s. 11 d., a cotland 6 s. 11 d. (PRO SC 6-877/21.)

[339] In the absence of comprehensive lists of tenants and tenements for the first half of the four-teenth century, it is not possible to measure the impact of *censum* policy on the Holywell peasant in this period. Professor Raftis (*Estates*, p. 225 and accompanying notes) has suggested a less than idyllic condition for the peasants of Ramsey manors put *ad censum* at this time due to the lack of concentration in customary lands and the probable consequent decline in the need for village wage labour by the tenant. At a time when cultivation was not at its peak, "The cash

For the tenant *ad censum* there was a definite uniformity to the rents to be paid. The *censum* itself being fixed, so too were the customary rents. As a result, a single virgate *ad censum* rendered an annual combined money rent of just under 17 shillings (16s. 5d. ob.q.), a cotland paid 8s. 6d. ob. The croft, at 3s. 4d., would have paid a total of 3s. 8d.

The sketch just given of tenurial structures and landholding patterns in Holywell-cum-Needingworth from the 1250's to 1370 is a rough and incomplete one, but the absence of sufficient records — especially detailed account rolls — prevents a more penetrating study of conditions during the period. Nevertheless, even the severely limited materials available point to the existence in Holywell of a tenacious, resilient and enterprising peasantry from the latter thirteenth century through the middle of the fourteenth century. Tenacity is first found in the survival of families themselves. Out of 104 known family groups residing at some point in the village between 1252 and 1370, only 33 remained for one generation or less, or for periods of from three to 40 years (31 %). Eighteen families disappeared only after two generations (17 %), and six families after three generations of settlement (6 %). On the other hand, 48 more families (46 %) did not disappear at all, but were in their second, third or even fourth generation by 1370.[340] Furthermore, of the 57 disappearing families, not all had been characterized by a peripheral involvement in manorial and village life. On the contrary, many had displayed a determination to identify themselves with the community and earn a living with whatever means were available and practical. It was not an easy task, however, as the inability of 33 families to remain longer than a generation testifies. But even among this short-term group an attempt was made: 14 families engaged in the brewing of ale, and of these, seven were able to maintain themselves for at least 20 years and five from between 10 and 20 years. In addition, three short-term families attempted to make a living through the performance of an essential service such as butchering and at least survived the 10-year point before disappearing. Moreover, at least nine of these families had reached a point of stability that enabled them to assume the responsibilities of court jurors and even manorial reeves during

renting of villein holdings and the sale of services meant that more of the burden of maintaining stable agrarian revenues was being thrown upon the peasant." (*Ibid.*, p. 223.) His conclusion is that "Although any peasant might desire the free disposition of his own labour acquired by this block commutation ... neither the ease of hiring labour nor the general economic conditions of the late thirteenth century, could have favoured this ad censum agreement in the eyes of the villein." (*Ibid.*, p. 225.)

[340] See *infra*, Chapter III, for a more detailed examination of demographic questions in Holywell, p. 166 *et seq.*

their limited residence.[341] This is not meant to imply, however, that such families were all necessarily prosperous. Obviously several were not. Six were characterized by members who were either described as poor in surviving records,[342] or fined for gleaning offenses — itself an indication of poverty. What remains of interest, however, is the fact that of 33 short-term families, only seven were unable to maintain residence for longer than 10 years. Whether they finally gave up and moved on or simply starved out is not known — the surviving records give no information — but the fact remains that they were an exception: the majority of families displayed a determination to "hang-on" as long as it was possible to do so.

But not all Holywell families in the latter thirteenth and earlier fourteenth centuries were short-term residents, and this in itself is illustrative of a tenacious peasantry. Some 24 families disappeared only after two or three generations of residence, while 48 did not disappear at all. No doubt the holding of land contributed to the prolongation of settlement, although it is more than likely that not all such families were generously provided with land — if at all. However, the importance of land cannot be overlooked: families such as the Grays, the Geres, the Mokes, the Palmeres and the Franklyns were customary tenants — of some kind — from as early as the second decade of the fourteenth century and at least into the 1350's and 1360's. The Hemyngtons, the Cranfelds, the Houghtons, the Beaumeyses, the Asplonds, the Carteres, the Brayns and the Nicholases — all long-term families — had kept a firm grip on customary properties from at least the 1350's and into 1370, while the Hunnes, the Lawemans, the Lanes, the Riptons, the Scots and the Godfreys had been holding-on to customary properties for over a century — from as early as the 1250's.[343]

---

[341] For further amplification of these questions, see *infra*, Chapter III, p. 208 *et seq.*

[342] Isabella de Walmesford, for example, was a Needingworth brewster in 1294 but was unable to pay her fine as she was "pauper" (BM.Add.Ch. 39597.).

[343] Even the maintenance of the blood right to property may be suggested as one aspect of this peasant tenacity. Although the lord of the manor would have favoured the custom as a means of ensuring labour for the demesne, the fact that the peasants themselves could sometimes dispute over who had more right to a tenement is indicative of an unwillingness to relinquish property and claims in property. A striking example of this may be found in the intra-familial conflict between Sampson Gilbert and his sister Maycusa over a virgate in 1294 (See *supra*, p. 59 note ⚡172), and Sampson's tenacity is further exemplified by the fact that he was not a resident of the vill in 1294 — nor thereafter — and, further, that he was in all probability the Sampson "the Candle-Maker of Needingworth" who was busy obtaining a stall (*selda*) in St. Ives in 1301 (PRO SC 178/95). In short, although not an active member of the local community and deriving his livelihood primarily as a tradesman, he was still unwilling to give up his property rights — even to his sister.

In addition, the families cited above were also able to maintain positions of major responsibility in the village throughout the late thirteenth and early fourteenth centuries and on past the middle of the fourteenth century.[344] More fundamental than the evidence of a group of main or leading peasant families in the community is the illustration they provide of peasants determined to maintain themselves in major positions from generation to generation.

But the Holywell peasantry of the latter thirteenth and earlier fourteenth centuries was also a resilient and enterprising peasantry. Perhaps the most striking indications of its resilience occurred in the years following the onslaught of the Black Death. Despite the loss of 15 families — and the replacement of only six — between 1340 and 1360, the manor was not afflicted with any serious vacancy problem. Only three crofts were without tenants in the mid-1350's, and even these had been filled by the 1360's. In addition, of the 15 families disappearing during the plague-infested years, only six were known customary families, while, further, only three were of major status in the village itself;[345] the bulk of the village families active in land and the exercise of responsible positions managed to survive the plague years unscathed.[346] Furthermore, by 1370 it was members of these families who stood at the beginning of a new chapter in Holywell's tenurial history as leaders in the accumulation and expansion of properties. However, even among lesser families — those neither deeply involved in land nor the official hierarchy of the village — an ability to sustain the shocks of the mid-century was in evidence. At least 16 such families managed to come through the plague years without serious injury and remained an additional 50 years or even longer.[347]

---

[344] See *infra*, Chapter III, p. 208 *et seq.*

[345] For further investigation of this question, as well as the classification of families in Holywell, see *infra*, Chapter III, p. 206 *et seq.*

[346] There were three major families, however, who, although they survived the plague years, sustained mortal wounds in the process. Thus the Franklyn, Laweman and Cranfeld families had all been of major importance in the village before the Black Death, but after its first visitation only the Cranfelds — in the person of Richard — managed to maintain their former position. All three, however, were gone by the early 1370's.

[347] Indeed, the one time in Holywell's earlier fourteenth-century history when the ability of especially major families to absorb severe shocks had been sorely tested — and the time when several had failed the test — occurred in the famine-riddled second decade of the century. Between 1310 and 1320, 12 families disappeared, among them being two of major rank, seven of intermediate rank, while only three minor families disappeared. This in itself is worth noting, since it may indicate that the major families — being, in all probability, the most seriously committed to land — were especially sensitive to famine conditions and liable to suffer heavily from them, whereas the minor group — being less directly dependent on land — sustained the immediate

Finally, Holywell from the late thirteenth century to 1370 also provides evidence of an enterprising peasantry. Given the scarcity of large — or even modest — parcels of land before the third quarter of the fourteenth century, the fact that 72 families managed to survive even past their second generation is significant. For some of those not involved in the customary structure, a village trade became the means of subsistence. Note has already been made of the number of short-term families engaging in the brewing of ale or in serving as butcher. In addition, there were over two dozen more families active in ale-brewing in the first three-quarters of the fourteenth century, the majority of which were of minor rank[348] but nevertheless in residence for two generations or longer. Furthermore, the Holywell peasant was not adverse to seeking opportunities away from home. Thus, in the early fourteenth century, the names of at least seven Holywell and Needingworth peasants can be found in the rolls of the St. Ives fairs taking up houses, shops and stalls.[349] On the other hand, opportunities for employment existed on the manor itself, whether as officials or *famuli*.[350]

Moreover, even despite the limited amount of land available in Holywell prior to the latter fourteenth century, examples can be found of peasants enterprising enough to take advantage of the few land opportunities that did exist. The exploitation of the land market, for example, enabled Richard le Eyr to make a modest career out of buying, selling, leasing or otherwise disposing of property, while in 1339, when 11 acres of demesne were put out on lease, four villagers joined forces to take them up jointly. The point to be made is that when and where opportunities existed, Holy-

---

shock more readily, if not more comfortably. For a contrary opinion, however, see Postan and Titow, "Heriots and Prices on Winchester Manors." *Economic History Review*, 2nd. series. XI (1959).

[348] See *infra*, Chapter III, p. 233 *et seq.*

[349] PRO SC 2-178/95. Sampson (Gilbert ?), "Candle-Maker" of Needingworth, took up a stall in 1301. Others were: William Kylleneth (1301/2: "unam rengiam domorum"), Henry Tiffayne (1314: "quartam cameram ... Domus"), John Raven (1314: medietatem ... dimidie rengiae"), William Bacoun (several small transactions from 1314 to 1324), John Scot (1318: "rengiam") and William de Halywell (i.e. Hamond) (1324: "rengiam").

[350] No lists of Holywell *famuli* exist from the early fourteenth century, but in the late 1300's positions such as that of ploughman were being taken up by local villagers, and frequently by villagers of modest background. Thus, Thomas Deye, who was to become a major tenant and village figure after 1400, seems to have begun his climb as *akerman* in 1392. Similarly, the reeve of Holywell in 1313 was Robert, son of Elena, while Robert Sky — representative of another small family — was reeve either of Holywell or Slepe in 1289 (BM.Add.Ch. 39736). In addition, the Cranfeld family appeared in the first decade of the fourteenth century but did not begin to assume any major position in the village until the 1320's, when Roger de Cranfeld began serving as reeve.

well seldom failed to provide men willing to take advantage of them.

Served, then, by characteristics of tenacity, resilience and enterprise, the Holywell peasantry had, by 1370, come through over a century of profound agrarian shifts and shocks without any cataclysmic changes to its outward structure. Neither the end of the era of high farming by the late thirteenth century, the famines of 1317/19, a growing demographic slump, nor the attack of the plague in 1349 radically altered the disposition of acreage throughout the village before 1370. The tenant population continued to remain stratified into large, middling and smallholders, with the balance tipped in favour of the last two groups, while the gap separating the large tenants from the small was narrow — with a tenurial ladder where top rungs stood at 18 acres. Throughout, a core of villagers had consistently managed to emerge who dominated the occupation of the land while even peasants not involved in tenure to any considerable degree had, through determination and enterprise, been able to survive and endure through the exploitation of opportunities presented by local trades and manorial occupations.

But by 1370, Holywell-cum-Needingworth stood on the brink of a new era in its land history. The declining fortunes of demesne farming over the next 50 years were to result in major revisions in administrative policy by the abbey, with the eventual release of the demesne to the peasants and the introduction of money rent as the basis for all tenures. This, coupled with a continuing fall in local population, would create challenges and opportunities for the peasantry that would again put their tenacity, resilience and enterprise to the test. How the test was met is the purpose of the next chapter to investigate.

Appendix I

Tenants* and Tenements in Holywell-cum-Needingworth, 1252

Agnes	1 forera
Alan, son of Richard	1 v
Albreda	1 cr
Ayse, Radulph	1 c (with Radulph Godfrey)
Bakun, Robert	1 v (with Stephan Edwyn)
Benet, Richard	1 v (with Radulph, son of Roger)
Bonde, Alexander	1 c
Clericus, Reginald	1 v
Cullefinche, William	1 c
Edusa	1 cr
Edwyn, Stephan	1 v (with Robert Bakun)
Galfridus, son of Rannulph	1 c
Gere, John	1 c; 1½ c
Gilbert, son of Walter	1 v
Godfrey, Radulph	1 v (with Radulph Ayse)
Godrich, Radulph	1 c
Godward, Alice	1 c
Gray, William	1 c
Hoki, Hugo	1 v; 1 forera
Hugo, son of Richard	1 c
Hunne, Stephan	1 v
Juliana	1 cr; 1 forera
Kyng, Richard le	1 c
Lane, Robert in	1 v
Laweman, Richard	1 v
Laweman, Robert	1 v
Laweman, William	1 c
Mareys, Henry	1 cr; 1 forera
Margaret	1 cr
Messer, Nicholas le	1 v
Molendinarius, Roger	1 cr
Prepositus, Henry	1 c
Prinaithe, Henry	1 cr
Radulph, son of Godrich	1 cr
Radulph, son of Roger	1 v (with Richard Benet)
Robert, son of Mauger	1 c; 1 r
Russell, Richard	1 cr
Ryptone, Robert de	1 v
Samuel, Radulph	1 cr
Scot, Radulph	1 v
Scot, Walter	1 c
Selede, Robert	1 cr
Sutor, Richard	1 cr

* Customary tenants, only.

Toly, Hawysia	1 v
Tulle, Richard	1 c
Turtleberne, Richard	1 cr; 1 forera
Venelle, Agnes in la	1 v

Appendix II

Tenants and Tenements in Holywell-cum-Needingworth, 1371

Asplond, John	1 v (op)
Asplond, Thomas	1½ a
Attewelle, John	1½ c (op)
Attewelle, Robert	1/2 v, 1/4 v (cens)
Balde, Richard	1 a
Baroun, John	1 cr (arent)
Baroun, William	1 cr (arent)
Beaumeys, John	1 v (op)
Beaumeys, Walter	1 v (op)
Berewell, William	2 a
Bernewell, Thomas	1 a
Bigge, William	1 a
Bokenham, John	2 a
Botiller, William	2 a
Bran, John	1 cr (cens)
Brayn, Reginald	1 pl, 1 r
Brayn, Richard	1 v (op)
Brian, William	1/2 a
Brouning, John	3 a (with John Colner)
Brunne, Simon	7 a, 1½ r; 1 pecia
Cabe, Hugo	1 a
Caldecote, Thomas	1½ a (with John Fyn Sr.)
Cartere, Thomas	2 c (op)
Catun, John	2 a; 1 a
Celere, William Sr.	1 cr (cens)
Celere, William Jr.	1 cr (cens)
Clerk, John	1 a
Cok, Robert	2 a; 1 pecia
Colle, Roger	1 a
Colner, John	3 a (with John Brouning)
Coupere, Thomas	1 a
Cranfeld, Cristina de	Drihirst meadow
Cranfeld, Richard	1 cr (cens); 1 c (cens); 1/2 a
Crouch, Ivo atte	1 a; 1 a
Daye, Robert	1 cr (arent)
Essex, John	9 a, 1 r; 3 a
Fannell, Robert	1 cr (arent)
Fisser, John	1 a
Fisser, Simon	1 a
Flesshewere, Nicholas	1 cr (cens)

FRERE, John	2 a
FYN, John Sr.	1½ a (with Thomas Caldecote)
GODFREY, Adam	1 v (op)
GODFREY, Nicholas	12 a, 1 r
GOODMAN, Andrew	1 v (op); 1 forera
GOODRICH, Thomas	1 cr (cens)
GRAY, Richard	1 v (op)
GURTON, Richard	1/2 a
GUTFORD, John	6 a; 1 pecia
GUTFORD, Robert	4 a
HAMOND, John	1 a; 1/2 v (op)
HARDY, Nicholas	1 cr (cens)
HAUT, Simon	1 a; 3 a
HEMYNGTON, John	1 a; 1 a; 2 c (op); 1 cr (cens)
HEROW, John	1½ a
HOGGE, Edward	1/2 a
HOGGE, Thomas	1 a
HOUGHTON, Robert	7 a; 3 a; 1 a; 1/2 v (cens); 1/2 c (op)
HROFF, Adam	1 a
HUNNE, Agnes	1/2 v (cens)
HUNNE, John	1 a
HUNNE, Thomas	1 v (op)
LANE, Nicholas in	1 a; 1/4 v (cens); meadow (Flegholm); 1 v
LEIGHTON, William	2 a
LENEHERT, John	2 a
MACHYNG, William	2 a
MERTON, John	1 v (op)
MILNERE, Robert	1 cr (cens)
MOKE, Robert	1/2 v (op)
NICHOLAS, John	meadow (Flegholm); 1 v (op)
NIEL, John	1 a
PALMERE, William	1 v (op)
RAVEN, John	11 a
POPE, John	1 a
PYE, Benedict	1 a
RAVEN, William	1 a; 1 c (cens)
REVE, William	1 a; 1 c (cens)
REYNOLD, John	1 a
SANDE, John	1 c (op)
SCHARP, Nicholas	2 a (with William Scharp)
SCHARP, William	2 a (with Nicholas Scharp)
SCOT, Nicholas	1 v (op); 1 c (op)
SCOT, William	1/2 v (op)
SEWEYN, Thomas	3 a
SHEPPERD, John	1 a
SHEPPERD, Nicholas	3 r; 3 a; 1 c (op)
SKYNNERE, John	1 c (op)
SOMO, Robert	2 a
SWOLD, John	1 a

THATCHER, Richard	1/2 v (op)
WEBBESTER, William	1½ a
WHITE, Hugo	1 pecia
WILLIAM the Parson	1 pecia
WOLAC, John	2 a
WRIGHT, John	2 a; 1 a
HENRY ... ? ...	6 a

CHAPTER II

STRUCTURES AND PATTERNS OF TENURE, 1370-1457

With the coming of the 1370's, Holywell-cum-Needingworth witnessed the beginning of what was to be a lengthy period of dramatic alterations in the tenurial lives of its peasants. Throughout the Ramsey estate complex, the 1370's and 1380's were years of stabilization and modest recovery in demesne administration, but by the 1390's the cancer eating away at the body of the manorial organization had progressed too far to permit any return to the "golden days"of agricultural production characteristic of the thirteenth century.[1] By the eve of the fifteenth century, productivity on Ramsey estates was stagnating, and even such measures of attracting tenants as increased commutations or long-term leases of demesne that had enjoyed some warm success in the 1370's and 1380's were beginning to lose their effectiveness as more and more tenements remained vacant or fell into varying stages of disrepair.[2] Despite attempts to continue direct demesne exploitation past 1400, the estates were entering into "the deepest and most prolonged depression in ... abbey history",[3] and the struggle proved to be a losing one. On some manors, the end came early: by the close of the first decade of the fifteenth century demesne cultivation had been abandoned and the demesne let-out to farm on six manors, including Holywell.[4] On others, it was drawn-out, but by the 1450's it was over, and a centralized administration of demesnes had been replaced by the local "farmer".

The effects of this gradual strangulation of the demesne economy from the last quarter of the fourteenth century — but especially after 1400 —

---

[1] For a detailed examination of conditions on Ramsey estates from the 1370's into the fifteenth century, see Raftis, *Estates*, pp. 259-66 and Chapter X (p. 281 *et seq.*). Similar conditions throughout England — characterized by a growing trend to "farm" manorial demesnes — and beginning as early as the middle of the fourteenth century have been well summarized by Postan, CEH, I, p. 587 *et seq.* See also F. R. H. DuBoulay, *The Lordship of Canterbury*, G. A. Holmes, *The Estates of the Higher Nobility in 14th-Century England*, Chapter IV; and, for a very general treatment, May McKisack, *The Fourteenth Century, 1307-1399* (Oxford, 1959), p. 331 *et seq.*, p. 340 *et seq.* and pp. 347-48.

[2] See Raftis, *Estates*, pp. 259-66 and Chapter X (p. 281 *et seq.*)

[3] *Ibid.*, p. 292.

[4] *Ibid.*, p. 266.

were to be not insignificant for the lives of the peasants of Holywell-cum-Needingworth. The eighty years from 1370 to 1450 witnessed deep changes in the structuring and responsibilities of tenure within the village, while, from 1400, a population decline aggravated by plagues almost a generation earlier finally made its impact felt and joined with trends heightened by some 30 years of leasing policies to contribute to a modification by the peasant of his attitude towards the nature and permanence of his tenurial commitment. Finally, although the 1370's inaugurated a period of increased availability of land — from demesne and fen leasing policies — and, supported by factors of population decline, thereby contributed to new possibilities for the extension, consolidation and concentration of tenements, the Holywell peasant found himself competing for land not only with his local neighbors but indeed with the whole region as peasants from as close as St. Ives and from as far north as Broughton and Warboys appeared in the village mainly for the purpose of acquiring tenements in the demesne and fen. All told, the years between 1370 and 1450 constituted a time of new opportunities for some individuals and families and new hardships for others, of changes in tenurial structure and profound alterations in tenurial attitudes and burdens. Especially was it a time of new challenges[5] as old forms of land-holding were redefined or completely abandoned by a manorial organization trying to keep itself from slipping into an already opened grave. How the Holywell peasant was affected by the changes between 1370 and 1450, and how he reacted to them shall be examined to the degree permitted by the surviving records.

As already noted in the previous chapter, one change in Holywell's tenurial structure manifesting itself by 1370 concerned the availability of land.[6] Although the sheer amount of land in the village had not undergone any particular increase or decrease from the early 1300's, there were more tenements available in terms of the resident population than had been the case a generation earlier. One reason for this lay in a declining population. By 1370, there were some 53 family groups resident in Holywell, as contrasted to 61 thirty years earlier.[7] Between the plague-ravaged years of 1340 and 1360 alone, 15 families had disappeared from the village, while only six had moved in to take their place. Essentially, it was a problem of replacement, and it had been a problem since the second decade

---

[5] For a provocative study of the "challenging" conditions of late fourteenth-early fifteenth-century rural England, see A. R. Bridbury, *Economic Growth: England in the Late Middle Ages* (London, 1962), pp. 52-55 and 83-92.

[6] See *supra*, p. 66.

[7] See *infra*, Chapter III, p. 167.

of the century,[8] for in the 50 years between 1310 and 1360 the village had lost a total of 42 families and witnessed the immigration of only 38.[9] Consequently, by 1370 there had been a definite readjustment in the potential amount of available customary land per family, especially as the number of families in the village was closely approaching the number of full customary tenements (45).

What resulted, however, was not a more equalized share in customary land per family. Out of 53 families clearly resident in the village, only 31 were involved in holding customary land (60 %), and of the 31 families, 11, or 35 %, controlled 55 % of the villeinage, or 26 out of a total of 47 parcels.[10] Certainly the aggravated population problems and the impact of plague from the mid-century had played a part in thinning the ranks of the customary families, but they had not done so to a sweeping degree. For example, out of 19 families disappearing from the 1340's to 1370, only seven were families involved in the customary structure. Consequently, not enough old customary families had been removed to the extent that a large proportion — or a majority — of the villein tenements could have been "thrown open" to the village population at large. Thus, among the customary tenant families in 1370, 10 had been customary tenants for at least 50 years by 1370.[11] Six other families first showed concrete signs of customary involvement in the 1350's, but they were all families that had been of major importance in the community for at least 20 years before that time and consequently may have been, in fact, customary tenants for as long a period. What is clear is that six additional families involved in the customary structure in 1370 were *new* families — having appeared first only after the plague — and that four more families, who had, in each case, been resident in the village from at least the first decade of the century, first appeared as customary tenants — indeed,

[8] The best study to date of the declining replacement rates in fourteenth-century England is that of Professor Sylvia Thrupp: "The Problem of Replacement-Rates in Late Medieval English Population." *Economic History Review*, 2nd. series. XVIII (No. 1, 1965), pp. 101-119.

[9] In contrast, in just the decade between 1300 and 1310, whereas eight families had disappearred from the village, 16 new families had moved in to more than replace them and fill the gap. See *infra*, Chapter III, p. 167 a.

[10] There were still 17 virgates, 15 cotlands and 13 crofts in villeinage in 1370, but only 12 virgates, 14 cotlands and the 13 crofts were full units. There were seven half-virgates, two one-quarter virgates and two half-cotlands, for a total of 47 customary tenements comprising 45 full units.

[11] Based on notices of work derelictions from court rolls between 1288 and 1339 and from property commitments in the 1252 extent in the cases of families surviving to 1370 from the 1250s and still retaining customary lands.

in two cases began to emerge as anything more than minor or peripheral families — only by 1370. In short, despite the shock of the plague and factors of continued population decline, certainly 10 — but probably even 16 — village families involved in customary land managed to survive the perils into the 1370's, while seven families, in one way or another, fell victim to them, leaving only 10 more families (six of them recent arrivals) to divide up what proprietary spoils there were.[12]

And just exactly what "spoils" there were is a good question. Of the four "old" families first appearing as customary tenants in 1370, only two managed to lay their hands on tenements larger than crofts: the Skynneres and the Shepperds, both of them holding cotlands, and then only one apiece. The other two — the Barouns and the Deyes — had to be content with crofts, although the Barouns were able to hold two — between two men. On the other hand, of the six newly-arrived families, three settled in as croftholders (Hardy, Miller and Flesshewere), one occupied a full cotland (Sande) and one a full virgate (Merton). The remaining family — the AtteWelles — fared best of all. Two men — Robert and John (father and son) — between them held one and a half cotlands and three-quarters of a virgate, or a total of four individual pieces: a cotland and a half cotland (John), and a half-virgate and a quarter-virgate (Robert). The families who seem to have really benefited most of all, therefore, were those that had already been customary tenants before the plague years and who survived them. Thus, by 1370 the Beaumeyses had two virgates, the Brayns a virgate and a croft, the Carteres two cotlands, the Hemyngtons two cotlands and a croft (held by one man, John), the Houghtons a half-virgate and a half-cotland (also held by one man, Robert), the Hunnes a virgate and a half-virgate, the Lanes a virgate and a quarter-virgate, the Cranfelds a croft and two cotlands (again held by one man, Richard the son of Roger), and the Scots a virgate, a half-virgate and a cotland.[13]

The early 1370's were witnessing, then, an intensified trend towards the concentration of customary tenements in fewer hands.[14] It was a trend that became more pronounced over the subsequent 30 years. By 1397, the 45 units in villeinage had been fragmented into some 50 separate

---

[12] There was one other family represented among the 1370 customary tenants that has been omitted from the above summary because it was not a long-term family in the 1370's — the Celeres — who held two crofts, and who were also outsiders.

[13] See Chapter I, Appendix II.

[14] In terms, not of families, but of individuals, out of 39 customary tenants in 1370, eight, or 21 %, had two or more customary tenements.

parcels,[15] held in that year by only 37 persons, 35 of whom represented only 24 village families.[16] All told, by the eve of the fifteenth century, eight men again — or 22 % of the 37 tenants — held two or more customary tenements, while 12 village families (50 %) controlled 31 parcels, or 62 % of the customary land.[17] In terms of overall village family population, in 1370 11 families out of 53 had dominated the customary structure, while only 20 more families were even active in it. In 1397, out of a probable 50 families resident in the village,[18] 12 controlled more than half the customary land, with further interest in customary land displayed by only 12 more families. Within 30 years, the number of village families *not* involved in the customary structure had grown from 40 % (1370) to over 50 % (1397).

This does not mean, however, that from 1370 the number or percentage of land — or property — less families in Holywell was increasing. As pointed out earlier, by 1370 there were new sources of opportunity in land in Holywell — a not insignificant part of which had been made available as early as 1362:[19] the demesne and the marsh. In 1370, some 74 acres of demesne were being let out. For 16 of these acres — seven in Schepenfurlong and nine in Oxhowe — the account roll gave no names of tenants, stating only that they were held by "customaries" (*custumarii*). However, the names of the tenants of the remaining 58 demesne acres were inscribed on the roll. All told, they were held by 16 persons. One was an outsider — John Frere — holding two acres. The remaining 15 were all Holywell residents, representing 11 village families. Of the 11 families, eight were customary families as well — i.e. holding customary tenements — and together they accounted for 33 of the 58 acres, or 57 %.

The second recent source of tenements was the marsh, but here the Holywell villager faced stiff competition from outsiders. Doubtlessly the

---

[15] The fragmentation may have been the result of a temporary readjustment in population between 1370 and 1390, during which years 16 new families had moved into the village while only eight had vanished, bringing the total number of families in Holywell by 1390 to a new high. Thereafter, however, the demographic slump resumed, with 15 families disappearing between 1390 and 1400, while only four new families took up residence. In the next 50 years, the village witnessed the arrival of only 11 new families, as contrasted with the loss of 29. See *infra*, Chapter III, p. 167.

[16] Two croftholders — William Dammesson and John Fagg — cannot be identified as local people.

[17] See Table III.

[18] The figure is only a conjecture, since the number of families between 1390 and 1400 was swiftly dropping.

[19] See *supra*, p. 60 *et seq.*

long-standing right of other Ramsey manors to pasture in the Holywell fens helped account for this,[20] but whatever the reasons, the renting of the fen grasses by the 1370's occasioned a flood of interested persons. Thus, in 1370 over 52 persons were recorded as having properties in the marsh, and of these over 40 were outsiders. Some came from St. Ives, others from Wistow, Warboys, Caldecote and Broughton. Only 12 Holywell people — representing 12 resident families — had marsh tenements, accounting for only 30 to 40 acres of a total exceeding 120.[21]

Taking into consideration, then, demesne and fen as well as straight customary tenements, a known 39 village families were holding at least one of the three kinds of property in 1370, or 74% of the families in residence. However, not all the 39 tenant families were generously provided with land in 1370. As indicated earlier,[22] some 46% held properties less than 10 acres in size, and an additional 13% held more than 10 acres but less than a virgate (18 acres). In terms of individuals, out of 52 village tenants (i.e. resident in Holywell), 29 held properties of 10 acres or less, or 55%. On the other hand, if all the known tenants in 1370 are taken into consideration — outsiders as well as residents — a total of 70 persons held properties of 10 acres or less (73%), and 61 of these were holding less than five acres (64%).

But, as already emphasized, the 1370's stood at the beginning of a new chapter in Holywell's tenurial history. Leasehold policies of the abbey, a continual waning of population strength, and the availability of demesne and fen resulted in a flurry of activity in land over the next 80 years, the general effect of which was a decrease in the number of true smallholders and an increase in the number of persons controlling 20 acres or more. That such a readjustment in land distribution was already foreshadowed in 1370 in the evidence of individuals holding multiples of tenements has already been noted.[23] However, a pattern was not really firmly set until the first decade of the fifteenth century. Thus, in 1392, out of 58 known tenants, 32, or 55%, still held 10 acres or less; 21 (36%) held between

---

[20] See *supra*, Chapter I, p. 62, notes ♯ 184 and 185.

[21] The uncertaintly about the acreage stems from the fact that at least two Holywell villagers — Nicholas in the Lane and John Nicholas — accounted for the whole of Flegholm marsh, whose size was not stated. Since the other individual marshes (Eestlang, Merslake, Dichfurlong) averaged some 28 acres each, it is likely that Flegholm fell near the same figure. If it was comparable in size to the smallest known marsh — the 23 acre Merslake — then the total acreage held by Holywell people was approximately 40, since 10 villagers held 17 acres. The figure "30-40" has been employed to cover even further overestimation of Flegholm.

[22] See *supra*, p. 58.

[23] See *supra*, p. 64.

11 and 20 acres; and five (9 %) held 21 acres or more. In 1400, almost the same proportion prevailed: 34 (58%) at 10 acres or less, 19 (32%) at 11 to 20 acres, and six (10 %) at 21 acres or more.[24] (See Table I). One reason for this stability in property distribution from 1370 through 1400 is no doubt to be found in a temporary arrest of population decline between the 1370's and the 1390's. However, it was a short-lived arrest. By 1400, there were only 50 families settled in the village, and the number continued to drop thereafter.[25] Consequently, by 1405 the first significant readjustment in property disposition was observable. In that year, out of 48 known tenants, the number of persons holding 10 acres or less had dropped to 19, or 39.6%. Nineteen persons (39.6 %) held from 11 to 20 acres, while 10, or 20.8 %, held 21 acres or more. The number of persons holding 21 acres or more had risen, by 1405, by four from 1400 or five from 1370.

TABLE I

DISTRIBUTION OF ACREAGE AMONG HOLYWELL TENANTS, 1392-1457

Year	No. at 1-10 a.	No. at 11-20 a.	No. at 21 a.+	Total
1392	32	21	5	58
%	(55)	(36)	(9)	
1400	34	19	6	59
	(58)	(32)	(10)	
1405	19	19	10	48
	(39.6)	(39.6)	(20.8)	
1409/13	22	17	16	55
	(40)	(30.9)	(29.1)	
1414/18	32	13	22	67
	(47.8)	(19.4)	(32.8)	
1419/33	25	20	16	61
	(41)	(33)	(26)	
1437/50	26	15	25	66
	(39.4)	(22.7)	(37.9)	
1451/57	20	11	18	49
	(41)	(23)	(36)	

[24] Unfortunately for purposes of tabulation, account rolls from 1392 on give no detailed information on holdings in the fen. The 1370 list of tenants was a unique record, therefore. Subsequent reports of fen holdings are condensed and summary in character. However, from 1392 the fen grasses reserved for Holywell people seem to have amounted to only 27 acres, one rod in Flegholm marsh. The remaining 100 acres were let out in blocs to customaries of Slepe, Wodehurst, Broughton and Caldecote. See PRO SC 6-877/22, 23, 26, 27, 28, 29, 30.

As a result of the lack of details on fen tenants, therefore, all lists of properties and propertyholders in Holywell beginning in 1392 will be incomplete, in so far as the 127+ acres of marsh cannot be assigned to any specific individuals.

[25] See infra, Chapter III, p. 167.

Between 1409 and 1413, however, when 55 tenants were accounted for, the number of people at 21 acres or more had increased by six (16, or 29.1 %), while the number at 10 acres or less had risen to 22 (40 %). Indeed, through the remainder of the second decade of the fifteenth century, as the number of tenants increased (67 between 1414 and 1418), so too did the number of persons at 10 acres or less (32, or 47.8 %). On the other hand, the 1420's, the 1430's and the 1440's — during which decades the number of tenants wavered between 61 and 66 — again witnessed an advance by the tenants at 21 acres or more and a reduction in the number at 10 acres or less. (See Table I).

Breaking-down the distribution of acreage in Holywell even further (See Table II), it is seen that between the 1390's and the 1450's, the number and percentage of tenants at five acres or less underwent a general — if irregular — reduction, but that they were at no time negligible. Indeed, with only two exceptions (1409/13 and 1419/33), they managed to account for over 30 % of all the known tenants in Holywell for almost 50 years from the last decade of the fourteenth century through the middle of the fifteenth century. On the other hand, Table II shows that persons holding between six and 10 acres fluctuated widely from just over 4 % (1405) to 23 % (1419/33), while the "middling" tenants — between 11 and 17 acres — wavered between percentages of eight and 18 until the 1450's. Tenants of from 18 to 25 acres first held steady, then dipped,

TABLE II

DISTRIBUTION OF ACREAGE AMONG HOLYWELL TENANTS, 1392-1457

Year	5a. or less.	6a-10a.	11a-17a.	18a-25a.	26a-29a.	30a.+
1392	26	6	8	15	3	0
%	(45)	(10)	(14)	(26)	(5)	(0)
1400	26	8	6	13	4	2
	(44)	(14)	(10)	(22)	(7)	(3)
1405	17	2	7	14	4	4
	(35.4)	(4.2)	(14.6)	(29.2)	(8.3)	(8.3)
1409/13	15	7	10	9	6	8
	(27)	(13)	(18)	(16)	(11)	(15)
1414/18	22	10	8	11	4	12
	(33)	(15)	(12)	(16)	(6)	(18)
1419/33	11	14	5	22	3	6
	(18)	(23)	(8)	(36)	(5)	(10)
1437/50	21	5	7	17	3	13
	(31.8)	(7.6)	(10.6)	(25.8)	(4.5)	(19.7)
1451/57	16	4	9	12	1	7
	(33)	(8)	(18)	(25)	(2)	(14)

rose and dipped again, while persons at from 26 to 29 acres rose and then dropped. Those at 30 acres and above rose, dropped, rose and dropped again. It is possible, based on the figures in Tables I and II, to state generally that the smallest holdings in Holywell were steadily reducing in number from the 1390's through 1413, that holdings of from 11 to 20 acres were very gradually declining and that the largest holdings (over 20 acres) were increasing over the same period. During the half-decade between 1414 and 1419, however, whereas smallholding activity advanced again, so too did largest tenements, while other tenements experienced a decline. From 1419 through 1433, on the other hand, smallholdings again retreated in the face of larger property concentrations, while the period from 1437 to 1450 was a time of extremes: the highest percentage of smallholds since the second decade of the century, and also the largest percentage of "big" concentrations (21 acres or more) of the century. Finally, the 1450's witnessed a general increase in all property categories with the exception of those in excess of 20 acres, which were again on the wane.

Equally important, however, as any statements about broad, general trends in Holywell's tenurial pattern from the 1390's to the 1450's is the evidence of fluctuations — sometimes even wide fluctuations — within those trends. If it can be said that, on the whole, the number and percentage of tenants holding 10 acres or less underwent a reduction over the 60 years, it must also be emphasized that, although the number and percentage of tenants above the 10 acre level advanced, they did not do so steadily or with even any special degree of continuity. In short, what is most striking about the tenurial pattern in Holywell over the first half of the fifteenth century is the aspect of fluctuation. Admittedly a degree of this fluctuation is to be explained by the constantly-changing number of tenants from the 1390's to the 1450's, and it is for this reason that the figures of Tables I and II cannot be pressed too far. Nevertheless, despite such grounds for caution in interpreting Holywell statistics, the fact of fluctuation still remains, and it is this, together with the trend of tenants at 21 acres or more to increase in number, that must be examined more closely.

It is generally agreed by scholars at present that the late fourteenth century and fifteenth century in England was a time of improvement for those members of rural society known as the smallholders or the landless.[26] The continuing demographic slump of the late 1300's, together with policies such as demesne leasing, increased the amount of land available, and

---

[26] See esp. Postan, CEH, I, p. 630 *et seq.*

this, coupled with low rents and high wages, made it possible for many smallholders — and even landless men — to be "promoted" up the rural tenurial ladder.[27] This does not mean that throughout England previous smallholders or landless men suddenly became large landholders. It simply means that, given the demographic and economic factors that obtained, the opportunity was often present in many villages for persons to acquire land — or add to their holdings — to a degree not possible or practical almost a century earlier, in the years of critical land-hunger. That such an opportunity was also present in fifteenth-century Holywell and was taken advantage of has already been demonstrated. What needs to be examined now is how much a part "promotion" really played in the village — especially among the lower strata of tenants — and, given the fact of fluctuation in tenurial involvements, to attempt to determine how consistently the new opportunity in land was exploited.

Table III is a listing of all known Holywell-cum-Needingworth tenants between 1392 and 1457, together with a tabulation of their total properties in terms of acreage at specific periods over the first half of the fifteenth century.[28] From the information in Table III, it can be seen that between 1392 and 1451, 34 persons began their Holywell tenurial careers as tenants of five acres of land or less.[29] Of these, 24 were tenants for anywhere from five to over 30 years, and none showed signs of promotion into any of the upper strata of tenants in the village. In short, they all began by holding five acres or less and they ended in the same position. Only two, in fact, increased the size of their already modest holdings: Nicholas Oky,

---

[27] Professor Postan, for one, has very ably and persuasively discussed this question of "social promotion" in CEH, I, pp. 630-32.

[28] The year 1396/97 has been omitted because the account roll for that year is incomplete, listing only customary tenants. PRO SC 6-877/23. This was also the last account roll to specifically name the virgaters and cotlanders in Holywell. Villagers listed as customary tenants at that time and still present and active in the village after 1400 are assumed to be still retaining their customary properties unless there is clear evidence to the contrary. In general, confirmation of the wisdom of this assumption has frequently been found in court roll notices of work derelictions, account roll tabulations of *opera* excused individual villagers for illness, and by later statements in the Ramsey Court Book indicating that certain villagers retained customary virgates or cotlands for several years after 1397.

[29] Some persons have been omitted from this figure. For example, Nicholas in the Lane, tenant of an acre in 1392 and 1400, is excluded because he was not beginning in Holywell but rather quite literally ending his life. Prior to 1392, he had been a virgater but had surrendered his tenement to his son John by 1392. Similarly, persons have been omitted who indeed held less than five acres but who were listed as tenants only once. Finally, such a person as Robert Rokysdon has been excluded because there is evidence that Robert was a cleric who — most importantly — was probably seldom, if ever, in residence in Holywell.

TABLE III

TENANTS AND TENEMENTS IN HOLYWELL-CUM-NEEDINGWORTH, 1392-1457

	1392	1400	1405	1409/13	1414/18	1419/33	1437/50	1451/57
ALBRY, William						20a	21a	
ARNOLD, John	1a	1a						
ARNOLD, Simon						9a		
ARNOLD, Thomas						1a	1a	12a
ASPLOND, John	19a	19a	19a	19a	19a	24a		
ASPLOND, John						26a	26a	
ASPLOND, John							37a, 2r	10a
ASPLOND, Richard					5a	10 ½a	23a	
ASPLOND, Rosa								23a, 3r
ASPLOND, Thomas	1a	1a						
ATTEWELLE, John (I)	17a							
ATTEWELLE John (II)		2a	28 ½a	26 ½a	26 ½a	35 ½a	45 ½a	9-3 ½a
ATTEWELLE, Robert	27 ½a	32 ½a						
BAKER, John	18a	18a	20a	29a	13a			
BAKER, Roger					18 ½a		3 ½a	21 ½a
BAKER, Thomas					2a			
BAKER, John (II)							19 ½a	19 ½a
BAROUN, John	1a	1a	1a					
BAROUN, Nicholas				10a	28a, 1r	25a	17a,¼r	17a,¼r
BAROUN, William	2a	2a	1a	1a	1a			
BAROUN, Thomas					1a	19a		
BAROUN, Alice								11a
BATE, John					2a	23 ½a	33 ½a	23 ½a
BEAUMEYS, John		19a	19a	29a	30a		13a	1a
BEAUMEYS, Walter	18a							
BEAUMEYS, Richard								11a
BENET, William							10a	
BERNEWELL, Thomas	1a	1a						
BOTILLER, William				12 ½a				
BOTILLER, Thomas				12 ½a				
BLAKWELL, John						15a		
BLOSSOUM, John						7a		
BRAMPTON, John			1a					
BROOK, Richard				1a				
BOTHE, William							11a	
BRAYN, John	20a							
BRAYN, Nicholas	9a							
BRAYN, Reginald			8 ½a, 1r					
BRAYN, Thomas			9a	3a, 3r	2a			
BRYAN, John						20a,2r		
BRYAN, William							1a	
BRYS, John							37a	

	1392	1400	1405	1409/13	1414/18	1419/33	1437/50	1451/57
CADEMAN, Thomas						9a		
CARTERE, William	10a	19a	14½a	6½a	6½a			
CARTERE, John		2a	2a					
CHAPLYN, William							19a	
CRISTEMESSE John (I)	2a	2a	2a					
CRISTEMESSE, John (II)						19a	34a	45a,¼r
CRISTEMESSE, Richard						20a	22a	22a
CRISTEMESSE, Roger						9a	24a	30½a
DALLYNG, Simon						18a	30a	33a
DAMMESSON, William	1a	1a	1a	1a				
DEYE, John	2a	2a	2a					
DEYE, Thomas	11a	10a	12a,1½r	17a,1½r	17a,1½r	18a	19½a	½a
DEYE, John (II)						4a, 4r		
DEYE, William						2a		
EDWARD, John Sr.	29a	29a	30a	2a	2a	31a	30a	21½a,½r
EDWARD, John Jr.						36a	30a	32a
EDWARD, Thomas	27a	27a	29a	40a	40a			
EDWARD, Richard		19a	19a	39a	40a			
ELYOT, John							21a	42a
ELYOT, William								12a
FAGG, John	1a							
FAUKON, John							5a	1a
FLESSHEWERE, Richard	5a							
GODFREY, Adam	18a	18a						
GODFREY, John	12a,1r		18a	18a	18a	18½a	19a	
GODFREY, Nicholas	10a	10a	18a	19a	38a		21a	
GODFREY, Richard		1a	1a	7a,3¼r		7a,3¼r	7a,3¼r	
GODFREY, Reginald						1½a		
GODFREY, Roger						28a	28a	14a
GODEMAN, John	10a							
GODSOULE, John	1a							
GODWYNE, John					10a			
GRAY, John		10a						
HARDY, Nicholas	2a	1a						
HALYDAY, Simon	18a							
HARROS, William						2a		
HEMYNGTON, John	2a	1a	32a	34a	22a			
HEMYNGTON, Adam						22½a,1r	42a	22a
HEMYNGTON, Thomas			33a		33a	33a	22a	22a
HEMYNGTON, John (Jr)								20a
HOUGHTON, Agnes	5a							
HOUGHTON, Robert		3a						
HOUGHTON, Roger	12a	37a	23a, ¼r					
HUNNE, Agnes			1a	1a	1a			

	1392	1400	1405	1409/13	1414/18	1419/33	1437/50	1451/57
HUNNE, John	18a	9a						
HUNNE, John							22a	
HUNNE, Thomas	24a	11a	11a	47a	47a			
HUNNE, William	2a	2a		12a	13a	31a		
HUNNE, Robert								19a
HURLEYBY, William		1a	11a	11a	11a	11a	10a	10a
JOYE, John					3a			
KYNG, Henry		1a						
KYNG, John					10a			
KYNG, William					10a			
LANE, John	22½a	22½a						
LANE, Nicholas	1a	1a						
LANENDER, John						19a	22a	21a
LANENDER, Richard						18a		
MARTYN, Thomas							1a	1a
MACHYNG, William			1a	1a	1a			
MERTON, John	18a	19a	19a	20a	40a			
MERTON, Richard		11a	11a	15½a,1r	10a	10a		
MERTON, Alice						15½a		
MERTON, Thomas						10a	37a,2r	
MILLER, Roger	15½a	5½a	9½a,1r					
MILLER, Robert		10a						
MILLER, William					9½a,1r	23a	23a	12a
MILLER John							12a	
MORICE, John			1a	13½a	13½a			
MURYELL, Radulph			1a	1a	1a	1a		
NICHOLAS, John	18a	18a	18a	23a,½r	23a,½r	24½a	4a	4a
NICHOLAS, Thomas	18a	18a	20½a,½r	37a	4a	4a		
NICHOLAS, Simon						19a	3a	15a
OKY, Nicholas						3a	4a	4a
PALMERE, John	17a	28a	31a	32a	32a			
PORTER, John Sr.	19a							
PORTER, John Jr.	9a	1a						
PORTER, Thomas			1a		10a	1a	9a	15a
PORTER, William					10a	10a		
PORTER, Nicholas							1a	
POPE, William		1a						
PYCARD, Thomas			1a					
PALFREYMAN, William					9a	9a	1a	
POLLARD, William					1a			
PEEK, William						2a		
PENY, John						6a,¼r		
PERYNGTON, John						20a		
PROMYTH, John						19a		
PULTER, John							9a	

	1392	1400	1405	1409/13	1414/18	1419/33	1437/50	1451/57
REVE, Richard	12a	12a						
REVE, William	2a							
ROKYSDON, Robert				1a	1a			
ROGGER, Thomas							1a	1a
SANDE, John	19a	19a	22a,¼r	22a,¼r	23a,¼r	28a	20a	21a
SANDE, William	1a							
SCHARP, Richard	3½a	27a	27a	28a	28a			
SCHARP, Nicholas		2a, 3r	2a	4a	5a			
SCOT, Nicholas	18a	18a						
Scot, Thomas	10a	18a	20a	22a, ½r	22a, ½r	10a		
SCOT, John			12a		47a	31a	31a	17a
SCOT, Richard			19½a	19½a	20a			
Scot, Laurence			19a	19a	10a			
SELDE, John				1a	1a	8a	4a	2a
SELDE, Roger					3a			
SEMTIOUN, Johanna					32a			
SEMTIOUN, Thomas					32a			
SEWALE, Adam				12a	2a	2a	1a	1a
SEWALE, Roger			1½a, ½r	1½a, ½r	13½a, ½r	17½a	1a	1a
SEWALE, Thomas				3a		1a		
SEWALE, John					3a			
SEWALE, RICHARD							2½a	½a
SEWALE, Robert							1a	1a
SEBERNE, John				19a				
SHEPPERD, John Sr.	14a	14a	37a	37a	50a	47a	47a	54a
SHEPPERD, Elena	3a							
SHEPPERD, Nicholas	3a,3r				2a		6a	
SHEPPERD, William		13a,3r	13a,3¼r	13a,3¼r	13a,3¼r			
SHEPPERD, Katerina			25½a	27a	29a			
SHEPPERD, John Jr.							28a	51a
SMYTH, Thomas	1a	1a	12a	12a	12a			
SMYTH, William	2a	2a				19a	2a	
SMYTH, John		11a				19a		
SMYTH, Radulph			1a					
SMYTH, Richard						10a		
SPERCOLL, John	2a	1a						
SPERCOLL, William	1a	1a						
STAYARD, John		1a						
STOWE, William	2a							
TAYLLOR, John			7a, ½r	26a	24a, ½r			
THELLER, John							37a	
TOWNESENDE, Richard							19a	
TOWSLONDE, John							1a	1a
VALENTYNE, Thomas						10a	1½a	1½a
WADEHILL, John					3a			
WODECOK, John						13a	12a	12a

	1392	1400	1405	1409/13	1414/18	1419/33	1437/50	1451/57
WILKYN, Thomas							1a	1a
WATTES, Richard						10a	19a	9a
WRIGHT, William			2a	3a	4a	4a	15a	26a
WRIGHT, Robert					2a			
WRIGHT, Alan							19a	
WRIGHT, John							1½a,¼r	1½a,¼r

II. — SELECTED FAMILY PROPERTIES, 1392-1457

	1392	1400	1405	1409/13	1414/18	1419/33	1437/50	1451/57
ARNOLD	1a	1a				10a	1a	12a
ASPLOND	20a	20a	19a	19a	24a	60a	86a	33a
ATTEWELLE	44a	34a	28a	26a	26a	35a	45a	9a
BAKER	18a	18a	20a	29a	33a	?	23a	41a
BAROUN	3a	3a	2a	11a	30a	54a	17a	17a
BEAUMEYS	18a	19a	19a	29a	30a	?	13a	12a
CRISTEMESSE	2a	2a	2a	?	?	50a	86a	97a
DEYE	13a	12a	14a	17a	17a	24a	19a	½a
EDWARD	56a	75a	78a	81a	82a	67a	60a	53a
GODFREY	40a	29a	37a	44a	63a	55a	68a	14a
HEMYNGTON	2a	1a	34a	67a	55a	55a	42a	42a
HUNNE	44a	22a	12a	60a	68a	40a	22a	19a
MERTON	18a	30a	30a	33a	30a	75a	37a	—
NICHOLAS	36a	36a	38a	60a	60a	47a	7a	19a
PORTER	28a	1a	1a	10a	11a	9a	16a	—
SCOT	28a	36a	68a	60a	100a+	41a	31a	17a
SHEPPERD	20a	27a	75a	77a	94a	47a	81a	54a
SMYTH	3a	14a	13a	12a	12a	29a	2a	—
WRIGHT			2a	5a	4a	4a	27a	27a

who held three acres in the 1420's and early 1430's, had increased his property by one acre from 1437 into the 1450's, and Nicholas Scharp, who began as a tenant of two acres, three rods of land in 1400, added two more acres by 1409 and another acre by the middle of the second decade of the century. Of the other 22 small tenants, not only did their holdings not expand, but in the cases of six men they diminished. Thus, William Baroun held two crofts *in arentata* from the 1390's through 1400, but by 1405 he had relinquished one of the crofts. Nicholas Hardy held two acres in 1392, but only one acre in 1400. John Faukon held five acres in the 1440's but only one in the 1450's. Thomas Sewale was holding three acres at the beginning of the century's second decade, but 10 years later he held only one acre, and John Spercoll was another to hold two acres in 1392 and only one acre in 1400.

However, not all the persons who began at the bottom of the tenurial ladder stayed there. There were 10 men who initially held very small properties but who indeed "promoted" themselves. Thus, John Bate held only two acres in the middle of the second decade of the fifteenth century. In 1433, however, he received 12 acres of land and meadow formerly held by the villager Thomas Hemyngton,[30] and probably during the 1420's had also acquired a cotland once held by John Morice.[31] By 1350, he had gained an additional 10 acres of land and meadow — once held by John Palmere. His properties were reduced in the 1450's only because John had released his cotland to his son, John Bate Jr., in 1452.

John Hemyngton was another smallholder who raised himself up the tenurial ladder. Beginning with two acres in the 1390's, by 1404 he had taken up a virgate vacated by John Raven and an acre formerly held by Thomas Bernewell.[32] In addition, he served as beadle from 1403 through 1409, which brought him a cotland in officio. Thus, by 1405, John Hemyngton's properties had leaped from two acres to 32 acres. There followed a reduction of 11 acres in 1413 — an acre and his cotland — which left him 21 acres until his death in 1419.[33]

William Hunne, another smallholder at two acres in 1392 and 1400, was able to obtain a vacant acre, croft and cotland in 1412 and 1413,[34]

---

[30] BM.Harl.Ms. 445. 15ʳ. "Ad letam predictam (i.e. 1433) venit Johannes Bate et cepit de domino xij acras (terre) et prati nuper in tenura Thome Hemyngton, Tenendas eidem Johanni et Johanni filio suo ad terminum vite eorum ad voluntatem domini secundum consuetudinem manerii, Reddendo et faciendo inde in omnibus sicut predictus Thomas nuper fecit. Et dat in gersuma iij capones."

[31] The fact of John Bate's cotland — and, indeed, John Morice's — is witnessed by the Court Book in an entry for December 1452, in which John surrendered to his son "unum cotlandum quondam Johannis Moryse edificatum cum una domo cum aliis suis pertinentiis..." (BM.Harl. Ms. 445, 238ᵛ.) Since John Morice (Moryse) ceased to be recorded as a tenant after 1418, it may be suspected that John Bate had taken up his property in the 1420's.

[32] BM.Harl.Ms. 445, 38ʳ. "Ad curiam ibidem tentam die veneris in crastino sancte Margarete virginis anno supradicto (i.e. 1402) Johannes Hemyngton cepit de domino unam acram terre dominice cum pertinentiis in Nyddyngworth iacentem super Oxhowe quam Thomas Bernewell prius tenuit, Tenendam eidem Johanni ad voluntatem domini secundum consuetudinem manerii ad terminum vite sue, Reddendo inde domino per annum xij d. terminis consuetis. Et dat domino de gersuma viii d." The virgate is first mentioned in the account roll of 1403/1404 (PRO SC 6-877/28).

[33] The cotland was surrendered by John to Thomas Hemyngton (BM.Harl.Ms. 445, 85ʳ). John's death was noted in the court roll of 1419. He had also received two acres and a cottage — vacated by John Cristemesse — in 1407. (BM.Add.Ch. 33447, 36ᵛ.)

[34] BM.Harl.Ms. 445, 81ʳ, 85ʳ, 86ʳ.

an additional croft in 1414,[35] and, finally, a virgate, *placea* and selion of meadow from John Seberne in 1433.[36] William Hurleby began holding a croft *in arentatum* in 1400, and within a year he was able to pick up a cotland left vacant by Nicholas Fannell.[37] Thomas Porter was tenant of an acre of demesne in 1405. He received a cotland in 1410,[38] had relinquished it by 1415,[39] and then, in 1424, he and Simon Arnold took up and shared a virgate left vacant by the villager William Cartere.[40] At some time in the 1440's he had added five more acres, for in 1451 he surrendered his properties to his son, Thomas Jr., consisting of five acres, a half-virgate and a cottage, or an approximate total of 15 acres of land.[41] Richard Scharp started with three and a half acres of demesne in 1392 — two of them held jointly with the villager John Cristemesse — and took up a total of 24 acres of arable and meadow in 1396.[42] Roger

---

[35] PRO SC 6-878/3.

[36] BM.Harl.Ms. 445, 151ʳ. "Johannes Seberne sursum reddidit in manus domini unam placeam et j virgatam terre cum terra dominica et cum j selione prati in Salmade quondam in tenura Johannis Taylor ad opus Willelmi Hunne, Tenendas eidem Willelmo et Alicie uxori sue ad voluntatem domini ad terminum vite eorum secundum consuetudinem manerii, Reddendo inde per annum xx s. iiij d. ob. terminis consuetis equales portiones et faciendo per annum in omnibus sicut predictus Johannes facere consuevit. Et dictus Willelmus et Alicia dictam placeam bene et sufficienter reparabunt et sustentabunt sumptibus eorum propriis durante toto termino predicto. Et dant in gersuma iii s. iiii d."

[37] *Ibid.*, 20ᵛ.

[38] *Ibid.*, 74ᵛ.

[39] In 1415, the cotland was taken up by Roger Sewale. BM.Harl.Ms. 445, 93ʳ: "Rogerus Sewale cepit de domino j cotlandum cum terra dominica adiacente et j croftum quondam Willelmi Reve et j acram terre apud Buryhegge ad finem ville, Tenenda sibi et Helene uxori sue ad voluntatem domini ad terminum vite eorum, Reddendo et faciendo domino omnia servitia et consuetudines inde debita et consueta secundum consuetudinem manerii prout Thomas Porter reddere et facere consuevit pro eisdem, et habet moram super cotlandum predictum. Et dat in gersuma ij s."

[40] BM.Add.Ch. 33447 (Ramsey Papers: Vol. III), 61 d.

[41] *Ibid.*, f. 97.

[42] *Ibid.*, 25 d: "Anno predicto (i.e. 1396) domini Edmundi abbatis videlicet tercio die Kalendi junii venerunt Ricardus Scharp et Margareta uxor eius de Niddingworth et ceperunt de ffratre Johanne de Empyngsham tunc celarario Ramesiensi xix acras terre arabilis et v acras prati adiacentes nuper in tenura Ricardi attebrok, Tenendas eisdem Ricardo et Margarete uxori sue a festo sancti michaelis proximo futuro post diem confectionis presente usque ad finem et terminum vit e eorum, Reddendo inde annuatim celarario Ramesiensi qui pro tempore fuerit triginti sex solidos argenti ad quattuor anni terminos per equales porciones, videlicet ad festum sancti Andree, Annunctionis beate marie, translationis sancti Benedicti et Nativitatis beate marie, et si ita continget quod predictus redditus in parte vel in toto ad aliquod terminum prenominatum per (...) aretro esse contigerit quod tunc bene liceat celarario supradicto dictam terram et pratum a predictis Ricardo et Margareta retinere et pro libito suo inde disponere sine contradictione aliquali. Et dant domino de gersuma xij d."

Sewale, tenant of a little over an acre and a half in 1405, picked up Thomas Porter's cotland in 1415,[43] and four more acres — vacated by Richard Scharp — in 1425.[44] Nicholas Shepperd progressed — slowly and modestly, to be sure — from three acres in 1392 to six acres in the 1440's, and Thomas Smyth, holding an acre of demesne in 1392, was able to take up a cotland by 1404. Finally, William Wrighte, who began with two acres in 1405,[45] picked up small pieces of property in 1406 (one acre), 1413 (one acre) and 1414 (a messuage). By 1428 he had been elected beadle — providing him with a cotland — and he was still active in that position in 1437. Along the way, he also managed to acquire a half-virgate, bringing his total properties to some 23 acres in the 1440's.[46]

Promotion was therefore not unknown to the smallest tenants in fifteenth-century Holywell, but it must be admitted that it was not a phenomenon that ran rampant among them. Although a total of 10 men can be cited who began holding five acres or less and subsequently increased their holdings (either within or beyond the five-acre stage), a perusal of Table III will reveal the names of 51 tenants[47] in the five-acre or below category who either were temporary or transient tenants or, if they remained in the village, did not add to their properties or else reduced them further. Substantial promotion trends, therefore, are not to be sought among Holywell's smallest tenants, but rather within the ranks of those who were already semi-virgaters or full virgaters when they began to expand. One reason for this is not too difficult to find: it was a question of money. True, more actual land was technically available from the 1390's than at any previous time since perhaps the early thirteenth century.[48] But this did not necessarily mean that everyone in the village had an equal chance of obtaining some of it. In the case of customary tenements, for example, family claims — the blood right — could be invoked. In addition, local villagers could find themselves in competition with outsiders for available properties. The large number of such persons descending upon the fens in 1370 has already been pointed out, and further, between 1392 and 1450, out of 182 persons holding land in the village, 33 were also outsiders (18%). In the last analysis, however, the real key to obtaining land was

[43] See *supra*, p. 123, note # 39.

[44] BM.Add.Ch. 33447, f. 63.

[45] He had been first listed as holding the two acres in 1404 (PRO SC 6-877/28).

[46] The existence of the half-virgate, as well as William's retention of his cotland, is evidenced by his transfer of these tenements to his son in 1451 (BM.Harl.Ms. 445, 235ʳ).

[47] Including tenants recorded only once.

[48] See *infra*, Chapter III, p. 166 *et seq*.

money; and here the advantage lay with persons already holding 10 acres of land or more, or with persons who, if they themselves were meagerly supplied with land, were members of families that displayed a serious involvement in land.[49] Thus, of the 10 peasants already cited who began with less than five acres but promoted themselves up the tenurial scale, five were either direct or related members of landed families. John Bate, for example, was the son-in-law of John AtteWelle, a tenant of over 25 acres since the early 1400's. John Hemyngton was the scion of a long established and substantial customary family.[50] William Hunne sprang from a villein family that had controlled some 44 acres of land between three members as early as 1392. Thomas Peter was a member of a family that had held some 28 acres in the 1390's, and Nicholas Shepperd was holding his three acres in 1392 when another relative, John Shepperd, was holding 14 acres, and, by the time Nicholas had graduated to a six acre holding, John had acquired 47 acres.

Promotion, therefore, was especially marked among those persons in the village already significantly involved in land. Thus, four members of the Asplond family were able to advance the total acreage controlled by the family from 19 acres in 1392 to 86 acres in the 1440's. John Atte-Welle, a smallholder in 1400, was granted his father's virgate and a quarter in 1401,[51] and in 1419 he obtained an additional half-virgate from William

---

[49] There was, indeed, from the 1370's a trend for opportunities in land to become available for several contemporary members of one family. Prior to 1370, only the Laweman, Scot, Beaumeys, Gere and Eyr families could confidently be cited as boasting two or more tenants at any one time. The majority of families appear to have been centred about one tenement, in which several members sometimes maintained an interest. In cases where this was not in evidence, presumably landless members engaged in activities such as brewing or else emigrated — either permanently or temporarily. Thus, among the Cartere family, Richard Cartere appears to have been the tenant in the first 30 years of the fourteenth century, which probably accounted for John Cartere being off the manor — with permission — from 1339. On the other hand, it should be pointed out that families in Holywell were seldom very large even in the early fourteenth century, so that the number of members excluded from land would not have been great. In any event, with the demographic decline quickening from the middle of the century, more tenements fell vacant, with the results that can be seen from Table III. Thus, three members of the Asplond family were tenants in one period. The AtteWelles boasted two contemporary tenants, as did the Bakers and the Nicholases. The Cristemesses had three major tenants at one time, as did the Edwards (1400-1405), the Godfreys (1437-49), the Hemyngtons (1451-57) and the Shepperds (1414-18). Mertons boasted four (1419-33), as did the Scots (1414-18).

[50] John's father, John Hemyngton, had been a double-cotlander in 1370, while a Thomas Hemyngton had been a virgater before 1375, when his widow Cristiana succeeded to his virgate "terre native" (PRO SC 2-179/40).

[51] BM.Harl.MS. 445, 17^v: "Ad eandem curiam Robertus atteWelle reddidit sursum in manus domini unam placeam edificatam et unam virgatam terre et unam quarteriam terre servilis

Palfreyman.[52] Indeed, the fact that John AtteWelle had managed to
obtain a total of some 45 acres by the 1440's,[53] made it possible for at
least three other persons to increase their own holdings. Specifically,
in 1451 John granted to Simon Dallyng — parish *rector* and manor *firmarius*
— and John Shepperd his virgate, cotland, quarter-virgate and smaller
bits of land — a total of some 33 acres, thereby raising the latter's acreage
to 55 and 54 acres, respectively.[54] Finally, in 1454 John Elyot, a carpenter
by trade and also John AtteWelle's son-in-law, who, with his father William,
had arrived in the village only in the 1440's and had acquired a virgate
in 1444,[55] increased his own properties to some 42 acres by the acquisition
of John AtteWelle's half-virgate, which was transferred to him by his
mother-in-law, Margaret.[56]

   Other villagers who experienced promotion in the first half of the fifteenth
century may be cited. Nicholas Baroun, initially a 10-acre tenant in

---

et iij acras terre de Penilond ad opus Johannis filii eius, Tenendas per servitium et consuetudinem
ad terminum vite in omnibus sicut idem Robertus inde facere consuevit. Et dat domino de gersuma xl d."

[52] B.M. Harl. MS. 445, 122[r]. "Willelmus Palfreyman sursum reddidit in manus domini mense
predicta dimidiam virgatam terre cum tota terre dominice ad opus Johannis atteWele, Tenendas
sibi et Margarete uxori sue ad terminum vite secundum consuetudinem etc., Reddendo et faciendo inde per annum sicut predictus Willelmus reddere et facere consuevit. Et dat in gersuma ij s."

[53] The fact of the additional 10 acres is witnessed by a grant of John AtteWelle's of 1451 to
Simon Dallyng and John Shepperd of his virgate, quarter virgate, demesne land and a cotland
(*Ibid.*, 235[r]).

[54] *Ibid.* "Mense Maii (i.e. 1451) Johannes atteWell sursum reddidit in manus domini per
manus Ballivi unum mesuagium, unum cotlandum, unam virgatam et unam quarteriam terre
cum terra dominica et prato in Salmade ad opus Simonis Dallyng et Johannis Shepperd, Tenenda
eisdem Simone et Johanni a festo sancti Michaelis archangelis ultimo preterito usque ad finem
et terminum vite eorum ad voluntatem domini secundum consuetudinem manerii, Reddendo
inde domino per annum et faciendo in omnibus sicut predictus Johannes reddere et facere consuevit. Reservate prefato Johanni atteWell et Margarete uxori sue durante vita sua placea et
dimidia virgata terre nuper Willelmi Palfreyman de sustentatione tam in reparacione domorum
quam redditum solvendo sumptibus ipsorum Johannis et Margarete durante vita ipsorum. Et
dant domini de gersuma. xl d"

[55] *Ibid.*, 204[r].

[56] *Ibid.*, 247[r]: "... Margareta nuper uxor Johannis atteWell sursum reddidit in manus domini
dimidiam virgatam terre cum tota terre dominica de novo adiacente cum vestura eiusdem terre
dominice que nuper fuerunt in tenura dicti Johannis atteWell viri sui et eiusdem Margarete (...)
per unam copiam et quondam in tenura Willelmi Palfreyman ad opus Johannis Elyot et Alicie
uxori sue filie dictorum Johannis atteWell et Margarete, Tenendam eisdem Johanni Elyot et
Alicie ad terminum vite eorum ad voluntatem domini secundum consuetudinem manerii, Reddendo inde domino per annum et faciendo in omnibus sicut predictus Johannes atteWell reddere
et facere consuevit. Et dant domino de gersuma vj s. viij d."

   Three years earlier (1451), John Elyot and his father, William, had added a cotland and two
crofts vacated by William Baroun and John Shepperd (*Ibid.*, 235[r]).

1413, had almost tripled his properties by 1416, when he took up a virgate vacated by Nicholas Godfrey.[57] John Beaumeys obtained John in the Lane's virgate and an acre of demesne in 1401[58] and an additional cotland vacated by William Hunne Sr. in 1416.[59] The entire Cristemesse family was able to take advantage of vacancies and the land market to extend the family's total holdings from two acres at the turn of the century to over 50 acres by the third decade. So, too, with the Edwards. Already a large tenant family in 1392 at 56 acres, by the third decade of the fifteenth century they were holding over 80 acres of land. The Godfreys, as a family, remained in control of properties exceeding 25 acres from the 1390's until 1450. Still further examples would be, among individuals, Thomas Hunne, who progressed from 27 acres in 1392 to 47 acres by the second decade of the fifteenth century, William Miller, from just over 9 acres to 23 acres in the 1420's, Thomas Nicholas (from 18 acres in 1392 to 37 acres by the second decade of the fifteenth century), John Palmere (17 acres in 1392 to 32 acres by 1413), Thomas Deye (from 11 acres in the 1390's to just over 19 in the 1440's), John Scot (from 12 acres in 1405 to over 30 acres from the second decade of the century through the 1440's), John Shepperd, who began with 14 acres in 1392 and advanced steadily to over 40 acres in the 1420's, 1430's and 1440's and to an excess of 50 acres in the 1450's; and among family groups, the Mertons, the Nicholases, the Scots, the Shepperds and the Wrights.

The point to be emphasized, therefore, is that although promotion played a part in virtually every strata of fifteenth-century Holywell tenants, the persons — and families — most frequently being promoted by accumulating more land were those with an already solidly established background in land. They were the villagers who could reasonably afford the cost involved, since the early fifteenth century was a time in which tenure was being converted more and more into a cash or money rent condition. Demesne was available, to be sure, and after 1409 all but 80 acres of it had been thrown onto the market, but it was not free — the rent averaged a shilling an acre. So too with customary tenements. Although the latter fourteenth century witnessed a return of several virgates and cotlands

---

[57] BM. Harl. Ms. 446, 95ᵛ: "Nicholus Baroun cepit de domino j virgatam terre quondam Nicholi Godfrey cum tota terra dominica adiacente et cum j selione prati in Salmede simul cum medietate de Benehill, Tenenda sibi et Helene uxori sue ad voluntatem domini ad terminum vite eorum, Reddendo inde per annum pro predicta virgata terre, terra dominica et selione predicta prout predictus Nicholus reddere et facere consuevit et pro medietate de Benehill x d. terminis consuetis. Et gersumavit ij s."

[58] *Ibid.*, 17ᵛ.

[59] *Ibid.*, 96ʳ.

to the *ad opus* category,[60] by 1409 this too had been abandoned by the abbey, and the introduction of the *novum censum* soon after put all customary tenements on a cash basis: 18 shillings a virgate, nine shillings a cotland.[61] Consequently, although a large amount of land was available after 1400, its tenure was limited to those villagers who could pay for it. In addition, there is yet another aspect to be considered. As R. H. Hilton pointed out in his study of the Leicestershire estates, the increased availability of land in the latter fourteenth century and the fifteenth century did indeed result in an increase in the size of tenements, but very often, since the increase favoured the more substantial and economically secure elements of the population,[62] although the number of peasant holdings over 20 or 30 acres grew, this growth often prevented promotion from the lower tenurial ranks. In short, it resulted in a new kind of "land-hunger". This appears to have been operative in Holywell, for although examples can be given of smallholders improving their position relative to acreage, it was not particularly widespread and very rarely indeed did a peasant at five acres or less move up the ladder into either the semi-virgater, virgater or even larger categories of tenants. In general, promotion was dominated by peasants of the middle rank or above. There were very few peasants in Holywell who qualified as fifteenth-century Horatio Algers.

What remains, after a consideration of the acreage patterns in fifteenth-century Holywell, is a picture of a community in which there was emerging a small group of peasants engaged in the acquisition of large concentrations of properties of 30 acres or more. Specifically, in 1400, 59 persons held an approximate total of 594 acres, but 12% (69 acres) was controlled by two men: Robert AtteWelle and Roger Houghton. In 1405, 638 acres were held by 48 persons, but 6% of the tenants (three men — John Edward, John Hemyngton, and John Shepperd) held 14% (99 acres) of the land. From 1409 to 1413, 55 persons held some 889 acres, 31% of which (275 acres) was controlled by seven men: Thomas Edward, Richard Edward, John Hemyngton, Thomas Hunne, Thomas Nicholas, John Palmere and John Shepperd — or 13% of the tenants. By the 1440's, a peak had been reached, with over 350 acres being held by only 10 men, or 15% of the tenants. In this respect, then, Holywell was witnessing a development of extremely large property-holders similar to that observed by Hilton on the Leicestershire estates,[63] as well as by Hallam in a recent examination

---

[60] See *infra*, p. 139 *et seq.*
[61] See *infra*, p. 144 *et seq.*
[62] See Hilton, *The Economic Development of some Leicestershire Estates*, pp. 100-29.
[63] *Ibid.*

of South-Lincolnshire Crowland Abbey manors in the middle of the fifteenth century.[64]

But if Holywell tenants took part in a more general trend of property accumulation in the fifteenth century, their participation was not especially characterized by an overwhelming consistency in land acquisition. As already indicated earlier,[65] there was a striking degree of fluctuation to individual dealings in land. A study of Table III, for example, will reveal some 43 persons whose property concentrations did not remain stable during the time they were tenants. In some cases, the acreage diminished from a previous high point, while in others it rose and fell, and rose and fell again, like a teeter-totter. The probable reasons for this fluctuating pattern, as well as the light it casts on the nature of tenurial involvements itself in fifteenth-century Holywell, require a closer investigation.

The fluctuating pattern to tenurial involvements in Holywell after 1400 points to the existence of a vacancy phenomenon in the village at that time. It is termed a "phenomenon" because it cannot really be called a "vacancy problem", since Holywell was not the scene of large blocs of land lying unclaimed or unwanted for long stretches of time.[66] What vacancies there were — and there were many — were mostly of short-term duration: frequently a year or a little more, but seldom longer.[67]

---

[64] H. E. Hallam, "The Agrarian Economy of South Lincolnshire in the Mid-Fifteenth Century." *Nottingham Mediaeval Studies*, XI (1967), pp. 86-95. It should be noted, however, that the growth of the 30-acre or more group of peasants on the three manors (Spalding, Holbeach and Gedney) studied by Hallam was not as pronounced (a total of 16 men, or 39 %) as at Holywell. Also in the South-Lincolnshire region, there was a larger proportion of smallholders at five acres or less, accounting for 75 % of the tenants at Spalding, 53.2 % at Holbeach and 70.9 % at Gedney (*Ibid.*, p. 92).

[65] See *supra*, p. 112 *et seq.*

[66] The sheer evidence of statistics of acreage held at given periods is witness to this fact: virtually all the land available was occupied until the 1450's, when there may have occurred the first really critical vacancy situation. Specifically, there had been over 950 acres of land — including customary tenements, demesne and even fen properties — available and occupied from the second decade of the fifteenth century. Between 1451 and 1457, however, evidence can be found of only a little over 600 acres being held by a small number (49) of tenants.

[67] The one very clear exception to this was recorded in 1441, when Simon Dallyng, the parish rector, took up three tofts and five acres which were described as having been in the lord's hands "for many years (per multos annos)". BM.Harl.Ms. 445, 188ʳ: "Mense Augusti anno domini Johannis Stowe abbatis vjᵗᵒ Simon Dallyng clericus cepit de domino j toftum nuper in tenura Willelmi Hunne cum terra adiacente, unum toftum cum pertinentiis nuper Thome Arnold, unum toftum nuper Katerine Shepperd cum pertinentiis et quinque acras terre dominice super Oxhowe, Overbrerecroft et Stonydole que omnia predicta per multos annos remanserunt in manus domini, Tenenda eidem Simone ad voluntatem domini Johannis ad terminum vite sue secundum consuetudinem manerii, Reddendo inde per annum ij s. terminis consuetis et faciendo alia debita et consueta. Et gersuma condonata."

The entries in the Court Book bear this out with their repeated employment of the words "recently" (*nuper*) or "once" (*quondam*) to describe the previous disposition of a tenement then being granted out to a villager, thereby implying that the holding of the property had not been continuous but that it had reverted to the direct control of the abbey for a period of time in the absence of immediate claimants. Furthermore, however, the many short-term vacancies in Holywell in the first half of the fifteenth century were not all the result of families dying out or otherwise disappearing and leaving no heirs to invoke blood claims. They frequently involved properties either taken up off the open market or transferred within a family and subsequently surrendered. Some were even the result of heirs declining to advance blood claims. Indeed, these facts are especially significant because they reveal that the nature of tenure in Holywell by the fifteenth century had undergone serious alteration from the fourteenth century. Specifically, the keynote of fifteenth-century tenurial practice in Holywell was impermanence. More and more, familial continuity in tenure was being neglected or, in some cases, ignored by the peasant. In a great number of cases, the individual commitment to land assumed a temporary character, and the number of peasants who built-up and maintained intact collections of property which were then passed on to heirs grew smaller as the years progressed. This can be immediately illustrated by a consideration of acreage statistics for specific families as given in Table III, Part II. Thus, the Asplonds had controlled some 20 acres in the 1390's. By the 1440's the family had expanded to over 80 acres, but no attempt was made to preserve this bloc intact, for by the 1450's it held only 33 acres. The AtteWelle family had been represented by two men holding a total of over 40 acres in 1392. One of them—John— had rid himself of 15 of his 17 acres by 1400, but shortly thereafter a second John received Robert AtteWelle's tenement of some 26 acres — a good example of familial continuity.[68] By the 1420's, he had increased his property to just over 35 acres,[69] and to 44$\frac{1}{2}$ acres by the 1440's. John had no sons, but he left two daughters, Johanna and Alice, both of whom were married and living with their husbands in the village: the wives of John Bate and John Elyot, respectively. In 1451, however, John transferred over 30 acres of his property not to either of his sons-in-law but to two other villagers: Simon Dallyng and John Shepperd.[70] This left John and his wife Margaret with just a little over 12 acres, and it was

[68] See *supra*, p. 125, note ‡ 51 for text.
[69] See *supra*, p. 126, note ‡ 52 for text.
[70] See *supra*, p. 126, note ‡ 54 for text.

not until 1454 — after John's death — that his widow released a half-virgate to her son-in-law and daughter, John and Alice Elyot.[71] This was an aspect of familial continuity, but a severely truncated one. No attempt had been made to preserve the integrity of either John AtteWelle's original or later property concentrations. It cannot, of course, be assumed that John had ignored the possible interests or needs of his daughters and their husbands. It is possible that neither John Bate nor John Elyot desired the bulk of their father-in-law's tenements. But whatever the domestic agreements involved, the AtteWelle case in an example of the weakening of the integrity of familial property in fifteenth-century Holywell.

The Beaumeys family had held a virgate, or 18 acres, in the 1390's in the person of Walter Beaumeys. Walter was dead by 1400, and his son John succeeded to the virgate, while John's son — also named John (Jr.) — acquired a virgate and an acre of demesne in 1401 from John in the Lane, who then left the village (as did the entire family).[72] Thus, by 1405 the Beaumeys family — in the persons of John Sr. and Jr. — were holding some 37 acres of land. By 1408, however, John Sr. had himself left the manor — without permission — and his virgate was not taken up by his son. The latter, however, added a cotland to his properties in 1416 — a cotland that had recently been held by William Hunne.[73] It was this cotland that John finally transferred to his son Richard in 1452.[74]

[71] See *supra*, p. 126, note # 56 for text.

[72] BM.Harl.Ms. 445, 17^v: "Ad letam cum curia ibidem tenta xv° die mensis Octobris Johannes in the Lane reddidit sursum in manus domini unam placeam edificatam et unam virgatam terre servilis ad opus Johannis Beaumeys junioris, Tenendas eidem Johannis Beaumeys in bondagio ad voluntatem domini etc. ad terminum vite per servitium et opus in omnibus sicut Johannes in the Lane inde facere consuevit etc."

"Ad eandem curiam, idem Johannes Beaumeys cepit de domino unam acram terre dominice quam dictus Johannes in the Lane prius tenuit, Tenendam eidem Johannis Beaumeys ad voluntatem domini ad terminum vite sue, Reddendo inde per annum xii d. terminis consuetis. Et dat domino de gersuma ii s."

[73] *Ibid.*, 96^r: "Johannes Beaumeys cepit de domino j cotlandum cum tota terra dominica eidem pertinenti nuper Willelmi Hunne et quondam Rogerii Bachesley, Tenendum sibi et Katerine uxori sue ad voluntatem domini ad terminum vite eorum secundum consuetudinem manerii, Reddendo et faciendo in omnibus prout predictus Willelmus reddere et facere consuevit. Et gersumavit ij s." It should be noted that William Hunne himself had only held the cotland from 1413 (*Ibid.*, 86^r).

[74] *Ibid.*, 239^r: "Mense Junii anno predicto (i.e. 1452) Johannes Beaumes sursum reddidit in manus domini per manus Ballivi unum cotlandum edificatum cum terra et prato adiacente quondam Rogerii Bachesley simul cum una acra terre super middylfurlong quondam in tenura dicti Rogerii ad opus Ricardi Beaumes filii sui, Tenenda eidem Ricardo ad terminum vite sue ad voluntatem domini secundum consuetudinem manerii, Reddendo inde domino per annum et faciendo in omnibus sicut predictus Johannes pater suus reddere et facere consuevit. Et dat domino de gersuma ij s."

What had become of the virgate over the years is not known, but it had been given up at some point because by the 1450's the entire family holding had shrunk to about 12 acres — a full 18 acres less than what it had been in the second decade of the century, and six acres less than what it had been at the end of the fourteenth century.

The Edward family held 56 acres in the 1390's, rose to over 80 acres in the second decade of the fifteenth century, but, by the 1450's, they were holding a little less land than that with which they had begun. Along the way, properties of John Edward (I) had been only partially claimed by his son Richard,[75] the remainder being taken up by Thomas Hunne.[76] On the other hand, the same Richard Edward's tenements — including the lands he had taken up from his father — were claimed by his son, John (III),[77] while those of Thomas Edward were unclaimed by other Edwards, being dispersed instead among the Smyth, Wodecok, Cristemesse and Nicholas families.[78]

The Merton and Shepperd families were alike in that they managed

---

[75] B.M. Harl. Ms. 445, 55ʳ: (1407) "Ricardus Edward cepit de domino unam solaciam et dimidiam virgatam terre ad censum, unum cotlandum in opere, unam acram terre dominice in Stonydole, unam rodam terre in le Smethe cum prato in S(almede) adiacente quondam patris sui, Tenenda etc. Reddendo in omnibus sicut Johannes Edward pater suus pro eodem reddere consuevit. Et gersumavit xiii s. iiii d."

[76] Ibid. "Thomas Hunne cepit de domino unam placeam edificatam cum j domo et dimidiam virgatam terre adiacente quondam Johannis Edward, Tenendas ad censum, Reddendo inde in omnibus sicut predictus Johannes Edward pro eodem reddere consuevit."

[77] Ibid., 144ᵛ (1431): "Johannes Edward junior cepit de domino j virgatam terre cum nova terra dominica et j cotlandum et dimidium cum terra dominica cum j acra terre in Stonydole, j acram, j rodam terre in le Smethe et dimidiam acram prati in Salmade nuper Ricardi Edward patris sui, Tenenda eidem Johanni et Alicie uxori sue ad voluntatem domini ad terminum vite eorum secundum consuetudinem manerii, Reddendo inde per annum et faciendo in omnibus sicut predictus Ricardus nuper fecit. Et dat domino in gersuma iij s. iiij d."

[78] Ibid., 105ʳ: (1419) "Ricardus Smyth cepit de domino j placeam cum dimidia virgata terre nuper in tenura Thome Edward cum tota terra dominica cum vestura eiusdem eidem de novo assignata, Tenendas sibi et Margarete uxori sue ad voluntatem domini ad terminum vite eorum secundum consuetudinem manerii, Reddendo inde per annum et faciendo in omnibus prout predictus Thomas reddere et facere consuevit. Et gersumavit j aucam et j caponem."

— Ibid., 141ʳ: (1430) "Johannes Wodecok cepit de domino j cotlandum et parcellam gardini quondam Willelmi Spercoll et nuper Thome Edward cum j acra terre super le Smethe et j acram terre in Stonydole nuper eiusdem Thome, Tenenda sibi ad voluntatem domini ad terminum vite sue secundum consuetudinem manerii, Reddendo et faciendo sicut predictus Thomas nuper fecit. Et reparabit dictum cotlandum etc. et gersuma ij s." This cotland eventually found its way into the hands of the Nicholas family by the 1450's (Ibid., 247ʳ). — Ibid., 146ʳ: (1432) "Johannes Cristemasse cepit de domino unum messuagium cum j virgata terre dominice de novo cum j buttera in Salmede quondam Thome Edward, Tenenda sibi et Agnete uxori sue ad voluntatem domini ad terminum vite etc. ..."

to build up concentrations of property over the first half of the fifteenth century that sometimes reached peaks three or four times the size of their initial blocs, but once having reached these new levels, they made no effort to retain them from one generation to another. On the other hand, families such as the Godfreys, Hunnes, Nicholases, Deyes and Scots went even further: they ended-up holding less land in the 1450's than they had held half a century earlier.[79] Finally, as a further illustration, one acre alone in Nethbrerecroft passed through six pairs of hands between 1400 and 1455, each tenant representing a different family group.[80]

The examples of the families cited above, however, are not meant to imply that there was a total disinterest in familial claims to property in fifteenth-century Holywell. Even in the cases already given of families failing to retain or transfer complete collections of properties from one generation to another, there were instances when the blood right was in fact invoked. The Edwards, for example, kept some properties within family hands, as did the AtteWelles and the Beaumeyses. The Hunnes especially exhibited a crazy-quilt pattern of retention, intra-familial conveyance and extra-familial dispersal of property. John Hunne, a semi-virgater, died in 1404 with heirs, but his half-virgate was left unclaimed for two years, until 1406, when it was then taken up by William Palfreyman.[81] Two virgates of Thomas Hunne passed from the family also, one going to Richard Lanender in 1431,[82] the other to John Promyth in 1432.[83] On the other hand, another John Hunne received a virgate from the property of William Hunne in 1438,[84] and Robert Hunne was granted a virgate by his father — William — in 1451.[85] Among other families, the Hemyngtons are a good example of the traditional generation-

---

[79] Thomas Scot, in particular, offers a very good example of the non-retention of familial property. In 1424, he transferred a cotland to his son-in-law, Thomas Valentyne (*Ibid.*, 124ᵛ), but in 1437 Thomas Valentyne transferred the same cotland to Richard Wattes (BM. Harl. Ms. 445, 165ʳ).

[80] Another factor which may have favoured the ascendancy of intermediate tenants into higher ranks — and thus helps explain the fluctuations in numbers in that group — was the abbey practice of allowing discounts (See Raftis, *Estates*, pp. 288-89) on properties to encourage tenure. With conditions of land-holding made easier through reduced rents and *gersumae*, the middling tenant found it possible to add to his holdings to a degree not in evidence prior to the last years of the fourteenth century. Unfortunately, the surviving records are not full enough to permit a real examination of this question; the bulk of evidence preserved deals heavily with the large tenant.

[81] BM.Harl.Ms.445, 44r.

[82] *Ibid.*, 144ᵛ.

[83] *Ibid.*, 146ʳ

[84] *Ibid.*, 172ʳ.

[85] *Ibid.*, 235ʳ.

to-generation retention of lands. John Hemyngton transferred a cotland to Thomas Hemyngton in 1413,[86] and the remainder of his properties — over 40 acres — went to his son Adam shortly after 1419. Adam, in turn, released some 20 acres to his own son John in 1449.[87]

In short, familial retention of property was not obsolete in Holywell in the first half of the fifteenth century. It was, however, overshadowed by non-familial interests. Thus, between 1397 and 1457, although such a source as the Court Book recorded a total of 43 cases of familial retention of property — 24 instances of blood right inheritances and 19 cases of direct conveyance within a family — there were 21 cases of direct conveyance outside a family, and, most important, 98 instances of land being taken up from the open market that had fallen vacant and been unclaimed by heirs or relatives of former tenants: a total of 119 recorded cases of property passing from one family group into another. Couple these facts with the evidence of fluctuation in acreage concentrations in individual hands over the years, and the conclusion is inescapable that by the fifteenth century in Holywell, the day of total commitment — of the concentration of individual interests upon the tenement and the further identification of the family's interests with the preservation of the tenement — was over.

One probable reason for this alteration in the peasant's commitment to land was to be found in the increasing ubiquity of leasehold tenure, and particularly of the life-lease. Leasehold itself was not new to Holywell in the fifteenth century. It could be found in local records as early as 1279, but the practice gained momentum after the Black Death. By 1363, approximately a dozen life-leases could be traced in the acount roll, and by 1370 their number had tripled. The years from 1390 and on through the middle of the fifteenth century, however, constituted the golden period of the life-lease. One hundred and thirty-six of the 149 Holywell entries in the Court Book alone were life-leases, and they applied to all categories of land, from smallholds to virgates.[88]

Doubtlessly, the increased adoption of the leasehold *ad terminum vite* facilitated the accumulation of larger properties by specific individuals and families.[89] By negating the perpetuity of tenurial commitments, the life-lease contributed to the extremely fluid conditions of the fifteenth-

---

[86] BM. Harl. Ms. 445., 85ʳ.

[87] *Ibid.*, 226ᵛ.

[88] The texts already given from the Court Book are examples of tenure *ad terminum vite*.

[89] This has already been suggested by Hilton in his *The Economic Development of some Leicestershire Estates*, p. 129.

century Holywell land market in helping to create a psychological climate in which the peasant no longer had to view his relationship to tenure as necessarily permanent.[90] This was no doubt even further intensified after 1409, when all properties in the village were converted into money-paying tenures and work services were abandoned. Henceforth, not only was the impermanence of tenure supported by the term quality of the lease, but by the elimination of work reponsibilities it no longer required from the peasant a heavy investment of his time and family resources. As a result, not even the life-lease was adhered to strictly. Virtually all the properties that changed hands between 1400 and 1457 in Holywell were originally taken up by their tenants for life, but only rarely were they retained that long.[91]

The impermanent character of tenurial commitments, the rapid turn-over in lands and the fluctuations in acreage concentrations in the first half of the fifteenth century were indicative further that land was being exploited by villagers — and outsiders — for quick profits and, frequently, for purposes other than cultivation. That exploitation was a factor to property-holding is reflected in several official notations concerning the dilapidation and deterioration of properties after 1400. In 1405, John Palmere and Margaret Hunne were each fined twopence in the court for failing to make repairs to their properties.[92] In the same year, John Asplond Sr. had his tenement seized because it was in ruins and he could not find a pledge for himself.[93] In 1409, John Tayllour was fined for

---

[90] This is admittedly a difficult and sensitive problem, but it nevertheless requires more investigation than it has received up to now and more than can be given in this restricted study. Postan writing in the CEH, I, doubts that the life-lease had any special effects on the peasant's actual title to property or even made any deep impression on his economic position (pp. 615-16). However, one cannot overlook the possible psychological effect of the life-lease as an impermanent or limited commitment to property, and although such a question is extremely hard to measure, it cannot be ignored.

[91] One of the rare cases was John AtteWelle, who received his father's properties in 1401 *ad terminum vite* and who released them to Simon Dallyng and John Shepperd only after 50 years — in 1451, three years before his death. On the other hand, Thomas Valentyne received a cotland from his father-in-law Thomas Scot in 1425 *ad terminum vite*, but he gave it over to Richard Wattes 12 years later, in 1437. Since Thomas Valentyne was still alive in the 1450's, he had not surrendered his cotland in 1437 because he felt the end to be near.

One additional factor in encouraging a quick turn-over in land was doubtlessly the increasing reduction of entry fines from the late fourteenth century (see *infra*, p. 146 *et seq.*). With *gersumae* for even full virgates declining to a nominal level — including the rendering of a chicken or a goose — the willingness to take up such properties was no doubt stimulated even further.

[92] PRO SC 2-179/49.

[93] PRO SC 2-179/50: "Et Johannes Asplond senior habet unum tenementum ruinosum et fere depositum. Et non invenit plegium. Ideo preceptum est ballivo seisire."

not having repaired his tenement,[94] and Thomas Hemyngton was fined for the same in 1413.[95]

Similarly, the Court Book contains several references to dilapidated properties. Obligations to repair and maintain tenements, often at the tenant's own expense, were sometimes imposed as conditions for holding specific pieces of land.[96]

It is doubtful that this incidence of disrepair to properties is to be fully explained by poverty. Villagers such as the Asplonds, Tayllours, Hunnes, Edwards and Hemyngtons, for example, were active participants in the land market as well as being found among the village and manorial officials. It is consequently difficult to accept that they were so financially destitute as to be unable to maintain tenements if they cared to do so. The answer must be, then, that they did not care to do so, because they were using their properties for purposes other than cultivation or settlement. Indeed, it is most difficult to imagine families like the Asplonds, the AtteWelles, the Edwards, the Hemyngtons, the Hunnes, the Nicholases, the Scots and the Shepperds — and even an individual like Simon Dallyng, the parish priest — amassing the number of acres they did at certain times for the purpose of putting them under seed, especially since such cultivation would have required a population large enough to provide sufficient labourers for the task, and it was this inability to find adequate supplies of labour that had contributed to the abbey's abandonment of demesne cultivation by 1409. Consequently, it is more than doubtful that properties were being put under seed. On the other hand, there is reason to believe that it was being put "under the hoof", and that the heavy dealings and quick turn-overs in land were at least partly the result of pastoral activities. The number of land transfers recorded in the Court Book concerned with small parcels of land of only a few acres or fractions thereof helps

---

[94] PRO SC 2-179/52. "Et quod Johannes Taillour non reparavit tenementum suum. Ideo ipse in misericordia (ij d)."

[95] PRO SC 2-179/54. In addition, the roll of the autumn *curia* of 1430 is virtually a list of directions on the repair of generally deteriorated conditions throughout the village.

"Ponitur in pena quod le Rautedyche mundetur infra septimanam sub pena cuiuslibet defecti xx d.

"Et quod fossatum vocatum fendyche iuxta Claylake mundetur citra festum Nativitatis Sancti Johannis sub pena j defecti xld.

"Et quod le mershdyche mundetur citra festum Nativitatis Sancti Johannis Baptiste sub pena cuiuslibet defecti xld.

"Et quod cursus aque in Nyddyngworth mundetur infra vj dies sub pena cuiuslibet defecti xii d." (BM.Add.Ch. 39480.)

[96] See BM.Harl.Ms. 445, 85ʳ., 124ᵛ, 128ᵛ, 132ᵛ, 141ʳ, 150ᵛ, 172ʳ.

support this suspicion,[101] but even more direct confirmation is to be found in the court rolls from 1398 through 1456. In 14 of these sessions, there were recorded over 39 cases of villagers fined for acts of trespass while pasturing their animals — and especially sheep.[102] Interestingly, foremost among the most frequent offenders were such names as Attewelle (1398, 1402, 1405, 1443), Hemyngton (1398, 1402, 1456), Hunne (1398, 1437), Scot (1398, 1402, 1432) and even Simon Dallyng, the rector of the church, sometime *firmarius* of the manor and an active dealer in land from the 1430's.[103] Indeed, the problem of pasturing seems to have reached serious proportions in the first half of the fifteenth century, and the impression is given that, more than at any time in the late thirteenth or early fourteenth centuries, there were more four-legged creatures at large in Holywell than two-legged ones, especially as court rolls from as early as the second decade of the century began recording byelaws intended to closely regulate pasturing activities. The fact that these bye-laws had to be repeated — and even amplified and the penalties for their infraction stiffened — from decade to decade strongly suggests that they were not having the desired effect.[104] In any event, there was more

---

[101] The Court Book entries for Holywell contain 56 cases of the transfer of properties of one acre to five, six or seven acres, while the cellarers' rolls preserved in the British Museum under the general title "Ramsey Papers" contain 40 such transfers between 1406 and 1454. (BM.Add. Ch. 33447.) That small properties were frequently associated with pastoral activities has been recently emphasized by H. E. Hallam, "The Agrarian Economy of South-Lincolnshire in the Mid-Fifteenth Century", p. 87.

[102] The 39 cases are not the total number of pasturing offenses between 1398 and 1456, but only those committed by local residents with sheep or calves. Others — not tabulated here — frequently involved outsiders, and animals from horses to pigs.

[103] Simon, who acquired some 18 acres in 1431 (BM.Harl.Ms. 445, 144v), an additional eight acres in 1441 (*Ibid.*, 188r), and added over 30 acres more in 1451 (*Ibid.*, 235r) — at which time he was also *firmarius* — was cited twice for trespass in 1455 and once in 1456.

1455: (BM.Add.Ch. 34322) "Et quod Simon Dally rector ibidem est communis transgressor cum animalibus suis in prato apud Millefeld ad nocumentum omnium tenentium ... Et quod idem Simon Dally transgressionem fecit simili modo cum porcis suis tam in granis quam in herbis ad nocumentum totae villatae."

1456: (PRO SC 2-179/67). "Et quod Simon Dally clericus persona ibidem fregit bilegem pascendo bidentes suos ibidem ad nocumentum ..."

[104] In 1413 (PRO SC 2-179/54): "Ordinatum est quod nulla bidentes mittentur in parcum de Nyddyngworth in aliquo tempore", and in 1419 (PRO SC 2-179/56): "Et quod nullus mittat aliqua animalia in stipula frumenti citra festum (...) sub pena xl d. domino et xl d. ecclesie." In 1423, it was further declared (PRO SC 2-179/57): "Ponitur in pena quod nullus depascat in le Falowfelde citra festum pasche sub pena xx d. domino et xx d. ecclesie"; and "Et quod nullus mittat animalia in campo frumenti citra finem autumpnalis sub eadem pena." This was followed in 1437 (PRO SC 2-179/63) with: "Ponitur in pena quod nulla animalia ponatur in le millefeld absque custode sub pena xl d. domino et xl d. ecclesie"; and "Et quod nulla animalia

concern over animals and pasturing in the court rolls of the earlier 1400's than there had ever been in the entire fourteenth century, and the conclusion is inescapable that after 1400 a potent factor — perhaps even the predominant one — in the tenurial involvements of Holywell's peasants was the raising of stock, and probably the raising of sheep. It is certainly consistent with the patterns of property concentration and the fluctuations within those patterns already described.[105]

The increased availability of properties in Holywell from the 1370's, the fluctuating trend in accumulations and the ever-advancing impermanence of tenurial commitments especially after 1400, as well as the rise in land investment for exploitational purposes were the more striking aspects of the tenurial pattern in late-mediaeval Holywell-cum-Needingworth, but it can be proposed that they might not have assumed the proportions they did had there not been an equally pronounced and simultaneous readjustment in the basic conditions or terms of land-holding, specifically in a growing emphasis on money rent alone as the essential responsibility of tenure as opposed to the performance of works or a combination of rents and services. Properties taken up on a lease for a straight money rent — even if the terms specified *ad terminum vite* — did not require of the peasant the heavy investment of time and labour that a tenement *ad opus* did. In addition, the eventual conversion of all properties in Holywell after 1409 into exclusively money-paying tenements also made it easier for the transient speculator or the outsider with adequate capital to invest in property since the obligation of contributing to a local labour force had been eliminated. Nevertheless, although tenure based on money

neque bidentes veniant in le falwe sine custode sub pena predicta." In 1443 (PRO SC 2-179/64), it was stated: "Et quod nullus ponat animalia in le falufelde citra festum Inventionis Sancti Crucis ...", while in 1452 (PRO SC 2-179/66) the court roll noted: "Et preceptum est quod nullus custodiat bidentes suos in le Falowfeld citra festum pasche sub pena vj s. viij d." Finally, in 1456 the problem was still being attacked (PRO SC 2-179/67): "Et preceptum est quod nullus ponat neque pascat bidentes suos in prato de (...) ...."

There is a further aspect to the economic activities of Holywell peasants after 1370 but especially after 1400 that is reflected in the heavy turn-over in lands and the investment in livestock, although the Holywell records do not permit its investigation in detail. It is the indication given by such activities of liquid capital. The ability of peasants to accumulate and then divest themselves of land regularly and also obtain large numbers of animals points to individual economic activities being based strongly on cash foundations. How much this was really an intensification over conditions in the early fourteenth century, however, cannot be adequately determined: the evidence of the Subsidy Rolls of 1327 and 1332 of heavy concentrations of movables for several peasants and peasant families equally suggests liquid capital resources as being a potent factor in village economy even at that period.

[105] See *supra*, p. 112 *et seq.*

rent obviously had its advantages, it did not act as an all-inclusive liberating force in the village. As indicated earlier, a large proportion of Holywell tenants in the fifteenth century still remained smallholders, and no doubt many were obliged to do so because of limited funds. Promotion and significant expansion, on the other hand, tended to be dominated by persons who could quite literally afford the burdens of tenure. Precisely how extensive these burdens were, and what persons displayed an ability to cope with them, must now be examined more closely.

Although the last quarter of the fourteenth century and the first half of the fifteenth century witnessed a new advance in money rents for land, the complete transformation of the terms of tenure did not occur until the second decade of the fifteenth century. Prior to that time, the abbey not only retained tenure *ad opus*, but increased it as well, in a serious attempt to win profits from demesne cultivation. As already pointed out in the preceding chapter,[106] by 1370 25 of the 45 full customary tenements in the village were *ad opus*, or 56 %. (See Table IV). In 1391/92, the number *ad opus* was 24, or 53 %. Twenty-five and a half were *ad opus* in 1396/97, $26\frac{1}{2}$ in 1400 and $27\frac{1}{2}$ in 1401. From 1403 through 1405, the number was stabilized at 26 (58 %). This had been accomplished by a return of virgates and cotlands to the *ad opus* category, the lesser-obligated crofts being kept wholly in commutation. However, as already noted, the abbey was fighting a losing battle in demesne cultivation.[107] Even as virgates and cotlands were taken out of commutation between the 1370's and the early 1400's, the need to commute — or sell — assessed annual *opera* reasserted itself. In 1370/71, 498 *opera* out of 3179 were sold, or 16%. By 1391/92, the proportion had risen to 32 % sold (965 out of 2977). In subsequent years the percentages sold were as follows: 1399/1400 — 30% ($1015\frac{1}{2}$ out of 3352); 1400/1401 — 33% ($1145\frac{1}{2}$ out of 3546); 1401/ 1402 — 38% ($1250\frac{1}{2}$ out of 3318); 1403/1404 — 43% (1460 out of 3424); and 1404/1405 — 42 % (1409 out of 3326). (See Table V).

Whether this sale of *opera* — accounting for over a third of assessed works from 1400 — was the result of a serious shortage of labour is not fully known.[108] That there may have been an insufficient supply of labourers

---

[106] See *supra*, p. 72.

[107] See Raftis, *Estates*, pp. 263-66, for a detailed consideration of this problem on Ramsey manors in the latter fourteenth century. For more general treatments of the problem of labour shortage in late mediaeval England, the works of Postan (CEH, I), and also McKisack and Alec Myers (*England in the Late Middle Ages*. Baltimore, 1961) offer good summaries.

[108] The number of acres sown in Holywell in 1399/1400 had been 167 (PRO SC 6-877/24). In 1400/1401, only $147\frac{1}{2}$ acres were sown (PRO SC 6-877/26), and the number had slipped to 140 acres by 1401/1402 (PRO SC 6-877/27). (Reference is to *demesne* acres only.)

TABLE IV

CUSTOMARY TENEMENTS IN HOLYWELL, 1370-1413

	VIRGATES				COTLANDS			
	Op.	Cens.	Off.	Vac.	Op.	Cens.	Off.	Vac.
1370/1371:	15	2	0	0	10	2	3	0
1391/1392:	14	3	0	0	10	1	4	0
1396/1397:	14½	2½	0	0	11	1	3	0
1399/1400:	13½	3	1/2	0	12	3*	0	0
1400/1401:	14½	2½	0	0	13	1	1	0
1401/1402:	14	3	0	0	13	1	1	0
1403/1404:	14	3	0	0	12	2	1	0
1404/1405:	14	3	0	0	12	2	1	0
1408/	10	4	0	3	12	2	1	0
1409:	0	17	0	0	0	15	0	0
1412/1413:	0	17	0	0	0	15	0	0

	CROFTS			
	Op.	Cens.	Arent.	Vac.
1370/1371:	0	8	4	1
1391/1392:	0	7	5	2
1396/1397:	0	7	5	2
1399/1400:	0	8	5	0
1400/1401:	0	8	5	0
1401/1402:	0	8	5	0
1403/1404:	0	6	6	1
1404/1405:	0	6	6	1
1408/	0	6	6	1
1409:	0	6	6	1
1412/1413:	0	6	6	1

* One cotland in *arentatum*.

DISPOSITION OF OPERA IN HOLYWELL, 1355-1409

	1355/56	1362/63	1370/71	1391/92	1399/1400	1400/1	1401/2	1403/4	1404/5	1408/9
WINTER										
Assessed	1120	1047	1640	1510	1794	1820½	1680	1720	1840	1408
Sold	0	29½	161	492	559	741	723½	839	937	471
Performed	1079	1142	1650	1028	1774	1079½	984½	843	902	937
Holydays	0	0	0	10	0	0	0	0	0	0
Illness	0	0	0	0	0	0	8	12	0	0
SUMMER										
Assessed	360	365½	400	418	390	615½	600	520	546	NOVUM
Sold	0	0	72	147	131½	233	188½	257	234	
Performed	360	366	312	271	258½	382½	411½	241	312	CENSUM
Holydays	0	0	0	0	0	0	0	0	0	
Illness	0	0	16	0	0	0	0	22	0	
AUTUMN										
Assessed	784	805	824	743	882	984	824	944	904	NOVUM
Sold	0	0	88	162	206	171	202	240	238	
Performed	732	718	696	542½	592	621	442	512	586	CENSUM
Holydays	54	87	40	38	73	84	80	0	80	
Illness	0	0	0	0	0	8	0	12	0	
POST A.										
Assessed	192	214	315	306	286	126	214	240	26	NOVUM
Sold	0	0	177	164	119	4½	136½	124	0	
Performed	192	183	158	140	129	43	63½	90	26	CENSUM
Holydays	0	23	0	0	39	27½	14	25	0	
Illness	0	0	0	0	0	0	0	0	0	
TOTALS										
Assessed	2456	2431	3179	2977	3352	3546	3318	3424	3326	1408
Sold	0	29½	498	965	1015½	1149½	1250½	1460	1409	471
Performed	2363	2409	2816	1981½	2753½	2126	1901½	1686	1826	937
Holydays	54	110	40	38	111	111	94	25	80	0
Illness	0	0	16	10	0	8	0	46	0	0

is possible, but it cannot be certain that it was critical. For one, the number of workers (*operarii*) mustered for *precariae* in 1371, 1392, 1400 and 1402 was, with only one exception (1392), in excess of the numbers that had been produced in the first half of the fourteenth century (See Table VI), and the fact that there was no *precaria* in 1401 or 1404 may indicate that, given the reduced size of the demesne by that time, the harvesting needs had been fully met without recourse to "extra" days.[109] By the same token, the fact that there were no recorded vacancies in *ad opus* customary tenements from 1370 through 1405 (see Table IV) further indicates that villagers did not shrink from holding such properties out of fear of being unable to meet the work obligations they imposed. However, what may be obscuring the point here is the fact that the actual amount of demesne under cultivation — and hence requiring work — was steadily shrinking in size. Thus, it is more than probable that the situation prevailing involved, first, that the abbey desired to maintain demesne cultivation but that the supply of labour was not sufficient to meet the needs of the full, integral demesne. Thus, the demesne was gradually nibbled away through leases to the peasantry, and what was retained required a heavy concentration of tenants *ad opus* to guarantee its labour needs being met. These were, in fact, met, and, because the amount of acreage under cultivation had shrunk considerably, the full complement of *opera* itself was not required and the surplus was consequently sold. Admittedly, this is speculation, but it may be argued that it is not an unreasonable explanation to the otherwise perplexing question of why the abbey felt it necessary to keep 27 customary tenements *ad opus* when the amount of demesne under cultivation in the first decade of the fifteenth century averaged 151 acres,

TABLE VI

LABOUR FORCE AT *PRECARIAE*, 1308-1402

	1308	1356	1363(1)	1363(2)	1371	1392	1400	1402
Labourers	112*	144*	110*	80**	122**	90**	188**	120**
Famuli	?	?	?	?	17	12	20	20
Total	112+	144+	110+	80+	139	102	138	140

* "custumarii"
** "operarii"

[109] The fact that the *precariae* workers from 1356 through 1402 were consistently designated "operarii" in the account rolls, whereas the labourers in 1308 had been termed "custumarii", prompts the suspicion that much of this labour force may have come from outside the village and been hired for the immediate seasonal need.

and it further renders more understandable the willingness of Holywell villagers to keep such tenements filled at a time when the population — and consequently the labour force[110] — was in fact at a low ebb.[111] Finally, it is also consistent with the fact that although customary tenements were being filled, the incidence of villagers taking up more than one *ad opus* tenement between 1370 and 1400 was slight when compared with the number of villagers holding multiple properties at rent. Thus, in 1370/71, out of 38 persons holding customary properties, eight were tenants of more than one, but only four held more than one tenement *ad opus*, and in all but one case the total work obligations owed by each equaled or were less than the *opera* of a full virgate. In 1391/92, out of 38 customary tenants again, 11 held more than one but only two held them *ad opus*, and neither's *opera* total exceeded a virgate's. In 1396/97, 32 persons held customary properties of whom seven held more than one tenement, but only three held *ad opus*, and the work obligations of each were equal to those of a full virgate. In short, despite the growth of multiple tenants from 1370, few had multiples of *ad opus* tenements,[112] and the few who did — with but one exception — were unwilling to commit themselves to more than a virgate's share of *opera*. In this, the insufficiency of labour supply no doubt played a significant role.

Despite the increased emphasis on *ad opus* tenure between 1370 and 1409, however, the place of money rent in land-holding in Holywell was steadily advancing. Indeed, it was even present in the *ad opus* arrangement, for the sale of works amounted to a form of commutation, and it is at least a possibility that *ad opus* virgaters and cotlanders were paying — in addition to the immutable customary rents — some three shillings a year for commuted *opera*.[113]

---

[110] It should be noted, however, that this "willingness" to fill *ad opus* tenements had some limitations, especially when considered in terms of recorded failures to perform works or the poor performance of work. Thus, the incidence of work derelictions in Holywell sky-rocketed from the 1370's. See *infra*, Chapter IV.

[111] See *infra*, Chapter III, p. 166 *et seq.*

[112] Eliminating duplication of such multiple *ad opus* tenants who held continuously from 1370 through the 1390's, the corrected total number of villagers who held more than one customary property *ad opus* from 1370 through 1397 is seven: Thomas Cartere (1370), John Hemyngton (1370), John AtteWelle (1370-1392), Nicholas Scot (1370), John Sande (1391-97), John Palmere (1396) and Richard Edward (1396).

[113] This is purely speculative. The number of works sold — and their total value — are known, but whether or not each cotland and virgate shared equally in the commuted number is not indicated. If they did, dividing the amount of revenue by the number of tenements *ad opus* yields the following portions: 1370/71 — 1 s. 8 d.; 1391/92 — 2 s. 8 d; 1399/1400 — 3 s. 5 d.; 1400/1401 — 3 s. 1 d.; 1401/1402 — 3 s. 4 d.; 1403/1404 — 3 s. 8 d.; 1404/1405 — 3 s. 9 d.

More certain, however, is the evidence of customary tenements *ad censum*, *in arentata*, and demesne leases on money terms. Naturally, until 1409 the holding of properties *ad censum* was low, since the number of tenements *ad opus* had been increased. Thus, in 1391/92, one-third of the customary tenements in Holywell were held exclusively for money rents, including *censa* and *arentata*. (See Table IV). In 1396/97, 34 %; in 1399/1400, 42 %; in 1400/1401, 37 %; in 1401/1402, 38 %; and from 1403 through 1405, 37 %. Throughout, the *censum* rate itself remained unchanged from the level fixed in the early fourteenth century, at 15s. for a virgate, 7s. 6d. for a cotland and 3s. 4d. for a croft. Crofts *in arentata* continued to be separately valued at three shillings (one croft), four shillings (three crofts) and five shillings (one croft).[114]

The year 1409 witnessed the elimination of *ad opus* tenure in Holywell, and the subsequent putting of all customary virgates and cotlands *ad censum*. At first, it appears that the abbey simply put all units into the traditional *ad censum* category,[115] but at some point between Michaelmas of 1409 and Michaelmas of 1412 this had been further readjusted by the introduction of the *novum censum*. This raised the *censum* rate — thereby allowing the additional elimination of the old customary rents — and fixed it at 18s. a year for virgates and 9s. a year for cotlands.[116] Since this was accompanied at the same time by the release of over 230 acres of arable demesne land and 26 acres of demesne meadow to the customaries and the remaining 80 acres of demesne arable and 23 acres of meadow to the *firmarii* John Benet and John Pulter, all land in Holywell was held strictly for money rent from the second decade of the fifteenth century.

What needs to be emphasized, however, is that the *censum* rates for customary tenements in Holywell, although redefined *ca.* 1410, did not undergo any *reduction*, either in the post-plague generation or after 1400,

---

[114] The balancing of crofts *ad censum* and *in arentata* from 1403 resulted in one more croft *in arentatum* being valued at four shillings (PRO SC 6-877/28).

[115] PRO SC 6-877/30. The transition occurred between the winter and summer work seasons of 1409, or from the feast of Pentecost, when it was stated in the account roll that no works were owed "quia customarii ad censa".

[116] The precise date of the introduction of the *novum censum* in Holywell is not known, due to the lack of account rolls for 1409/10, 1410/1411 and 1411/1412. Raftis has noted that the change occurred around 1410 on most Ramsey manors and that the *censum* was not uniform: at Slepe, for example, the *censum* for virgates was reduced by two shillings (*Estates*, p. 266, and Appendix I, p. 267). It should be added that the *novum censum* in Holywell affected only virgates and cotlands. Crofts — either *ad censum* or *in arentata* — were not involved. It should further be noted that the *novum censum* — whether intentionally or not is unknown — corresponded closely to a rent of a shilling an acre for virgates (18 s. = 18 a.) and cotlands (9 s. = 9/10 a.).

from its early fourteenth-century levels of 15s. and 7s. 6d. With regard to the acres of demesne let-out to the peasants, the rents per acre remained unchanged over the second half of the fourteenth century and through the first decade of the fifteenth century. A readjustment in their rents did not occur until *ca.* 1410 — after 1409 but before 1412. Thus, as early as the 1330's, 11 acres of demesne (in "le Smethe") had been let-out at a rate of a shilling an acre.[117] This value of 12d. an acre in le Smethe remained unchanged through 1409. By 1412, it had been reduced — to 10d. an acre. Similarly, acres in Benehill, Malwode, Schepenfurlong, Middilfurlong, Overebrerecroft and le Brache were valued at either 14 d. or 12 d. or 2 s., but they were not reduced until the second decade of the fifteenth century. On the other hand, values in Oxhowe and Bury-hegge did not change at all, remaining stable at 12 d. and 10 d. an acre respectively through 1418, when the account roll series breaks off for over 30 years. In Stonydole and Nethbrerecroft rents were readjusted earlier — by 1404, but upwards — from 14 d. to 2 s. an acre, and they remained in force until after 1409, when they were again altered, with the rates subsequently at 12 d., 14 d. or 18 d. an acre. Only in Braynesdole were acreage values *reduced* early (from 2 s. to 18 d. or 14 d.) in the fifteenth century.

In general, then, a reduction of demesne acreage values had occurred in Holywell, but not until the second decade of the fifteenth century, and then the newly "revised" values appear to have remained in force throughout the rest of the first half of the century.[118] In short, at a time when land values — in terms of rents — were steadily — and sometimes rapidly — falling throughout England[119], values in Holywell, with regard to demesne, appear to have been falling slowly and then only slightly,

---

[117] PRO SC 6-877/18.

[118] The account rolls document the stability of the revised rents through 1418. After that date the accounts are missing for the next 31 years, but sporadic entries in the Court Book tend to confirm their retention. For example, in 1425 John Peny received three acres and a quarter in le Brache and three acres in Schepenfurlong, paying, respectively, 2 s. and 3 s. 6 d. (14 d.C) — the same rents obtaining in 1418 (BM.Harl.Ms. 445, 128ᵛ). In 1440, William Smyth took up one acre in Stonydole, paying 12 d. annual rent — a rate unchanged from 1418 (*Ibid.*, 183ʳ). Finally, in 1447, John Theller and John Bry received acres in Stonydole, Oxhowe and Overe-brerecroft bearing rents unchanged from 1418 (*Ibid.*, 217ʳ⁻ᵛ), and in 1451 Alice Herle (Baroun) received an acre in Middilfurlong, whose rent was still 10 d. (*Ibid.*, 235ʳ.)

It should further be noted that when 123 additional demesne acres were released to the peasants between 1409 and 1412, they were released with a value of 12 d. an acre (PRO SC 6-878/2).

[119] The phenomenon of declining values in land has been carefully and thoroughly summarized by Postan, CEH, I, pp. 589-91 and p. 630.

while values for customary tenements seemed not to have fallen at all but were, on the contrary, raised.[119] This, however, is actually quite deceptive. As Professor Postan has noted,[120] a more sensitive index to declining land value is found in entry fines, or *gersumae*, and here the Holywell evidence is of a rather heavy drop in property value. Unfortunately, the very few account rolls of the first three-quarters of the fourteenth century do not give any adequate information on *gersumae* in Holywell, so a precise comparison of Holywell entry fines before 1390 with those after 1390 is not possible. Nevertheless, a general comparison is not prohibited, for it is doubtful that Holywell *gersumae* of the early fourteenth century were radically different from those on other Ramsey manors. Thus, entry fines for virgates varied anywhere from 10 shillings to over 60 shillings, with an average of 30 shillings to 40 shillings, while half-virgates (or cotlands) paid from six shillings to 40 shillings.[121] In contrast, the *gersumae* for Holywell recorded in the Court Book from 1400 through 1457 definitely point to a drop in land value. Indeed, the highest entry fine set down in the entire period was 26 shillings. It occurred twice, once in 1414, for a virgate and two acres of demesne, and once in 1416, for a half-virgate. Otherwise, the rates for virgates ran from 40 d. (1401) to 13 s. 4 d. (1419 and 1420), with other entry fines for cotlands, half-virgates and additional land parcels of varying size and composition ranging from threepence to 13 s. 4 d. In addition, the number of entry fines payable in kind — chickens, geese or hens — grew from 1410, so that a full virgate could be had for three chickens in *gersuma* in 1424, six chickens in 1427, and six geese in 1432.[122]

The fact that land value was in fact decreasing in Holywell by the early fifteenth century, and that tenure was coming to be dominated by money rent — a condition that was total after 1409 — does not necessarily mean that land-holding itself was an especially cheap or inexpensive practice. The income to the abbey from money rent through various types of rentals of arable and fen in the latter fourteenth century was not insignificant, accounting for over £13 in 1370/71, over £28 in 1403/1404,

---

[120] CEH, I, p. 589.

[121] See Raftis, *Estates*, pp. 237-38 and Appendix IV, pp. 248-49. Rates in the non-Ramsey Oxfordshire village of Cuxham ranged from 20 s. to 50 s. for a half-virgate (Harvey, p. 174). For entry fines on Winchester estates in the latter thirteenth and early fourteenth centuries, see Postan and Titow, "Heriots and Prices on Winchester Manors", p. 392 *et seq.*

[122] Why the *gersumae* varied so widely in Holywell at this time cannot be readily determined. Tenements of the same size, for example virgates, could command entry fines from a chicken to over 13 s. Possibly the entry fine was an index to the condition of the land itself, but the question cannot be investigated due to the limitations of the sources.

over £31 in 1408/1409 and over £66 in 1412/1413.[123] Not surprisingly, the rent obligations of individual peasants could be considerable as well, growing in amount according to the number of acres taken up and held.

The full extent of these money rents can perhaps best be seen from the following table (Table VII). Listed are individual peasants, with estimates of the rents owed by them in specific years up to 1418. Projection cannot be safely extended beyond that year due to the absence of account rolls for 31 years. The rent estimates themselves are based on information of personal holdings in account rolls from 1370 through 1418, and, after 1397, on supplementary data found in the Court Book, and are the combined sums due from: (1) small tenements, (2) customary rents from *ad opus* properties (prior to 1412), (3) *censum* and *arentatum* payments, and (4) demesne and/or fen leases. Due to the incomplete nature of the sources, they cannot hope to be exhaustive, but they are at least an index to the general and minimal rent obligations incumbent upon individual peasants.[124]

The structure of money rents in late fourteenth — early fifteenth-century Holywell was far-reaching. Few peasants were untouched by it, and no tenants were immune. In addition, after 1409 it became inescapable for tenants, and, since there was a rough equation of a shilling to an acre after that date, this fact no doubt contributes to an explanation of the continuing number of tenants at less than 10 acres over the first half of the century. On the other hand, it must be admitted that it did not prevent the accumulation of large concentrations of property by specific industrious peasants, but it cannot be known with certainty that the heavy emphasis on money rent *facilitated* accumulation. There is at least one case in which it did not. William Cartere had been a half-virgater *ad opus* in the 1390's and through the first decade of the fifteenth century. In addition, he held five acres of demesne from 1404 for five shillings' rent. By 1410, however, he had given up his half-virgate, retaining seven acres of land for seven shillings' rent. It seems likely that the prospect of keeping his half-virgate, for a total of 16 acres for 16 shillings, was too great a demand

---

[123] This estimate includes rents from *censa, arentata*, fen and demesne leases and rentals of other properties. By comparison, profits from *opera* sales in 1370/71 amounted to just over 42 s. Those in 1403/1404 to over five pounds.

[124] For the sake of greater convenience, the amounts given in Table III have been further abbreviated by the elimination of pence, half-pennies and farthings. Thus, a tenement of a virgate *ad opus* actually yielded a full customary rent of 22 d. ob.q. This has been uniformly shortened to "22 d." Similarly with other entries. The primary concern has been to show the *minimal* rents in shillings owed by individual peasants, although in some cases it is definitely known that the rent owed was higher (in terms of a few pence), and in others it is a probability.

TABLE VII

ESTIMATES OF MINIMAL RENTS DUE FROM HOLYWELL PEASANTS, 1371-1418

	1371	1392	1400	1401	1402	1404	1405	1409	1413	1414	1416	1418
ARNOLD, John			2s	2s	2s							
ARNOLD, Simon					2s							
ASPLOND, John	12d	3s	3s	3s	3s	3s						
ASPLOND, Richard											12s	12
ASPLOND, Thomas	2s	14d	14d	14d								
ATTEWELLE, John I	20d	3s										
ATTEWELLE, John II			4s	4s	22s	22s	22s	22s	25s	25s	25s	25
ATTEWELLE, Robert	11s	15s	22d	22s								
BAKER, John		18d	12d	12d	12d	3s	3s	3s	7s	7s	7s	7
BAKER, Roger												18
BAKER, Thomas									3s	3s		
BAROUN, John	4s	4s										
BAROUN, Nicholas									4s	4s	4s	4
BAROUN, Thomas												4
BAROUN, William	4s	7s	4s	4s	4s	4s	4s	4s	4s	4s	4s	4
BATE, John									?	?		
BEAUMEYS, John I	18d											
BEAUMEYS, John II		2s	2s	2s	2s	2s	12d				9s	9
BEAUMEYS, Walter	18d	18d										
BERNEWELL, Thomas	2s	14d	14d	14d	14d							
BOTILLER, William & Thomas									40s			
BRAMPTON, John									?			
BRAYN, John	3s	8s										
BRAYN, Nicholas		13d										
BRAYN, Reginald	12d	12d	12d	12d	12d							
BRAYN, Richard	18d											
BRAYN, Thomas			13d					3s	4s	3s	3s	3s
BROOK, Richard										18d	18d	
CARTERE, John			3s	3s	3s	3s						
CARTERE, Thomas	2s											
CARTERE, William	2s	25d	10s	11s	6s	6s	6s	7s		7s	7s	7s
CRISTEMESSE, John		28d										
CRANFELD, Cristina	15s											
CRANFELD, Richard	15s											
DAMMESON, William	3s	3s	3s	3s	3s	3s	3s	3s	3s	3s	3s	3s
DEYE, John	5s	5s	5s	5s	5s	5s						
DEYE, Robert	4s											
DEYE, Thomas		4s			2s	2s	4s	5s	5s	5s	5s	5s

	1371	1392	1400	1401	1402	1404	1405	1409	1413	1414	1416	1418
ᴀRD, John		17s	19s	19s	19s	18s	20s					
ᴀRD, Richard								18s	38s	38s	38s	38s
ᴀRD, Thomas		10s	17s	17s	17s	20s	20s	31s	39s	39s	39s	39s
ꜰREY, Adam	18d	18d	22d									
ꜰREY, John		12s										
ꜰREY, Nicholas I	12s											
ꜰREY, Nicholas II		9s	8s	8s	8s	8s	8s	18s	18s	18s	18s	27s
ꜰREY, Richard		3s	3s	3s	3s	3s	3s	6s	6s	6s	6s	6s
ᴇMAN, Andrew	18d											
ᴇMAN, John		13d										
ʀICH, Thomas	3s											
ᴡYNE, John										?	?	?
ʏ, John			8s	8s								
ʏ, Richard	22d											
ᴏND, John	25d											
ᴅY, Nicholas			2s	2s	2s							
ʏNGTON, John	8s	4s	12d	2s	12d	10s	10s	10s	10s	10s	10s	10s
ʏNGTON Thomas									4s	13s	13s	13s
ɢHTON, Agnes		6d										
ɢHTON, Robert	22s	3s	3s	3s	3s	3s	3s	3s				
ɢHTON, Roger		7s	30s	30s	30s	41s	41s	33s				
ɴE, Agnes	8s											
ɴE, John	12d	22d		12d								
ɴE, Thomas	22d	30s	14d	14d	14d	12d	12d	12d	10d	10d	10d	10d
ɴE, William		14d	2s	2s	2s							
ᴇ, John in the		5s										
ᴇ, Nicholas in the	5s	12d	12d	12d	12d							
ʜYNG, William	5s					12d	12d	12d	10d	10d	10d	10d
ᴛON, John	22d	22d								14d		
ᴛON, Richard		6d										
ɴERE, Richard		13d										
ɴERE, Robert		13d										
ɴERE, Roger	3s	4s	8d	8d	8d	6s	6s	6s				
ᴇ, Robert	13d											
ʀICE, John							4s	16s ?	16s ?	16s ?	16s ?	16s ?
ʀYELL, Radulph				14d		2s	2s	2s	14d	14d	14d	14d
ᴏLAS, John	76s	22d										
ᴏLAS, Thomas		22d				2s	2s			4s	4s	4s	4s
ᴍERE, John		20s		13s	13s	18s	18s	18s	45s	45s	45s	45s
ᴛER, Thomas						2s	2s	2s	14d	14d	14d	14d
ʀD, Thomas							4s					
ʀEYMAN, William									9s	9s	9s	9s
ᴀRD, William											4d	4d

	1371	1392	1400	1401	1402	1404	1405	1409	1413	1414	1416	1…
POPE, William			4s									
REVE, Richard			26d	3s	3s							
ROKYSDON, Robert								?	?	?	?	
SANDE, John	13d	27d			13d	13s	13s	13s	17s	19s	19s	1?
SANDE, William		12d										
SCHARP, Nicholas			19d	5s	5s	5s	5s	6s	6s	6s	6s	(
SCHARP, Richard		3s		3s	3s	2s	2s	2s	3s	3s	3s	?
SCOT, John				15s					35s	35s	35s	3?
SCOT, Laurence								5s	5s	5s	5s	?
SCOT, Nicholas	2s	18d										
SCOT, Richard						12d	12d	12d	10d	18d	18d	1?
SCOT, Thomas							2s	2s	3s	3s	3s	?
SCOT, William	13d											
SELDE, John								4s	4s	4s	4s	?
SELDE, Roger										5s	5s	?
SELEDE, John		?										
SEMTIOUN, John & Thomas										27s	27s	
SEBERNE, John								?				
SEWALE, Adam								4s	4s	2s		
SEWALE, Roger						12d	12d	12d	10d	10d	20d	2?
SEWALE, Thomas								4s	4s			
SEWALE, John										3s	3s	?
SHEPPERD, Elena	5s	5s										
SHEPPERD, John III	12d	17s										
SHEPPERD, John III				15s	31s	31s	39s	39s	46s	46s	46s	5?
SHEPPERD, Katerina						13s	28s	28s	28s	28s	28s	
SHEPPERD, Nicholas I	9s	2s										
SHEPPERD, Nicholas II										12d	12d	?
SHEPPERD, William			2s	2s	2s	2s	5s	5s	4s	4s	4s	?
SMYTH, Radulph						4s	18d	18d				
SMYTH, Thomas		14d	14d	14d	14d	14d	14d	14d	14d	14d	14d	1?
SMYTH, William		4s										
SPERCOLL, John			14d	14d	14d	14d						
SPERCOLL, William			14d	14d	14d	14d						
STAYARD, John			3s									
TAYLLOR, John						7s	7s	7s	4s	6s	6s	?
WRIGHT, John	7s											
WRIGHT, Robert									2s			
WRIGHT, William						4s	4s	3s	3s	4s	4s	?

on his resources. As for those villagers who did build-up large concentrations of property — at times for rents exceeding 40 shillings — the only legitimate conclusion that can be made is that they accepted the rents as an accomplished fact and obviously were able to do so because their own financial resources were extensive enough to meet them.[125]

Truly, then, although the holding of property exclusively for money doubtlessly inhibited the expansionist hopes of some peasants, it did not paralyze tenurial involvements in Holywell. It did, however, restrict the accumulation of extensive holdings to peasants with capital enough to bear the rent obligations — just as the holding of larger customary tenements *ad opus* had previously been restricted to those able to meet the labour obligations. In short, this simply means that the altered basis of land-holding did not prevent the growth of individual property concentrations nor especially inhibit the activities of peasants whose primary interest was speculation in or exploitation of land opportunities.[126] That there were such people active in Holywell in the late fourteenth and first half of the fifteenth century has already been established. What remains to be considered is the degree to which they were connected with the village itself.

Land-holding peasants in Holywell-cum-Needingworth from the 1370's to the 1450's can be divided into two fundamental categories: locals and outsiders. By "locals" is meant those tenants who, either singly or with families, are known to have been actually resident in the village. "Outsiders", on the other hand, simply refers to peasants who held land in Holywell but did not display any signs of actually living there.[127] Taking the latter category first, 17% of the known tenants in Holywell between the 1370's and the 1450's were non-residents or outsiders.[128] Two men — John Benet and John Pulter — served as *firmarii* of the manor from the second decade of the fifteenth century through at least the 1430's,

---

[125] This can especially be proposed in the cases of peasants who acquired large blocs of properties — over 30 acres — and also displayed an involvement in pastoral activities. Not only would they need the capital sufficient to support heavy rents, but also enough capital for investment in livestock.

[126] Indeed, it is not impossible that the exploitational aspect of tenure was encouraged by the elimination of a commitment to *opera*.

[127] This is based on a failure to find any indication of residence through such a source of village life as court rolls.

[128] Omitted from consideration are peasants leasing parcels of the Holywell fens, since names were given only once — in 1370/71. If names were known for subsequent periods, they could have been included, and the proportion of outsiders would probably be slightly raised. The actual number of known tenants is 211, of which 36 were clearly outsiders.

thereby assuming responsibility for over 100 acres of demesne at a rent of 60 shillings.[129] The remaining outsiders maintained land interests in the village for periods of from one year to 50 years, although the majority were short-term investors — i.e. they held properties for less than 10 years. Despite the acute impermanence of their tenures, however, 16 persons managed to take up properties of more than 10 acres, and 10 of the 16 were tenants of at least virgates or their equivalents. On the other hand, 14 were strictly smallholders, being tenants of five acres of land or less for the brief time they held Holywell properties.

The remaining 83 % of the Holywell tenants from the 1370's to the 1450's — some 71 persons — were all local residents. They, in turn, represented 63 individual family groups.[130] Of these, 64 persons (37%) represented 28 families (44%) who were "newcomers" to the village in the sense that they had not taken up residence until after the Black Death. Furthermore, 11 of these "new" families (39%) were able to establish themselves as tenants of intermediate or larger rank (i.e. 10 to 18 acres, or above 18 acres) either immediately or soon after their arrival. To accomplish this, at least eight did not even shrink from becoming villein families. Thus, the AtteWelles, who first appeared in the 1350's, were substantial villein tenants by 1370, with John AtteWelle holding a cotland and a half *ad opus* and Robert AtteWelle a half-virgate and a quarter-virgate *ad censum*. Indeed, so far had the identification with the villeinage gone that Robert was also serving as reeve in 1370/71.[131] Similarly with the Baker and Haliday families. First appearing in the 1380's, by 1392 both John Baker and Simon Haliday were *ad opus* virgaters. The Mertons, taking up residence after the Black Death, were able to sustain an *ad opus* virgate in 1370. The Sandes first appeared in 1370 — with John Sande an *ad opus* cotlander — as did the Thatchers, with Richard Thatcher

---

[129] Benet and Pulter were first recorded as *firmarii* in the account roll for 1412/13, and they retained the position through 1418. Thereafter the accounts break off until 1449, at which point Simon Dallyng was *firmarius*. When he first assumed the post is not known, but he had been in the village since the 1430's. No trace of John Benet is found after 1418, but John Pulter was tenant of some nine acres in free properties in 1449, owing a rent of 5 s. 8 d. He appears, further, to have been a resident of St. Ives, for in 1420 he presented one Thomas Pulter to the rectorship of the Holywell parish church (See *A Short History of the Parish Church of Holywell-cum-Needingworth*, Appendix II.)

[130] Simon Dallyng, the parish priest, is included among these tenants because he was actually in residence, at least from the middle 1450's. Prior to that time — from 1443 to 1453 — he was Master of Trinity Hall at Cambridge. He retained his rectorship of Holywell until 1461, when it was ceded to William Dallyng (*Ibid.*).

[131] PRO SC 6-877/21.

a half-virgater *ad opus*. Lastly, the Palfreymans appeared shortly after 1400, and in 1406 William Palfreyman had taken up a half-virgate *ad opus* previously held by John Hunne. Of later-arriving new families, the Elyots took up residence in the 1440's, and almost immediately John Elyot had acquired a virgate.[132] So too with the ubiquitous Simon Dallyng. Appointed rector in 1423, he was already taking up 18 acres of land in 1431.[133] The Lanenders appeared first in 1420, taking up a virgate, and by 1431 two members of the family were holding a total of a little over 36 acres. The Valentines, who arrived in the 1420's, were holding a customary cotland in 1424, while the Wodecoks first appeared in 1430, at which time they acquired a cotland and three acres of demesne. The point to be emphasized is that of newly-arriving families in Holywell in the late fourteenth and first half of the fifteenth centuries, a little over 40% quickly established themselves as intermediate or major tenants, and that they did so regardless of the conditions or commitments required, whether they were money rents or villein obligations.[134]

---

[132] John Elyot was first noted in 1443, and he took up his virgate in 1444 (BM.Harl.Ms. 445, 204r). Since there was no mention of the family name in the 1430's, the Elyots probably arrived around 1440, and the fact that John was described as a carpenter by trade may explain the rapidity with which he took up over 18 acres of land: at a time of reasonably good wages for craftsmen, he would no doubt have commanded a quite decent income. On the other hand, one cannot rule out the possibility that John was simply a fast worker. After all, not only had he acquired a virgate by 1444; he had also married Alice AtteWelle.

[133] BM.Harl.Ms. 445, 144v. The tenure was a joint one, established with Richard Wattes, an outsider.

[134] This last point is deserving of special note, for it adds weight to the suspicion — most recently advanced by Professor Postan (CEH, I, pp. 610-17) — that land and the local or regional status it conferred on its tenant could be, in many ways, more important to the peasant than strictly legal definitions of freedom or servility. That such should be in evidence in the late fourteenth century should not be surprising — examples of freemen taking up villein land in Holywell and assuming villein services, as well as of free families being transformed into villein families through probable peasant intermarriages in the latter thirteenth century have already been observed (The Geres and Eyrs, for examples, were free in the 1250's but villeins by the early 1300's). In addition, studies by Helen Cam and R. H. Hilton have touched upon the question in recent years. Nevertheless, the fact still bears noting — especially in light of the yet fully unresolved question of the peasant discontent in parts of England that flared up in the Kentish and East Anglian riots traditionally labelled "the Peasants' Revolt" of 1381. The more the student is confronted with evidence of peasants in the 1370's, 1380's and 1390's virtually choosing to assume villein properties and their consequent obligations, the more must he wonder about the validity of attributing major significance to questions of villein status in the violence of the 1380's.

Finally, it should be pointed out that the fact that families such as the AtteWelles, Bakers, Mertons, etc. became Holywell villein families does not mean that they were freemen becoming villeins. The original residences of these families cannot be traced, and it is not unlikely that

Not all incoming families after the Black Death assumed large properties immediately or soon after their arrival, however. Seven (25 %) were resident for at least a generation before individual members began serious involvement in tenure. Thus, the Cristemesses, who had moved in during the 1360's, were smallholders for the remainder of the fourteenth century, and through the first two decades of the fifteenth century. Not until the 1420's did the family display a heightened interest in property, but it then did so to an intense degree, until by 1437 three members of the family controlled a total of 63 acres. The Millers, also arriving in the 1360's, were a croft-holding family in 1370, and not until the 1390's had they risen to the level of cotlanders, and their next — and final — advance (to 23 acres) was delayed until the second decade of the fifteenth century. The Porters appeared first in the 1370's, but not until the 1390's had they become a customary family holding a virgate and a half.[135] The Scharps, who arrived in the 1350's, were smallholders until the late 1390's, when the family's fortunes improved primarily through the efforts of one member — Richard — who acquired some 27 acres in 1396.[136] The Sewales appeared in the 1370's, but it was not until the second decade of the fifteenth century that they rose from the smallholder category to cotlanders. The Bates had been present over 30 years before they rose above 10 acres in the 1430's, while the Arnolds had been resident even longer — since the 1370's — before they obtained more than 10 acres in the 1450's. On the other hand, 10 other families taking up residence in Holywell in the late fourteenth and first half of the fifteenth centuries failed to rise above the category of tenants holding less than 10 acres of land: the Flessheweres, the Godsoules, the Hardys, the Kyngs, the Martyns, the Muryells, the

---

they were villeins in their original localities. This, however, does not alter the significance of their Holywell activities. If a distaste, or even violent aversion, to villeinage or villein commitments and obligations was really a burning issue, then it can be wondered why such mobile families would leave one locality to re-establish themselves as villeins elsewhere. Using the AtteWelles as an example, since they appear to have been pastorally involved after 1400 and were able to adjust to the *novum censum* — and add even more acreage later — with little or no difficulty, the family could have taken up pieces of demesne and fen at a straight money rent instead of customary tenements — unless their primary concern was not one of villienage as opposed to non-villeinage but rather a maximum of land for a minimum of expense and investment. Some further confirmation of this point is possibly reflected in the fact that, in the surviving court rolls' records of failures to work between 1369 and 1396, John Baker was presented twice, John Sande three times, John Merton three times, and John AtteWelle and Robert AtteWelle a total of eight times.

[135] It should also be noted that 1392 marked the highest land concentration of the Porters — 28 acres, all but one of which were held *ad opus*. By the second decade of the fifteenth century, the family's properties totalled 20 acres, and they continued to decline thereafter.

[136] BM.Add.Ch. 33447, 25ᵛ. See *supra*, p. 123, note ♯ 42 for text.

Okys, the Popes and the Seldes. Nevertheless, despite this fact, five managed to maintain residence for a little over a generation,[137] while three stayed in the village for over 70 years.[138]

Not all local persons and families active in property-holding in Holywell in the late fourteenth and first half of the fifteenth centuries were newcomers, however. Between the 1370's and the 1450's, there were 107 persons holding property at one time or another who represented 34 village families that had been settled from before the onslaught of the Black Death. Of these, 10 families (29 %) were holding 10 acres of land or less in 1370 and continued to do so as long as they remained.[139] Thus, the Bernewells held an acre in 1370 and continued to do so through 1400, after which trace of them is lost. The Fannells were croftholders, the Machyngs tenants of an acre or two,[140] the Spercolls of two to three acres, the Godriches of a croft, and the Hroffs of an acre. The Skynneres, on the other hand, were cotlanders, while the Hamonds and the Mokes were half-virgaters. None of these families, however, expanded its holdings, and all were either in or beginning their last generation of residence. Specifically, the Bernewells, who had first appeared a little after 1300, would be gone by 1410. The Fannells were gone by 1420, after over a hundred years' residence, as were the Machyngs, after almost 80 years' residence. The Spercolls, the Godriches and the Hamonds, all of whom had been settled in the village as early as 1300, had disappeared by 1410, 1400 and 1380, respectively, while the Mokes and the Skynneres, resident from the first decade of the fourteenth century, were literally in their last years in 1370: both were gone by 1380. In addition, there were four other "old" families in 1370 who would not endure past the first decade of the fifteenth century and who, although all substantial tenants in 1370, experienced declines in their properties over subsequent years. Specifically, the Brayns were

---

[137] The Flessheweres, who appeared in the 1350's, disappeared in the 1390's. The Muryells were resident from the 1390's into the 1430's, the Popes from the 1370's to the second decade of the fifteenth century, the Godsoules from the 1390's to the 1420's, and the Hardys from the 1360's to the second decade of the fifteenth century. The Essex family, on the other hand, appeared in the 1360's, held 12 acres in the 1370's and were gone by the 1380's.

[138] The Okys arrived in the 1380's and were still present in the 1450's, as were the Seldes, who had appeared first in the 1370's. The Kyngs had been residents from the 1350's to the 1440's. Finally, the ninth family — the Martyns — had arrived in the 1420's and were still present in the 1450's.

[139] One family — the Brooks — were not recorded as holding any land in 1370, but they held at least an acre in the second decade of the fifteenth century just before they disappeared.

[140] William Machyng held two acres in 1370, but from 1405 through 1418 he was listed at only one acre.

a virgate-holding family in 1370, in the person of Richard Brayn. By 1392, they had managed to increase their acreage: John and Nicholas Brayn between them held some 29 acres of customary and demesne land. However, in 1400 neither John nor Nicholas still held his tenements, leaving only a Reginald Brayn with a little over eight acres and Thomas Brayn with nine acres. By 1414, only Thomas remained — holding a croft (*in arentatum*) and an acre of demesne.

The Carteres had been represented in 1370 by Thomas Cartere, holding two cotlands *ad opera* — a total of some 20 acres. By 1392, Thomas was gone, and William Cartere was holding a half-virgate *ad opus* and an acre of demesne. He managed to add nine more acres of demesne by 1400, at the same time a John Cartere was holding two acres of demesne. However, William had relinquished his half-virgate by 1410. He remained for another 10 years — holding a little over six acres and then disappeared, as did the entire family.

The Godeman and Gray families were less prolonged in their property declines. In 1370, Andrew Godeman had been a full virgater *ad opus*. By 1392, only John Godeman remained, and he was a cotlander. Similarly with the Grays. Richard Gray was an *ad opus* virgater in 1370, but by 1392 no Gray held customary land. In 1397, however, John Gray re-established the family's place among the customary tenants — but as a cotlander — while at sometime around 1400 a Roger Gray held — briefly — a half-virgate. Thereafter — until the 1420's — John Gray's cotland was seemingly the family's only tenement.[141]

Whereas 14 old Holywell families experienced either no expansion or a decline in properties over the late fourteenth and early fifteenth centuries, six (18%) were able to promote themselves from modest to major positions, although the process was not necessarily rapid. The Deyes, who had been present from the second decade of the fourteenth century, were a smallholding family in 1370, and it was not until the 1390's that they advanced to the level of cotlanders. This, in fact, was accomplished through the efforts of Thomas Deye, who was serving as one of the manorial ploughmen (*akerman*) in 1392 and consequently received a cotland *in officio*. Indeed, it was this Thomas who alone managed to increase the holdings of the family. By 1409 he was holding a little over 17 acres, and although he surrendered his cotland to his son-in-law John

---

[141] John Gray converted the tenure of his cotland from *ad opus* to *ad censum* in 1399. As for Roger Gray, he did not hold his half-virgate in 1397, but he was presented for not coming to the autumn *precaria* in 1400, which would indicate his being a customary tenant in that year. By 1405, however, his half-virgate had been taken up by John Palmere. (PRO SC 6-877/29.)

Shepperd in 1417,[142] he replaced it with a virgate, which he retained through the 1440's.

The Bryans, resident from the 1330's, had not been recorded as tenants at all during the late fourteenth century, and it was not until the 1420's that John Bryan held two customary cotlands. The family's serious involvement in property was short-lived, however. By 1424, John had transferred his tenements to Roger Cristemesse.[143] The Edwards, on the other hand, experienced a relatively spectacular property jump. Present from before 1300, they were not among the tenants of 1370. Nevertheless, by 1392 Thomas Edward was holding one virgate *ad opus* and a half-virgate *ad censum*, while John Edward held a full virgate *ad censum* and a cotland *in officio* for serving as reeve.[144] Five years later — in 1397 — John's son, Richard Edward, was also a tenant, holding a half-virgate *ad opus*, and by 1405 all three men controlled a combined total of some 78 acres of land. Thereafter, the family consistently maintained properties exceeding 50 acres.

The Smyths, also resident from the late thirteenth century, were another family to rise in the tenurial scale, although to a more limited degree. They grew from three acres in 1392 to 14 acres in 1400 and reached their peak in the 1430's, when just under 30 acres of land were in the family's control. Similarly with the Tayllours. Resident from the 1330's, they finally managed — in the person of John Tayllour — to briefly hold a little over 25 acres in the second decade of the fifteenth century. The Wrights, on the other hand, although present from the second decade of the fourteenth century, were especially late in promoting themselves. Smallholders through the 1420's, it was not until the 1440's that the family properties exceeded 20 acres.

Fourteen additional old Holywell families (41%), however, were characterized by a fundamental consistency in that they were among the principal tenants — i.e. holding 11 acres or more — from the 1370's and never retreated from that position as long as they remained in residence. Furthermore, 10 of these families were already major tenants (18 acres or more) in 1370 and remained so — even to the point of increasing their acreage

---

[142] BM.Harl.Ms. 445, 101ʳ: "Thomas Daye sursum reddidit in manus domini j cotlandum cum tota terra dominica adiacente de novo ac vestura eiusdem terre dominice ad opus Johannis Schepperd, Tenenda eidem Johanni et Agnete uxori sue ad terminum vite eorum, Reddendo inde in omnibus prout predictus Thomas Daye reddere et facere consuevit. Et dat in gersuma iii s. iiii d." John Shepperd had married Agnes Deye in 1412 (*Ibid.*, 80ᵛ).

[143] *Ibid.*, 124ᵛ.

[144] PRO SC 6-877/22.

in nine cases. Thus, the Asplonds were tenants of some 19 acres in 1370, which were increased to 24 in the second decade of the fifteenth century. By the 1440's the family was controlling over 80 acres. The Beaumeys family held two virgates in 1370, and although their properties declined by the 1390's, they still remained at the virgate level — and continued to do so until the 1440's. The Godfreys held 30 acres in the 1370's, 40 in 1392, and over 60 acres by the second decade of the fifteenth century. The Hemyngtons controlled over 20 acres in 1370, over 30 by 1405 and over 40 in the 1440's. The Houghtons remained at over 20 acres through 1405, while the Hunnes, in the two decades from the 1370's to the 1390's, had grown from 28 acres to 44 acres, and less than 20 years after that they had reached 60 acres. The Lanes never fell below 20 acres, and the Nicholases grew from 18 acres of land and some 27 acres of meadow in 1370 to 60 acres by the second decade of the fifteenth century. The Palmeres rose from 18 acres to just over 30 acres in the early 1400's, and the Scots grew from 37 acres in 1370 to over 90 acres of arable and meadow after 1414. A similar rise was experienced by the Shepperds, who stood in the intermediate range (15 acres) in 1370 but who held some 94 acres — part of which (meadow property) was held jointly with the Scots — by the second decade of the fifteenth century.[145]

To summarize, then. Out of 76 persons appearing as major tenants (over 18 acres) in Holywell from the 1370's to the 1450's, 13 were outsiders, or 17%. On the other hand, 63 were residents, of which 40 persons (53%) represented 11 old families that had been settled from before the Black Death, while the remaining 23 (30%) were all newcomers, representing 12 families that had established residence since the middle of the fourteenth century. Similarly with those peasants holding 10 acres or less during the same period. Out of 62 known persons, 19 were outsiders, or 30.7%. On the other hand, 32 — representing 20 families — were newcomers (51.6%), while only 11 (17.7%) were members of 10 families that had been established since at least the early fourteenth century. In short, major tenures tended to be concentrated in the hands of the older established families, while the lesser properties were dominated by members of newly-arrived families, followed by outsiders.

What was, in effect, crystallizing in Holywell from the late fourteenth century was a group of local peasants who, in both their tenurial and

---

[145] Three other families stayed above 10 acres from the 1370's until their disappearances: the Reves — gone by 1405 — the Ravens (emigrated without permission by the 1390's) and the Cranfelds — gone by 1390.

administrative involvements, were nothing less than yeomen. They were not specifically labelled "yeomen" in surviving records, but this does not alter the fact that they were in reality occupying a position characteristic of the emerging yeomanry throughout England at the time. Granted that most — if not indeed all — of the major local tenants in Holywell were legally unfree, this in itself does not prevent their being classified as yeomen. It has long been recognized that although the strict sixteenth-century definition of a yeoman was a "40 shilling freeholder", in actual fact not all yeomen were freeholders,[146] and that the best application, of the term is as a description of status in rural society.[147] Specifically, the yeoman is understood to have been a peasant "identified with the soil and its interests",[148] and especially a man whose proprietary interests were, when compared with his community as a whole, extensive — usually exceeding 30 acres.[149] In fifteenth-century Holywell, at least this qualification was met by 21 men.[150] If, further, the sixteenth-century requirement of a minimal 40 shilling annual income is applied to these Holywell tenants, it will be found that they qualified on this point as well. Not that any precise record of their incomes has survived, but it can be suggested that their individual rent obligations provide a clue as to their income, accounting, as they do, for a part of their annual expenses. Thus, prior to 1419, it is known that John AtteWelle was owing rents of 25 s., John Edward (II) 20 s., Richard Edward 38 s., Nicholas Godfrey 27 s., Roger Houghton 41 s., Thomas Hunne 30 s., John Palmere 45 s., John Scot 35 s., and John Shepperd Sr. 55 s., while, after 1419, rents usually equalled a shilling an acre, so that all the above tenants were obligated to rents of at least 30 shillings *per annum*.

---

[146] This fact was early noted by R. H. Tawney, *The Agrarian Problem in the Sixteenth Century* (New York, n.d. orig. pub. 1912), p. 28, and subsequently emphasized by Mildred Campbell, *The English Yeoman under Elizabeth and the Early Stuarts* (New Haven, 1942), p. 16, who pointed out that "the freeman or free tenant of the earlier period ... formed merely the nucleus of the yeoman's ancestors and were by no means his only ones." G. M. Trevelyan, *Illustrated English Social History*, Vol. I (London, 1954), observed that the yeoman could be either a freeholder, a capitalist farmer, or a peasant with secure tenure holding at an unalterable rent, while Alec Myers, *England in the Late Middle Ages*, p. 135, has stated that the term can be used to describe "prosperous peasants generally, whether freeholders, customary tenants or tenants at will."

[147] See Campbell, p. 27; Tawney, p. 28.

[148] Campbell, p. 27.

[149] Hallam, "The Agrarian Economy of South-Lincolnshire ..." equates the peasants holding over 30 acres with the "class of yeomanry" (p. 93).

[150] John Elyot, William Hunne, John Neaumays, John Attewelle, John Bate, John Cristemesse, Roger Christemesse, John Edward (II), John Edward (III), Thomas Edward, Richard Edward, Nicholas Godfrey, John Hemyngton, Adam Hemyngton, Roger Houghton, Thomas Hunne, Thomas Merton, Thomas Nicholas, John Palmere, John Scot, John Shepperd.

Finally, the late fourteenth and fifteenth-century yeoman was further characterized by the occupation and exercise of a specific administrative responsibility in his locality. Particularly, it has been stated, that in places where there was no resident gentry, "the yeomen were the obvious leaders in the community".[151] Here, too, the Holywell group noted above qualified, with all but two men exercising positions of official responsibility in the community more than once, from jurors to beadles, ale tasters to *collectores redditus*.[152] In terms, therefore, of local occupation, capital, place in village affairs and even of activity in property transfers and acquisitions,[153] Holywell from the late fourteenth century witnessed the local enactment of a scene from a larger drama being played throughout England at the time: the emergence and crystallization of a group of villagers displaying the characteristics of the yeoman. However, the term "yeoman", despite its frequent application to fourteenth- and fifteenth-century England, is, with all its legal and social ramifications, more properly the creature of the sixteenth and seventeenth centuries. Therefore, although it can be used for the late mediaeval period, it is perhaps more accurate to refrain from definitely classifying men such as the AtteWelles, the Edwards, the Scots and others as "yeomen", but rather to settle on calling them "proto-yeomen". If not, strictly speaking, yeomen in name, they were nevertheless an unmistakable part of the nucleus of that social group which, throughout the country, was swiftly evolving into the full-fledged yeomanry of the Tudor era.

But whether related to the emergence of the yeoman group or not, Holywell-cum-Needingworth was, from the late fourteenth century through the first half of the fifteenth century, the scene of a steady transformation in tenurial structure. Despite the increased availability of land resulting from population decline and the abbey's abandonment of demesne cultiva-

---

[151] Campbell, p. 61, and esp. Chapter IX, p. 314 *et seq.* where the domination of local official positions by the yeomanry is emphasized.

[152] John Elyot was not recorded as holding any offices prior to 1457, William Hunne held but one, and John Beaumeys two. The number of official involvements for the others are as follows: John AtteWelle — 10, John Bate — 3, John Cristemesse — 5, Roger Cristemesse — 6, John Edward (II) — 6, John Edward (III) — 10, Thomas Edward — 5, Richard Edward — 6, Nicholas Godfrey — 15, John Hemyngton — 9, Adam Hemyngton — 10, Roger Houghton — 9, Thomas Hunne — 3, Thomas Merton — 8, Thomas Nicholas — 5, John Palmere — 14, John Scot — 7, John Shepperd — 9.

For further discussion of the question of official responsibility in Holywell, see *infra*, Chapter III, p. 206 *et seq.*

[153] Campbell, pp. 72-73, has noted that the yeoman group was characterized by a consistent traffiking in land.

tion, shares in land had not been equalized throughout the village. The proportion of smallholders still remained large, and if the sheer number of persons occupying the top rungs of the tenurial ladder had not increased to any major degree, the top of that ladder had been extended to new heights. Aided by recurrent vacancies and a gradual turning-away from familial and perpetual commitments to properties throughout the village, large blocs of land were concentrated in the hands of particularly industrious and opportunistic peasants to an extent impossible one hundred years earlier. It was, indeed, a time of challenge, but the challenge was most effectively — and profitably — met by the already prosperous peasant. The result for the ambitious and capable peasant was a new level of prosperity, a higher level of wealth. For the less prosperous peasant — who could be just as ambitious — the result was not necessarily abject poverty or devastating misery, but it may be wondered if it did not provide a check on his ambitions. Whereas in the early fourteenth century the acquisition of a cotland or, more especially, a virgate — in short, from 10 to 20 acres — could have raised him and his family to a major position in the village, the attainment of similar properties after the 1370's, but especially after the first decade of the fifteenth century, would have brought him only to an intermediate position. The gulf separating the highest from the lowest ranks of tenants had grown wider — and possibly even more difficult and expensive to cross — than ever before.

Chapter III

FAMILIES IN HOLYWELL-CUM-NEEDINGWORTH:
PATTERNS OF SETTLEMENT AND PLACE IN THE VILLAGE

In the preceding two chapters attention was directed to an investigation of Holywell peasants as tenants from the 1250's to the 1450's. Since records of land and land tenure were the earliest to survive for the Middle Ages, and since land itself plays a major role in the lives of any peasant group, this was not inappropriate. However, the picture thereby obtained — of a peasantry stratified into categories of large, middling and small tenants, of major and minor tenant families, of tenacity, resilience and enterprise relative to land — is neither a complete nor even a reasonably approximate picture of the totality of peasant life in late mediaeval Holywell-cum-Needingworth. As frequently indicated, the number of persons and families involved in land-holding at any one time between the 1250's and the 1450's did not exhaust the number of persons and families residing in the village. In addition, it must be recognized that, given the limited amount of land divided into tenements and the infrequent and sparse evidence of any excessive fragmentation of tenements, the number of persons and families neither directly nor deeply involved in the manorial and tenurial structure was not insignificant. Furthermore, even among peasants heavily committed to land and the manorial organization, the totality of their energies was not exclusively expended in purely agricultural affairs: the Holywell peasant was not a man who was "wound-up" every morning at dawn and sent out into the fields where he remained until dusk. In short, he was not only a tenant — if he was a tenant at all. He was also a member of a family group, of a tithing group, sometimes of an occupational group, and, in some cases, of an activity group in local government. He was, in effect, a member of a village community, and it is this village community, with its networks of interpersonal relationships, its governmental institutions, its human and economic structures, that is seldom — if ever — revealed by the demesne-oriented, tenure-conscious records originating from the manorial administration. Nevertheless, despite the disregard of the village by manorial records, the village was just as important a part — and in some cases an even more important part — of the peasant's experience as the manor.

Fortunately for the student, the fact of the village and its variety ot institutions — whether personal, economic or governmental — is nof

merely a subject of speculation. The survival of "manorial" court rolls
provides him with some record of and guide to village life in the later
Middle Ages.[1] It remains an imperfect record and guide, since court
roll series are not always continuous, while, further, even those which
do survive are not exhaustive catalogues of village and peasant experience.
Indeed, that a full picture of any mediaeval community can ever be realized
is admittedly a more than remote probability. Human emotions and
motives for action, for example, are not easily found in any documents
of an administrative or legal nature, and the mediaeval peasant has left
the modern investigator no directly written or dictated records of his
experience — no chronicles, no "Paston Letters", no individual works
of major literary art. Nevertheless, the manorial court rolls, concerned
as they were with a variety of village institutions — from the regulation
and enforcement of manorial and community custom, inter-personal
relationships of an economic nature, public order, to even the protection
of individual rights and obligations — are an extremely important means
for extending the historical perceptions of the peasantry beyond the narrow
limits imposed by account rolls, surveys, extents or charters, where the
peasant is frequently either a cipher or a name but invariably only a
tenant and a cog in the great wheel of the manorial organization. Through
court rolls, he can be at least partially rescued from this anonymity and
seen more clearly as a human being of flesh and blood, who brews ale,
complains of trespasses on his property, beats his neighbor's wife, practices
a trade, cooperates (or does not cooperate) with his neighbors in matters
of work or investment, marries, buys, sells or leases land, or stands as
surety for his friends. But perhaps most important of all is the evidence
court rolls provide of the fact of the village itself as a human community,
an institution whose governmental, economic and social structures both
influenced and engaged the lives of its peasants in ways barely even indicated

---

[1] For a highly useful survey of the importance of manorial court rolls for the study of mediaeval
English village society, see J. A. Raftis, "Social Structures in Five East Midland Villages," *Economic History Review*, 2nd. series. XVIII (No. 1, 1965), pp. 83-100.

Although traditionally described as "manorial" court rolls, the courts themselves covered
a variety of business only a small part of which was manor or demesne-oriented (*exodus* of *nativi*,
work derelictions, trespasses on the demesne), while the lord of the manor received the profits
of justice. Otherwise, court business involved both national (ale assizes, the keeping of the watch,
the frankpledge system) and local village institutions (personal trespasses, debts, land transfers,
etc.) and might just as easily — and with more precision — be termed "village" court rolls. In
support of this may be cited the fact that the heading of the court rolls themselves — giving the
location and date of the session — always employed the formula "Visus (or Curia) apud Halywell ..." and not "apud manerium de Halywell."

by demesne- and production-oriented manorial records, and within which the peasant is revealed more fully as an individual, not merely as a tenant, whose life, although affected in varying degrees by the manor, was not exclusively absorbed by it.

The main purpose, therefore, of this and the subsequent chapter is to examine that aspect of the Holywell peasant's life in the later Middle Ages that was not irrevocably bound to the manor and the tenurial commitments to that institution, but whose focal point was rather the village community. This is not meant to block-off the manor or to ignore its influence. On the contrary, familial status in the village was frequently and closely related to involvement in the customary structure, while such matters as the extent to which customary law was applied in the court and even the social importance of individuals themselves were either dependent on, or coloured by, the degree to which villagers were involved in the manor and were villeins of the abbot of Ramsey. What is meant, however, is to attempt to reveal further dimensions to the peasant's life, dimensions that found their fullest expression not within the manorial and tenurial structures but within the village, of which the manor was a part. To accomplish this, investigation shall draw heavily on information supplied in the surviving Holywell court rolls from the late thirteenth century and into the 1450's. Admittedly, the survival of such records for Holywell has not been suffocating. The rolls of only 53 court sessions between 1288 and 1456 have been preserved,[2] but they are continuous enough that no decade except the 1340's remains unrepresented between the 1280's and the 1450's. Thus, there is one roll from the 1280's,[3] three from the 1290's,[4] three from the first decade of the fourteenth century,[5] three from the second,[6] three from the 1320's,[7] five from the 1330's,[8] four

---

[2] The total of 53 sessions is further broken-down into 39 views of frankpledge (*visi franciplegii*) and 14 *curiae*. For further elaboration of this question, see *supra*, Introduction.

[3] PRO SC 2-179/5. *Visus* of 16 October, 1288.

[4] BM.Add.Roll 34337: 1292; BM.Add.Roll 39597: *Visus*, 25 January, 1294; and PRO SC 2-179/10: *Visus*, 10 December, 1299.

[5] PRO SC 2-179/11: *Visus*, 17 October, 1301; PRO SC 2-179/12: *Visus*, 4 February, 1306; PRO SC 2-179/15: *Visus*, 1307.

[6] PRO SC 2-179/16: *Visus*, 16 December, 1311; PRO SC 2-179/17: *Visus*, 27 January, 1313; PRO SC 2-179/18: *Visus*, 28 (?) January, 1318.

[7] PRO SC 2-179/21: *Visus*, 23 October, 1322; PRO SC 2-179/22: *Visus*, 6 December, 1326; PRO SC 2-179/25: *Visus*, 14 December (?), 1328.

[8] PRO SC 2-179/26: *Visus*, 1332; PRO SC 2-179/29: *Visus* and *Curia*, 1338; PRO SC 2-179/30: *Visus* and *Curia*, 31 December, 1339.

from the 1350's,[9] two from the 1360's,[10] three from the 1370's,[11] three from the 1380's,[12] four from the 1390's,[13] seven from the first decade of the fifteenth century,[14] two from the second,[15] two from the 1420's,[16] three from the 1430's,[17] one from the 1440's,[18] and three from the 1450's.[19] Furthermore, these rolls supply over 2900 individual entries concerning over 800 individual Holywell peasants, ranging from names of officials to pleas of debt, trespass, assault, infractions of brewing regulations, licenses for marriage and for permission to leave the manor, work derelictions, and other miscellaneous business.[20] Their number and content permit investigation of at least the following questions: people, families and groups in late mediaeval Holywell, their settlement patterns and place in the village, their involvement in local occupations and government, and, on a broader scale, patterns of inter-personal and inter-group cooperation and intra-village harmony and cohesion. The present chapter shall concern itself with questions of family and group activities in Holywell from the late thirteenth to the mid-fifteenth century, while Chapter Four shall focus on an investigation of patterns of cooperation and cohesion within the village.

[9] PRO SC 2-179/35: *Visus*, 24 October, 1353; PRO SC 2-179/35: *Curia*, July, 1354; PRO SC 2-179/36: *Visus*, 27 October, 1356; BM.Add.Roll 39583: *Visus*, 15 October, 1359.

[10] BM.Add.Roll 39860: *Curia*, 16 July, 1364; PRO SC 2-179/38: *Curia*, 19 July, 1369.

[11] PRO SC 2-179/39: *Visus*, 25 October, 1372; PRO SC 2-179/40: *Visus*, 29 October, 1375; PRO SC 2-179/41: *Visus*, 29 October, 1378.

[12] PRO SC 2-179/42: *Curia*, 16 July, 1386; BM.Add.Roll.: *Visus*, 8 October, 1386; PRO SC 2-179/42: *Curia*, 26 July, 1389.

[13] PRO SC 2-179/43: *Visus*, 23 October, 1391; PRO SC 2-179/44: 2 November, 1394: PRO SC 2-179/44: *Visus*, 24 April, 1396; BM.Add. Roll. 34817: *Curia*, 21 July, 1398.

[14] PRO SC 2-179/45: *Visus*, 15 October, 1400; PRO SC 2-179/47: *Curia*, 21 July, 1402; PRO SC 2-179/48: *Curia*, 27 June, 1403, and *Visus*, 3 October, 1403; PRO SC 2-179/49: *Curia*, 29 July, 1405; PRO SC 2-179/50: *Visus*, 15 October, 1405; PRO SC 2-179/52: *Visus*, 28 October, 1409.

[15] PRO SC 2-179/54: *Visus*, 25 October, 1413; PRO SC 2-179/54: *Curia*, 27 July, 1419.

[16] PRO SC 2-179/57: *Visus*, 24 November, 1423; PRO SC 2-179/59: *Visus*, 26 July, 1428.

[17] BM.Add.Roll. 39480: *Curia*, 12 July, 1430; PRO SC 2-179/61: *Visus*, 15 October, 1432; PRO SC 2-179/63: *Visus*, 29 November, 1437.

[18] PRO SC 2-179/64: *Visus*, 11 November, 1443.

[19] PRO SC 2-179/66: *Visus*, 2 October, 1452; BM.Add.Roll. 34322: *Visus*, 18 June, 1455; PRO SC 2-179/67: *Visus*, 26 July, 1457.

[20] "Entry" here means simply a separate item in a court roll. Under the term of "miscellaneous business" are included cases of gleaning offenses, licenses of concord, defaults, essoins, and the recording of village by-laws.

I

"Families in Holywell-cum-Needingworth: Patterns of Settlement 1300-1450"

Any attempt to precisely determine the population of Holywell-cum-Needingworth at any period from the late thirteenth century to the middle of the fifteenth century is an exercise in futility and frustration. As with virtually all other mediaeval communities — whether rural or urban — a complete census is out of the question. In addition, the inclusion of only tenants in the 1252 extent, the truncated nature of the 1279 Hundred Roll survey, the failure of account rolls prior to 1370 to record customary tenants, and the absence of the Poll Tax returns for Huntingdonshire in 1377 seriously inhibit even a general estimate of population along traditional lines.[21] Nevertheless, the existence of two subsidy returns for 1327 and 1332, the break-down of tenants supplied by account rolls from 1370, the Court Book, and, most importantly, the survival of court rolls beginning in the late 1200's, provide some tools for at least attempting to determine the number of families resident in the village during the fourteenth and first half of the fifteenth centuries. In addition, since these records supply the names of over 800 individual Holywell adult peasants from the 1250's to the 1450's, it is further possible to offer some suggestions as to the minimal number of adults most probably in residence as well.

Between the 1250's and the 1450's, record has survived of at least 140 families[22] maintaining themselves in residence in Holywell-cum-Needingworth for anywhere from two years to over two-hundred years.[23] By 1300, there were 66 separate families resident in the village. The next 10 years witnessed the disappearance of eight of these families, but the immigration of 15 new families, with the result that by 1310 73 families were settled in the community. There then began a decline in the number

---

[21] For a discussion of the use of extents, accounts, the Hundred Rolls and the Poll Tax returns in estimating mediaeval population in England, see J. C. Russell, *British Medieval Population* (Albuquerque, 1948), pp. 17-147. For a more succint summary of current methods in estimating mediaeval English population, see Postan, CEH, I, pp. 561-63.

[22] By "families" is meant groups of persons with a common surname who further display ties of blood or marriage.

[23] The sources of information for the number of families are those already cited: the extent of 1252, the 1279 Hundred Roll, the fourteenth and fifteenth-century accounts, the fifteenth-century Court Book and the court rolls from 1288 to 1456. Upwards to 50 % of the families known come from court rolls alone.

of settled families that was to continue into the middle of the fifteenth century. In the decade between 1310 and 1320 — a decade during which the English countryside as a whole was ravaged by serious famines between 1314 and 1317 — 12 families disappeared, while only six new families took up residence, thereby bringing the number of families settled in 1323 down to 67. (See Table I). The decline continued, with the loss of 17 families between 1320 and 1340 as contrasted with the acquisition by the village of only 11 replacement families, while the further loss of 15 families — and the replacement of only six — between the plague-infected years from 1340 to 1360, brought the number down to 52 by 1360. For forty years thereafter, the downward trend in settlement was arrested. For the first time since 1310, the number of families taking up residence in the village outweighed the number disappearing, so that by 1390 the families resident in Holywell had risen to 61 (See Table I).

TABLE I

FAMILIES IN HOLYWELL-CUM-NEEDINGWORTH, 1300-1450

Year	Old	New	Disappeared	Total
1300	66	—	—	66
1310	58	15	8	73
1320	61	6	12	67
1330	59	6	8	65
1340	56	5	9	61
1360	46	6	15	52
1370	48	5	4	53
1380	47	12	6	59
1390	57	4	2	61
1400	46	4	15	50
1410	40	1	10	41
1420	35	3	6	38
1430	33	3	5	36
1440	31	2	5	33
1450	30	2	3	32

That this new wave of immigration to Holywell occurred simultaneously with the abbey's attempts to stimulate a profitable period of demesne cultivation by increasing the availability of land and fen for money rent[24] was in all probability more than coincidental. The drop in resident families by 1360, coupled with what appears to have been an escape from the

[24] See *supra*, Chapter II, p. 112 *et seq.*

more catastrophic economic effects of the plague,[25] no doubt made Holywell moderately attractive to outsiders in more devastated localities. By the release of parts of the demesne and the bulk of the fen, this attraction no doubt increased, and the result was the immigration of 21 new families within 30 years. However, just as the abbey's hopes for increased profits and productivity from the revived demesne cultivation were short-lived, so too was the arrest of the decline in settlement. By 1400, 15 families had disappeared — more in a decade than had been lost in the 30 years between 1360 and 1390 — while the immigration, or replacement, rate had dropped as well. As Table I shows, in the 50 years from 1400 to 1450, the village lost a total of 29 families, of which only 11, or 38%, were replaced, until by 1450 the number of families settled in the village had reached a low point of 32. In short, in the 150 years between 1300 and 1450, the number of families in Holywell had dropped by 52%. In addition, the years between 1310 and 1330 and the decade of 1390 to 1400 were especially crucial. The former marked the beginning of the decline in settlement — with a greater drop in village families between 1310 and 1340 than occurred during the plague-infected years from 1340 to 1370. Similarly, the 10 years from 1390 to 1400 witnessed, after a mild recovery in settlement, the inauguration of the second downward trend that continued unarrested past the middle of the fifteenth century.

A decline in the number of families settled in Holywell in the fourteenth and early fifteenth centuries does not of itself necessarily indicate a decline in overall population as such. A decrease in the number of families does not always mean a decrease in the size of families, for example. However, there is additional evidence to indicate that Holywell was indeed the scene of serious population decline from the second decade of the fourteenth century, and that, consequently, the village was being affected by a demographic set-back that was common throughout England from as early as the last decade of the 1200's.[26] This may first be seen in an estimate

---

[25] See *supra*, Chapter I, p. 31.

[26] The literature on the English demographic decline of the fourteenth century is vast, but more recent and useful studies are: Postan, CEH, I, pp. 560-70; "Some Economic Evidence of Declining Population in the later Middle Ages," *Economic History Review*, 2nd. series, II (1949-50), pp. 221-47; "Heriots and Prices on Winchester Manors," *Economic History Review*, 2nd. series. XI (1959) (with J. Z. Titow); K. F. Helleiner, "Population Movement and Agrarian Depression in the Later Middle Ages," *Canadian Journal of Economics and Political Science*, XV (1950), and, more recently, CEH, IV, Chapter One; J. C. Russell, *British Medieval Population*, pp. 246-81; J. M. W. Bean, "Plague, Population and Economic Decline in England in the Later Middle Ages," *Economic History Review*, 2nd. series, XV, pp. 423-37; and Sylvia Thrupp, "The Problem of Replacement-Rates in Late Medieval English Population," *Economic History Review*, 2nd. series, XVIII (1965), pp. 101-19.

of the number of adults[27] actually known to be in residence in the village at given points over the years (See Table II). Unfortunately, no estimate of the total human population is really practical. The number of children, for example — boys or girls under 12 years of age — is virtually unknown, given the uncertainty of determining infant and child mortality,[28] and it is further highly unproductive to speculate. In addition, surviving documents did not necessarily record every person living in the community. As already noted, the extent and account rolls concerned themselves exclusively with tenants — and then only with the tenant himself, not the members of his household. Tax lists of subsidies assessed on movables in 1327 and 1332 accounted only for persons above a minimal exemption point, and even then the number of persons able to evade the tax altogether could be high.[29] Finally, court rolls — although a most comprehensive source

TABLE II

NUMBER OF RESIDENT ADULTS IN HOLYWELL-CUM-NEEDINGWORTH, 1300-1450

Year	Adults
1300	251
1327	172
1332	177
1360	120
1370	131
1380	140
1390	142
1400	134
1410	129
1420	112
1430	116
1440	100
1450	91

[27] Adult is here understood to mean any male over the age of 12, the age at which males were bound to be in a tithing group, and, consequently, were legally responsible. For the sake of convenience alone, the same age has been employed in the case of females as well, since it is more than likely that when a woman is mentioned in a court roll as a brewster, a gleaner or a participant in a hue and cry she is at least past her twelfth year.

[28] See Russell, pp. 208-14.

[29] For a discussion of the demographic problems presented by the early fourteenth-century subsidy rolls, see J. F. Willard, *Parliamentary Taxes on Personal Property, 1290 to 1334: A Study in Mediaeval English Financial Administration* (Cambridge, Mass. 1934), pp. 174-82. Unfortunately, the one tax record which attempted to include at least all persons — male and female — above the age of 14, and which may have suffered from only a small percentage of under-enumeration — the Poll Tax of 1377 (See Russell, pp. 120-121, 124-30) — is missing for Huntingdonshire.

of information on local people — are useful for estimating population only if a fairly close series has survived, but although reasonably close groupings have been preserved for Holywell, it cannot be pretended that every adult villager was accounted for, since only those who had business before the court were noted. Consequently, an attempt to estimate the total population of Holywell in specific years is subject to many dangers. All that can be fruitfully suggested are listings of numbers of known adults, mindful throughout that the proposed figures are by necessity *under-enumerations* of adult population as well as total population. However, although the adult population figures are under-enumerations, it is not unlikely that they do not under-enumerate by too much. The intimacy of village life and the wide range of business brought before the court, for example, suggest that the majority of adults in the community did in fact have their names recorded at one time or another in its rolls, whether as officials, law-breakers, suitors or complainants. Furthermore, the method of calculation used has attempted to correct possible under-estimation by not being confined to one document only for a specific year. Thus, in the figure for 1300, although there is no court roll or account roll for that year, the court rolls of 1292, 1294, 1299, 1301, 1306 and 1307, as well as the account roll of 1307/8, have been utilized in such a way that any person present in the village in the 1290's who was present also in the seven years after 1300 has been counted as being present in 1300. In addition, where evidence exists of a man having sons or daughters, it is assumed also that he has a wife. Similarly, with the figures for 1327 and 1332, not only have the names from the subsidy rolls for those years been counted, but also those of persons noted in court rolls both before and after the years in question. What results, therefore, are more than likely lists of the numbers of resident adults that, although imperfect and probably short of the actual total numbers, are not short by too great a margin.

From Table II, then, it can be seen that in 1300 there were a definitely known 251 adults resident in Holywell. Assuming an under-enumeration of total population of about 20%, a probable overall population of just over 300 is obtained. [30] By 1327, on the other hand, the decline that had

---

[30] 251 is the exact number that would have resulted had the number of families — 66 — been multiplied by Russell's figure of 3.8. (See *British Medieval Population*, p. 31. Although Russell proposes 3.5. as a multiplier for households, he believes the index in pre-plague years was probably closer to 3.8. Thus, 66 × 3.8 = 250.7 = 251.) However, Russell's multiplier was designed to account for households — wives and children — and therefore, it can be seen that it would have been inadequate for Holywell, since 251 was the number of known adults. Therefore, J. Krause's

first been noted among settled families in 1320 was observable in the reduced number of known adults in the village: 172.[31] In subsequent years, the size of the known adult population declined, as did the number of settled families, with an arrest and a mild recovery between 1370 and 1400. Thereafter, a second decade of decline set in, until by 1450 the size of the known adult population in the village — as well as the estimated total population — had declined by 64 % from 1300.

It is definite, then, that Holywell was experiencing a decline in resident population from as early as the second decade of the fourteenth century and on into the 1450's. What remains indefinite are the reasons for the decline, although there are some clearly observable patterns in family settlement and family sizes that can be noted. If, in the final analysis, they do not completely explain the phenomenon, they at least throw light on its development.

One obvious factor in the decline of Holywell's population during the fourteenth and first half of the fifteenth centuries lies in the settlement patterns of individual families. As already noted, between the 1250's and the 1450's, some 140 separate families took up residence in the village. Not all were present simultaneously, however, and not all established what was to become, in effect, permanent residence: that is, residence for three generations or longer, or in excess of 80 years. Specifically, out of 132 local village families, 49 may be classified as having been permanently settled (35 %), or for three generations or longer (See Table III). An additional 32 families maintained residence for two generations, or from just over 40 to 80 years (23 %) (See Table III), while a total of 51 families (36 %) remained settled no longer than a generation, or for less than 40 years (See Table III). Eight additional families (6 %) cannot be classified as either long, intermediate or short-term residents because they first appeared in the village only after the 1420's, and the absence of consistent

---

proposal of a multiplier of 4.5 ("The Medieval Household: large or small ?" *Economic History Review.* 2nd. series IX (1956-57), p. 420 *et seq.*) is undoubtedly closer to estimating overall population, since 66 multiplied by 4.5. gives 297. In all probability, the number of persons in the village — adults as well as children — was a little over 300. Consequently, it may be suggested that the tabulations of adult population in Table II underestimate overall population by about 20 %.

[31] It should be noted here that the years 1327 and 1332 provide a good example of the drawbacks of using such sources as subsidy rolls. The roll for 1327 accounted for only 47 tax-paying adults — or 27 % of the known number. That of 1332 listed only 60 persons, or 34 %. If Russell's multiplier of 3.8. had been applied in each case, the result for 1327 would have been close to the number of adults (47 × 3.8 = 178.6), but since the process is for estimating total population, it would have been short. In 1332, on the other hand, the result would have been nearer the probable total population: 40 × 3.8 = 228.

TABLE III
FAMILIES IN HOLYWELL-CUM-NEEDINGWORTH

FAMILY	EARLIEST DATE	LAST DATE	RESIDENCE GROUP
ALEYN	1288	1353	II
ARNOLD	1378	1455	II
ASPLOND	1294	1457+	I
ATTEWELLE	1356	1454	I
AVENAUNT	1288	1301	III
AYLBERN	1322	1328	III
AYSE	1252	1326	II
BACOUN	1252	1301	II
BALDEWYNE	1313	1372	II
BAKER	1392	1457	II
BARKER	1307	1391	I
BAROUN	1313	1457	I
BATE	1400	1456	II
BEAUMEYS	1307	1457	I
BERNEWELL	1306	1402	I
BERCAR'/SHEPPERD	1288	1457+	I
BOLOYGNE	1322	1339	III
BOTWRYTE	1306	1356	II
BENEYT	1252	1288	III
BRADENACH	1372	1391	III
BRAYN	1288	1419	I
BROOK	1288	1424	I
BRYAN	1339	1438	I
BRUN	1288	1339	II
BUNDELEG	1275	1332	II
BURTON	1437	—	IV
CALDECOTE	1313	1375	II
CAMPION	1353	1356	III
CAPPE	1292	1318	III
CAPUD VILLE	1294	1313	III
CARTERE	1288	1418	I
CARPENTER	1294	1346	II
CLAROT	1326	1353	III
CLAVIGER	1288	1294	III
CLERVAUS	1279	1326	III
COLYERE	1288	1307	III
COLYN	1292	1326	III
CONSE	1306	1339	III
CLERK	1252	1339	I
CRISTEMESSE	1362	1457+	I
CROUCH/CRUCEM	1332	1370	III
CURPEL	1306	1311	III
CURTEYS	1294	1416	I
CUSSTE	1301	1353	II

Family	Earliest Date	Last Date	Residence Group
CRANFELD	1307	1370	II
DEYE	1318	1457	I
EDWARD	1292	1457+	I
ELENE	1301	1313	III
ELYOT	1443	—	IV
ESSEX	1370	1392	III
EYR	1252	1400	I
FABER/SMYTH	1279	1456	I
FANNELL	1294	1419	I
FISHERE	1299	1328	III
FLESSHEWERE	1353	1392	III
FRANCEYS	1288	1301	III
FRANKLYN	1279	1362	I
FREYSANT	1288	1332	II
FYCHYEN	1288	1299	III
GERE	1252	1356	I
GEROLD	1322	1339	III
GODALE	1288	1307	III
GODEMAN	1288	1397	I
GODFREY	1252	1457+	I
GODRYCH	1252	1370	I
GODSOULE	1400	1420	III
GRAY	1252	1438	I
GUNNE	1288	1313	III
GYBBE	1307	1402	I
HAMOND	1288	1400	I
HARDY	1370	1418	II
HALIDAY	1375	1392	III
HEMYNGTON	1322	1457+	I
HILDEGAR	1250	1299	II
HOUGHTON	1252	1409	I
HROFF	1338	1400	II
HUNNE	1252	1457+	I
KYLLENETH	1288	1294	III
KYNG	1362	1440	II
LANE	1252	1402	I
LANENDER	1416	1454	III
LAWEMAN	1252	1372	I
LEGGE	1294	1339	II
MADDE	1294	1372	III
MARIOT	1299	1307	III
MARTYN	1419	—	IV
MAY	1279	1313	III
MACHYNG	1339	1418	I
MERTON	1356	1443	I
MOKE	1301	1378	II
MOREL	1252	1294	II
MILLER	1299	1448	I

Family	Earliest Date	Last Date	Residence Group
Muryell	1400	1429	III
Newerk	1372	1391	III
Nicholas	1306	1457	I
Oky	1428	1452	III
Palfreyman	1406	1423	III
Palmere	1306	1437	I
Pellepar/Skynnere	1306	1372	II
Pollard	1279	1311	III
Portam	1279	1318	II
Porter	1372	1418	II
Prepositus/Reve	1252	1410	I
Prondhele	1299	1339	III
Pope	1370	1402	III
Pye	1288	1307	III
"Radulphi"	1292	1332	III
Raulyn	1306	1353	II
Ravene	1332	1404	II
Reynold	1338	1370	III
Ripton	1252	1346	I
Rille	1375	1391	III
Russell	1252	1356	I
Sande	1370	1454	I
Scharp	1353	1418	II
Scot	1252	1457+	I
Selde	1372	1451	II
Selede	1252	1353	I
Semen	1294	1307	III
Sewale	1353	1456+	I
Sewyn	1370	1400	III
Slogh	1386	1396	III
Sky	1288	1318	III
Snowe	1394	1423	III
Spercoll	1288	1402	I
Tayllour	1339	1443	I
Thatcher	1370	1386	III
Thurberne	1437	—	IV
Thurkyll	1288	1318	III
Toly	1252	1318	II
Tony	1307	1328	III
Tiffayne	1288	1353	II
Touslond	1443	—	IV
Valentyn	1432	—	IV
Venelle	1252	1339	I
Walmesford	1288	1299	III
Webbester	1400	1405	III
Wilkyn	1427	—	IV
Wodecok	1430	—	IV
Wright	1318	1451	I

records after 1456 makes it impossible to accurately determine the lengths of their settlements. (See Table III).

At first glance the fact that 51 of Holywell's known 140 families from the mid-thirteenth to the mid-fifteenth century failed to maintain residence for longer than a generation appears sobering. However, even among the 51 short-term families, only 11 (22 %) remained for less than a decade — or 8% of all the known families settling in the village. Twenty-one families managed to stay from 11 to 20 years (41 %), while 19 remained from three to four decades (37 %). Indeed, what is perhaps more significant is the fact that a total of 69 families (49 %) established and maintained residence for longer than 50 years, and that 37 families (26%) even passed the century-mark (See Table IV).[32]

TABLE IV

FAMILY SETTLEMENT PERIODS (IN DECADES)

Term	Number of Families
1-10 Years	11
11-20 Years	21
21-30 Years	9
31-40 Years	40
41-50 Years	11
51-60 Years	8
61-70 Years	7
71-80 Years	6
81-90 Years	7
91-99 Years	4
100-200 Years	34
201 Years+	3

The failure of 51 families to maintain residence for longer than a generation, and the settlement of 32 additional families for more than one but less than three generations between the 1250's and the 1450's, must be taken into consideration, however, in any attempt to investigate the decline in resident population in the village throughout the fourteenth and first half of the fifteenth centuries. The fact that not a decade passed from 1300 to 1450 in which at least two families did not disappear from the village (See Table I) need not have been injurious to overall settlement — as

[32] It should be further noted that of the 49 permanent families, 37 were able to attain a major position of importance in the administrative life of the village, whereas the majority of minor families — those not involved in local government or administration — were of short-term residence.

long as the village could count on gaining at least an equal number of new persons or families through immigration to replace its losses. However, this was something the village could not count on, in fact. In only four decades did the number of incoming families and persons exceed the numbers that had been lost: 1300-1310, 1360-1370, 1370-1380 and 1380-1390.[33] In all other decades, immigration failed to fill the gaps left in the village's population.

If immigration to Holywell did not remedy its demographic problems, emigration from Holywell does not seem to have been one of their major causes either. The leaving of their home manors to seek employment, land, marriage and even education by villeins was a well-established practice throughout the Ramsey estates from the latter thirteenth century,[34] and the abbey had made provisions for regularizing this emigration at an early date.[35] The names of persons consequently given permission to remain abroad were normally inscribed in the court roll of the view of frankpledge.[36] As a result, it is possible, with a reasonably continuous series of rolls, to tabulate the number of persons living away from the manor — both licitly and illicitly, since the court attempted to take note of fugitive villeins as well as those licensed to emigrate. The resulting total may not necessarily be complete, since rolls have not survived from every year, but it can nevertheless serve as an index to the movement of villeins from their home community.

In fourteenth-century Holywell — from 1311 to 1396 — emigration from the manor was not especially heavy. The number of persons licensed to be abroad in any one year for which records have survived never exceeded four, while, as Table V further shows, the cumulative loss of persons to

---

[33] For the number of families, see Table I. In terms of persons, the village witnessed the disappearance of 13 in 1300-1310 and the acquisition of 30. From 1360-70, six were lost and six gained. Nine disappeared in 1370-80, but 16 more replaced them. Finally, in 1390-1400, six persons were added, where only two had been lost.

[34] For a detailed discussion of emigration from Ramsey manors in the late thirteenth, fourteenth and fifteenth centuries, see Raftis, *Tenure and Mobility*, pp. 139-82.

[35] For a frequently nominal annual payment of a chicken or two, Ramsey villeins were given license to be abroad, provided that they maintained their home tithing group affiliation and consequently returned for the view of frankpledge. See Raftis, *Tenure and Mobility*, p. 139.

[36] In rolls of the late thirteenth and early fourteenth centuries, the names of licensed *nativi* usually were placed at the end of the roll. By the second half of the fourteenth century, they were shifted to the beginning section, immediately after the names of the jurors and under the general heading "Chevagium". After 1400, however — when emigration from Ramsey manors suddenly assumed new, high proportions — the names were frequently recorded twice: the beginning of the roll reserved for persons licensed to be off the manor and a section at the end of the roll listing persons abroad illicitly (*sine licentia*).

TABLE V

EMIGRATION OF HOLYWELL CUSTOMARY TENANTS, 1311-1456

FOURTEENTH CENTURY
(1311-1396)

YEAR	MEN	WOMEN	TOTAL (Annual)	CUMULATIVE TOTAL
1311	2		2	2
1313	3	1	4	4
1326	3		3	7
1338	3		3	9
1339	3		3	10
1353		1	1	11
1359	4		4	12
1373	2		2	12
1375	3		3	13
1378	2		2	13
1386	2		2	13
1391	3		3	14
1394	2		2	13
1396	2		2	13

FIFTEENTH CENTURY
(1400-1456)

YEAR	MEN	WOMEN	TOTAL (Annual)	CUMULATIVE TOTAL
1400	8	1	9	9
1402	9	2	11	13
1403	9	2	11	13
1405	11	2	13	17
1409	11	2	13	17
1413	12	2	14	20
1423	9	2	11	20
1428	9	2	11	20
1432	7	2	9	22
1437	7	1	8	22
1443	5		5	26
1452	5	1	6	27
1455	5		5	27
1456	6		6	28

the village — since only one of the persons leaving Holywell during the period covered is known to have returned — was only 13.[37] In addition, of a total of 14 persons leaving the manor between 1311 and 1396, only four did so without permission.[38] The remaining 10 had all sought and received license to be abroad.[39]

With the opening of the fifteenth century, however, Holywell experienced, along with virtually all other Ramsey manors,[40] a sudden and intensified movement of persons off the manor. (See Table V). In 1400, eight people were abroad. Two of the eight had left before 1400.[41] In addition, four persons did not represent villeins who had recently left, but were instead descendents of a previously emigrated villein who appear to have been recorded in an attempt by the abbey to keep an account of even the progeny of fugitive *nativi*.[42] Specifically, in 1400 the homage reported that four members of the Gere family — John, Simon, Alan and Alan Jr. — were abroad. Since the last Geres to be actively present in the village had disappeared by the 1360's,[43] it can only be assumed that they had "jumped" the manor, and that the court took almost 50 years to "catch up" with the fact and then did so with respect to their descendents.

In any event, between 1400 and 1457, Holywell witnessed the loss of a total of 28 persons through emigration, the majority of whom had left without license.[44] However, despite the fact that most were fugitive *nativi*, there was little real effort exerted to recover them. The court roll repeatedly ordered the seizure of all their goods and chattels, but little seems to

---

[37] Reginald Brayn, *nativus* and licensed to be abroad from 1356 through the 1380's, had returned by 1394.

[38] In 1313, Nicholas Godrich had left the manor *sine licentia*, as had Johanna Curteys, who had not only left without permission but married as well (PRO SC 2-179/17). Alexander Cartere had fled by 1326, and John the son of Matthew and done the same in 1339.

[39] Those licensed to be abroad were: from 1311, Adam Godrich and Alexander Brun; from 1326, William Hamond and William Gere; from 1338, John Cartere; from 1339, John the son of Nicholas; from 1353, Joanna Smyth; from 1359, Reginald Brayn; from 1375, Adam Gray; and from 1391, Thomas Smyth.

[40] See Raftis, *Tenure and Mobility*, p. 133.

[41] Adam Gray and Thomas Smyth were reported gone in 1386 and 1391, respectively.

[42] See Raftis, *Tenure and Mobility*, p. 133.

[43] In 1359, William Gere was reported as still being *extra feodum* — where he had been since 1326. He was the last Gere mentioned in local records before the notice in the 1400 court roll, since John Gere, Nicholas Gere and Joanna Gere had been the only members of the family still resident in the 1350's and no trace of them was found after 1356.

[44] All told, out of the 28 persons leaving Holywell between 1400 and 1457, only seven initially did so with permission, and even these seven appear to have consistently defaulted in their obligations to return for the annual view of frankpledge.

have been accomplished by this measure — if, indeed, it was even carried out.[45] In addition, in a great number of cases the whereabouts of the fugitives was known and dutifully set down in the court roll. Indeed, several of the Holywell fugitives had even moved to other Ramsey manors. Thus Andrew Miller was at Chatteris in 1400 and at Upwood in 1402. Alan Gere remained at Chatteris from 1400 through 1403, while Robert Gere was present there from 1405 through 1409, followed by Simon Gere in 1423. Among other Ramsey manors, Over claimed Margaret Raven and her mother from 1402 through 1432, St. Ives William Hunne from 1405 through 1409, Ramsey John Smyth in 1428 to 1432, Chatteris Nicholas Hemyngton in 1428, Abbots Ripton Robert Sande in 1443, whence he had moved to St. Ives by 1452. Thomas Sande was at Warboys before 1443, while John Sande was at Hemmingford Abbots in 1457. Others went to communities that, if not part of the Ramsey complex, were nevertheless either in Huntingdonshire or in nearby counties. In Huntingdonshire, Bluntisham claimed Adam Gray (1400-1409), Colne Thomas Smyth (1400-1405), John Smyth (1400-1405), Broughton claimed John Gere (1405-1413), Somersham John Gere (1428-1437) and St. Neots John Sande (1443). Still others were found in Cambridgeshire and Ely,[46] Northamptonshire[47] and even Kent.[48] The locations of very few, in fact, remained unknown. Only in the cases of Matilda Hunne (1400), John atte Lane (1402), John Raven (1403), Thomas Hunne (1413), Margaret Raven (1437) and Thomas Sande (1443) could the homage report that they were *extra feodum*, "sed ubi ignorant".

The loss of 28 persons by Holywell through emigration over 57 years, although not to be minimized, was nevertheless not very heavy when compared with other Ramsey manors over the same general period. For example, Broughton had lost 31 by 1455, Warboys 52 by 1458, Weston, Brington and Bythorn 54 by 1457, Wistow 42 by 1458, Houghton 51 by 1458, Graveley 33 by 1457, Abbots Ripton 36 by 1455, Therfield 29 by 1455, Barton 59 by 1455, Ellsworth and Knapwell 48 by 1456,

---

[45] The fact that the same command was issued every year indicates it was not being put into practice. Probably the fact that emigrating *nativi* frequently took their chattels with them explains its not being done.

[46] John Smyth was at Ely in 1423, John Gere in Willingham (Camb.) in 1432, John Smyth Jr. in Bassingborne (Camb.) in 1432, whence he moved to Orwell in 1443, where he was both "uxoratus et medicus" (PRO SC -179/64), and Joanna Baker was at Ely in 1452, who may or may not have been "uxorata" but who was with a Walter Coke.

[47] John Raven was at Rothwell, Northants., in 1402.

[48] Alan Gere remained at Ereth in Kent from 1400 through 1413.

and Cranfield 36 by 1458.[49] Indeed, Holywell stood, along with Elton, Upwood, Shillington and Hemmingford Abbots, among the manors that lost the least numbers through emigration.[50] Furthermore, in terms of families, only three appear to have been virtually eliminated or crippled as a result of flight from the manor in the fifteenth century: the AtteLanes, the Ravens and the Sandes. The AtteLanes were totally lost to the village by John atte Lane's flight in 1402, since he was the last known male member of the family line in the village. The Ravens also seem to have left in a body in 1402, almost immediately after the death of John Raven Sr. His widow, daughter Margaret and son John emigrated, having abandoned the paternal inheritance of a virgate, with the two women taking up residence at Over and John, after a short stay at Rothwell in Northamptonshire, disappearing. As for the Sandes, four male members — John, John Jr., Robert and Thomas — had all left Holywell by 1443 for St. Neots, Hemmingford Abbots, Abbots Ripton and Warboys, respectively, leaving only a John Sande Sr. and still one more John Sande Jr., with his wife Alice, in the village. By 1454, John Sr. was dead, and only John Jr. and Alice remained.[51]

During the almost century and a half between 1311 and 1457, then, Holywell had lost a definitely-known grand total of some 38 persons through emigration. In addition, these 38 people had been representatives of 17 separate families, of which only four had seen their place in the village seriously diminished or completely erased as a result of their emigrations. However, such figures can be misleading. For one, it is highly probable that more people actually left the village during the fourteenth and fifteenth centuries than ever were reported in court rolls. The reason for such a statement is, first, the evidence of a large number of transients in Holywell. Over 200 persons came into and moved out again from the village in the course of the 1300's and early 1400's. Some, of course, were purely outsiders, residents of other villages, who simply happened to have some business in Holywell.[52] Others, however, were servants, hired labourers

---

[49] See Raftis, *Tenure and Mobility*, Tables, pp. 160-66.

[50] *Ibid.*, Elton had lost 26 by 1458, Upwood 18 by 1457, Shillington 22 by 1458 and Hemmingford Abbots 27 by 1458.

[51] In the fourteenth century, only the Gere family had been totally lost to the village through emigration.

[52] For a discussion of this phenomenon on Ramsey villages as a whole, see Raftis, *Tenure and Mobility*, pp. 129-38. The number of outsiders holding properties in Holywell in the latter fourteenth and early fifteenth centuries may be cited as one example of this. So, too, may John Bigge, reeve in 1346/47, who was specifically described in the account roll of that year as being a resident of Broughton ("non habet mansum suum in haliwell sed in Broughton.") PRO SC 6-877/18.

or craftsmen.[53] They came and went virtually as they pleased, with no official record kept of their comings and goings, even when they displayed signs of being in residence for a year or longer. The reason for this is most likely to be found in their not being part of the customary structure of the manor. It is significant, for example, that all the Holywell *nativi* leaving the village in either the 1300's or the 1400's both with and without license whose names were recorded in court rolls had this one thing in common: they were all members of customary tenant families. The impression is therefore left that the abbey took pains to regulate — or at least note only the movements of members of families involved in the customary structure of the manor, since they were responsible — either actually or potentially — for a large part of the manorial labour force. Consequently, it is equally likely that the abbey was not so immediately concerned with the movements of persons and families outside the customary structure, and thus their migrations would have been scarcely noted.[54]

This, in fact, seems to have been the case in Holywell. Of the 51 one-

---

[53] In the category of occasional labourers can doubtlessly be placed such people appearing only once as guilty of trespasses, as, for example, the appropriately named Walter Careles, guilty of trespass in 1372, or Thomas Fole, described as a "perturbator pacis" in 1394. Other types were the temporary ale-brewers such as Katerina de Pydele (1288-94), Johanna le Typeler (1311), Elena Rabyn (1359), Agnes Paddok (1359); butchers, such as John de Drayton (1301), Reginald Handy (1286), Alexander Pergrave (1339); and even practitioners of the world's oldest profession, such as Ivette Brabon, "communa meretrix" in 1306.

[54] This policy has a two-fold significance. First is the fact that the practice was not changed even during the years of growing labour shortage after the middle of the fourteenth century. The only alteration was that of listing progeny of fugitive customary tenants. Indeed, the *reductio ad absurdum* of this practice was reached in 1416, when a Richard May was listed as a fugitive in the cellarer's roll for that year (BM.Add.Roll. 34609) and whose name was repeated in subsequent rolls through 1552 ! (BM.Add.Roll. 34614.) Since there had not been any sign of a member of the May family in the village since 1313, the abbey had apparently failed to note the family's exodus when it had occurred, catching up with the fact only a century later. Having finally done so in the early fifteenth century in the person of one who was probably a great-grandson of last resident May, it then refused to abandon its claims for another hundred years.

A second aspect of the importance of the practice of recording the migration of only customary tenants, their relatives and descendents lies in the light this casts on the meaning of villeinage itself (See Raftis, "Social Structures in Five East Midland Villages." *Ec.H.R.* XVIII, pp. 93-94). The impression is given of a status whose full implications seem to have applied the more the individual was involved in the land-holding structure of the manor. In short, restrictions to villein mobility — in so far as there were restrictions in the sense of demanding license — came to be imposed only when commitment to customary tenure was present. The villein not involved in the customary structure would appear to have had a very real and complete freedom of mobility. The question cannot be investigated in any detail in the present study due to the limitations in examining one single community, but it is one which calls for further and more widely-based study.

generation or short-term families resident in the village between the 1250's and the 1450's, for example, it cannot be assumed that all simply died out. The Kylleneth family, for one, had not. Present in the village in 1288, when the wife of William Kylleneth had been fined sixpence for unjustly raising the hue and cry on William Cartere,[55] they were last mentioned in 1294, when William himself acted as a pledge for Isabella de Walmesford for an ale infraction.[56] They disappeared from the local records immediately thereafter, but they had not perished, only moved, for in 1301 William was in St. Ives, taking up possession of "unam rengiam domorum".[57] In a few other cases, although the fact of emigration is not as clear as in the example of William Kylleneth, it is highly probable. Thus, the Colyn family was last mentioned in the 1320's, at a time when at least two male members and two female members (possibly wives) were still present in the village. So too with the Maddes: Robert Madde disappeared shortly after 1322. Finally, the Clavigers, Nicholas and Matilda, who had flourished from 1288 through 1313, had left at least one son, Hugo, who first appeared in 1322. He had most certainly left the village soon after, however, for his name was last mentioned in 1326. On the other hand, William Bacoun had been active in Holywell from 1292 through 1306. He had even held a croft in the 1290's, but he surrendered it by 1299, and as there were seemingly no further members of the family to succeed to it, another villager — Robert Mariot — was elected to it, with William himself acting as his pledge.[58] He then remained in the village at least another seven years, for he was a juror in 1306,[59] but he left sometime later, for in 1314 he too was in St. Ives, where he and his wife Matilda took up a messuage.[60] So too, with the Legge family, whose members had appeared in peripheral positions in the village from 1294. They were last mentioned in 1338, but by the 1350's Legges were also turning up in St. Ives.[61]

The point to be made, therefore, is that court rolls did not necessarily take account of all local people leaving the village, but rather devoted primary attention to those connected in some way with customary tenure,

---

[55] PRO SC 2-179/5.

[56] BM.Add.Roll. 39597.

[57] PRO SC 2-178/95.

[58] PRO SC 2-179/10.

[59] PRO SC 2-179/12.

[60] PRO SC 2-178/95. William and Matilda surrendered the messuage in 1319 to Radulph of Benygton, and in 1323 and 1324 William and Matilda engaged in further land transactions (*Ibid.*).

[61] PRO SC 2-178/95.

and that, consequently, the number of persons — and even whole families — moving away from Holywell was no doubt larger than the issuing of *exodus* licenses would indicate. However, there is no reason to believe that this unreported emigration was ever so heavy as to account for demographic decline in the village from the second decade of the fourteenth century through the middle of the fifteenth century. On the contrary, as already indicated, a crucial element in the decreasing settlement of Holywell lay not so much in the sheer disappearance of families or individuals in the village, but rather in the failure of the village to find sufficient replacement for the numbers lost. Indeed, as Professor Thrupp has recently stressed, the demographic crisis of late mediaeval England was primarily a replacement crisis,[62] and in Holywell its seeds could be found not so much in the failure of the village to keep people at home or attract sufficient numbers of newcomers to fill the gaps left by her wandering children, but rather in the local families themselves, in their diminishing ability to adequately replace or reproduce themselves.

Admittedly, the investigation of the replacement capabilities of individual families in fourteenth- and fifteenth-century Holywell is difficult. Ideally, it requires consideration of birth-rates, death-rates — infant, child and adult — and also marriage-rates. Unfortunately, the nature of surviving records prohibits investigations of some and seriously restricts pursuit of these questions. Specifically, since account rolls were concerned almost exclusively with the peasant as a tenant and court rolls with him as a legally responsible adult — i.e. over the age of 12 — the matter of determining a full picture — or even a close approximation — of the total number of births in the village, as well as per couple, is impossible. Furthermore, even though it is frequently possible to discover that a particular villager was married, it is not always easy to establish direct family ties among adults bearing the same surname. In cases where a family is first represented by only one male and his spouse, the identification of subsequent males within a 10 to 20 year period with the same surname as surviving male children of the initial couple is probably justified. In other cases, however — or in later generations preceded by the presence of two or more male members of the same family group, it is virtually impossible to determine whether the several males in one generation are sons of one parent or rather cousins. On the other hand, there are a few instances in which the records — court rolls, and, in the early fifteenth century, the Court Book — do indicate paternity, so that in such cases some picture of the number of surviving offspring of a couple is possible. On the whole, how-

---

[62] *Ec.H.R.* XVIII, pp. 101-119.

ever, such clear and direct information is exceptional, and the only really practical course open to the investigator is to attempt to determine the general reproductive powers of a total family group, particularly in terms of the number of representatives present in a generation, and to eschew precise identification of paternal ties.[63]

[63] This emphasis on paternal relationship in Holywell is not a denial of the possible importance of matronymics in the formation of surnames. The practice of children taking surnames of maternal rather than paternal identification appears to have been an early one, however, and in the very few cases in which it did occur in Holywell the maternal name soon became the official surname of the family and was subsequently passed down through male lines. Thus, the Cusste family was first represented in 1299 by Robert, who was identified both as "Robertus Custe" and "Robertus filius Custe" — apparently a shortening of "filius Custancie". Within 20 years, however, the surname had became "official" and was being passed from father to son. A similar case was that of "Robertus filius Elene", who bore that identification as a juror in 1301. By 1311, it had been transformed into the surname "Elene", and it was as such that Robert was subsequently known.

In addition to the adoption of surnames from a mother's Christian name, there were some Holywell families that took their surnames from occupations or from what was probably the site of their homestead in the village, as well as from names of communities of original residence. Thus, the Hemyngtons appeared in the 1320's and were initially, "de Hemyngton". The Houghtons, on the other hand, were initially known as "de Houghton", although the family was traceable back to a Simon Fikebert. The Bernewells were "de Bernewell" in the first decade of the fourteenth century, but "Bernewell" alone sufficed by the 1330's. Among local geographical names, the Capud Ville family from the 1290's to 1313 may be cited, as well as the "in the Lane", "atte Brook" and "ad Crucem" families.

Occupational or craft names were adopted by the Cartere, Carpenter, Miller (Molendinarius), Reve (Prepositus), Skynnere (Pellepar), Smyth (Faber), Baker, Tayllour, Wright and Shepperd (Bercar') families, although there is little evidence — save in the case of the Faber/Smyths — that the families in question were consistently engaged in the occupations denoted by their names. In addition, in three of the above cases, the surnames were Anglicized by the 1350's: Bercar' had become "Shepperd," Prepositus "Reve" and Faber "Smyth".

In addition to surnames, however, there is the striking evidence of only a small number of distinct Christian names within village families. From a sampling of 610 Holywell peasants from the late thirteenth century to the mid-fifteenth century, the most popular male names were: JOHN (borne by 139 men), ROBERT (59 men), RICHARD (53 men), WILLIAM (171 men), NICHOLAS (41 men) and THOMAS (41 men). Among women's names, the most frequently encountered were: JOHANNA (27 women), MARGARET (21 women), MATILDA (18 women) ALICE (28 women), and AGNES (21 women). Other names carried — and the number of persons bearing them — were as follows:

MEN

ADAM	15	PETER	3
ASPELON	3	RADULF	22
ALAN	1	RANULPH	2
ANDREW	5	REGINALD	8
ALEXANDER	6	ROGER	17
EGIDIUS	1	SAMPSON	1

In terms of general family replacement, then, it may be observed that several Holywell families were experiencing difficulty in abundantly perpetuating themselves from one generation to another in the fourteenth and early fifteenth centuries. Some, in fact, were dying out either through lack of male or any offspring. Thus the Aleyn, Ayse, Benet, Clerk, Avenaunt, Morel, Ad Crucem, AtteWelle, Venelle, Barker, Colyere, Fychyen, Raulyn,

GALFRIDUS	11	SIMON	11
GILBERT	4	STEPHAN	8
HAMO	4	THURKYLL	1
HUGO	6	SEMANNUS	1
HENRY	13	MATTHEW	3
IVO	1	MICHAEL	2
BARTHOLOMEW	1	WALTER	8
LAURENCE	2		

WOMEN

ANNE	1	KATERINA	9
AMITIA	2	LETITIA	2
ARTYN	1	LUCIA	1
BEATRIX	5	MARIOTA	7
CRISTINA	8	MAYCUSA	1
EMMA	8	SARRA	3
ELENA	20	SIBILLA	2
IVETTE	2	JULIANA	5
ISABELLA	11	ROYSEA	8

Most interestingly, there was not one instance of any woman being Christened "Mary" — not even in the Cristemesse family. The closest to it was MARIOTA, which was one of the less popular female names. Among men, not only were names such as JOHN, ROBERT, RICHARD, WILLIAM and THOMAS especially popular: they were also sometimes numbingly repeated from generation to generation within the same family. The Hunnes, for example, survived for over 200 years and repeated the names of Thomas, William and especially John. By 1400, in fact, out of eight male Hunnes present then or thereafter, one was named Thomas, two William and five John, with even one Johanna. The Asplonds, from 1318 to 1457, boasted four members named John, one Johanna, one Robert, one Roger, one Thomas, and one Richard — this last being especially worthy of note not for his own name but for that of his second wife, a woman with perhaps the most unusual and singularly beautiful name in the village: Artyn.

The AtteWelles repeated the name of John three times (with one Johanna) between 1356 and 1454. The Barouns were attached to John (three times) and William (twice), the Beaumeys repeated John three times. The Shepperd family boasted six members named John, while the Bryan, the Cartere, the Edward, the Gere, the Godfrey, the Hemyngton, the Laweman, the Nicholas, the Sande and the Wright families displayed similar attachments to the names of John, William, Richard, Robert and William. However, despite the temptation of the investigator to view this monotonously repetitious naming pattern as a sign of a lack of imagination, it is likely that the repetition of names was deliberate and purposeful: an as expression of familial continuity and identity. As such, it is a subject deserving of further investigation — ideally involving several communities — and the present writer hopes to undertake such a study in the near future.

Tiffayne and Sky families all disappeared from the village, being last represented by females, while the Deye family boasted only one adult male surviving into the 1450's.[64] On the other hand, several families, instead of producing only females who survived into adulthood, seem to have produced no surviving descendents at all and subsequently died out. At least 26 families seem to have fallen victim to this fate.[65]

The inability or failure to provide more than one or two males in a generation, however, was characteristic of more than just the families tabulated. With few exceptions, a decrease in the number of surviving members — in several cases amounting to a bare sustaining of the line through one male — was widespread among Holywell's families, and especially after the middle of the fourteenth century. The Shepperds, the Hunnes, the Asplonds, the Edwards, the Smyths, the Godfreys and the Nicholases were the exceptions, although even here the village was far from being overrun with their progeny after 1350 or even after 1400. Indeed, it had never been. For one, the number of males was never really excessive in any generation. With the Asplonds, for example, there had been but two adult males in the first half of the fourteenth century. The next generation merely replaced them, and of the two mid-century Asplonds, one — Thomas — died childless by 1405, whereas John (II) had two sons: John (III) and Richard. Richard was without issue, and John (III) had only two sons: Roger and John (IV). As for the Shepperds, it is virtually impossible to discern paternal lines in the family, although it

---

[64] From cellarers' rolls of the fifteenth century, it is learned that Thomas Deye had also had two sons, William and John (BM. Add.Roll. 33447, f. 53, 55). One — William — died childless, and apparently unmarried. John was dead by 1428 (*Ibid.*, 65 d) and had one son — Richard — who did not enter records until the 1460's (*Ibid.*, 111 d).

[65] I.e. Baldewyne, Brayn, Bryan, Broun, Bundeleg, Cartere, Cranfeld, Curteys, Fannell, Flesshewere, Franklyn, Godeman, Godrich, Gray, Hamond, Houghton, Laweman, Molle, Palmere, Porter, Reve (Prepositus), Ripton, Russell, Selede, Skynnere & Spercoll. That they were not families whose last-known members emigrated from Holywell is almost a certainty. All were customary families, and because of this fact their migration would have been recorded in the court rolls. Seven non-customary families, however, may either have died out or moved away, since, as already indicated, it was not the policy of the manor to keep special watch over the movements of such persons (the Bernewells, the Botwrytes, the Brooks, the Caldecotes, the Cappes, the Capud Villes). Even here, however, migration cannot be taken for granted. The Bernewells, for one, were settled from 1306 throgh 1402, and the last representative of the family was recorded for over 33 years before disappearing. Similarly with the Botwrytes: Simon and Matilda had flourished in the first decade of the fourteenth century, but the last Botwryte survived to 1356. The Brooks, too, seem to have simply died out, having never been really prolific. The Caldecotes, as well, stayed from 1313 to 1375, but they too suffered from an acute shortage of males, as did the Scharps, who could boast only four men from the 1350's through 1418.

is known that William Shepperd was the only son of Elena Shepperd —
presumably the widow of Peter Shepperd — leaving John (II) as the
likely father of both Nicholas (I) and John (III). As there were subsequently four adult Shepperd men in the village in 1400 (John III, John
IV, Nicholas II and William), the appearance of only two more males
— John V and VI — in the next 50 years was barely an adequate replacement. It guaranteed the continuation of the line, but it did not maintain
the family's strength.

Turning to other families, the AtteWelles, who ended in the 1450's
because of the survival of only female issue, had never been especially
prolific, as was also the case with the Barouns and the Beaumeys family,
both averaging one male per direct line in every generation from the
second half of the fourteenth century. The Brayns had been afflicted
by a decreasing number of males, as had even the Edwards, with Thomas
Edward dying without issue and John (II) being succeeded by only two
sons, of whom Richard (II) left but one son (John IV) and John (III)
none. Among the Scot family, Richard Scot was survived by only females.[66] Even the Smyth family was thinly-spread by the mid-fifteenth
century, as were the Godfreys. About the only families who managed
to maintain a truly adequate replacement rate after the turn of the fifteenth
century were the Hunnes, the Nicholases and the Wrights. Other village
families were producing about one male per couple per generation.

The demographic crisis in Holywell from the fourteenth century through
the middle of the fifteenth century was, then, indeed primarily a replacement
crisis, and although families afflicted with the problem can be cited as
early as the first half of the fourteenth century, the situation became acute
especially after the middle of the century. But demonstrating the existence
of the problem does not necessarily give the reasons for it, and, unfortunately,
the nature of surviving Holywell records does not permit the investigator
to find those reasons. Whether it was a question of high infant, child
and adult mortality or a dropping birth-rate is simply not known. Small
amounts of evidence for almost any one of such explanations could be
drawn from the Holywell records. For one, it might be suggested that
a possible early death-rate is reflected by the examples of wives outliving
husbands. Thus, Rosa Asplond outlived her husband, John (III), who
was dead in 1457. However, since John (III) had first appeared in 1398,
he was well over 60 at the time of his death. So too with John AtteWelle

---

[66] Richard Scot left two daughters: Agnes, who married the newcomer William Lanender
in 1416 (BM.Harl.Ms. 445, 97r), and Alice, who was a servant of John Nicholas in 1424 (*Ibid.*,
124v).

(II). Although he was dead in 1454 and survived by his wife Margaret, he had first appeared in 1401, and he too was consequently over 60 when he died. The same appears to have been true of John Shepperd (II). He was dead in 1401, but his wife Katerina survived him at least through 1418.[67] However, as John had first appeared in 1353, he too must have been over 60 when he died. Even Thomas Nicholas, who died between 1424 and 1427 and was survived by his wife Margaret, who married Thomas Cademan of Hemmingford Abbots in 1427, was probably a man in his late 50's at death, since he had first appeared in the records in 1392, holding a virgate *ad opus* and consequently may be assumed to have been about 20 at the time. Roger Sewale, also, who flourished from 1402 to his death in 1431 and was survived by his wife Helena, was most likely middle-aged when he died. In fact, a study of the dates between which late fourteenth- and early-fifteenth-century Holywell men flourished reveals that out of 117 men, 38 were active in the village for documented periods of time of from one to 19 years, 36 for from 20 to 30 years, 17 from 31 to 40 years, 19 from 41 to 50 years, and seven for over 50 years. Since all had to be at least 12 years of age when first mentioned in court rolls, while some appeared initially as tenants or officials, and even as married men, a crude approximate initial age for the individual men would be 20. As a result, by adding 20 to the number of years covered by a man's documented village life, it may be proposed that out of 117 men resident in Holywell between the second half of the fourteenth and the second half of the fifteenth century, 32 % lived less than 40 years, 31 % survived into their 40's, 15 % into their 50's, 16 % into their 60's and 6 % exceeded 70 years. In short, 79 men, or 68 %, lived to middle age or longer.

This, of course, does not prove anything significant about death-rates, since there is no way of knowing how many individual children may have been born who never survived infancy or chilhood. However, if overall death-rates remain hidden, there are some interesting aspects to birth patterns — not rates — that are reflected, although obliquely, in the records. Specifically, among the Asplonds, John (III) had two sons: John (IV) and Roger. John appeared initially in 1437, as a married man, and since he did not begin to exercise positions of official responsibility in the village until the early 1450's, he was most likely about 20 in 1437.[68] The second son, Roger, appeared first in 1457. He too was married at the time, but the absence of any mention of him prior to that date suggests

---

[67] BM.Add.Roll. 33447, f. 43 d.

[68] The age at which an office such as juror tended to be assumed for the first time was around 30 years. See *infra*, p. 216.

he too was in his 20's in 1457. John (III), then, would have been in his late 30's when John (IV) was born, while he would have been in his mid- or late 50's when Roger was born. So, too, with John AtteWelle (II). By 1444, his daughter Alice was married to John Elyot, a very recent immigrant to Holywell. She was still living in 1454, as was her mother, Margaret, although John AtteWelle was dead. She was no doubt a very young woman, then, when she married, having been born probably in the 1420's, when her father was already middle-aged.

John Beaumeys (III) was another villager whose only son, Richard, was apparently born when he was middle-aged, since Richard first began to appear in the 1450's (i.e. 1452), with his birth probably having occurred in the 1420's or 1430's, when John would have been over 40, or close to it. Similarly, John Shepperd (III) appeared first in 1400 — and lived 40 more years — and was most likely born in the 1370's or early 1380's, when his father would have been close to 40. In addition, since his mother, Katerina, outlived her husband, John (II), by some 17 years at least,[69] she was apparently several years his junior — perhaps even 20 years younger.[70]

The two sons of John Cristemesse (I) — Richard and Roger — were also men who seem to have been born in their father's older years. Since both appeared first in the 1420's, were already married and yet had some 30 years of activity in the village still ahead of them,[71] they were most probably in their 20's or early 30's at the time and would have been born between 1390 and 1400, when their father was in his late 50's.

Among other village families in which similar situations most probably occurred were the Nicholases — with John (III), son of John (II), most likely born in the 1370's, when his father was in his 30's; the Palmeres, where John (fl. 1392-1437), if he was the son of William (II — 1353-78), was probably born in the late 1360's or 1370's, when his father was over 40; and the Wrights, where William (III) was the son of William (II) and was born also during his father's middle years.

Given the stubborn resistence of the surviving Holywell records to divulging all their secrets, it cannot be stated that the above instances of what, for want of a better term, may be called "delayed paternity"

---

[69] John (II) was dead by 1401, but Katerina was still living — and an active tenant — in 1418. How much longer after that date she survived is not known, since the account rolls, which bore witness to her presence, broke off after 1418 for 31 years.

[70] Katerina Shepperd was first noted in the 1370's, as an ale-brewer in 1372, 1375 and 1378.

[71] Richard Cristemesse appeared in 1424, with his wife Margaret, and was still present in 1455. Roger was first noted in 1428, with his wife Agnes, and he was still present in 1456.

were representative of all or most village families from the second half
of the fourteenth century. But even if restricted to just the persons named,
an interesting pattern is revealed. For one, in many cases it is apparent
that the mothers of the children in question were younger than their
husbands — in several instances, most likely much younger. The example
of Katerina Shepperd has already been cited as one. There were, however,
others. Rosa Asplond outlived her husband, and as John (IV) was probably
born between 1410 and 1420 and Roger in the 1430's, she was not her
husband's age if she was the mother of both, and it is known that she
was married to John (III) in the 1430's. So too with Margaret AtteWelle,
wife of John (II). She outlived her husband, and their daughter, Alice,
had married the newcomer John Elyot by 1444, who, as she was living
in 1454, was most likely a young woman when married, having been born
sometime in the 1420's when her mother was also a young woman —
probably 10 and possibly 20 years younger than her husband. In all the
other cases cited above where sons were born after their fathers had reached
middle age, younger mothers may be proposed as well. It is not impossible,
of course, for a child to have been born to both a middle-aged father and
mother, but to assume that all or most were such cases is to stretch the
limits of probability.

The evidence indicates, therefore, that in some cases Holywell men
were becoming fathers in their middle years or later, and by younger
wives. Whether or not this means that they were becoming fathers for
the first time, as well as husbands, at a later age is simply unknown. There
is very little indication of a proliferation of bachelors in the village: between
1400 and 1456, for example, the number of men whose wives were actually
known by name was 48, while there were an additional 15 male members
of village families who were married but whose wives' names have not
been preserved, for a total of 63 married men. As there were some 60
more men in the same period representing village families, but about
whose marital status no information has come down, a little over half
of the men in the village in the first half of the fifteenth century were
certainly married. In addition, as can be seen from just the examples
of the "late-born" sons referred to above, there were obviously men in
late fourteenth- and early fifteenth-century-Holywell marrying in their 20's.
Consequently, the possibility that the middle-aged fathers noted above
were in second marriages cannot be discounted. But if they had been
married previously, they had either not had any children, or none of
their children had survived. Thus, there is no real certainty in the matter,
for whether a man married young and married a young wife, or married
late — or a second time — and also chose a younger wife, does not explain

the minimal replacement-rates in the village's families. And since it is difficult to believe that Holywell men and women from the middle of the fourteenth century were almost all afflicted with some bizarre form of galloping sterility, the failure of village families to do more than barely replace themselves from one generation to another must be ascribed to more plausible causes. Possibly, there was a high rate of infant, child and even adult mortality, resulting from conditions not yet fully explored — perhaps a general atmosphere of infection and contagion partly stemming from years of plague but especially intensified by accelerated mobility. This has been suggested by at least one major scholar, who has termed the period from the mid-fourteenth century through the mid-fifteenth century "the golden age of bacteria",[72] and the fact that 32 % of the known men of Holywell families between 1350 and 1450 died before or during middle-age, coupled with the small number of children reaching adult age during the same period, could be interpreted as substantiating such a view.

On the other hand, still another possibility could be advanced, although it is purely speculative and must remain so until the question is given attention by scholars. Specifically, it is a question of the possibility of "family planning", or more precisely, of a possible change in the peasant's attitude towards marriage and family. As already noted in Chapter II, alterations in manorial policy relative to the basic conditions of tenure — themselves responses to a general agrarian decline in England from the middle of the fourteenth century — had contributed to a change in the Holywell peasant's attitude to land and the permanence and familial character of tenurial commitments. This in itself marked a striking break with long-standing peasant traditions relative to land. Consequently, if his attitude towards land and his relationship to it were undergoing revision, it is surely not impossible to wonder if the peasant's attitude towards marriage and family were equally being revised — especially as the two — land and family — had been intimately related to one another prior to the late fourteenth century. Specifically, in the thirteenth century and even into the first half of the fourteenth century, land, for the peasant, was truly a family affair. Tenure *ad opus* predominated, and the security of a peasant's tenure hinged on his ability to acquit the work obligations incumbent upon his tenement, which, in turn, contributed to the generation of large families. This not only guaranteed the fulfilment of labour duties, it further secured the tenement in the family's hands from one generation to another. Even among families not possessed of

---

[72] Sylvia Thrupp, "The Problem of Replacement-Rates ...", *Ec.H.R.* XVIII, p. 118.

much — or any — land, and consequently dependent upon employment as day labour for their subsistence, a large family — although imposing strain in the matter of adequately providing the necessities of life — could possibly have been desired as supplying several "wage-earners" for the maintenance of the family as a whole. From the middle of the fourteenth century, however, rural economy and society suffered severe shocks, both from recurrent visitations of plague and a growing stagnation in agricultural production, and in their wake came high periods of mortality, changes in the nature of tenure, and profound shifts in the distribution and utilization of land. It is not impossible, then, that to some peasants the unhealthy conditions — bacteriologically speaking — that obtained resulted in a re-evaluation of the desirability of reproducing in large numbers. This may have been extended further by the changes in tenurial obligations, which, in their growing de-emphasis of *ad opus* terms culminating in their practical elimination in Holywell in 1409, no longer necessitated the large family as a source of labour. In addition, the increasing impermanence to tenurial commitments — amounting to a repudiation of the family's identification with a tenement through successive generations — also made the large family unnecessary and perhaps, for some, undesirable. Even among the so-called "labouring" group — those peasants not heavily involved in land — the high premium on labour from the late fourteenth century, and, most importantly, the intensified mobility of this group, could have militated against large families, since it would have been easier to move about the countryside from job to job with one or two children in tow than with half a dozen.

This is, admittedly, pure speculation, and the Holywell evidence neither especially confirms nor denies it. But the possibility of the peasant — or at least of some peasants — deliberately choosing to limit the size of his families[73] as a result of probabilities of survival, changes in tenurial

---

[73] To speak of "family limitation" or "family planning" implies both direct and indirect methods of keeping the number of offspring to a minimum. Whether contraceptive techniques were widely utilized in the period is simply not known. That techniques themselves were available is scarcely to be doubted. Anglo-Saxon and Celtic penitential manuals, for one, had much earlier displayed a high degree of familiarity with such techniques, both in their more sophisticated and less delicate aspects. That techniques were known, then, is admitted; what still awaits investigation is the extent to which they were employed. See J. T. NOONAN, *Contraception*, Cambridge, Mass., 1967.

Among indirect methods of family planning, men could delay marriage until their middle years or later, hoping thereby — if marriage was to a younger woman — to restrict the span of their own reproductive years, for the delaying of marriage may point to a de-emphasis of the importance of generating offspring as soon as possible. On the other hand, the choice of a middle-aged or older woman for a marriage partner was also a possibility, while it may further be suggested

obligations, commitments and practices, and mobility patterns cannot be totally disregarded until the question has been more closely explored. To even suggest it is not to reject other causes or explanations of population decline and low replacement-rates, since such a phenomenon as the demographic crisis of the late English Middle Ages was most likely the result of several factors, not merely one. Plague, infection, high mortality all had a role to play, but it can be proposed that so too did the psychological climate in the countryside, and it is this psychological climate that still very badly awaits investigation.

Finally, there is yet another possible factor to be considered in the declining settlement and shrinking population of Holywell in the fourteenth and early fifteenth centuries. Specifically, it is a question of the availability of the means of subsistence. It is perhaps belabouring the obvious to state that if a people do not have enough land or opportunities for employment providing them either directly with enough food or the money to acquire enough food to sustain life, some persons are going to starve to death, but the question can be asked with respect to Holywell if, in fact, there is evidence of such conditions obtaining in the fourteenth and fifteenth centuries. Did the facts that 51 village families failed to maintain residence longer than a generation, that 32 other families disappeared within or shortly after their second generation of settlement, and that family sizes in general tended to shrink have any connection with an inability to maintain minimal levels of subsistence? However difficult it is to investigate, it is nevertheless a question that must be asked.

In terms of the historiography of the mediaeval English manorial community, the question of subsistence has traditionally reduced itself to a question of land. Most recent estimates have concluded, further, that the amount of land necessary to maintain a family at a subsistence level — defined as providing "an income large enough to make it unnecessary for the family to depend on regular employment for wages, yet not so large as to permit the family to live wholly on the proceeds of rents or to enable it to work its holding entirely or mainly by hired labour" — was roughly between 12 and 15 acres.[74] This, it is also maintained, was

that the monogomous marriage itself is an implied form of family planning. It is to be hoped that a study now being conducted by Professor Michael M. Sheehan of Toronto on the incidence of bigamy among parishioners in the diocese of Ely in the late fourteenth century will cast additional light on this question.

[74] Postan, CEH, I, pp. 618-20. See also Hilton, *A Medieval Society*, pp. 114-15, 121-22. The most recent summary of this question may be found in J. Z. Titow, *English Rural Society*, 1200-1350 (Cambridge, Mass., 1969). Unfortunately, this book reached me when the manuscript was in the press.

generally the holding of the semi-virgater, and it is he who is presently considered to be the representative English peasant of the thirteenth and early fourteenth centuries.[75] Not that he was always in the majority. Postan, for example, has suggested, from a study of several estates of the bishops of Winchester and Worcester, the abbeys of Glastonbury, St. Peter's (Gloucester) and the Lancastrian estates of East Anglia in the late thirteenth century, that their number scarcely exceeded a third of the total peasantry.[76] But despite their numbers, "their mode of existence, their standards of life ... approached nearest the characteristic type of medieval peasant".[77] They were, in short, representative of the "average household",[78] and that is asserted to have been characterized by a life at the subsistence level.[79]

If the semi-virgater — or the peasant holding from about 12 to 15 acres — was representative of rural England and was "living on the very edge of subsistence",[80] the family holding 10 acres or less is alleged now to have been insufficiently provided with land and consequently to have been living below subsistence — or, in some cases, just meeting it (often through supplementing their income by employment as hired labour). Most recent scholarship has termed all those at 10 acres or less "small-holders",[81] who, further, comprised roughly one-half of the peasantry and who "had holdings insufficient to maintain their families at the bare minimum of subsistence".[82] On the other hand, the only group of the

[75] CEH, I, pp. 618-20 ; Hilton, pp. 114-15, 121-22. CEH, I 112. Neither Postan nor Hilton has made any firm statement as to the amount of land necessary for subsistence from the mid-fourteenth century, but since 12 to 15 acres, or a semi-virgate, was allegedly required for the generally still productive late thirteenth and early fourteenth centuries, it is probable that, given the increasing stagnation of agricultural production from the middle of the fourteenth century, the amount of land would most likely have to be increased — to perhaps 20 acres — to give the peasant a reasonably safe margin, while the holder of 12 to 15 acres, though still able to subsist, would be at the very edge.

[76] CEH, I, p. 619.

[77] Ibid.

[78] Hilton, A Medieval Society, p. 122.

[79] CEH, I, pp. 618-20; Hilton, A Medieval Society, pp. 121-22. See also Postan, "Investment in Medieval Agriculture," The Journal of Economic History, XXVII, No. 4 (December, 1967), pp. 576-87. "So small were the holdings of the great majority of medieval serfs, so low was the yield of their lands, and so great were various compulsory payments weighing upon customary tenancies that the net produce of an average medieval small holding was only just sufficient to sustain a family on the margin of the barest subsistence." (p. 585.)

[80] Hilton, A Medieval Society, p. 114.

[81] Postan, CEH, I, p. 622. This represents a change from earlier scholarly estimates, especially of Kosminsky, who tended to equate an inadequate supply of land with five acres or less. See Studies, p. 217.

[82] CEH, I, p. 622. Although, again, the reference is primarily to the late thirteenth century,

peasantry considered to have been able to maintain themselves at a relatively comfortable level was that holding virgates and above: men at roughly 30 acres or more. These are said to have constituted the "village rich",[83] whose general prosperity was demonstrated by their activity in local markets — as buyers, and lessors — in the loaning of money to their neighbors and by their service as pledges,[84] and as village and manorial officials.[85]

The importance of all this for Holywell can be briefly stated. If the peasant population of mediaeval England living at a subsistence level is normally associated with the possession of semi-virgates or their equivalents — between 12 and 15 acres — and if the below-subsistence population held 10 acres or less, then the student of Holywell-cum-Needingworth in the latter thirteenth and earlier fourteenth centuries is dealing with a population almost entirely living at a subsistence level or below it. Specifically, the Holywell virgate — it will be recalled — was roughly 18 acres of arable,[86] with, under the three-course rotation employed on the manor, only about 12 usable acres a year. Consequently, the Holywell virgater corresponded closely to the average semi-virgater in other parts of England and should have been living at a subsistence level or just slightly above it. Furthermore, the Holywell semi-virgater and cotlander — holding about 10 acres — were, by modern definition, smallholders. In addition, the size of this smallholding population itself — whether in the 1250's or after 1370 — was always large, accounting for over two-thirds of the peasantry in the mid-thirteenth century and just over a half from the 1370's to 1400.[87] Consequently, since the overwhelming majority of Holywell tenements until the fifteenth century — even the largest — were modest in size — with some 90% of the population still holding less than 20 acres by 1400[88] — it should follow that the majority of Holywell peasants in the late thirteenth and fourteenth centuries were living at, just above or below a subsistence level, and that, as a result, the chances for survival should have been slim.

The evidence, however, does not especially support this supposition. For one, the survival of 37 village families for longer than a century, coupled

---

the conclusion can probably be extended into the fourteenth century, when agrarian output went into a general decline and prices began to fall.

[83] CEH, I, p. 624.

[84] Ibid., pp. 625-28.

[85] Hilton, A Medieval Society, p. 152.

[86] See supra, p. 6 et seq.

[87] See supra, Chapters I and II, passim.

[88] See supra, p. 112 et seq.

with the survival of another 11 families for over 80 years but less than 100, is not insignificant. More specifically, however: out of eight families holding virgates — or 18 acres — in 1252, one (Toly) survived 66 years into the second decade of the fourteenth century (1318), three survived for a little over 80 years longer (Clerk, 87 years; Venelle, 87 years; Ripton, 87 years), one lasted for another century and a half (Lane) and one was still present 200 years later (Hunne).[89] Out of 17 semi-virgater and cot-lander families, nine failed to survive into the last two decades of the thirteenth century, but one lasted at least another 36 years (Benet), one 49 years (Bacoun), one 74 years (Ayse) and five survived for over a century more (Godfrey, Prepositus/Reve, Godrich, Gere and Gray). Even between the 1280's and the 1350's, 18 customary families — holding between 10 and 18 acres of land — were able to survive in the village, and several did so in such a way that indicates they were more than merely subsisting. Specifically, the Asplonds — controlling one virgate — were able, in the persons of Robert and John (I), to serve on at least four court juries between 1322 and 1339, while in the subsidy rolls of 1327 and 1332, Robert and John were assessed taxes against 23 s. 4 d. and 30 s. and 23 s. 4 d. and 20 s. of movables, respectively.[90] The Brayns — also a virgate family — supplied constables, capital pledges, jurors and ale tasters for the village over the first half of the fourteenth century, while John Brayn (I) was taxed on over 20 shillings' of movable property in 1327.[91] The Bruns were frequent jurors and tasters, while Richard Cartere, a juror and frequent ale taster, had movables valued at 23 s. 4 d. in 1327 and at 37 s. 6 d. in 1332.[92] The Cranfelds, who seem to have been cotlanders before 1370[93] and co-sharers of 11 acres of demesne with three other villagers, supplied jurors and reeves in the first half of the fourteenth century, while in 1332 two members of the family had movables valued at a total of 35 shillings.[94] The Franklyns

---

[89] In addition, only the Hunnes expanded their holdings to any appreciable degree, and then not until the latter fourteenth century.

[90] PRO E. 179/122-4. The tax of 1327 was a 20th on all movable property above 10 shillings; that of 1332 was a 15th. See Willard, *Parliamentary Taxes on Personal Property* ... The assigning of a virgate to the Asplonds is based on the fact that the family controlled but one virgate in 1370 and continued to do so until after 1400.

[91] PRO E. 179/122. He paid 16 d. tax against 26 s. 8 d. of movables. In 1332, on the other hand, he was taxed on only 10 shillings' of property (8 d.) (PRO E. 179/124).

[92] PRO E. 179/122-4.

[93] A cotland and a croft and a half-acre of meadow were the only properties held by Richard, son of Roger Cranfeld, in 1370 (PRO SC 6-877/21).

[94] Roger Cranfeld was taxed 16 d. against 20 shillings' of property. His son Richard paid 12 d. against 15 shillings'-worth. In 1327, Roger had paid 18 d. on movables valued at 30 shillings (PRO E. 179/122-4.)

provided two jurors and a taster and possessed over 20 shillings' of movables in 1327 and 1332.[95] The Geres supplied constables, capital pledges and jurors for the village, and in 1327 and 1332 two members of the family were worth over 50 shillings in movables.[96] Members of the virgate-holding Godeman family were found on juries as well as among ale tasters,[97] as were the Godriches.[98] The Grays, too — another virgate family — were frequent jurors, while in 1327 the family as a whole was worth over 80 shillings in movable property and over 90 shillings in 1332.[99] The Hamonds provided at least one juror and stood in the middle range of tax-payers in both 1327 and 1332.[100] The Lanes, holding a virgate, served as both jurors and tasters, while the Nicholases — also a virgate family — were found as jurors and tasters, and in 1327 and 1332 the family controlled movables valued in excess of 20 shillings and seven pounds, respectively.[101] In addition, the Palmeres and Riptons — both virgate families — supplied jurors, tasters and even constables for the village.[102] The Colyns provided a juror, the Beaumeys family both jurors and tasters,

[95] In 1327, Richard was assessed 16 d. against 26 s. 8 d. of movables and 16 d. again — against 20 shillings — in 1332. PRO E. 179/122-4). In addition to being a frequent juror, Richard also acted as a personal pledge on at least 13 different occasions.

[96] In 1327, Robert Gere (II) paid 18 d. against 30 shillings of movables, his father Richard paying 16 d. for 26 s. 8 d. (PRO E. 179/122). In 1332, two John Geres paid 12 d. and 2 s. 8 d. on 15 shillings and 40 shillings, respectively. (PRO E. 179/124.)

[97] In addition, Robert Godeman was taxed 2 d. 4 d. q. on 35 shillings' of movables in 1332. PRO E. 179/124.

[98] William Godrych was taster in 1288 and 1294 and a juror in 1299, 1301 and 1306. In 1327, Simon Godrych was taxed 16 d. on 26 s. 8 d. of movables.

[99] In 1327, Robert Gray was taxed 2 s. on 40 shillings' of property. Radulf paid 16 d. on 26 s. 8 d. and Margaret paid 10 d. on 16 s. 8 d. of movables. The total tax paid by the family was 4 s. 2d. against movables valued at £ 4. 3 s. 4 d. (83 s. 4 d.). In 1332, Robert paid 4 s. for 60 shillings' of property, while Isabella Gray was taxed 2 s. 6 d. against 37 s. 6 d. worth of movables. The total tax for the family was 6 s. 6 d. The total value of movables thereby taxed: 97 s. 6 d., or £ 4. 17 s. 6 d.

[100] In 1327, Henry Hamond was taxed 16 d. against 26 s. 8 d. of movables, while in 1332, Hamond of Haliwelle paid 2 s. tax on 30 shillings' of movables. PRO E. 179/122-4.

[101] Stephan Nicholas was a juror in 1326 and taster in 1321. Robert was a juror in 1332, as was Richard in 1338 and 1339, while Nicholas was elected taster in 1339. In 1327, Stephan paid 14 d. on 23 s. 4 d. of movables. In 1332, he paid 2 s. for 30 shillings, while 4 s. — against 60 shillings — were collected from Richard Nicholas, 2 s. ob. q. from Robert (on 30 s. 11 d.), and 2 s. from Matilda (on 30 s.). Thus, in 1332, four member spaid a total of 10 s. ob. q. in tax on movables valued at £ 7. 10 s. 11 d.

[102] Adam de Ripton was a juror in 1294, constable in 1299 and 1301 and taster in 1311 and 1313. William Palmere was a juror in 1311, 1321, 1332, 1338 and 1339 and elected taster in 1338.

the Ad Portams a juror, and the Hunnes a juror and taster before the middle of the century.[103]

Just as interesting as the major role in village life being exercised by customary families holding between 10 and 18 acres of land in the first half of the fourteenth century is the fact that at least three other families either not involved in the customary structure or, if so, but marginally — as croftholders — achieved similar status. Thus, the Brooks provided at least two jurors, the Fannells were represented among the village tasters at least four times by one man, while the Edwards boasted two jurors and one taster in the family before 1350.

Indeed, the subsidy lists of 1327 and 1332 are of some assistance in forming a picture of economic levels in the village, although it must be realized that not all villagers had large stores of movable property, and their absence does not necessarily indicate poverty. Nevertheless, in terms of tax-payers for the subsidies of 1327 and 1332, although almost half the village's residents were indeed considered too poor in movables to be taxed,[104] out of 28 families taxed in 1327, 19 fell between 23 and 30 shillings' worth of property (68%), and 13 — out of 32 — the same in 1332 (41%).[105] In terms of persons, out of 47 persons taxed in 1327, there were only two at the cut-off point of 10 shillings. Three had property between 13 and 17 shillings in value, 21 had goods worth from 20 to 27 shillings, 19 had properties valued from 30 to 40 shillings, and two were worth 60 shillings. In 1332, out of 59 taxpayers, nine were at the cut-off point of 10 shillings, six at 15 shillings, 21 between 20 and 30 shillings, 12 from 31 to 40 shillings, eight between 41 and 60 shillings, and three at over 60 shillings. In short, in either year, roughly two dozen villagers had from three to four times the amount of movables possessed by the lowest-taxed persons.[106] Combining the values of movables possessed by

---

[103] Two other customary families, the Lawemans and the Scots, also served as important officials in the village, but in each case it was to be expected, since both were double-virgate families, controlling about 36 acres.

[104] The exemption point was 10 shillings of property. As 28 families paid the tax of 1327 — whan there were some 64 families in the village — about 56 % of the families were excluded. That they were all too poor, however, cannot be too readily assumed, since it was quite possible to evade the tax altogether. See Willard, *Parliamentary Taxes on Personal Property.*

[105] It should be noted that of the 28 families taxed in 1327, only two were free families — Clervaus and Gibbe — with Thomas Gere alone representing a free branch of an otherwise villein family. In 1332, Alexander Gere was probably a representative of the free branch of that family, while the Gibbes were also present. Otherwise, 34 families were villein families.

[106] For a comparison with another Ramsey village taxed in the late thirteenth century (1295), see Raftis, "The Concentration of Responsibility in Five Villages," *Medieval Studies,* XXVIII (1966), pp. 115-16, and esp. p. 116, note ♯ 19, where, out of 34 villagers paying the 11th in Wistow,

individual members of village families, the values of separate family properties have been set-out in Table VI. Out of the 39 families thus presented, it can be seen that four were especially rich in movable properties: Beaumeys, Laweman, Nicholas and Scot. In the cases of the Laweman and Scot families, this is not surprising, since they constituted the largest customary tenant families in the village at the time, both being in control of two virgates, or some 36 acres each.[107] The Beaumeys family, too, may have been a double virgate family — they were by 1370 — but the Nicholas family was but a single virgate family, and remained so until the 1380's or 1390's.[108]

The next wealthiest families — the Brooks, the Grays and the Hamonds — were not more than virgaters, however, while the Fabers and the Fannells were not known to have been customary tenants at all before the end of the fourteenth century. Even among families controlling between 20 and 50 shillings' of movables, the Bercars, the Carpenters, the Edwards, the Eyrs, the Cusstes, the Gibbes, the Legges, the family "of Richard" and the Ravens were not customary tenants during the period.

The point to be made is that, despite the normally modest size of tenements in Holywell, especially during the late thirteenth and first half of the fourteenth century — before any pronounced trend towards multiple tenements in a family took root[109] — which should have resulted in a peasantry displaying signs of bare subsistence — or even below-subsistence living — the village boasted 15 customary families that, based on the subsidies of either 1327 or 1332, were possessed of personal movables valued at over 30 shillings, or three times above the lowest rank of taxation, as well as nine families not involved in the customary structure, and also giving no evidence of any real land involvement, who fell into the same "tax bracket". It is consequently difficult to imagine such families living at a rough "subsistence" level.

But the evidence of personal movable property is not the only means

eight were between 11 and 18 shillings, 14 between 21 and 29 shillings, nine between 31 and 39 shillings and three between 40 and 44 shillings.

[107] Three members of the Laweman family held two virgates and a cotland in 1252, but the family held no customary properties by 1370. The Scots, on the other hand, held two virgates, or their equivalent, from 1252 through 1370.

[108] Only one virgate was held in 1370, but two were in the family by 1392.

[109] Indeed, the concentration of multiple tenements in individual hands could not really begin until the population had itself undergone extended decline; hence the delay of the phenomenon until the years between the Black Death and 1370, its arrest for 20 years thereafter as population gradually increased, and its resumption after 1400, when the slump in settlement began again.

TABLE VI

TOTAL WEALTH IN MOVABLES OF TAX-PAYING HOLYWELL FAMILIES
1327 AND 1332

| | 1327 | | 1332 | |
FAMILY	PERSONS	VALUE	PERSONS	VALUE
ASPLOND*	2	46s.8d	2	50s
BEAUMEYS*	2	53s.4d	2	120s.12d
BERNEWELLE	—	—	1	10s
BRAYN*	1	26s.8d	1	10s
BROOK	2	56s.8d	2	75s
BERCAR'	1	20s	—	—
BUNDELEG*	1	30s	—	—
CARTERE*	1	23s.4d	1	37s.6d
CARPENTER	—	—	1	30s
CLERVAUS**	1	40s	—	—
CLERK*	1	30s	1	20s
CRANFELD	1	30s	2	35s
CUSSTE	1	13s.4d	2	45s
EDWARD	—	—	2	30s
EYR	—	—	1	25s
FABER	2	50s.2d	2	53s.5d
FANNELL	—	—	2	65s
FRANKLYN*	1	26s.8d	1	20s
FREYSANT	1	20s	1	10s
GERE**	1	30s	2	45s
GERE*	1	26s.8d	3	45s
GODEMAN*	—	—	1	35s
GODRICH*	1	26s.8d	—	—
GEROLD	—	—	1	10s
GRAY*	3	83s.4d	2	97s.6d
GYBBE**	1	30s	1	37s.6d
HAMOND*	2	46s.8d	2	90s.7d.ob
HOUGHTON	—	—	1	45s
HUNNE*	1	30s	1	45s
LEGGE	1	20s	—	—
LAWEMAN*	3	97s.4d	5	140s
NICHOLAS*	1	23s.4d	4	150s.11d.q.
PALMERE*	—	—	1	10s
PRONDHELE	—	—	1	10s
"RICARDI"	1	40s	—	—
SCOT*	2	63s.4d	3	117s.6d
RAVEN	—	—	1	23s.1d.ob.
SKYNNERE*	1	10s	—	—
TIFFAYNE	1	10s	1	14s.6d

* = customary family

** = free family

of determining just how large a role subsistence living played among Holywell's families. The fact that 49 families were able to survive for anywhere from three generations to over 200 years is in itself highly significant. This is not to deny, however, that several families no doubt found it difficult to maintain themselves. Between 1288 and 1339, for example, 29 families were able to maintain but short residence — that is, less than 40 years. It cannot be assumed, however, that all disappeared through starvation. At least seven — the Avenaunts, the Fischers, the Fychyens, the Godales, the Mariots, the Skys and the Walmesfords — came to an end because of the generation or survival of only female offspring. The remainder either died out or moved away,[110] although there is no way of determining the exact fate of all. That they may have died out or emigrated as a result of an inability to subsist cannot be discounted. An examination of five Ramsey manors in northern Huntingdonshire during the same period — the late thirteenth and first half of the fourteenth centuries — reveals the existence of a large body of peasants who wandered from vill to vill, attempting to survive on the edge of the community, as servants, tradesmen, butchers, and then moving on.[111]

However, even if it be readily admitted that these families may have moved away because of an inability to "make ends meet" or else died out through starvation — rather than through an equally probable failure to generate offspring — it is clear that not all families supplied with little or no land were doomed to quick extinction. The Fabers, the Fannels, the Pollards, the Russels, the Seledes and the Spercolls, for example, were either not tenants of any land or of only a very few acres — even less than five — and yet each family survived from at least the late thirteenth century for periods of from 101 (Selede) to over 177 years (Faber/Smyth). In addition, eight other villein families outside the customary structure[112] survived through two generations, for periods of from 44 (Fressant) to 65 years (Tiffayne).

The point to be emphasized is that neither the modest size of customary tenements nor the failure to be supplied with land at all necessitated either a subsistence existence or starvation and extinction in Holywell

---

[110] One customary family — the Colyns — apparently died out, since they were last represented by only one person and no record survives of their being *extra feodum*. One non-customary family — the Kylleneths — are known to have emigrated to St. Ives (PRO SC 2-178/95).

[111] The villages examined were Broughton, Warboys, Wistow, Upwood and Abbots Ripton. Unfortunately, no representatives of the vanishing Holywell families turned up in those communities, which may mean either that they did in fact die out at home or else moved to other villages.

[112] Baldewyne (1313-72), Botwryte (1306-56), Carpenter (1294-1346), Cusste (1301-53), Fressant (1288-1332), Legge (1294-1339) Raulyn (1306-53), and Tiffayne (1288-1353).

prior to the middle of the fourteenth century. Indeed, the size of tenements — even the small virgate — did not prevent families like the Clerks, the Edwards, the Fabers, the Fannells, the Grays, the Hamonds, the Lanes, the Lawemans, the Nicholases and the Scots from boasting anywhere from three to six members in one generation prior to 1350. It is clear that subsistence in Holywell prior to the Black Death did not depend exclusively, therefore, on land, nor for that matter did prosperity. That land was an important element in the survival process, as well as in conferring status, is not at all denied, but the fact that a large number of peasants between the last decade of the thirteenth century and the middle of the fourteenth century was encountered in court rolls loaning money to their neighbors, serving as frequent personal pledges and regularly exercising positions of official responsibility — in short, behaving in a manner normally identified with the peasant at 24, 30 or even 40 acres in other parts of England — when, in fact, very few Holywell peasants had anything near 30 acres, or even 24 acres of land, points to a peasantry capable of surviving and, in many cases, more than subsisting but rather prospering despite limited proprietary resources. In fact, the question of subsistence itself may have been unduly clouded by a heavy emphasis on the place of wheat in the peasant's diet. It is normally proposed that subsistence depended on the holding of so many acres because they were necessary to produce a specific amount of wheat whereby a family might live. Yet in Holywell, where the number of acres under the normal virgater's and semi-virgater's or cotlander's control was modest, it may be that wheat was not a *sine qua non* for a subsistence diet, but rather something else: rye and peas, for example,[113] and — an intriguing possibility — fish. Indeed, in such a village as Holywell, lapped by the waters of the Ouse on one side and nudged by fens on another, where royal commissions to fish were being granted as late as the reign of Henry VI and whose fishing possibilities were attracting the tenants of the Bishop of Ely as early as the late thirteenth century, the place of fish in a subsistence diet cannot be entirely overlooked.[114]

---

[113] The abbey, for one, was employing large amounts of rye in its payments in kind to its *famuli* in Holywell around 1300 (See Raftis, *Estates*, p. 205), while from the 1370's equal portions of wheat and peas were given out, at a normal rate of four bushels every six weeks (*Ibid.*, Table XLVI, p. 208).

[114] See *Calender of the Patent Rolls*, Henry VI, Vol. IV (1452-1461): London, 1910; p. 556, 612, for commissions "de kidellis" in the fifteenth century in Holywell waters and involving Holywell peasants. For the bishop of Ely, see *Carts.* I, p. 216. In an agreement of 1294 between the bishop and the abbot of Ramsey, it was stated that "lada, quae ducit de Nydyngworthe usque magnam ripam ... est communis piscaria omnium communicantium .... "

But whatever the ultimate explanation, the fact remains that in Holy-well during the late thirteenth century and first half of the fourteenth century, despite the limited amount of land available to them, a large number of peasants was surviving. More than that, they survived for considerably long stretches of time and were able to assume and maintain places of importance in village life that, in other localities, were normally the prerogative of peasants more generously supplied with land. In short, the evidence is of a community where, although a not insignificant number of peasants and peasant families could be poor and could fail to maintain residence beyond a generation, an equally significant number of families survived through two and three generations, occupied important places in village government, administration and general community life and, when it came time to be taxed, were taxed on personal movables at least two times above the exemption point — and all on a tenement foundation that should have guaranteed only a subsistence income. Indeed, such peasants were surviving. But they were also more than subsisting,[115]

[115] A possible clue to the thriving conditions of a large number of Holywell peasants at this time may come from their economic interests being regional, and not simply local. Professor Raftis has done much to emphasize the broad extent of peasant mobility on Ramsey estates as early as the late thirteenth century, and frequent reasons for such mobility were the application of a skill or the taking up of land in neighboring — and even distant — villages (See *Tenure and and Mobility*, Part III, Chapters 6-8, and esp. p. 151). The pursuit of such interests would not even always necessitate the peasant's abandoning his home community. That Holywell villagers may have had sources of income from outside the manor is therefore a possibility, although I have been unable to find direct evidence of it to any considerable degree. For example, an investigation of court rolls for the northern-Huntingdonshire vills of Broughton, Warboys, Wistow, Upwood and Abbots Ripton from the 1280's to *ca.* 1350 has failed to reveal the activities of any major Holywell people in those communities, while the same has resulted from a study of court rolls for the nearby village of Hemmingford Abbots in the same period. However, rolls from the St. Ives courts from 1301 to 1356 have supplied details on at least 14 property transactions in that town involving Holywell people. In addition, the majority of the transactions did not involve pieces of land but rather houses, shops and stalls, beginning in 1301 with the taking up of a stall by Sampson "the Candle-Maker of Niddingworth". Among other Holywell people noted were: Henry Tiffayne, John Raven, John Scot and William de Halywell (i.e. Hamond). PRO SC 2-178/95.

In short, there is at least some evidence of Holywell people engaging in economic activities outside the village, and the likelihood of there having been many more than known by name is real. The incidence of outsiders in Holywell, for example, reflects the heavy mobility of the peasantry in the region at the time, and although Holywell people do not appear in court rolls — as outsiders — of neighboring Ramsey villages does not at all prove or suggest that they were an exceptional lot who never went outside their own boundaries. On the contrary, the probability is that they were as mobile as their neighbors, and, being situated on the Ouse as the village is, their interests may not have been restricted solely to Huntingdonshire but rather could have taken them into other counties. Several instances can be cited, for example, of locals emigrating

and if subsistence was not an overwhelming problem in Holywell prior
to the Black Death — when population, although beginning to decline,
was still at a high point — then it is most improbable that it was a major
problem after the Black Death, when population continued to thin-out,
more land became available, mobility intensified and the concentration
and consolidation of larger tenements — for purposes of quick exploitation
more than for cultivation — dominated the village.[116] Therefore, although
there were certainly poor peasants in late mediaeval Holywell,[117] and even

to Cambridgeshire and even Kent in the early fifteenth century (see *supra*, p. 178). There is
no real reason for discounting the possibility of a similar far-ranging mobility earlier in the village's
history.

[116] Specifically, if a family like the Seldes could move into the village in the early 1370's and
be content to hold only a croft (received in 1407) through two generations as its "core" tenement,
they were obviously not worried too much about starving to death, especially when — given the
willingness of the abbey to still issue *exodus* licenses as well as its inability to really do much about
fugitive *nativi* — they could have left at any time. The same observation could, in fact, be made
about any number of small-holding families in the late fourteenth and first half of the fifteenth
centuries, while the fact that immigration to Holywell was a consistent factor throughout the
fourteenth and fifteenth centuries is a powerful indication that the village held very real attractions.

[117] One index to poverty conditions in the village may be found in fourteenth-century court
roll presentations of villagers guilty of "gleaning wrongly", since the right to glean was a recognized
form of village welfare (see Raftis, "Social Structures ..." *Ec.H.R.* XVIII, pp. 92-93). Thus,
in 1288 the wives of Nicholas Godfrey and Thomas Bundeleg were gleaners. In 1301, the children
of Radulf Seman were presented for gleaning wrongly. Nicholas Godfrey's wife — Margaret
— was presented again in 1307 and 1321. Also gleaning in 1307 was the daughter of Galfridus
Maryot. In 1318, seven villagers were fined for gleaning offenses: Alice Ripton, Margaret ad
Crucem, Matilda Colyn, Sibilla and John Cappe, Katerina Legge and Alice Godrych. In 1326,
Nicholas de Ripton gleaned, as did a transient — Margaret, wife of "Big John" ("uxor Magni
Johannis") in 1339. In 1353, seven villagers again were presented for gleaning wrongly: the
wives of Nicholas Russell, and Nicholas Scharp, Joanna le Smyth, Agnes Bernewell, Matilda
Campion, Caterina Raulyn and Agnes Granit (a transient). Matilda Campion gleaned again
in 1356 — along with yet another transient, Margaret le Warden. In 1378, Agnes Hemyngton
gleaned, as did John Tayllour in 1386, John Wright and William Langeton (another transient)
in 1391, and the son of William Patrik (transient) in 1394. Finally, in 1394 Margaret Scharp
and Agnes Deye were fined for gleaning wrongly.

All told, the surviving rolls from the late thirteenth and fourteenth centuries record a total
of only 30 instances of wrongful gleaning, involving only 28 persons. Interestingly, the two periods
of heaviest gleaning were 1318 and 1353 — the first during the decade of famine, the second only
a few years after the Black Death. In addition, of the gleaners representing resident families,
only one — Margaret Godfrey — gleaned wrongly three times — and then spread over a period
of 34 years — while two gleaned wrongly twice (Matilda Campion and Margaret Scharp) and
20 gleaned wrongly only once. Compared with five other Ramsey Huntingdonshire villages,
Holywell's incidence of gleaning was not extraordinary. Thus Wistow recorded 25 gleaning
offenders; there were 27 at Upwood, 10 at Broughton, six at Abbots Ripton and 27 at Warboys
(See Raftis, "Social Structures," *Ec.H.R.* XVIII, p. 92).

destitute, desperate and starving peasants, they were not overwhelmingly predominant, while the securing and maintenance of a subsistence level of life as well as of even more overtly prosperous levels were, despite proprietary limitations, capable of realization and were, in fact, realized by several villagers and families. Consequently, Holywell's fourteenth- and fifteenth-century population crisis was not, in the last analysis, the result of a subsistence crisis. Rather it was indeed a part of the general demographic malaise settling over the English rural landscape at the time, a decline which had possibly been conditioned by initial over-population at the end of the thirteenth century, started on its course by the famines of the second decade of the fourteenth century, intensified by the savage attacks of the Black Death in the middle of the century and subsequently sustained by repeated visitations of plague through the 1380's[118] and by a general atmosphere of contagion and infection — all against a background of agrarian stagnation — and possibly also assisted by changing peasant attitudes regarding the institutions of matrimony and family. But whatever its final explanations and causes, its effects were felt in virtually every part of England, with consequent declines in rural settlement — even to the complete desertion of some villages.[119] If Holywell was spared its full force — which may have been due partly do the ability of Ramsey administration to make continuous adjustments in manorial policy to meet new situations as they arose, partly to a generally vigorous peasantry with solid experience in the art of survival and capable of making adjustments of their own in order to continue to both survive and even prosper, and partly also to sheer chance — the village was nevertheless far from immune to the crisis, and although it survived, the wounds it suffered in the process were both very real and very deep.

---

[118] See Postan, CEH, I, p. 570; and Postan and Titow, "Heriots and Prices," *Ec.H.R.* XI, p. 392 *et seq.*

[119] See M. W. Beresford, *The Lost Villages of England* (Lutterworth, 1954).

II

"FAMILIES IN HOLYWELL-CUM-NEEDINGWORTH: PLACE IN VILLAGE
STRUCTURE, 1288-1457"

The preceding pages were devoted to a discussion of the settlement
patterns of Holywell families in the fourteenth century and first half of
the fifteenth century, together with an investigation of the general demographic trend in the community from 1300 to 1450. Furthermore, the
degree to which individual families involved themselves in the customary
structure of the manor has also been given attention.[120] However, it is
apparent that a description of the land or tenurial commitments of a
family does not provide a complete and exhaustive picture of its activities
and place in the local community. It may help clarify a family's place
in the context of the manor, but it says little of its place in the society
of the village. That there was indeed such a phenomenon as a village
society should no longer need special emphasis.[121] Although the manor
exerted a powerful influence and occupied a major place in the experience
of the local community, it has been pointed out, for one, that in Holywell
not all the resident families were involved in the manorial structure.
In addition, the court rolls provide glimpses of the existence of local institutions that were either not products of the manor or were not uniquely
dependent on it. Thus, the institution of the frankpledge — that organization of local residents into tithing groups for the purpose of maintaining
the peace and the initial reason for the existence of the *visus* — was of
ancient and non-manorial origin, with its roots deep in the Anglo-Saxon
period and having been reinforced by the Anglo-Norman kings.[122] So,
too, the existence of a local ale-brewing "industry" — regulated from
outside by royal assizes — was independent of the manor's presence.
Further, the incidence of pleas of debt, the enunciation and enforcement
of by-laws, the evidence of craftsmen, the punishment of violations of
the peace and personal trespasses, the movement of villeins throughout
the countryside for economic or family reasons, and even the evidence

---

[120] See *supra*, Chapters I and II, *passim*.

[121] The reality of the village community and experience in mediaeval England has been well
established by Helen Cam, Joan Wake ("Communitas Villae," *English Historical Review*, XXXVII
(1922), pp. 406-13); G. Homans, *English Villagers of the Thirteenth Century*, and, most recently,
by Raftis, *Tenure and Mobility*, and "Social Structures in Five East Midland Villages," *Ec.H.R.*
XVIII.

[122] See W. A. Morris, *The Frankpledge System* (Cambridge, Mass. 1910).

of varying degrees of capital resources as revealed by the early fourteenth-century subsidy lists all point to be existence of a village society with needs and institutions that went beyond the close and tight framework of the manor. Unfortunately, not all the institutions of this village society can be examined in any significant detail. The primary source for their study remains — at present — the court rolls, and they act as a window on the village, through which the modern investigator can peer as facets of local life pass by. However, some pass by quickly, or only occasionally, while, further, as with a window, the investigator's field of vision is limited. For this reason, therefore, such a factor as the local economic institutions of the village defies precise definition or description. That a village economy was a reality is recognized — the major role assumed by smallholdings, the evidence of intra-village debt structures, the practice of a craft or a trade and the accumulation of large stores of movable property bear witness to it[123] — but the nature of surviving Holywell records prevents an examination of its dimensions or component parts.

But if Holywell records — especially court rolls — do not permit detailed examination of many village institutions, they do allow some assessment of the places in local life occupied by individual families, especially with regard to responsibility for local administration and government. Therefore, based on the exercise of positions of official responsibility both within the village (e.g. jurors, tasters, constables, capital pledges) and manorial (e.g. reeves, beadles, bailiffs, ploughmen, *collectores redditus*) structures, it is possible to make some judgments as to the degree to which individual families were involved in the village — whether deeply or peripherally — and consequently to classify known families as being of major, minor or intermediate importance to the life of the community. In so doing, attention shall further be given to the relationship of such families to the manorial structure as well as to their patterns of settlement. That such questions demand consideration can no longer be doubted. The recent attention that has been given to the study of the family in history and in individual societies[124] especially demands that such an institution be investigated in the context of rural society and peasant culture, and no matter how limited the result of the investigator's labours, the attempt must nevertheless be made to assess the role and place of family groups in the life of the local community.

The local court in Holywell-cum-Needingworth was more than just

---

[123] See G. Duby, *L'economie rurale*, pp. 59-60, 61-2, 166 *et seq.*, 191 *et seq.*, 377 *et seq.*, 473; also Raftis, *Tenure and Mobility*, pp. 91-97.

[124] See Joan Thirsk, "The Family," *Past and Present*, No. 27, 1964.

a source of revenue for the abbot of Ramsey and a vehicle for enforcing customary tenurial obligations through the fining of villeins working carelessly or not working at all. It was the instrument whereby various village and national institutions and regulations were sanctioned and enforced. Violations of the peace, of the assize of ale, debts, private land transactions, personal complaints and infractions of local by-laws were all brought before it. As a result, aspects of local government and administration are almost uniquely reflected in the rolls of the court, especially the persons exercising positions of governmental and administrative responsibility. Even manorial officials — the reeve, the bailiff and the beadle — worked closely with the court, calling upon it to penalize derelictions of customary obligations and to enforce distraints made upon troublesome *nativi*, while these officials themselves were liable to presentment and amercement for their own derelictions of duty.[125] Consequently, because of the importance of the court in local government and administration, the rolls from 1288 through 1457 supply the names of 222 persons exercising positions of official responsibility — from court jurors, ale-tasters, capital pledges and constables to reeves, bailiffs, beadles and lesser manorial or agricultural officials (hayward, autumn reeve and custodian). In addition, of the 222 thus documented, 212 were representatives of 79 village families, and they displayed degrees of involvement in official life varying from the infrequent or sporadic to the intense and continuous. (See Table VII).

In short, out of a total of 140 known families resident in the village between the late thirteenth century and the middle of the fifteenth century, 56% involved themselves in the govermental and administrative structure of the community. But not all were necessarily of major importance because of this fact. Thirty-two of the 79 official families, for example (41%), were characterized by the undertaking of only one official position of responsibility during the family's residence, and they may therefore be classified as families of "lesser" or "intermediate" importance (Table VII: Group "B"). On the other hand, 47 families (59%) commanded

---

[125] An especially good example of the responsibility of the reeve to the local court — as well as an indication of the powers and duties of the reeve relative to the behaviour of customary families — is found in the Holywell court roll for 1313 (PRO SC 2-179/17), where Robert the son of Elena, reeve, was fined 6 d. for failing to prevent the marriage of Joanna Curteys to a villein of St. Ives. The marriage was illicit both because, as a *nativa*, Joanna had not secured permission to marry, and further had married outside the manor. The complete text itself — which reveals the full, almost comic extent of the whole affair, including the complicity of Joanna's mother Beatrix and Robert's failure to arrest her — can be found in Raftis, *Tenure and Mobility*, p. 274, no. 13.

TABLE VII

MAIN FAMILIES IN HOLYWELL-CUM-NEEDINGWORTH, 1275-1457

FAMILY	MEMBERS	NO. OF OFFICES	TIMES SERVED	ACTIVITY GROUP	RESIDENCE GROUP
ALEYN	1	1	1	B	II
ARNOLD	1	1	1	B	II
ASPLOND	7	5	44	A	I
ATTEWELLE	2	5	23	A	I
BACOUN	2	1	4	B	II
BAKER	3	2	23	A	II
BAROUN	3	4	9	A	I
BATE	1	2	3	A	II
BEAUMEYS	5	2	18	A	I
BRADENACH	1	1	5	B	III
BRAYN	8	4	26	A	I
BRIAN	2	2	3	A	I
BROOK	3	1	4	B	I
BRUN	2	2	6	A	II
CAPUD VILLE	1	1	1	B	III
CARPENTER	2	1	4	B	II
CARTERE	3	3	16	A	I
CLERK	2	2	4	A	I
COLYN	1	1	1	B	III
CRANFELD	3	2	9	A	II
CRISTEMESSE	3	5	16	A	I
CURTEYS	1	2	2	A	I
CUSSTE	1	1	1	B	II
DEYE	2	6	12	A	I
EDWARD	7	6	45	A	I
ELYOT	1	3	4	A	IV
EYR	3	2	7	A	I
FABER/SMYTH	2	2	4	A	I
FANNELL	2	2	5	A	I
FLESSHEWERE	1	2	2	A	III
FRANKLYN	3	2	8	A	I
FREYSANT	1	1	1	B	II
GERE	3	3	9	A	I
GODEMAN	7	4	13	A	I
GODFREY	6	6	25	A	I
GODRYCH	1	2	5	A	I
GRAY	7	5	18	A	I
GUNNE	1	2	3	A	III
HALIDAY	1	2	3	A	III
HAMOND	2	3	9	A	I
HEMYNGTON	3	4	20	A	I

Family	Members	No. of Offices	Times Served	Activity Group	Residence Group
Houghton	3	4	24	A	I
Hunne	7	5	26	A	I
Lane	4	2	9	A	I
Lanender	1	3	5	A	III
Laweman	7	4	20	A	I
Machyng	1	1	1	B	I
Madde	2	1	4	B	III
May	1	2	6	A	III
Merton	3	2	13	A	I
Miller	2	3	4	A	I
Moke	1	2	3	A	II
Muryell	2	2	4	A	II
Nicholas	9	6	36	A	I
Oky	1	1	1	B	III
Palmere	3	6	25	A	I
Portam	1	1	2	B	II
Porter	1	2	12	A	II
Prepositus/Revf	3	3	3	A	I
"Radulphi"	4	2	14	A	III
Raulyn	1	1	1	B	II
Ripton	1	3	6	A	I
"Elene"	1	2	2	A	III
Russell	1	1	1	B	I
Sande	3	2	7	A	I
Scharp	2	2	4	A	II
Selede	2	2	4	A	I
Scot	9	8	43	A	I
Sewale	3	4	7	A	I
Shepperd	5	6	22	A	I
Sky	1	1	1	B	III
Thurkyll	2	1	2	B	III
Tiffayne	1	1	1	B	II
Toly	1	1	1	B	II
Tooslond	1	1	1	B	IV
Valentyn	1	1	2	B	IV
Venelle	1	1	1	B	I
Wilkyn	1	1	7	B	IV
Wright	2	4	7	A	I

an unmistakably major importance in the governmental and administrative life of the village, since they held anywhere from two to nine offices during their term of settlement (Table VII: Group "A"). A closer examination of the offices held and the people holding them should prove instructive.

One of the most important positions in local government in Holywell was that of court juror. It was upon the jurors that the bulk of the court's operations devolved, being charged with the duty of making presentments of violations before the abbot's seneschal and declaring the truth of the numerous complaints brought before the court. They served as both an investigatory and declaratory body, and the heaviness of their responsibility was underlined not only be their being under oath,[126] but by their own liability to amercement for falsified or concealed presentments.[127] In addition, although the office of juror is seen in operation only during the sessions of the court, its responsibilities were not confined to one solitary day in the year, but rather engaged the energies of its holder throughout the period between court sessions, since only then could a thorough report of offenses and complaints — and judgments — be rendered. Consequently, the jurors' responsibility was both a continuing and time-consuming one. It was not a position of minor or incidental importance in the village; and therefore attention now turns directly to the Holywell jurors in an attempt to determine who they were, what qualified them to be jurors, and what — if anything — they had in common with each other.

As already noted, between 1288 and 1457, 222 men served as officials in Holywell-cum-Needingworth. Of these, 176 (80 %) were recorded as holding the office of juror for anywhere from one to over a dozen times.[128] In addition, 168 of these men represented 71 of the 79 "official" families (90 %). As for the men themselves, 78 (44 %) seem to have seen jury service but once. Twenty-five served twice, 21 three times, 15 four times, 10 five times, eight served six times, seven served seven times, three men served eight, nine and 10 times, and one served 11, 12 and 14 times. The representation of families among the jurors was equally diversified, therefore, extending from once (18 families) to 32 times (one family). (See Table VIII).

---

[126] The formula invariably accompanying presentments by the jury in the court roll was: "Et dicunt per sacramentum suum."

[127] This last was no idle or merely remote possibility. Holywell jurors were fined 3 s. 4 d. in 1288 for concealed presentments (PRO SC 2-179/5), 5 s. in 1294 (BM.Add.Roll. 39597) and 3 s. in 1301 (PRO SC 2-179/11).

[128] Eight capital pledges have been included in this total number of jurors, since they composed one-half the jury of the *visus* of 16 October, 1288 (PRO SC 2-179/5).

TABLE VIII

THE REPRESENTATION OF HOLYWELL FAMILIES ON JURIES, 1288-1457

Family	No. of Men	No. of Times
Aleyn	1	1
Asplond	7	31
Attewelle	2	17
Bacoun	2	2
Baker	3	19
Baroun	2	7
Beaumeys	5	13
Bradenach	1	5
Brayn	6	15
Brook	3	4
Brun	2	3
Bryan	1	2
Capud Ville	1	1
Carpenter	2	4
Cartere	3	12
Clerk	2	3
Colyn	1	1
Cranfeld	2	7
Cristemesse	3	8
Curteys	1	1
Cusste	1	1
Deye	2	3
Edward	7	32
Elene	1	1
Elyot	1	1
Eyr	3	5
Faber/Smyth	1	3
Fannell	2	2
Flesshewere	1	1
Franklyn	3	7
Freysant	1	1
Gere	2	8
Godeman	5	9
Godfrey	3	11
Godrych	1	3
Gray	5	11
Gunne	1	1
Haliday	1	2
Hamond	2	6
Hemyngton	3	11
Houghton	2	17
Hunne	6	18
Lane	4	8
Lanender	1	2

Family	No. of Men	No. of Times
Laweman	7	14
Madde	2	4
May	1	5
Merton	3	11
Moke	1	2
Nicholas	7	28
Palmere	3	14
Portam	1	2
Porter	1	10
Prepositus	1	1
"Radulphi"	2	9
Raulyn	1	1
Ripton	1	2
Russell	1	1
Sande	2	3
Scot	8	31
Selede	1	2
Sewale	2	3
Shepperd	4	16
Sky	1	1
Thurkyll	2	2
Tiffayne	1	1
Toly	1	1
Tooslond	1	1
Venelle	1	1
Wilkyn	1	7
Wright	1	3

in Holywell was not tightly confined to only a handful of special villagers through the fourteenth and first half of the fifteenth centuries. The fact that 71 of the village's known 140 families (or 51 %) exercised juratorial responsibility at one time or another is sufficient confirmation of the fact that Holywell's juries were not in the control of a narrowly-limited oligarchy of peasants. On the other hand, there is no reason for assuming that jury service was rotated among village families according to some obscure egalitarian principle. If 51 % of the families saw service over the course of the years, 49 % did not — and there are little or no grounds for believing that they ever did. Consequently — and in light of the fact that jurors, as other local officials, were elected to their positions by the homage — it is fair to suspect the existence of some specific principles of selection and eligibility obtaining in the village which resulted in some men and families being qualified for the office and others not.

Long-term residence in the village does not seem to have been one of the criteria for jury service. Admittedly, 61 of the 71 jury families — or 86 %

It is clear from the sheer number of men serving on juries — and the large number of families they in turn represented — that jury service — had been in residence for at least 10 years before their initial appearance among the jurors, but 10 families — or 14 % — had not. Rather, they were supplying jurors shortly after their arrival in the village. The Carpenters, for example, were not found in local records at all prior to 1294 — the year in which Robert Carpenter was a juror. Similarly with the Capud Ville family. The Maddes initially saw jury service in 1299, but the family seems to have arrived only five years earlier — in 1294. The Bakers, the Mertons and the Bradenachs were alike in that they first appeared as jurors — no record being found of them prior to their holding of the office. Nicholas Flesshewere was a juror in 1356, yet he appeared in the village only three years earlier. The Palmeres appeared in the village first in 1306, yet they were supplying a juror in 1311, while both the Porters and the Wilkyns were holding the office almost immediately after their arrivals. In addition, there were a dozen families of definitely long-term residence who apparently never saw jury service: the Barkers, the Bernewells, the Hroffs, the Machyngs, the Pollards, the Ravens, the Seldes, the Spercolls, the Tayllours, the Scharps, the Baldewynes and the Skynneres.

Long-term residence, therefore, was neither a prerequisite for nor a guarantee of jury service in Holywell. That it may have been a factor, of course, cannot be discounted but it was not the indispensable criterion. Other considerations were obviously involved.

It may be wondered if the answer may not be found in the frankpledge system. After all, it could be argued that since the court session — in the form of the *visus* — was a survey of activities within the various tithing groups, it would not be inconceivable to expect the capital pledges — the leaders of the individual tithing groups — to serve in the capacity of jurors. Such a phenomenon was noted, for example, by Maitland on the Ramsey manor of Gidding,[129] and a further example can be found at Hemmingford Abbots in 1291.[130] However, this does not appear to have been the case in Holywell — at least after 1288, when a jury of 16 was composed of eight capital pledges and eight other peasants.[131] There are, of course, no surviving lists of all the capital pledges in Holywell

---

[129] *Select Pleas*, II, p. 87; see also Seldon Society, IV, p. 110.

[130] PRO SC 2-179/7. The roll begins with the heading: "Nomina capitalium plegeorum juratorum ..."

[131] PRO SC 2-179/5. It should further be noted that the number of jurors in 1288 — 16 — was itself exceptional. Subsequent Holywell juries consisted of 12 men.

in the fourteenth century or of the number of tithing groups in the village. The court roll of 1288 — when the jury was partly composed of capital pledges — provides the names of eight tithing men,[132] and the name of yet another is found in the court roll of 1306.[133] As said, it is not known how many tithing groups there were in the village, but there were doubtlessly a dozen — and possibly even two-dozen — around 1300, when there were at least 251 adults in the village, although the number must needs have declined as the population itself shrank over the fourteenth century. But even if there were enough capital pledges to furnish 12 jurors, the important point to be made is that of the nine capital pledges actually known by name between 1288 and 1306, only four are recorded as having served as jurors subsequent to 1288: Robert Brayn Jr. (1313, 1318), William le Eyr (1306, 1313, 1322), Richard Gere (1294, 1299, 1301, 1306, 1313 and 1318) and Richard Laweman (1294). The remaining five did not appear as jurors. Even given the incompleteness of the court roll series, it is likely that these five men would have appeared as jurors at some point in either 1292, 1294, 1299, 1301, 1306 or 1307, if, in fact, they made up a pool from which jurors were drawn.[134]

Furthermore, there is another reason for discounting the exclusive identification of Holywell jurors with capital pledges, and it is a reason derived from numbers. Between 1288 and 1299, 38 identifiable men, representing at least 29 separate families, served on the four juries whose records are extant. If the 38 men were all capital pledges, there would have had to have been at least 38 tithing groups in the village around 1300, or an absolute minimum of 380 adults in the vill at that time. As there were only 251 known adults — both male and female — in Holywell in 1300, this is most unlikely.

Finally, the fact that the court roll of 1288, when eight capital pledges did play a role in the jury, took pains to distinguish between the *capitales plegii* and the *juratores*, pure and simple, indicates rather plainly that the jury was not the exclusive function of the tithingmen.

The exercise of juror responsibility, therefore, is not to be explained by the jurors necessarily being all capital pledges. Capital pledges could be jurors — and some were — but they were not jurors because they were capital pledges, anymore than long-term residents were jurors merely

---

[132] The eight were: Gilbert Arthur, Robert Brayn Sr., Robert Brayn Jr., Adam le Eyr, Richard Gere, Richard Laweman, Radulph the son of Roger, and Walter Scot.

[133] William le Eyr.

[134] The office of capital pledge, for example, appears to have been a continuing — and not an annual — one. Thus, William Eyr, capital pledge in 1306, was still a capital pledge in 1311.

because they were long-term residents. Similarly, it does not seem that jury service was dependent upon prior experience in other offices. Although 88 of the known 176 jurors — or 50 % exactly — served in other positions in village and manorial government and administration, in addition to being jurors, only 38 (43 %) held another office (or offices) prior to their initial appearance as jurors. Twenty-one had previously been ale-tasters, five had been constables, four capital pledges, two had seen service as reeves, four as beadles, one as ploughman and one as *custos autumpni*. Clearly the assumption cannot be made that to be a juror one had to have been first a taster, reeve or other official. Therefore, although experience and expertise may have played a part in the selection of some men for jury service, it alone was not a *sine qua non* for such service.

Two factors, however, appear to have been extremely important as qualifications for the office. One was age. Although it is most difficult to determine the ages of individual Holywell peasants in any given years, it is known that men did not appear in the court rolls until they had reached the age of legal responsibility in the village — 12 years, when it was necessary to enter a tithing group. In addition, the court rolls document that at least 44 of the known 176 jurors (25 %) had reached the age of legal responsibility and had been living and working in the village several years before they first appeared as jurors. Furthermore, since not one of the 44 displays the behaviour of an early adolescent in his earliest court roll appearances,[135] but rather all seem to have been in their late 'teens or early 20's at the time,[136] while the average length of time elapsing between their first appearance and their assumption of jury duties is 16 to 17 years,[137] they appear to have been at least in their early 30's when

---

[135] By "early adolescent" behaviour is meant being presented for such offenses as breaking-and-entering or being the subject of the hue and cry. This does not mean to imply that Holywell adolescents were necessarily fourteenth-century juvenile delinquents; it only suggests that when an initial appearance is made in the context of such offenses, it may be fair to suspect the subject of being very young and not yet fully adjusted to the more adult responsibilities now demanded of him.

[136] Their initial appearances in local records were either as a result of trespasses, failures to work, debts, licenses of concord or even land acquisitions.

[137] The 44 men — with the years between their initial appearance in local records and their first recorded jury service — are as follows:

ASPLOND, Thomas:	19 years	GODFREY, Nicholas II:	34 years
ASPLOND, Richard:	31 years	GODFREY, John II:	13 years
BAROUN, John II:	33 years	GRAY, William II:	11 years
BEAUMEYS, John I:	10 years	HAMOND, Stephan:	23 years
BEAUMEYS, John III:	27 years	HAMOND, John:	16 years
BRAYN, William I:	11 years	HEMYNGTON, John:	8 years

chosen as jurors. Although this admittedly accounts for only 25 %
of the known jurors, it may nevertheless be suggested that jury service was
indeed for men who were at least about 30 years of age, that is, for men
who had reached a minimal maturity in years, thereby ensuring their
sobriety and reliability in the office. This tends to receive further confirmation by the evidence of a number of peasants who exercised juratorial
responsibilities over extended periods of time — when the men themselves
would have been in their 40's, 50's and even 60's and 70's. Thus, John
Asplond (II) was a juror 10 times in 27 years, while John Asplond (III)
held the position at least nine times over a 48 year period, and John (IV)
served three times between 1437 and 1457. Robert AtteWelle was a juror
nine times in 32 years, and his grandson, John (II), served eight times
in 30 years. John Baker was a 12-time juror over a 27 year period, while
Roger Baker flourished as a juror between 1419 and 1443. All told, 39
men — out of a total of 98 — who held the office of juror more than once,
did so for periods of between 20 and 42 years.

But if a minimal age of about 30 appears to have been a factor in eligibility
for the office of juror, another — and perhaps the most important — factor
concerned the economic position of the peasant himself. Specifically,
out of 176 known jurors between 1288 and 1457, 147 (84%) were either
customary tenants on the manor or members of customary families.[138]

BRYAN, William I:	20 years	LAWEMAN, Simon:	12 years
CARTERE, William II:	15 years	LAWEMAN, William I:	19 years
CLERK, John:	23 years	LAWEMAN, Nicholas:	15 years
CRANFELD, Richard:	11 years	LAWEMAN, Richard II:	28 years
CRISTEMESSE, Richard	8 years	LANE, Nicholas:	11 years
CRISTEMESSE, Roger:	9 years	NICOLAS, Stephan:	16 years
CRISTEMESSE, John II:	20 years	NICHOLAS, Robert:	10 years
DEYE, Thomas II:	20 years	NICHOLAS, Thomas:	8 years
EDWARD, Nicholas:	25 years	NICHOLAS, John IV:	7 years
EDWARD, Thomas:	20 years	NICHOLAS, Simon:	11 years
EDWARD, Richard II:	12 years	SCOT, Thomas:	14 years
FABER/SMYTH, Thomas:	35 years	SEWALE, Roger:	17 years
FRANKLYN, Richard:	10 years	SHEPPERD, John II:	35 years
GODEMAN, John:	29 years	SHEPPERD, John III:	9 years
GODEMAN, Robert:	5 years	WRIGHT, William II:	26 years
GODFREY, Adam:	9 years		

[138] Twenty-nine men cannot be identified as customary tenants. Thus, members of the Brook
(3), Bradenach (1), Capud Ville (1), Carpenter (2), Smyth (1), Freysant (1), Gunne (2), "Rad-
ulphi" (2), Madde (2), Raulyn (1), Elene (1), Sky (1), Thurkyll (2), Tiffayne (1), Tooslond
(1) and Wilkyn (1) families are not found at any time holding either virgates, cotlands or crofts
or even indicated indirectly to be so. On the other hand, six men cannot be identified at all:
Gilbert Arthur, John Cous, Thomas Merale, Adam de Norton, Robert the son of Alan and Radulph

This does not mean, however, that all were necessarily large tenants:
Nicholas Flesshewere, for example, a juror in 1356 was only a croft holder,
while, if demesne and fen is included together with specifically labelled
customary land after the middle of the fourteenth century, out of 62 men
serving as jurors after 1350, it can be found that 28 held 20 acres of property
or more, whereas 24 held between 10 and 20 acres, and 10 held less than
10 acres. (See Table IX).[139] The tendency, then — as observed after the
middle of the fourteenth century — was for the jurors to be at least semi-
virgaters or cotlanders, or their equivalent, that is, tenants of 10 acres
of land or more, and it is not unlikely that a similar condition obtained
prior to 1350. Nevertheless, even then the ranks of the jurors were not
closed to the tenant of less than 10 acres, and although an involvement
in the customary structure of the manor was a predominant element
among the jurors, it was not an absolute prerequisite — as the example
of 29 families not showing any signs of customary tenure yet supplying
jurors demonstrates. That land — and, as Professor Raftis has recently
emphasized, "a real title to land"[140] — was an important factor in qualifying
a person for jury service cannot be denied, but perhaps the over-riding
consideration was general economic stability and security, whether its
foundation was in land or in other capital resources. This is given emphasis
by the subsidy rolls of 1327 and 1332, for example. Out of a total of 82
persons paying either the twentieth of 1327 or the fifteenth of 1332 — or
both — 28 were men who could be found among the jurors of the village,
or 34%, while, further, 25 of a total of 38 tax-paying families were "jury"
families (66%). Of the 28 men themselves, 20 (71%) were consistently
in command of movables valued at 20 shillings or more, thereby accounting
for 37 % of the 63 taxpayers in the same range. In addition, 20 of the
25 jury families (80%) were possessed of movables at 20 shillings or above,
accounting for two-thirds of the village families at the same level.[141]

The conclusion that can be drawn, then, is that Holywell jurors were
generally men of some economic substance, and that the majority in
the fourteenth and earlier fifteenth centuries were customary tenants

---

Tubbe are known only as officials; they do not appear in any other way in surviving court rolls,
account rolls or related records.

[139] The 62 persons named in Table IX account for 70 % of the 88 jurors after 1350. Tenurial
information on 24 men cannot be found.

[140] "Social Structures," *Ec.H.R.* XVIII, p. 85.

[141] Breaking this down even further, six families had movables valued between 10 and 19
shillings, of which two (one-third) were jury families. Seventeen families held properties worth
from 20 to 39 shillings, and 10 (59 %) were jury families. Finally, 13 families were possessed
of movables exceeding 40 shillings in value, and nine of these (69 %) were jury families.

TABLE IX

THE DISTRIBUTION OF LAND AMONG HOLYWELL JURORS, 1356-1457

TWENTY ACRES OR MORE:

ASPLOND, John III
ASPLOND, John IV
ASPLOND, Richard
ATTEWELLE, Robert
ATTEWELLE, John II
BAROUN, Nicholas
BEAUMEYS, John III
BRAYN, John II
CARTERE, William
CRISTEMESSE, Richard
CRISTEMESSE, Roger
CRISTEMESSE, John II
EDWARD, John II
EDWARD, Thomas
EDWARD, Richard
EDWARD, John III
ELYOT, William
GODFREY, Roger
HEMYNGTON, John
HEMYNGTON, Adam
HOUGHTON, Robert
HOUGHTON, Roger
HUNNE, Thomas II
LANE, Nicholas
LANENDER, John
SCOT, Nicholas
SCOT, John
SHEPPERD, John III

TEN TO TWENTY ACRES:

ASPLOND, John II
BAKER, John I
BAKER, Roger
BAKER, John II
BEAUMEYS, Walter
BRAYN, Richard
CARTERE, William II
CRANFELD, Richard
DEYE, Thomas II
GODEMAN, Andrew
GODFREY, Adam
GODFREY, Nicholas
HALIDAY, Simon
HAMOND, John
HUNNE, Thomas
HUNNE, John III
MERTON, John
MERTON, Richard
MERTON, Thomas
SCOT, Thomas
SCOT, Richard
SEWALE, Roger
SHEPPERD, Nicholas
SHEPPERD, John II

LESS THAN TEN ACRES

ASPLOND, Thomas
BAROUN, John II
FLESSHEWERE, Nicholas
GODFREY, Richard
HUNNE, William
SEWALE, Adam
SMYTH, Thomas
TOOSLOND, John
WILKYN, Thomas
WRIGHT, William II

or members of customary families. Furthermore, although examples can be found of men serving as jurors who were not customary tenants, customary status — with its commitment to the manor and the responsibility it thereby implied — was a regular feature of those men or families who saw jury service more than once. Specifically, out of 53 families who were represented on juries anywhere from two to 32 times, 48 (91 %) were families involved in the customary structure of the manor. In addition, of the customary tenant jurors or jury families, the majority were holders of at least semi-virgates or cotlands. Tenants of smaller units — e.g. crofts — were not prevented from assuming the office, but the number who did was never large. But especially noteworthy is the number of families who were capable of serving as jurors five times or more. There were 32 such families in the village, and although the majority were customary families, they serve as examples of families whose competence for the office was obviously quite real and, given the fact that jurors were elected to their post, recognized by the rest of the community. For although a large number of families saw jury service, not all did so repeatedly, despite their tenurial status, and the suspicion is left that sheer competence was therefore a more highly valued element than merely economic position. It is this that no doubt helps explain why some families more than sufficiently supplied with land — and consequently major figures in the manorial context — did not always achieve or maintain predominance in the ranks of the jurors. The premium was on competence, not tenurial status, and, as a final note, it may be suggested that if 32 families out of 71 (45 %) were chosen to provide jurors five times or more — or 37 men of a total of 176 (21 %) — the village was not plagued by a crippling lack of special competence.

Jurors, however, were not the only important officials in the village structure. The ale-tasters were possessed of equally heavy — and continuing — responsibility. Charged with maintaining the assize of ale on the local level and thereby regulating brewing practices — and even the quality of the brew — they too, like the jurors, were elected by the homage,[142]

---

[142] This question of the election of the tasters is deserving of more detailed investigation than the records for Holywell alone permit. It cannot be safely stated, for example, whether "election" meant "appointment", and it is further unclear just who did the electing. The tasters were normally elected during the court session, but the rolls give no special details on the process, being content to state either "homagium eligunt" or "electi sunt". It is possible that the villagers as a whole chose the tasters, but it is equally possible that their election was a matter for the jurors, or even the jurors and the abbot's seneschal. In the early fifteenth century, for example, the election of beadles for the manor was shared by villagers, jurors and the seneschal. Thus, in 1423 four men "electi sunt ad officium bedelli per totum homagium de quibus (name) electus est per

bound to maintain the duties of their office under oath,[143] and also liable
to amercement for dereliction of their responsibilities.[144] As a result,
the office required generally mature and sober men, and it may be expected
that qualifications similar to those obtaining for jury service would also
apply to the tasters. Indeed, upon close examination, it is found that virtually
the same *criteria* were operative. Specifically, between 1288 and 1457,
the names of 80 tasters have been preserved, 77 of whom represented 46
village families (See Table X). The 80 men held their office a total of
118 times, with 53 men (66%) holding once, 17 (22%) serving twice,
nine (11%) serving three times, while only one man served four times.
Out of the 46 village families seeing service as tasters, 21 did so but once,
eight served twice, six three times, three served four times, five served
five times, and one each six, seven and 10 times. Furthermore, 30 of
the families supplied only one man as taster, five provided two men, eight
furnished three men, two supplied four, and one boasted five members
who were tasters.

Most significant, however, is the fact that 56 of the 80 tasters — or 70%
— were men who also could be found among the jurors, while 42 of the
46 families (91%) were jury families.[145] Indeed, the impression is given
of a body of village families that dominated the ranks of both jurors and
tasters, and when investigation is extended to other positions of official
responsibility in the village and the manor, it is found that the same families
again appeared as supplying the required men. Thus, of nine known

---

senescallum et juratores." (PRO SC 2-179/57); and in 1428, four men were again elected beadles
"per totum homagium", of which one "electus per senescallum." (PRO SC 2-179/59.)

[143] Presentments of ale-infractions were not only frequently accompanied by the phrase "Tasta-
tores dicunt per sacramentum suum", but when the tasters were elected they were often described
as taking an oath ("... electus est et juratus").

[144] It should be noted that prior to the 1320's, the Holywell and Needingworth tasters appear
to have been most conscientious in the performing of their office, not being presented in any
of the surviving court rolls from 1288 through 1318 for dereliction of duty. In 1322, however,
the tasters were fined 6 d. each because they had not done their job well ("non bene officium suum
fecerunt"), and in every court roll thereafter — and into the 1450's — the tasters were invariably
amerced for failing to acquit their obligations satisfactorily. That this means, however, that
by the third decade of the fourteenth century the tasters were no longer taking their office seriously
cannot be assumed. It is possible that the lord was demanding a stricter application of brewing
regulations in order to increase his profits from fines. The question as such demands further
investigation, but ideally involving more than one village.

[145] In addition, only 12 of the families furnishing tasters were themselves involved in the village
brewing industry at the time of their official engagement. Thus, men of the Brayn, Brun, Cartere,
Clerk, Curteys, Faber, Flesshewere, Godfrey, Hamond, Hunne, Laweman and Shepperd families
were tasters at least in the same decade that other members of their families were presented for
infractions of the ale-assize.

TABLE X

ALE-TASTERS IN HOLYWELL-CUM-NEEDINGWORTH, 1288-1457

FAMILY	NO. OF MEN	NO. OF TIMES
ARNOLD	1	1
ASPLOND	3	5
ATTEWELLE	1	1
BAROUN	2	2
BATE	1	1
BEAUMEYS	3	5
BRAYN	5	10
BRUN	1	1
BRYAN	1	1
CARTERE	1	3
CLERK	1	1
CRISTEMESSE	1	1
EDWARD	3	5
ELYOT	1	1
FABER	1	1
FANNELL	1	3
FLESSHEWERE	1	1
FRANKLYN	1	1
GODEMAN	2	2
GODFREY	3	7
GRAY	3	3
GUNNE	1	2
HALIDAY	1	1
HAMOND	1	2
HEMYNGTON	1	1
HOUGHTON	1	1
HUNNE	3	4
LANE	1	1
LANENDER	1	1
LAWEMAN	4	5
MACHYNG	1	1
MOKE	1	1
MURYELL	2	4
NICHOLAS	3	3
PALMERE	1	1
PORTER	1	2
"RADULPHI"	3	5
RIPTON	1	2
SANDE	2	4
SCHARP	1	3
SCOT	4	6
SELEDE	2	2
SEWALE	1	1
SHEPPERD	1	1
WRIGHT	1	2

capital pledges between 1288 and 1306, seven were members of five families that also served regularly as jurors and tasters (See Table XI). The same obtained among the constables for the village — men charged with official peace-keeping obligations.[146] Fourteen families of juratorial or tastatorial rank dominated the constabulary, providing 16 of 18 known constables between 1275 and 1457, or 89 % (See table XI).[147]

TABLE XI

CAPITAL PLEDGE AND CONSTABULARY FAMILIES

| | Capital Pledges | |
FAMILY	No. OF MEN	ACTIVITY GROUP
BRAYN	2	A
EYR	2	A
GERE	1	A
LAWEMAN	1	A
SCOT	1	A
	Constables	
ASPLOND	2	A
BAROUN	1	A
BATE	1	A

[146] One of the responsibilities of the constable was the producing of armed men when required by the abbot or king. There is no record of whether Holywell ever sent any of its peasants to participate in the Welsh, Scottish or French campaigns from the late thirteenth century into the fifteenth century (the village is not found in the *Nomina Villarum* of 1316, for example), but the village was required to send armed "vigilatores" to the St. Ives Fair in the late thirteenth century. The rolls of the Fair Courts for 1275 (PRO SC 2-178/94), 1286 (PRO SC 2-178/96), 1290 (PRO SC 2-178/97), 1292 (PRO SC 2-178/98), 1299 (PRO SC 2-178/100) and 1301 (PRO SC 2-178/101) state this quite clearly. Holywell's quota was apparently six men (eight in 1290), and for the years documented the quota in men was met — but not always in arms. Thus, in 1275 both John Bundeleg and Radulf Scot came to keep the watch, but each was fined 6 d. for coming unarmed. The constables themselves came with the *vigilatores* and possibly helped make-up the full complement. According to the late thirteenth-century St. Ives' rolls, the village had two constables. Whether there were more is not indicated, but by the fifteenth century — at least in one year, 1455 — three were elected in the village. The office itself was apparently for a year, but of 18 constables whose names have been preserved from the late thirteenth century to the mid-fifteenth century, nine are known to have been elected to the position more than once, and at least six occupied it for two or more years in succession.

[147] Adam de Norton, constable in 1356 and a juror in 1359, cannot be identified with any village family. On the other hand, Thomas Valentyne, elected constable in 1432 and 1443, although not representing a jury family, was in fact related to one through marriage, as he had married Margaret Scot, daughter of Thomas Scot, in 1417 (BM.Harl.Ms. 445, 98r).

BRAYN	1	A
ELYOT	1	A
GERE	2	A
GODFREY	1	A
HUNNE	1	A
LAWEMAN	1	A
RIPTON	1	A
SCOT	1	A
SHEPPERD	1	A
SEWALE	1	A
VALENTYN	1	B
WRIGHT	1	A

Not only did certain families dominate the official structures of the village, however. When attention is turned to the more specifically manorial offices, the same families are again encountered as reeves, beadles, bailiffs and even in lesser capacities. Thus, out of nine reeves known by name between 1288 and 1391, eight were members of seven local families that were also found represented on juries or among the tasters.[148] (See Table XII). Similarly with the beadles. All the 24 known *bedelli* from the fourteenth and earlier fifteenth centuries were members of families that dominated the official structure of the village. (See Table XII). Bailiffs, on the other hand — at least from the late fourteenth century — tended to fall into the hands of outsiders, probably professional administrators. Thus, out of five bailiffs named after 1375 (See Table XII), three were not local men. Two men, however, were local villagers, and both represented leading official families.

Even the lesser positions of a manorial or demesnal orientation — the seasonal autumn reeves and custodians, the haywards, and the *collectores redditus* of the earlier fifteenth century — were invariably held by families that could be found regularly filling other manorial and village offices (See Table XII), while the same families also maintained control over the position of *Akerman* (ploughman), who was more of an exalted *famulus* than an official. (See Table XII).

What is evident from all this is that there was in Holywell-cum-Needingworth from the late thirteenth to the middle of the fifteenth century a very definite body of main peasant — and villein — families upon whom

---

[148] Only one man — John Bigge — reeve in 1346/47, was not a member of a local family at all. Instead, he seems to have been a professional administrator from outside, for in the account roll of 1346/47 it was stated: "Allocantur preposito xx s. ex grana abbatis in subsidium expensarum suarum quia non habet mansum in haliwell set in Broughton." (PRO SC 6-877/18).

TABLE XII
FAMILIES SUPPLYING MANORIAL OFFICIALS

FAMILY	NO. OF MEN	ACTIVITY GROUP
Reeve		
ATTEWELLE	1	A
CRANFELD	2	A
EDWARD	1	A
HAMOND	1	A
MAY	1	A
ELENE	1	A
REVE	1	A
Beadles		
ASPLOND	1	A
ATTEWELLE	1	A
BAKER	2	A
CRISTEMESSE	2	A
DEYE	1	A
EDWARD	2	A
GODEMAN	1	A
GODFREY	2	A
HEMYNGTON	2	A
HOUGHTON	2	A
HUNNE	1	A
LANENDER	1	A
MERTON	1	A
NICHOLAS	2	A
PALMERE	1	A
SCOT	1	A
WRIGHT	1	A
Bailiffs		
CRISTEMESSE	1	A
DEYE	1	A
Prepositi & Custodes Autumpni, Haywards, etc.		
BAROUN	2	A
CARTERE	1	A
DEYE	1	A
GODFREY	1	A
GRAY	1	A
HEMYNGTON	1	A
HUNNE	1	A
MILLER	2	A
NICHOLAS	1	A
OKY	1	B

Family	No. of Men	Activity Group
Palmere	1	A
Scot	1	A
Sewale	1	A
Shepperd	1	A
Collectores Redditus		
Asplond	1	A
Cristemesse	2	A
Edward	1	A
Nicholas	1	A
Palmere	1	A
Akermen		
Attewelle	2	A
Deye	1	A
Edward	1	A
Godeman	1	A
Gray	1	A
Houghton	1	A
Reve	1	A
Scharp	1	A
Scot	1	A

fell the responsibility for village and manorial government and administration. All told, 79 families participated in such activities at one time
or another. Not all, however, did so extensively or consistently. Fifty-
five of the families (71 %), for example, were very clearly of major importance,
since they saw service in two or more positions, although even here the
number of men supplied was from one to nine, and the number of times
the families exercised their diverse responsibilities varied from two to
45. On the other hand, 24 families, although attaining official status,
did so with respect to only one office, supplying anywhere from one to
three men and serving from one to seven times. As already indicated
above with respect to the jurors, the majority of the official families in
Holywell were committed to the customary structure of the manor. In
addition, it may be observed that the majority were families characterized
by long-term residence in the village. Specifically, 43 were permanent
families — capable of producing surviving sons sufficient enough to sustain
the family through three generations or longer. Eighteen were two-generation families, and 14 were short-term families. Indeed, although long-
term residence was not absolutely necessary for a frequent or even pro-

minent exercise of official responsibility by families,[149] the most active families were in fact of long-standing residence, although not all were necessarily consistent or continuous in their identification with the village's official life. For example, there were 12 families that enjoyed a special pre-eminence in the governmental and administrative structure of Holywell in that they managed to serve in five different offices or more, yet not all were continuously active as sources of officials during the length of their residence. Only five, in fact, displayed such continuity. The Asplonds were major officials almost continuously from 1318 through 1457, with the 1350's and the years between 1410 and 1420 the only decades in which they failed to appear in surviving records as officials. The AtteWelles similarly were to be found among the village or manorial officials from 1364 — not long after their arrival in the wake of the Black Death — through 1443, with but a brief spell of inactivity at the very beginning of the fifteenth century. The Edwards were consistently jurors from 1318 through 1457, while from 1370 they began to exercise additional positions. The Palmeres, too, in all their three generations from 1311 through 1423, maintained an active part in governmental and administrative affairs, while the Scots were a family that never really seemed to weaken in their official involvements from 1275 through 1457.

On the other hand, seven major — and especially involved — families either came to assume their roles late in their residence or served sporadically. The Cristemesse family, for one, although holding five offices a total of 16 times, did so between three men within a 25 year period, and that beginning in 1432, after the family had been settled in the community for some 60-odd years with no previous indications of activity. A similar "delayed" involvement was displayed by the Shepperd family, which only began to emerge as major in the 1350's — after over a half-century's residence — but thereafter pursued its new role with determination, boasting six men from 1356 through 1437 who held a total of five offices some 22 times.[150] The Deye family exemplifies both delayed and sporadic official

---

[149] For example, the short-term Lanender family produced one man who held three offices a total of five times. Similarly, the Mays of the late thirteenth century boasted one man who held two offices some six times, while the briefly ensconced four sons of the mysterious "Radulph" held the positions of juror and taster a total of 14 times in the space of 34 years (1292-1326).

[150] The probable explanation for the delayed starts of the Cristemesse and Shepperd families lies in the fact that it was not until late in their settlement — and almost simultaneously with their assumption of official responsibilities — that they became tenants to any significant degree. The Cristemesses, for example, did not begin to emerge from the category of smallholders until the 1420's. So, too, with the Shepperds. Prior to the middle of the fourteenth century, the family (under its Latin surname of "Bercar'") did not appear to have been customary tenants, a condition that had probably been rectified by the 1350's, when Peter Shepperd emerged as a juror (1356, 1359), for by 1370 the family at least controlled a cotland.

involvement. Resident from as early as 1318, it was not until 1375 that a member of the family was recorded as holding an office. In that year, Thomas Deye (I) appeared as bailiff, and in the next 30 years he held a total of six offices some 10 times. After his death, however, the official activity of the family severely contracted, with only Thomas Deye (II) serving as a juror, and then but twice (1428, 1430), although he lived over 50 years after 1400. The Godfreys, the Grays, the Hunnes and the Nicholases, although found as officials early, experienced lengthy periods in which no members of the families seem to have exercised official positions of responsibility. Thus, the Godfreys were supplying a constable as early as 1275, but there was not another official recorded in the family until over a century later, when Adam Godfrey was a juror in 1386. Thereafter, the family produced five more men who held a total of six offices some 24 times through 1451. The Grays, too, were active officials in the early fourteenth century, with four men serving as jurors and as taster some eight times from 1299 to 1318. Then, in the 1320's and 1330's, there were no signs of activity, and it only resumed in the 1350's. The Hunnes were represented early as well — by Robert, a taster and three-time juror between 1288 and 1301 — but there were then no Hunnes found as officials for 50 years, not, in fact, until 1353, when Thomas Hunne was taster. For a little over 50 years, thereafter, however, the family produced five men who held five offices some 21 times. Then followed a second period of restricted involvement, which witnessed only one member of the family — William (II) — serving as a juror (1437) between 1403 and 1457. Finally, members of the Nicholas family had been frequently found as officials in the 1320's and 1330's, but there was then a hiatus in their activity that lasted until the 1380's.

Indeed, the total number of long-resident and major families who consistently and continuously maintained a high degree of activity in village government and administration during the course of their settlement was not overwhelming. The Baroun, Hamond, Hemyngton, Lane, Miller, Sande, Selede and Wright families, for examples, were all late to begin serving as officials, and among them the concentration of responsibility in the Lane, Miller and Selede families was not particularly heavy. Among other major families, the Beaumeys experienced a reduction of their activity in the first half of the fifteenth century, although they had been generally prominent as officials from 1318 through 1389. The Bryans, the Clerks, the Reves and the Riptons enjoyed only brief periods of real activity, the Faber/Smyth family was only lightly involved but its two periods of activity were also separated by 90 years, while, finally, both the Fannell and Godrich families were active as officials only early in the fourteenth century, although both survived past the second decade of the fifteenth century. In fact, only five families genuinely exhibited an undeniable consistency and continuity in their major role,[151] and because the majority did not but rather experienced either solitary or intermittent periods of activity explains the involvement of such a number as 79 village families at one time or another in the governmental and administrative responsibilities of the community. Unfortunately, it is not possible to discover with any certainty why so few families continuously retained and exercised a major role in the village and why so many did not. In some cases, no doubt, the decline of a family's importance was the result of changing economic conditions, but examples could be cited of families who ceased to function as officials — or else declined in importance and activity — and yet remained semi-virgaters or virgaters (e.g. the Lanes, the Riptons, the Beaumeyses and the Deyes). On the other hand, the replacement crisis in the village's population over the fourteenth and early fifteenth centuries may have been a factor in the diminishing roles of some families: the preponderance of two-generation or short-term residents among the lesser active families at least suggests this. In addition, however, there is yet another possible factor involved — one that unfortunately cannot be adequately examined or weighed due to the nature of surviving records but which nevertheless cannot be entirely ignored. Specifically, it is a question of the willingness of individual families and peasants to in fact assume the responsibilities of different offices. That there was never any serious flight from responsibilities seems more than probable. The fact that 79 out of 140 village families, for a total of 222 persons, in a period of over 150 years exercised offices at all at least points to a community many of whose members were not violently disinclined to serve. Furthermore, if the history of the village is broken up into 30-year segments, it is found that the proportion of resident families serving at any given time was never negligible, with 32 % involved in the exercise of official responsibility around 1300, 48 % around 1360 and just over 40 % around 1450. Indeed, considering the probable time-consuming nature of the majority of offices, it is significant that the village never appears to have experienced any real crisis in filling them. That there may have been some kind of remuneration attached to such positions as juror and taster is, in fact, quite possible, although at the present stage of research into the mediaeval village community no information has been forthcoming as to what form it took, or even if there was any. There

---

[151] The Asplond, AtteWelle, Edward, Palmere and Scot families.

was, of course, very definite payment for manorial officials. Holywell beadles and ploughmen, for example, were not only allowed a regular food livery, but each received a cotland free of labour services and customary rent payments. The fact that account rolls contain no record of any payments to jurors or tasters does not necessarily mean that they received nothing; it may simply mean that, since such positions were essentially village-oriented, it was for the village to arrange its own form of compensation for services. But whether involving some form of remuneration or not, the governmental and administrative needs of the community consistently attracted enough men and families to meet them, and in several cases enterprising and resourceful men and families were actively engaged in filling them. This is evidenced by the example of the 12 families in the village's fourteenth- and fifteenth-century history that saw service in five different offices or more. All were long-term resident families, but, as already noted, not all commanded a major role in administration for the entire length of their stay. Nevertheless, several were alike in that they exhibited an ability to take advantage of local opportunities for expanding or solidifying their place in the community, and it may at least be wondered if their assumption of major offices may have resulted not only from their tenurial commitments and expertise but from a desire to exploit the offices for the prestige they doubtlessly conferred, thereby strengthening their place in the community. Thus, the Asplonds were a family already in residence in the last decade of the thirteenth century, at which time they were involved in the brewing of ale. A customary family as well — probably holding the virgate ascribed to the family in 1370 — by the second decade of the fourteenth century two Asplond men were active in the village — Robert and John (I) — both of whom served as jurors in 1322. They were also not insignificant holders of movable property, for in 1327 each was taxed on goods valued at 23 shillings, and in 1332, whereas John's (I) movables amounted to only 20 shillings, Robert's had risen to 30. Robert was no longer mentioned after 1332, but John survived through 1354, serving as a juror at least two more times — in 1338 and 1339. He may be assumed to have died in the late 1350's or early 1360's, after which the family was represented in the village by two other men: John (II) and Thomas. The former, an *ad opus* virgater from at least 1370 to his death, ca. 1405, served as a juror 10 times between 1369 and 1396 and was taster in 1396. Thomas, a juror three times between 1372 and 1378, was a smallholder, taking up an acre and a half of fen in 1370 and an acre of demesne by 1392. Both were apparently dead after 1405, and again two more Asplonds appeared in their place: John (III) and Richard. The former, beginning as a smallholder in

1404, was particularly active as an official. He was constable as early as 1403 — a post he held again many years later, in 1428 and 1443 — and a juror eight times from 1409 to 1445. Finally, he served as one of the *bedelli* in 1449. In addition, as he maintained an active role in government and administration, he also busily engaged himself in the fluid land conditions obtaining in the early fifteenth century, picking up a croft in 1423, a half-virgate and three acres of demesne in 1438, until by 1449 he controlled a virgate, a croft and six acres of demesne.

The other contemporary Asplond — Richard — was a modest property-holder throughout his career, as well as a sometime official. Not recorded as ever holding more than 10 acres, he came to accept official responsibilities late — in 1443, as taster, and later as constable (1452, 1455) and juror (1455).[152]

The final Asplond — John (IV) — was both more tenurially and officially involved than Richard. A juror in 1437, he again served in 1452 and 1457, was taster in 1452 and 1455, and *collector redditus* in 1455. In addition, between 1440 and 1457, he and his wife Margaret had absorbed over two and a half virgates of land previously in the hands of the Merton family.

The AtteWelles, unlike the Asplonds, provide an example of a family not only being able to move into the village and quickly become important tenants but major officials as well. Arriving in the wake of the Black Death,[153] by 1370 Robert AtteWelle was holding three-quarters of a virgate *ad censum* and serving as reeve, while his son John (I) was tenant of a cotland and a half *ad opus*. In 1372, Robert was serving as a juror for at least his second time — he had done so already in 1364 — and he was a juror eight more times between 1375 and 1396. Finally, although nearing the close of his life in 1396, he was holding down the position of ploughman. Dead by 1402, so too was his son, with the result that Robert had transferred all his properties to his grandson, John AtteWelle (II), in 1401. This John, who, with his wife Margaret, added still another half-virgate to his properties in 1419, continued the family's official in-

---

[152] Perhaps Richard had little interest in being an official at an earlier date, especially as his first court roll appearance had been a mildly spectacular one in 1432, when he and three other villagers (William Hawkyn, Thomas Wright and William Smyth Jr.) were presented because "post ultimam letam in ecclesia aperte vocaverunt juratores de leta falsos et periuratos." (PRO SC 2-179/61.) It is pointless to speculate on such an entry, of course, but one cannot help but wonder if the four men presented were done so because they had merely called the jurors "falsos et periuratos" or if, rather, their offense lay in their having done so "aperte".

[153] The name first appeared in the court roll for 1356, when Robert AtteWelle was fined both for trespass and for having the hue and cry raised on him by John Hamond. (PRO SC 2-179/36).

volvements, serving as juror at least eight times between 1413 and 1443, as well as being elected *bedellus* in 1423 and again in 1428.

The Cristemesse family first moved into the village in the 1360's but remained in obscurity until after 1400. Then two members appeared — Richard and Roger. The former acquired two cotlands from John Bryan in 1424, and by 1432 he was elected beadle.

The Palmeres and the Shepperds were families that initially served exclusively as jurors and tasters, only to branch out into other offices in the early fifteenth century. Thus, William Palmere (I) was elected a taster in 1332, but served as a juror six times from 1311 to 1353. William (II) acted as juror once — in 1378; and it was left to John Palmere to extend the family's involvements. A juror seven times from 1398 through 1437, he served as autumn reeve (1402) and custodian (1398), *collector redditus* (1414-18) and as beadle on at least seven occasions (1409, 1413, 1414, 1415, 1416, 1417, 1418). The Shepperds, for their part, were slow to assume a major role in the village, beginning as jurors only in the 1350's. Not until 1400, when William Shepperd served as constable, did their range of offices expand, and then it was confined to one man: John Shepperd (III), who, in addition to being a four-time juror between 1409 and 1432, served as autumn reeve in 1419 and 1430, autumn custodian in 1428, and both hayward and taster in 1437.

The Scots, on the other hand — commanding both a virgate and a cotland in 1252 — early assumed offices of differing responsibilities. Thus, Radulph Scot was a constable in 1275 and a juror in 1288, while Walter Scot was one of the capital pledges in 1288. Subsequent members of the family for the first three quarters of the fourteenth century acted regularly as jurors, and occasionally as tasters, but from 1389 to 1402 Thomas Scot (II) alone held five offices, from juror to autumn reeve, and including autumn custodian, beadle and *akerman*, while the family closed out the period much as it had begun: still in a major position, with John Scot a juror at least seven times from 1419 through 1457. In addition, just as the family displayed a willingness to assume offices, so too did it exhibit an ability to seize land opportunities, especially after 1400, when John Scot consistently joined with members of the Shepperd family in exploiting the meadow of Drihirst. Indeed, it is because the majority of the families just cited were adept at taking advantage of land opportunities, as well as a local industry such as ale-brewing, that their identification with office-holding may perhaps be seen as yet another means of securing or maintaining a place of pre-eminence in the community. It is surely a possibility that a family such as the Godfreys, for example, who became major tenants only by the last quarter of the fourteenth century, intensified their involvement in village administration from that time because it helped to confirm and solidify their newly-attained status. Of course, the study of village governmental and administrative institutions in mediaeval England is still at an early stage, and it is therefore not wise to speculate too widely on such question until investigation has gone deeper beneath the surface, but it may nevertheless be suggested that the regular holding of offices by specific families was as much an exploitational device as the juggling of properties on an open land market or sporadic involvement in local industry.

There were, then, in late mediaeval Holywell-cum-Needingworth a sizeable number of peasant and villein families who occupied main positions of importance in the life of the community, either to a major or lesser degree. Not only did they constitute the overwhelming majority of custo-mary tenants on the manor — whether virgaters, cotlanders or croft-holders — and consequently bore the responsibility for the working of the demesne and the sustaining of the manorial structure in general, but they were equally vital to the institutional life of the village, supplying the personnel that kept the machinery of local government and administration in working order. However, they were not the only families in the village over the fourteenth and first half of the fifteenth centuries. There were some 140 families settled or settling in the community during that period, but only 79 could be considered main families. Sixty-one families (See Table XIII) remained, who, from the standpoint of their non-involvement in government and administration, may be classified as minor families, although this does not necessarily mean that they were all peripheral to the life of the village or unimportant or even irrelevant to it. If not especially committed to the customary structure of the manor or directly concerned with responsibility for local administration, several still occupied a definite place in the community and either made some contribution to village life or derived benefits from it — or both. Specifically, out of 61 minor families, 14 were clearly on the periphery of village life (See Table XIII), almost all being characterized by short periods of settlement and displaying no signs of being either landholders or engaged in the performance of a service, craft or trade.[154] Thirty-one, however, were landholding families, some of whom were even customary tenants. Thus,

---

[154] The exceptions to the short residence were the villein Baldewyne, Caldecote and Legge families, who remained into their second generation, and the free Gibbe family, who were present as early as 1307 and were still maintaining some identification with the village in 1402, when Agnes Cartere, daughter of Thomas, paid 40d. for license to marry Nicholas Gybbe. BM.Harl. Ms. 445, 33ʳ,

the Ayses and Benets were both semi-virgate families in 1252 who survived into the early fourteenth and late thirteenth centuries, respectively, yet neither was productive of officials. Similarly with the Kyng family, the Mariots, the Popes, the Hardys, the Clarots, the Palfreymans, the Ravens, the Tayllours, the Thatchers, the Wodecoks and the Skynneres. All were, at one time or another, virgate, semi-virgate, cotland or croft-holding families, yet they remained apart from village administrative affairs, although four were in residence at least through two generations (See Table XIII).

TABLE XIII

MINOR FAMILIES IN HOLYWELL-CUM-NEEDINGWORTH, 1275-1457

(a = Tenant; b = craft, trade; c = peripheral family)

Family	Residence Group	Status in Vill	Family	Residence Group	Status in Vill
Avenaunt	III	c	Kyng	II	a
Aylbern	III	b	Kylleneth	III	c
Ayse	II	a	Legge	II	c
Baldewyne	II	c	Martyn	IV	a
Benet	III	a	Mariot	III	a
Barker	II	a, b	Morel	II	a
Bernewell	I	a	Newerk	III	c
Boloygne	III	b	Palfreyman	III	a, b
Botwryte	II	a	Pollard	III	a
Bundeleg	II	a,b	Pope	III	a
Burton	IV	b	Prondhele	III	c
Caldecote	II	c	Pellepar/Skynnere	II	a, b
Campion	III	b	Pye	III	c
Cappe	III	b	Raven	II	a
Clervaus	II	a	Reynold	III	b
Claviger	III	b	Seman	III	b
Clarot	III	a	Selde	II	a, b
Colyer	III	b	Spercoll	I	a, b
Conse	III	c	Slogh	III	a
Curpel	III	b	Snowe	III	b
Crouch	III	c	Tony	III	c
Essex	III	a	Tayllour	I	a
Fisher	III	a, b	Thurberne	IV	b
Franceys	III	a	Thatcher	III	a
Fychyen	III	b	Walmesford	III	b
Gerold	III	c	Webbester	III	a, b
Gibbe	I	c	Wodecok	IV	a
Godale	III	b	Hroff	II	a
Godsoule	III	a, b	Rille	II	b
Hardy	II	a	Tannator	III	c
Hildegar	II	a			

In addition to land tenure, however, 25 minor families — including nine tenant families — were engaged in the application of a skill or service. The Bundeleg family, for one, were the village millers in the late thirteenth and early fourteenth centuries,[155] while members of the Colyere, Walmesford, Pollard and Skynnere families were occupied in being village butchers in 1286, 1287, 1306 and 1307, respectively.[156] By far the greatest number, however, was engaged in the brewing of ale for village consumption.[157]

---

[155] John Bundeleg was specifically named as miller in 1288 and again in 1294, being noted in both cases because of fraud. In the former year he had been convicted of cheating Robert, the son of the reeve, and it was further set down that John "non est idoneus ad opus ville" (PRO SC 2-179/5). In 1294, he was fined 6d., being accused of having "graves mensuras."

[156] They were not the only butchers known by name, however. At least 13 men are known to have been butchers between 1286 and 1339. Four men were not resident villagers at all: Reginald Handy (1286), John de Drayton (1301), John Norgrave (1338) and Alexander Norgrave (1339). The remaining five were all local men: Matthew, son of Alexander (1299), William Custte (1306, 1307), William Laweman (1307), Richard Laweman (1311, 1313), Robert Russell (1311, 1313), but they were also all villagers of main status (Mathew, son of Alexander: taster-elect, 1318) or members of major (Laweman) or lesser official families (Custte, Russell).

[157] The brewing of ale was a veritable village industry, as the presence of the ale-tasters indicates. In late mediaeval Holywell it engaged the activities of at least 123 persons from 1288 through 1457, the majority of whom were women. Initially, there appear to have been two centres of brewing: one in Holywell proper, the other in Needingworth; and through 1332 the court rolls, in their presentation of ale-infractions, distinguished the brewers accordingly, with Needingworth being the site of the heaviest concentration — as the accompanying table shows — and which was further indicated by the fact that throughout the fourteenth century at least, the village

CONCENTRATION OF BREWERS IN HOLYWELL AND NEEDINGWORTH, 1288-1332

YEAR	NO. OF BREWERS (Total)	HOLYWELL	NEEDINGWORTH
1288	17	6	11
1294	13	3	10
1299	10	3	7
1301	8	3	5
1306	15	7	8
1307	13	4	9
1311	12	4	8
1313	11	4	7
1318	8	3	5
1322	5	2	3
1326	9	4	5
1328	8	3	5
1332	9	3	6

required three ale-tasters a year, one for Holywell, but two for Needingworth. After 1332, however, the location of the brewers was no longer specified. The number of persons involved, however, still remained generally not insignificant (see the following table), at least not until the fifteenth

Indeed, between 1288 and 1457, a total of 66 village families undertook this important occupation, 39 of which were main families (See Table XIV). Not all maintained a continuing interest in the business, however. Only nine families retained an identification with brewing that continued past one generation, and none was a minor family (See Table XV), but

century. By the end of the first decade of the century, however, a somewhat erratic pattern presented itself and continued through 1437. Thereafter, the brewing operations in the village seem to have declined sharply, although the evidence of the figures in the above table may in fact be quite misleading, since the number of tasters in the village by 1452 had been returned to three.

CONCENTRATION OF BREWERS IN HOLYWELL-CUM-NEEDINGWORTH, 1338-1457

YEAR	No. OF BREWERS
1338	7
1339	11
1353	6
1356	7
1359	10
1372	9
1375	7
1378	8
1386	8
1391	7
1394	6
1396	5
1400	7
1403	6
1405	6
1409	2
1413	4
1423	8
1428	2
1432	6
1437	5
1443	3
1452	2
1455	2
1457	1

(after having been reduced to two from 1403 to 1413, and from 1428 through 1443), and it is hard to conceive the necessity for three ale tasters in the 1450's if, in fact, only two women were brewing ale. The suspicion remains, therefore, that, despite the evidence of declining numbers in court rolls, the brewing of ale probably still retained its importance in the village in the earlier fifteenth century. The sparse account of brewers in court rolls from that time may have resulted either from failures by the tasters to present all offenders in court, or from the brewers themselves meeting the provisions of the assize and consequently not being liable to fine, or even from a declining interest in rigid enforcement of the assize itself by the court.

TABLE XIV

ALE-BREWING FAMILIES IN HOLYWELL-CUM-NEEDINGWORTH

FAMILY	No. OF BREWERS	No. OF TIMES	ACTIVITY GROUP
ASPLOND	2	6	A
AYLBERN	1	2	C
BAKER	1	6	A
BARKER	1	1	C
BERNEWELL	3	6	C
BOLOYGNE	1	5	C
BRAYN	1	1	A
BROOK	2	3	B
BRUN	2	9	A
BRYAN	1	1	A
BUNDELEG	1	3	C
BURTON	1	2	C
CAPPE	1	6	C
CARTERE	2	7	A
CLAVIGER	1	8	C
CLERK	5	17	A
COLYERE	1	2	C
COLYN	2	4	B
CRANFELD	1	3	A
CRISTEMESSE	1	2	A
CURPEL	1	1	C
CURTEYS	1	1	A
DEYE	4	12	A
EYR	2	2	A
FABER/SMYTH	7	19	A
FANNELL	1	1	A
FISHERE	1	1	C
FLESSHEWERE	1	2	A
FREYSANT	1	1	B
FYCHYEN	2	2	C
GERE	2	3	A
GODALE	1	1	C
GODFREY	2	4	A
GODSOULE	1	4	C
GRAY	1	1	A
HAMOND	1	1	A
HEMYNGTON	1	6	A
HOUGHTON	1	3	A
HUNNE	4	10	A
LAWEMAN	3	7	A
MACHYING	2	8	B
MADDE	1	1	B

Family	No. of Brewers	No. of Times	Activity Group
Merton	1	1	A
Moke	1	1	B
Molendinarius/Miller	1	1	C
Nicholas	1	5	A
Palfreyman	1	1	C
Pollard	1	1	C
Raulyn	1	1	B
Reynold	1	1	C
Rille	1	2	C
Russell	1	1	B
Scot	1	1	A
Selde	1	1	C
Seman	1	2	C
Sewale	1	1	A
Shepperd	6	26	A
Sky	1	1	B
Skynnere	3	4	C
Snowe	1	1	C
Spercoll	2	7	C
Thurberne	2	2	C
Walmesford	1	2	C
Webbester	2	3	C
Wright	1	2	A

TABLE XV

FAMILIES DISPLAYING A CONTINUING AND CONSISTENT INTEREST IN
ALE-BREWING

Family	Brewers	Times	Years Covered	Activity Group
Cartere	2	7	1326-1353	A
Clerk	5	17	1288-1339	A
Colyn	2	4	1299-1326	B
Brun	2	9	1288-1313	A
Deye	4	12	1378-1432	A
Brook	2	3	1313-1372	B
Faber/Smyth	7	19	1288-1423	A
Laweman	3	7	1288-1313	A
Shepperd	6	26	1359-1432	A

in fact seven were of major importance in the village.[158] Nevertheless, despite their prominence, brewing was not the exclusive property of the main families, and thus 27 minor families were also found among the brewing population of the village. For some, it was apparently a temporary occupation (e.g. Seman, Colyere, Godale, Curpel, Pollard, Walmesford, Molendinarius, Barker, Aylbern, Fischer, Reynold, Rille, Palfreyman, Snowe, Selde and Burton) engaging one member who was presented no more than twice. But for 11 families, it seems to have been a very definite livelihood. Either they featured one member who was presented for ale-infractions three times or more (e.g. Claviger, Cappe, Boloygne, Godsoule, Bundeleg), or two or more members of the family — either contemporaneously or in successive generations — were found brewing (e.g. Spercoll, Fychyen, Skynnere, Bernewell, Webbester, Thurberne). In the last analysis, the degree to which minor families were involved in brewing compared favourably with that of main families, for out of 39 of the latter, 21 displayed signs of a serious engagement in the practice — regardless of how long it continued — or 54%, whereas out of 27 minor families, 11 displayed the same kind of identification or 41%.

Finally, it may be noted that minor families in Holywell-cum-Needingworth were not all restricted to the exercise of only one local occupation or service. The Bundeleg family, for example, although millers during the last years of the thirteenth century, had either transferred or branched out to the brewing of ale by 1326, when Matilda Bundeleg was first noted as a brewer. The Colyeres and the Walmesfords had originally been butchers but later turned to brewing. The Fischers, although briefly engaged in brewing (1328), had also worked as hired labour — as indicated by a case of 1299 where the son of Thomas Fischer was charged with trespass and it was noted that he had been received by Ivetta Fychyen.[159] The Skynneres, who both brewed and acted on at least one occasion (1317) as butchers, may also have been practitioners of the skill their very name denoted, especially as the court rolls from 1306 to 1313 frequently took pains to write the name "le Skynnere". But the important point to be made is that, despite the purely economic motives that may have led specific families to engage in brewing and act as craftsmen, butchers and millers,

---

[158] It is interesting to note, however, that despite the large number of major and lesser families engaged in brewing in Holywell, only 12 (31 %) furnished tasters at or near the time of their involvement in brewing: Brayn, Brun, Cartere, Clerk, Curteys, Faber, Flesshewere, Godfrey, Hamond, Hunne, Laweman and Shepperd. In the majority of instances, tasters did not come from families other members of which were active brewers at the time the office was held.

[159] PRO SC 2-179/10.

they thereby helped to satisfy important needs of the community at large, and consequently the families themselves were not irrelevant to village life. Truly, the evidence of minor families performing essential services or exercising important skills, coupled with the readiness of a total of 79 other families to shoulder the several governmental and administrative responsibilities of the community, points to a village where few families had no place or no job to do. Indeed, out of all the known 140 families holding-down residence in Holywell from the late thirteenth century to the middle of the fifteenth century, only 14 can definitely be described as having occupied positions peripheral to village life, or 10%.

In the last analysis the question of the places of families in late mediaeval Holywell-cum-Needingworth reduces itself to a matter of service, and if the main families rendered very definite services to the manorial economy by upholding the customary structure and to the village by assuming the responsibilities of government and administration, minor families too rendered their own service, and especially in their brewing of ale and exercise of special skills they provided for very basic needs of all villagers, whether rich or poor, major or minor. Of course, it is always possible to speculate on what would have occurred had they not been present, and it may even be proposed that the services would then either have been rendered by the same families active in land and administration or supplied in some way through their efforts — by specially hired individuals. But it is really quite fruitless to speculate on this, because the fact remains that the minor families were there in Holywell and that they did render definite services for their neighbors, who, consequently, were in a very real sense dependent on them for much of the ale they drank, many of the cattle skinned and butchered, grain they needed milled and even hands to meet some of their work needs. In short, service was a concept that could — and did — work in more than one way in Holywell, and if several families served their neighbors' — and the village's — governmental and administrative needs, a not insignificant number served other needs — in some respects, more fundamental or basic needs. Consequently, the very question of family importance in the village becomes less easy to define. All tended to need each other for various services, and if major families may not have needed the minor families to actually survive, it may nevertheless be suggested that they needed them to continue in their major role, since they freed them of the necessity of providing all the services that a human community required.

On the other hand, the several service roles assumed by families and individuals in Holywell-cum-Needingworth indicates yet another aspect of mediaeval village society that still awaits a fuller and deeper appreciation and study: the fact of a vital and real peasant culture. Unfortunately, it is a subject that has yet to receive the attention it demands from historians, being still largely left to the anthropologist,[160] but it may be argued that it cannot be neglected much longer if mediaeval rural society is to be understood in terms more far-reaching than those of economics and law. Indeed, if that society is ever to be appreciated, it must be examined as expressing and resulting from a genuine peasant culture, and, at present, the most fruitful means of exploring that culture is by study of the institution of the family through the examination of specific families and individuals themselves. It is here that elements of service and responsibility most clearly stand out. It is here that the essential human dimensions of rural society most strongly assert themselves. Given the means for grappling with them now being afforded by local court rolls, they can no longer be ignored.

Finally, in all the ways whereby individuals could and did contribute to the economic, governmental and administrative needs of the village of Holywell-cum-Needingworth as a whole, the impression is left of a very real social group, a family — embracing and composed of many families — some of whose members were ambitious and powerful, others restrained and modest, but all of whom served one another by serving the various needs of the community at large. It is this final aspect of late mediaeval Holywell's experience — the group quality of the village and the degree to which its component parts were integrated into the whole and cooperated with each other on a more direct and personal level — that remains to be investigated, and it is this which forms the subject of the next — and last — chapter of this present study.

---

[160] See, for example, Robert Redfield, *Peasant Society and Culture* (Chicago, 1960).

CHAPTER IV

ASPECTS OF INTRA-VILLAGE COOPERATION AND COHESION IN HOLYWELL-CUM-NEEDINGWORTH, 1288-1457

At the close of the preceding chapter, attention was drawn to the peasants of late mediaeval Holywell-cum-Needingworth as composing a very real social group, a village whose members fulfilled the service needs of each other as well as of the whole. It is now necessary to go deeper beneath the surface of the village and attempt to discover how extensive this notion of service was, or, more precisely, to what extent villagers were really participants in what may be called a community. To determine, for example, that there was a group in the village that possessed and exercised the competence to satisfy village governmental and administrative needs, and another group that satisfied more fundamental needs by rendering essential services, may indicate ties of dependence between the two groups, but it does little to disclose how much — if at all — the two groups were *personally* involved with one another. Fortunately for the student, the survival of court rolls provides some tools for estimating the extent of inter-personal and, consequently, inter-group relationships in the village. The institution of the personal pledge, the records of land transfers, debts, references to joint working arrangements and intra-village marriages all contribute to forming a picture of a village in which cooperation between members of varying backgrounds and places in the community played a role. How extensive this role was — and even how consistently it emerged — forms the subject of this chapter, as an attempt shall be made to weigh the degree to which Holywell villagers were bound together by economic and personal ties to create a cohesive and inter-dependent community from the late thirteenth century through the middle of the fifteenth century.

One of the clearest examples of inter-peasant cooperation within Holywell-cum-Needingworth is afforded by the institution of the personal pledge. Fundamentally, it was a system of providing surety for the fulfilment of a court-incurred obligation — either the payment of a fine[1] or the

---

[1] It seems likely, for example, that the fines imposed during a court session were not necessarily paid on the spot. The existence of the need for a pledge itself suggests this, while account rolls frequently contained a section — "perquisitiones curie" — which indicates that it rested with the reeve to collect the total sum levied at the court from the responsible parties and render it to the lord at the time of the annual account.

performance of some specific task (e.g. amending of a trespass, solution of a debt) — and the peasant charged with such an obligation was bound to obtain another peasant who would agree to guarantee his future conduct. The securing of the pledge appears to have been the responsibility of the peasant himself,[2] and in almost all cases the pledge either had been obtained prior to the actual sitting of the court or was secured shortly thereafter.[3] The institution itself fulfilled needs for surety within village society that were beyond the scope of the tithing, or frankpledge, group — which was concerned primarily with keeping the peace — and the choosing of a pledge by a peasant, as well as the agreement of a peasant to serve as a pledge, were, in the last analysis, the result of a personal arrangement between villagers.[4] As such, therefore, records of the personal pledging activities of Holywell peasants can provide at least a tentative guide to the extent of inter-personal relationships within the village, specifically the degree to which members of different village groups — whether economic or activity groups — displayed a willingness to assume some responsibility for the actions of their neighbors and thereby helped them to maintain their membership in the local community, and, equally important, which neighbors they chose to support. For it was, indeed, basically a question of choice. Whether or not a peasant was restricted in his selection of pledges to members of his own tithing group — a question still not answered[5] — there are no cases of Holywell men being compelled to assume personal pledging responsibilities,[6] and consequently the number

---

[2] The phrase invariably used by court rolls to describe the securing of a pledge was "invenit plegium". For further discussion of this question, see Raftis, *Tenure and Mobility*, p. 101.

[3] The reason for this uncertainty stems from a lack of exact knowledge as to when the court roll itself was written. If it was a record of the session made at the time — which is possible, considering both its invariable employment of the present tense (e.g. "jurati dicunt ..., X querat versus Y") and occasional examples of rolls where names have been crossed out from a record, indicating perhaps an initial false writing — then the appearance of the pledge on the roll points to a prior arrangement between pledge and peasant, itself quite possible since it is likely that the agenda of a court was known in advance by the concerned parties. If, on the other hand, the court roll was drawn up shortly after the session — perhaps from notes made at the session — the pledge could have been secured during the interval and his name subsequently reported to the scribe.

[4] See Raftis, *Tenure and Mobility*, pp. 101-4.

[5] *Ibid.*, p. 101.

[6] Examples of pledging being imposed *alter alterius* — in cases of group trespasses, work derelictions or other group delicts — are surely instances of involuntary pledging, but they are also cases where the pledging was imposed almost as part of the penalty for the offense: the holding of a group of men responsible for the future conduct of each other in the wake of some joint misdemeanor. As such, they do not rightfully qualify as part of the scheme of *personal* pledging, being

of men who served as pledges, the frequency with which they did, and the persons they in fact pledged remains a not insignificant index to the cooperative and village-directed spirit of individual peasants and peasant families.[7]

Examination of the patterns of personal pledging in Holywell-cum-Needingworth is confined to only a little more than a half-century of the village's late mediaeval history, specifically to the years between 1288 and 1339, and, further, to only 16 years — or 19 court sessions — represented by court rolls scattered throughout the period, so that any attempt to obtain a comprehensive picture of intra-village pledging activities within the period is prohibited. It is not, however, the scarcity of court records after 1339 that curtails investigation of pledging at that point but rather the swift break-down of the institution itself from the middle of the fourteenth century. For reasons not yet fully understood, the employment of personal pledges in English villages after 1350 apparently fell into general disuse.[8] In Holywell alone, for example, this can be strikingly demonstrated by the fact that the records for 19 court sessions between 1288 and 1339 contained some 367 cases of personal pledgings, while in 19 court rolls between 1353 and 1405 only 63 instances can be found, the majority of them (57) coming from the years between 1353 and 1396 and almost exclusively confined to cases of hue and cry, housebreaking or assault, with the remainder

in nature quite impersonal. Thus, when the three ale-tasters were fined for failing to perform their office well in years from 1322 on, pledging *alter alterius* was imposed together with the fine, but no indication was given as to just who was to pledge whom within the group. Indeed, it may finally be suggested that the seemingly punitive employment of pledging *alter alterius* itself points to the normal importance of *personal* pledging, since it denied or took away what was probably considered a significant right to choose one's own surety.

[7] This is not to deny the possibility of profit as a motive for some men serving as pledges, however. Although very little information survives on the nature of the initial pledging arrangement, the probability that the pledge may have given his services for a price — to cover his own risk — cannot be entirely dismissed. (See Raftis, *Tenure and Mobility*, p. 102). In addition, it should further be noted that to be a pledge — particularly a frequent pledge — itself doubtlessly required some financial security on the part of the pledge, since he would be liable to amercement in the event of non-performance by his principal, and it is difficult to conceive a pauper undertaking such a risk, or even being seriously considered as fit to do so.

[8] See Raftis, *Tenure and Mobility*, pp. 103-4, for a discussion of the difficulties in appraising this decline. For one, it is suggested that with court rolls becoming shorter and more abbreviated in nature, pledges may have first simply been unrecorded. However, the careful inclusion of the names of pledges in cases of hue and cry or assault in post-1350 rolls makes this questionable. More likely is the observation that "the personal pledge seems to have lost its practical use" (*Ibid.*, p. 104), especially with the employment of more rigidly fixed fines that were paid without the need for a pledge (*Ibid.*, p. 103).

employed only in providing surety for villeins living off the manor.[9] Whatever the explanation, the summer of the institution was over by the middle of the fourteenth century. It limped its way through the remainder of the 1300's, until by the end of the first decade of the fifteenth century it had completely lapsed in Holywell.[10]

As indicated, however, between 1288 and 1339 the records of 19 court sessions — representing only 16 years — contained some 367 cases of personal pledgings.[11] The number of persons serving as pledges was 141, of which 115 were members of 63 village families, while 26 persons also served as pledges who were either outsiders or transients or village residents not identifiable with any known family group. The number of persons recorded as pledging but once in the years documented was high — 76 (54%) — while only 24 men pledged five times or more (See Table I). In terms of families, however, 34 pledged less than five times, with 29 pledging five times or more (See Table I). By far the families most active as pledges were those of major standing in the community (Group"A"). Thirty-five such families supplied 75 men acting as pledges and were

TABLE I

INCIDENCE OF PERSONAL PLEDGING, 1288-1339

PERSONS		FAMILIES				
Times	Number	Times	A.	B.	C.	Total
1	76	1	6	6	7	19
2	24	2	2	3	2	7
3	12	3	3	1	3	7
4	5	4	1	0	0	1
5+	24	5	5	1	1	7
		6+	18	3	1	22

[9] The number of pledgings in a session itself provides a good indication of the decline of the institution. From 1288 to 1339, the overall average of pledgings had been 25 a session, with a spread of from 16 (1338) to 51 (1318). From 1353 to 1396, the average was four a session, with a spread of from 0 (1369, 1375, 1389) to 10 (1356). In addition, 15 of the 57 pledgings between 1353 and 1396 — or 26% — were confined to the office of the constable, whereas prior to the middle of the century, only 15% of the known instances of pledgings had been handled by officials — reeves, bailiffs and beadles.

[10] The last reference to it occurred in the court roll for the *visus* of 15 October, 1405, when John Asplond had his tenement seized because of its dilapidated condition and his inability to find a pledge that he would repair it ("non invenit plegium"). PRO SC 2-179/50.

[11] The number was actually larger, but the roll of 1292 is badly damaged and virtually illegible, while that for 1307 is only partially intact: the first half of the roll is completely missing.

represented anywhere from one (six families) to 16 (one family) times. Only 22 men from 13 main families of lesser standing (Group "B") were found represented among the pledges (See Table I), although it was one of these families — Tiffayne — that was the most active in pledging of all village families. Whereas one of its members — Radulph — served as a pledge once in 1288, a second member — Henry, a juror in 1332 — pledged at least 24 times between 1306 and 1332, undertaking four principals in seven separate cases in one year alone (1326). Finally, 14 minor village families also engaged in pledging activities, supplying 19 men and the majority pledging once (seven families) but one pledging at least seven times (Pellepar/Skynnere). In addition, there were 26 men not associated with village families (Group "D") who accounted for a total of 36 pledgings.

In terms of the pledging activities of family groups, however, an interesting pattern emerges. First, the incidence of intra-familial personal pledging was not overwhelming. Although 36 of the 63 pledging families (57 %) engaged in intra-familial pledging, only 84 of the 367 cases of personal pledgings involved members of the same family, or 23 %. Again, the majority (62 cases) occurred within the ranks of the major families (21), with the next largest concentration found among 12 minor families (22 cases). Within 22 of the families, however, intra-familial pledging accounted for 50 % or more of all the families' known pledgings, and in 14 families, pledging was exclusively familial.[12]

Nevertheless, despite the significant role played by intra-familial pledging, the bulk of Holywell's recorded pledgings from 1288 to 1339 was not confined within family lines but was rather between members of different families.[13]

---

[12] *Group A:*   Asplond, Edward, Hemyngton, Houghton, Wright.
   Group B: Cusste, Venelle.
   Group C: Aylbern, Boloygne, Curpel, Fychyen, Mariot, Semen, Spercoll.
One possible reason for the low incidence of intra-familial pledging may lie in the effectiveness of family control or discipline over its members. In short, there was less intra-familial pledging because there were less intra-familial violations than obtained between individual villagers caught up in economic relationships.

[13] The word "family" is used here deliberately and is to be understood as referring to persons bound by discernible ties of blood or marriage. As to the question of how much pledging in Holywell was intra-clan, as distinct from intra-family, no positive answer can be given, since there is very little indication of clans having formed in the village. Even among the most prolific families, the survival of more than two continuous lines was seldom encountered. The demographic decline (and especially the growing replacement crisis of the fourteenth century) no doubt militated against the formation of clans, but whatever the reason the clan phenomenon was not characteristic of Holywell, and consequently it is not to be found operative in its pledging behaviour.

However, if the individual family did not seem to take precedence in the overall pledging pattern, the same cannot be said for the activity or economic groups to which families belonged. Specifically, out of 367 personal pledgings, 204 — or 56% — were cases of intra-group pledging. Major families (Group "A"), for example, although pledging 30 times for members of lesser main families, 22 times for minor families and 42 times for transients, outsiders or otherwise temporary persons (Group "D"), pledged 147 times within their own ranks (See Table II). Lesser families, in turn, pledged 15 times for members of major families, 10 times for minor families and nine times for transients, but 25 times within their own group. Likewise with minor families. Members were found pledging twice for major families, five times for transients and 24 times for other minor family members. The only group not found pledging predominantly within its own ranks was that composed of transients or outsiders (Group "D"). Only eight of their pledgings were within the group, the remaining 28 being spread throughout the minor and main family groups (See Table II). More precisely, 21 of the 35 major families engaged in pledging pledged predominantly within their own ranks, as did 13 of the 14 minor families. On the other hand, only four of 13 lesser families were so oriented.

It would be tempting to see in this pattern evidence of some kind of "class" solidarity, but the temptation should best be resisted. For one, the fact that families of major, lesser and minor rank tended to pledge more within their own groups than outside them may be the result less of a "class consciousness" than of a simple familiarity and closeness of experience. Main families — both major and lesser — being involved in both the customary structure of the manor and sharing governmental and administrative responsibilities in the village naturally worked together, and consequently they cooperated most frequently with those persons with whom they came into constant and intimate contact; hence the fact that they accounted for 217 of their 232 pledgings. On the other hand, main families, despite their pledging activities within their own ranks, still accounted for 32 of 71 pledgings within minor families, while they also assumed the majority (51 out of 64) of the pledgings required by transients.[14] Consequently, since a total of 36 main families undertook pledging responsibilities for minor or transient persons, it becomes increasingly more difficult to assign an exclusiveness in orientation to main families, while, further, the fact that the majority of their pledgings still remained

---

[14] Specifically, out of 48 main families — including 35 major (A) and 13 lesser (B) — engaged in pledging, a total of 36 pledged for members of minor families and for transients: 26 major families did so, and 10 lesser families.

TABLE II

INCIDENCE OF INTRA- AND INTER-GROUP PLEDGING, 1288-1339

GROUP A
(Major Families)

Pledges: 75	Pledgings: 241
GROUPS PLEDGED	No. OF PLEDGINGS
A	147
B	30
C	22
D	42

GROUP B
(Lesser Families)

Pledges: 22	Pledgings: 57
GROUPS PLEDGED	No. OF PLEDGINGS
A	15
B	25
C	10
D	9

GROUP C
(Minor Families)

Pledges: 19	Pledgings: 31
GROUPS PLEDGED	No. OF PLEDGINGS
A	2
B	0
C	24
D	5

GROUP D
(Transients)

Pledges: 26	Pledgings: 36
GROUPS PLEDGED	No. OF PLEDGINGS
A	12
B	1
C	15
D	8

---

within their own ranks may owe much to the fact that, first, they supplied the bulk of the pledges, and, secondly, the majority of pledgings required — in short, the majority of persons most active in the village and consequently coming before the court — were members of main families. In the final analysis, then, the pledging pattern indicates less that different groups tended to "stick together" than that main families simply constituted the "heart of village life",[15] and, furthermore, that despite the preponderance of group orientations to pledging, the fact that 77% of all the known pledgings were extra-familial points to the existence of a definite spirit of cooperation in the village prior to the middle of the fourteenth century. In addition, it remains to be noted that, just as certain village families displayed an ability to provide especially competent officials for the governmental and administrative needs of the community, so too did some families enter enthusiastically into the pledging structure. Thus, eight families — all of main rank — each boasted four men or more serving as pledges, or a total of 36 men pledging 80 times — 55 times outside the family.[16] Furthermore, some 16 families — again all of main rank — although not producing a large number of individual pledges, nevertheless had members who served as pledges anywhere from five to 24 times, or a total of 19 men pledging 160 times ![17]

---

[15] Raftis, "Peasant Mobility and Freedom in Mediaeval England." *Report of the Canadian Historical Association*, 1965, p. 128.

[16] E.g.

FAMILY	GROUP	MEN	PLEDGINGS
Capud Ville	B	5	7
Clerk	A	4	14
Colyn	B	4	10
Faber	A	5	11
Gray	A	5	15
Laweman	A	5	8
Nicholas	A	4	9
Prepositus	A	4	6

[17] The men were:

BEAUMEYS, Robert:	5	GODRICH, William:	5
BROOK, John:	5	GUNNE, Aspelon:	11
BRUN, Alexander:	8	GUNNE, Hugo:	9
CARTERE, Richard:	9	MAY, Richard:	10
ELENE, Robert:	5	PALMERE, William:	9
EYR, Richard:	5	RADULPHI, Richard Fil':	8
EYR, William:	6	RADULPHI, Robert fil':	7
FRANKLYN, Richard:	13	RIPTON, Adam de:	6
GERE, Richard:	10	TIFFAYNE, Henry:	24
GODFREY, Nicholas:	5		

Finally, there were a few instances in which inter-family pledging relationships were either multiplied in one year or repeated over a period of years. The Beaumeys family, for example, pledged the Fannells three times in 1322 alone. The Brayns pledged the Cusstes in 1299 and again in 1307, while the Bruns served as pledges for the Godriches in 1311, 1313 and 1318, as did the Gunnes in 1311 and 1313 also. The Bruns themselves were pledged by the Capud Villes in 1311 and 1313, who also pledged twice for the Hamonds in 1311. The Eyrs pledged the Lawemans in 1306 and in 1322, as did the Grays in 1311, 1313 and 1318 and the sons of Radulph in 1288, 1301, 1306, 1311 and 1313. The Franklyns pledged the Curteyses in 1307 and 1313. Godales were pledged by Geres in 1288 and also in 1306. The Asplonds were pledged by the Gunnes in 1299 and 1306 and by the Mays in 1301 and 1307. The Tiffaynes pledged the Russells in 1311 and 1313 and the Hamonds three times in 1326. The Fabers pledged the Clavigers in 1299 and 1301, and Carteres were pledged by Lawemans in 1338 and 1339. If the actual extent of the relationships between such families escapes detection, the fact of their repeated adoption of the pledging tie points not only to a degree of inter-family cooperation in the village, but to a continuing cooperation as well.[18]

This aspect of cooperation is further illustrated by the few surviving instances of inter-peasant relationships of a contractual nature from the late thirteenth to the mid-fifteenth century, specifically with regard to debts or licenses of concord usually issued to resolve debts. Unfortunately, in all but 11 cases the records give no information as to the nature of the debt — whether it involved money, tools or produce[19] — so that all that

---

[18] It should be noted, however, that although there was evidence of some continued cooperation between specific families, it was not especially long-lived — or, more to the point, permanent — so that such cases do not appear to have been thinly veiled instances of clan pledging, or pledging for an "extended family". Thus, in the examples given above of repeated formal pledging relationships, the number exceeded three times only once: the five-time pledging of Lawemans by the family of Radulph, 1288-1313. Even with the court roll series as interrupted as it is, if the relationships were more permanent or expressions of a clan tie, they could have been expected to reappear in other years, certainly more than two or three times.

Even the nature of the pledgings themselves tends to bear this out, since, in most cases of repeated or multiple pledgings, the relationships tended to differ each time, with only a few exceptions (e.g. Bruns pledging Godriches *extra feodum*, or Capud Villles pledging Bruns twice for ale infractions).

[19] A study presently being conducted of the village society of King's Ripton (co. Hunts.) by Anne REIBER DeWINDT (Toronto) sheds more light on inter-peasant debt structures than does Holywell, since, in several instances, the court rolls for that village carefully describe the nature of the debt, with some involving even the lending of livestock between villagers.

can usefully be gleaned from the court rolls is the fact that specific peasants entered into some kind of contractual relationship with each other. Thus, between 1288 and 1452, record has survived of some 77 instances of debts or licenses of concord involving 100 Holywell villagers representing 49 local families. In addition, there were three recorded cases of inter-peasant land leases — or attempted leases — involving five villagers from as many families, for an overall total of 80 contractual relationships involving 104 peasants from 49 village families.

The predominant number of villagers engaged in such activities came from major families. A total of 60 peasants representing 32 major families were involved in 62 of the 80 known contracts. As with pledging, so too with contracts the tendency was for families to be involved with other families of their own rank, but here again it was not exclusive. Fifteen families were recorded as exclusively engaging in contracts with other families of their own social rank,[20] but 34 families were not so confined. Thus, the Brayns, although involved in a license of concord with the Scots in 1294,[21] had borrowed money from an outsider in 1322 and sought license to resolve the matter.[22] The Scots, in addition to being involved with the Brayns in 1294, were creditors of the Lawemans and the Deyes in 1318, and, much later (1419) of the Hemyngtons,[23] while in 1403 John Scot had been in debt to William Webbester, a villager of minor rank.[24]

---

[20] Specifically, the Grays (Radulph) were owed money by the Franklyns (Richard: 5d.) in 1306, and the Semans (Radulph) were granted a license of concord with the Curpels (Reginald) in the same year. The Clerks (John) had licenses with the Franklyns (Richard) and the Mokes (William) in 1318, and the Lawemans (William) were in debt to the Scots (Nicholas) in the same year. The Deyes (William), too, were in debt to the Scots (Nicholas) in 1318, and in 1405 Thomas Deye (I) owed 10d. to Robert Miller, while in 1437 Thomas (II) had loaned money to John Wright. The Tiffaynes (John) were creditors of the Venelles (Robert) in 1322, and in debt (Joan) to the Brooks (Margaret) in 1326. The Bruns (Henry) were creditors of the Fannels (Stephan) in 1326, and the Scharps (Nicholas and Richard) of the Ravenes (John) and Houghtons (Robert: 6d) in 1378 and 1386, respectively. Robert Houghton not only owed money to the Scharps in the latter year, but he was the subject of a license with William Shepperd as well. The Porters (John) were creditors of the Fannells (Adam: 17d) in 1394, as were the Hunnes (William) in 1400. The Beaumeys (John) owed 3d. to the Nicholases (John) in 1405, and the Hemyngtons (John) were in debt to the Smyths (Thomas) and the Scots (Thomas) in 1407 and 1419, respectively. Finally, the Wrights (John) had borrowed from the Deyes (Thomas) in 1437, while, earlier, in 1318, the Mays (Beatrix) had loaned to the Mokes (William).

[21] William Brayn sought a license with Nicholas Scot in that year. BM.Add.Roll. 39597.

[22] The court roll is damaged at this point, but enough is preserved to indicate that Agnes Brayn sought a license "in placito debiti" with someone "de Overe" (PRO SC 2-179/21).

[23] The debt was between Thomas Scot and John Hemyngton, but Thomas never collected, for although the court set aside a day for settlement of the matter, it was noted in the margin that John Hemyngton was dead ("Mortuus"). PRO SC 2-179/56.

[24] PRO SC 2-179/57.

The Venelles, a main family of lesser rank, were in debt to the Tiffaynes in 1322, but earlier, in 1299, Radulph in Venelle had sought five separate licenses of concord with the Fychyens, Joan and Ivette,[25] a minor village family. The Franklyns, in three out of four cases, had been involved with other major villagers, but in 1288 Roysea le Franklyn had attempted to lease two and a half acres of land to Robert Russell. The Curpels — a minor family — had sought licenses of concord with members of both the Seman and Molendinarius/Miller families in 1306 to resolve debts,[26] while the Miller family further were in debt to the Fabers in 1306, to Egidius of Holywell in 1307, and, later, to the Bernewells in 1394, while they were creditors of the Deyes in 1405.[27] The Faber/Smyths — a family of major rank — were predominantly engaged with other major families,[28] but in one instance (1288) they attempted to lease land from Robert Sky, representative of one of the lesser main village families. The Hamonds, in the person of William, were in debt to an outsider in 1326,[29] while the Cusstes — a minor family — were both debtors and creditors of the outsider Matthew Half-ape in 1307.[30] The major family of Curteys, although debtors of both the Eyrs and the Hamonds in 1313,[31] were in debt to two outsiders in 1307 and 1313 as well as to the Brooks in the latter year.[32] The Eyrs, too, were involved with transients at least once, when Richard le Eyr was the creditor of Peter Saille in 1307,[33] as were the Ad Portams in 1311.[34] The Brooks, a lesser main family, although in debt

---

[25] PRO SC 2-179/10.

[26] PRO SC 2-179/5 and 12.

[27] In 1394, Thomas de Bernewell sought a license of concord to resolve a debt with Robert Miller (PRO SC 2-179/44), while in 1405 Robert was owed 10d. by Thomas Deye (I). PRO SC 2-179/50.

[28] In 1306, Gilbert Faber sought a license of concord with members of both the Molendinarius (Richard) and Hamond (Galfridus) families, while, in 1313, Peter Faber did the same with Nicholas de Ripton. Finally, in 1394, John Smyth was a creditor of Adam Fannell for an unpaid debt of 12d. and was awarded 10d. damages by the court. PRO SC 2-179/44.

[29] The roll is damaged so the name of the creditor is not decipherable, but William's pledge, Henry Tiffayne, was fined 6d. because of the failure of his principal to repay the debt.

[30] PRO SC 2-179/15.

[31] Beatrix Curteys was in debt to Matilda le Eyr, while William Curteys was in debt to William Hamond. PRO SC 2-179/17.

[32] In 1307, Thomas Curteys obtained a license of concord to settle a debt with the outsider Gilbert the Chapelyn (PRO SC 2-179/15), while in 1313 Beatrix Curteys was in debt to another transient, William le Tanherd, and William Curteys was in debt to John in le Brook (PRO SC 2-179/17).

[33] PRO SC 2-179/15.

[34] Matthew ad Portam was both a debtor and creditor of Caterina Ivette in 1311. PRO SC 2-179/16.

to a member of the Colyn family and creditors of a Tiffayne in 1318 and 1326, respectively,[35] were, as already noted, creditors of the Curteyses in 1313 and also creditors of the Asplonds in 1318.[36] The Riptons were creditors of both the Fabers and the Caldecotes in 1313, while, as noted above, the Russels were involved in an abortive attempt to lease land from a member of the Franklyn family.[37] The Palmeres were creditors of two outsiders in 1318,[38] and, much later — in 1405 — a Palmere was in debt for 5 d. to a member of the minor Webbester family. The Nicholases acted both as debtors and creditors, with Robert Nicholas securing license to resolve a debt with Matthew, son of Alexander, in 1318, and John Nicholas being the object of two licenses obtained by two transients in 1372. The Mokes appeared three times in 1318 as debtors — once to Beatrix le May, once to John Clerk and once to the outsider Henry de Landey.[39] The Asplonds were once in debt to the Brooks, and in 1391 Thomas Asplond was creditor of the transient Robert Clerk for 3 s. 8 d.[40] The Fannells — one of the most active families in the debt scheme — were variously in debt to Mathew, son of Alexander, in 1322, the Bruns in 1326, members of the Baroun family,[41] the Nicholases in 1391, the Porters in 1394, the Hunnes in 1400, the Smyths in 1394 and even to one outsider (William Stayard) in 1396. The Gerolds — a minor family — had an unpaid debt to an outsider (William Redburn) in 1326, as did the Prondheles in 1339 to an Adam of Somersham. The Barouns, in addition to their three-time involvement as creditors to the Fannels, were in debt to an outsider in 1364, as were the Shepperds in 1386.[42] The Bernewells — another minor

---

[35] In 1318, John in le Brook was in debt to Matilda Colyn and fined 3d. (PRO SC 2-179/18), while in 1326 Joan Tiffayne was fined 3d. for a yet unpaid debt to Margaret in le Brook (PRO SC 2-179/22).

[36] PRO SC 2-179/18. Specifically, John Asplond was in debt to John in the Brook and fined 3d. for non-payment.

[37] PRO SC 2-179/17. In addition, in 1313 Robert Russell impleaded his brother Thomas in court as a usurer, since Thomas — apparently in the name of interest for a loan — had taken off nine rings and three bushels of dredge from Robert, when, it was stated, he was not allowed to take more than 32d. by law. For his action Thomas incurred a fine of two shillings.

[38] Robert and Alexander le Moigne obtained a license of concord for settling a debt with William le Palmere in 1318. PRO SC 2-179/18.

[39] PRO SC 2-179/18.

[40] PRO SC 2-179/43.

[41] In 1356, Robert Fannell was in debt to William Baroun and sought a license for settlement (PRO SC 2-179/36), while in both 1394 and 1405 William Baroun was in debt to Adam Fannell (PRO SC 2-179/44 and 50).

[42] In 1386, John Shepperd was in debt to a Thomas Cribbe and sought a license for settlement. Remaining Shepperd debts involved Robert Houghton — creditor in 1386 — and Joan Eyr — debtor — in 1364.

village family — were in debt to the Millers in 1394 and to the rector of the parish church in 1403,[43] while, finally, the Cristemesse family — in the persons of John (I) and John (II) — were, respectively, in debt to the outsider John Messauger in 1405 and creditors to John Touslond in 1452 for 9 s. 10 d.[44]

All told, the court rolls indicate that 31 families engaged in relationships of a contractual nature with their neighbors two times or more,[45] and again the predominance of main families must be recognized, for 27 of the families thus active as borrowers or lenders were of major or lesser rank, although their dealings were not necessarily confined to other families within their own group. Indeed, 17 of the 27 main families — or 63 % — were involved in contracts with members of minor families or transients, so that, as with the pledging structure, so too the pattern of debt relationships points to a broadly-based spirit of cooperation within the village — dominated, to be sure, by main families, either as a result of their own extensive involvement in and identification with village life or, perhaps, stemming from a sense of responsibility for their less secure neighbors, but nevertheless a cooperativeness that was a distinctly recognizable pattern of village life.

The cooperative spirit was reflected not only in pledging and debt relationships, however. Notices of fines for group trespasses in the early fourteenth century — coupled with the imposition of pledging *alter alterius* — probably point to joint working arrangements between peasants, while, from the late fourteenth century, cases of direct land conveyances from one family to another indicate a probable degree of closeness and cooperation between the families. In terms of the former, although it is possible that all trespasses in the village could have been "lumped" together into one artificial group for the sake of convenience of court presentment, it is improbable that this was done, since group trespasses invariably constituted an item of court business separate and distinct from individual trespasses presented and fined in a session.[46] This, coupled with the fact

---

[43] Specifically, Thomas Bernewell was in debt to Robert Miller in 1394 and obtained a license for settlement (PRO SC 2-179/44), while Thomas again was in debt to the rector in 1403, a fact known from the imposition of a 3d. fine on the rector for failing to prosecute his charge of debt against Thomas (PRO SC 2-179/48).

[44] PRO SC 2-179/50 and 66.

[45] Specifically, 16 families did so twice, five did so three times, three did four times, four five times, two six times and one 11 times.

[46] In the years for which group trespasses were recorded, individual trespasses were presented as well. Thus in 1299, when one group of 11 peasants was fined, an additional 13 cases of trespass were penalized, each requiring an individual pledge. In 1306, when one group trespass involving

that the guilty parties were invariably pledged *alter alterius*, suggests that each member of such groups shared a definite responsibility for the misconduct of the group as a whole, and that consequently the specific offense being penalized had been committed in concert.[47] Thus, in 1299 Thomas Curteys and Alexander Brun were jointly fined 12 d. and pledged *alter alterius* for trespass against Isabella Hildegar,[48] while a group of 11 peasants composed of five representatives of as many major families,[49] one member of a lesser family,[50] one member of a minor family,[51] and four transients[52] was further presented for trespass in the same year.[53] In 1306, four peasants — two men of major rank[54] and two of lesser status[55] — were jointly presented for badly reaping. In 1307, five men had apparently worked together in a group, for they too were presented and fined for badly reaping,[56] while in 1318 four men were presented as a group for badly mowing.[57] Also in the latter year, Robert Scot and Katerina Brun were jointly fined for badly ploughing, which possibly reflected an agreement whereby Robert undertook to acquit Katerina's ploughing services. They were fined again, as well — together with William Moke and Alexander de Ripton — in the same year for a group trespass *ad damnum*.[58]

All told, between 1299 and 1318 a total of 33 peasants representing 23 families were presented in surviving court rolls for offenses of a group nature, thereby reflecting some probable joint working arrangements. In addition, the majority were members of major families,[59] itself a cause

---

four men and another involving two were presented, so too were seven other individual trespasses. Similarly, in 1307: two groups were noted, along with six individual trespasses. Again, in 1311, there was one "group" offense, and four individual offenses, and in 1318, when four distinct group violations were dealt with, there were five separate and individual trespasses fined as well.

[47] This interpretation of group fines as being reflections of a real group offense has been tentatively suggested by Raftis, "Social Structures in Five East Midland Villages," *Ec.H.R.* XVIII, p. 89.

[48] PRO SC 2-179/10.

[49] I.e. William Selede, William Godrich, Nicholas Clerk, Stephan Hamond and Richard Gere.

[50] I.e. Robert Aleyn.

[51] Isabella Hildegar.

[52] John the son of Henry, John Lylre, John Ivette and Paulinus, son of Juliana.

[53] The trespass itself was not revealed, being described only as "transgressio ad nocumentum" (PRO SC 2-179/10).

[54] Stephan Nicholas and Richard Franklyn.

[55] Robert and Galfridus Cusste.

[56] Reginald Clerk, Stephan Colyn, Radulph Gray, William Venelle and Thomas Curteys.

[57] William Moke, Robert Asplond, Reginald Clericus, John Hunne.

[58] PRO SC 2-179/18.

[59] Specifically, 22 persons were members of 17 families of major rank in the village. Six persons represented five main but lesser families, and four men were transients.

for no surprise since, as customary tenants, they would almost naturally be accustomed to working close to or with one another, so that, in the final analysis, the evidence of group or joint working relationship indicates less any unusual village phenomenon but rather mirrors a tradition of cooperation among peasant families, a tradition that could be found reflected even in the few surviving examples of joint tenancies, as when four villagers — from three families — joined forces to take up 11 acres of demesne in 1339,[60] or when groups of peasants formed about one main villager for the purpose of exploiting fen in 1370.[61]

Land transfers, on the other hand, may not reflect so much a spirit of mutual inter-peasant cooperation as they underscore what was a very powerful contractual element of the society itself.[62] Between 1393 and 1457, cellarers' rolls and the Court Book recorded some 26 inter-familial transfers of properties in Holywell, involving 34 local villagers representing 27 village families. Twenty-two of the families were main families — 21 of major, one of lesser rank — and five were minor families. Eight were involved in transfers — either as grantors or receivers — more than once. The Mertons, for example, received a croft from the Bernewells in 1393,[63] and they granted three-quarters of a virgate to the Godfreys in 1426,[64] and two virgates to the Asplonds in 1440.[65] The Beaumeys family received a virgate from the Lanes in 1401,[66] a croft from the Sewales

---

[60] Roger Cranfeld, John Carpenter, Nicholas Scot and Richard Cranfeld jointly held 11 acres of "le Smethe" dismissed by the abbot in 1339 for 5s. 6d. *per annum* and still being held in 1346/47. PRO SC 6-877/18.

[61] John Nicholas "et socii" held 40 pieces of marsh in 1370 for a total rent of 75 shillings, while Nicholas Shepperd "et socii" held three acres in Merslake, and Thomas Asplond "et socii" held an acre and a half in Dichfurlong. PRO SC 6-877/21.

[62] Indeed, this contractual aspect of the society — as contrasted to the stress often placed on status as determining some village operations (See Lipson, *Economic History of England*, Vol. I "The Middle Ages") — is evidenced throughout by the wide-spread existence of suretyship relationships, debt structures and joint working arrangements.

[63] BM.Add.Ms. 33447, 17ʳ. Thomas Bernewell transferred the croft to John Merton in the accepted manner of surrendering it to the lord "ad opus Johannis". In addition, Thomas' original tenure had been a joint venture with the villager John Spercoll, for the croft was described as having been held by both Thomas and John.

[64] Specifically, Alice Merton "sursum reddidit in manus domini j messuagium cum iij quarteriis terre et cum terra dominica adiacente nuper in tenura Ricardi Merton viri sui ad opus Rogerii Godfrey." BM.Harl.Ms 445, 132ᵛ.

[65] *Ibid.*, 182ᵛ. "Thomas Merton sursum reddidit in manus domini j mesuagium et j virgatam terre cum terra dominica et cum ij rodis prati in Salmade et j virgatam in le Smethe ad opus Johannis Asplond jun'."

[66] *Ibid.*, 17ᵛ.

in 1452,[67] and a cotland from the Barouns in 1457.[68] The Shepperds were the recipients of a cotland from the Deyes in 1417[69] and of a cotland, a virgate and a quarter from the AtteWelles in 1451.[70] The Nicholases transferred a virgate to the Smyths in 1427,[71] which they had themselves received from Thomas Merale in 1423,[72] and four acres to the Cristemesses in 1455.[73] The Cristemesses, for their part, were recipients also of two cotlands from the Bryans in 1424[74] and of a cotland and a half from the outsider John Blakwell in 1437.[75] The AtteWelles were granted a half-virgate by the Palfreymans in 1419,[76] transferred a little over 30 acres to the Shepperds (and Simon Dallyng) in 1451 and a half-virgate to the Elyots in 1454.[77] The Bakers transferred a virgate to the Godfreys in 1419,[78] and received a virgate from an outsider — Richard Townesende — in 1441.[79] The Godfreys, in addition to their grant from the Bakers in 1419, received property from the Mertons in 1426.[80] The Valentynes received a cotland from their in-laws, the Scots, in 1424[81] and transferred it to an outsider — Richard Watts — in 1437.[82] The Barouns granted out a virgate to another outsider — John Albry — in 1432[83] and a cotland to the Beaumeyses in 1457,[84] while the Asplonds were the recipients of two grants: a half-virgate from the Palmeres in 1438[85] and two virgates from the Mertons in 1440.[86]

To summarize at this point, then, there is evidence of a spirit of cooper-

---

[67] BM.Harl.Ms. 445, 238ᵛ.

[68] *Ibid.*, 256ʳ. The transfer was between Richard Beaumeys and William Herle — stepson of the late Nicholas Baroun.

[69] *Ibid.*, 101ʳ.

[70] *Ibid.*, 235ʳ. In addition, the tenure thereby established by John Shepperd over the properties was a joint tenure with Simon Dallyng, the parish priest.

[71] *Ibid.*, 133ᵛ.

[72] *Ibid.*, 121ᵛ.

[73] *Ibid.*, 250ᵛ.

[74] *Ibid.*, 124ᵛ.

[75] *Ibid.*, 165ʳ.

[76] *Ibid.*, 121ᵛ.

[77] *Ibid.*, 247ʳ.

[78] *Ibid.*, 121ᵛ.

[79] *Ibid.*, 188ʳ.

[80] *Ibid.*, 132ᵛ.

[81] *Ibid.*, 124ᵛ.

[82] *Ibid.*, 165ʳ.

[83] *Ibid.*, 146ʳ.

[84] *Ibid.*, 256ʳ.

[85] *Ibid.*, 175ʳ.

[86] *Ibid.*, 182ᵛ.

ation obtaining in Holywell-cum-Needingworth between 1288 and 1457, whether inter-family or inter-group in nature. Specifically, record exists of 87 separate village families engaging in cooperative relationships with each other, from pledging to joint working arrangements, contracts (debts) to transfers of land. In addition, only 24 families can be cited whose activities seem to have been confined to but one other village family (See Table III). Thirty-seven families, on the other hand, had dealings with five other families or more (See Table III). In terms of the frequency of relationships themselves, 50 families were involved with each other from one to five times, and 37 families again anywhere from six to over 20 times[87].

Equally significant as the number and scope of inter-family relationships, however, is the fact that such relationships were not necessarily intra-group relationships. In other words, families of a specific rank in the village — either major, lesser or minor — did not confine themselves

---

[87] In addition to relationships arising from pledgings, debts, working arrangements and land transfers, note should be made of yet another type of relationship: marriage. In the fourteenth century, it was recorded, for example, that Robert Gere married Johanna Brayn, a widow, in 1309 (BM.Add.Roll. 39693). In addition, personal relationships between the Bercars and the Franklyns were quite close in 1288: in that year, Katherine Franklyn, daughter of Rosa, was presented for having borne Walter Bercar's child out of wedlock (PRO SC 2-179/5). (There is no record as to whether or not Walter and Katherine ever did marry, but Katherine's name disappeared thereafter, while Walter was married in 1294, when both he and his wife were the object of a hue and cry raised by John Clerk, and it is not unlikely that the two probably had in fact married by the latter date.)

In the late fourteenth and early fifteenth century, record of at least a few more intra-village marriages has survived. It is known that Henry Kyng was married to a Rosa Shepperd, daughter of John, in 1393 (BM.Add.Ms. 33447, 19ᵛ). The freeman John Bate married Johanna AtteWelle in 1400 (*Ibid.*, 13ʳ), while Alice AtteWelle — daughter of John II — was married to John Elyot by 1443, and a second Alice AtteWelle married Simon Touslond in 1449 (*Ibid.*, 226ᵛ). In 1412, Agnes Deye, daughter of Thomas Deye (II), married John Shepperd (III) (*Ibid.*, 80ᵛ.) Alice Cartere — daughter of Thomas — married the freeman Nicholas Gybbe in 1402 (*Ibid.*, 33ʳ), while Agnes Scot married William Lanender in 1416, and Margaret Scot married Thomas Valentyne in 1417 (BM.Harl.Ms, 445, 97ʳ and 98ʳ).

Outside of the fact that the Gere/Brayn, Bate/AtteWelle, Elyot/AtteWelle, Touslond/Atte-Welle, Deye/Shepperd, Scot/Lanender, and Scot/Valentyn marriages of the fourteenth and fifteenth centuries were all examples of inter-marriages between main families, what is perhaps most interesting is the absence of any recorded heavy concentration of relationships between the respective families either prior to or following their unions in marriage. The contacts between the AtteWelles, the Deyes and the Scots, for example, and their respective sons-in-law were minimal, confined to single grants of land — which were perhaps endowments to the newly-weds. Thereafter, close cooperation does not seem to have been in evidence, which is either a result of a simple lack of adequate records, or, perhaps a further reflection of the weakening of the family bond already noted with respect to tenurial practices from the beginning of the fifteenth century.

TABLE III

EXTENT OF PARTICIPATION IN INTER-FAMILIAL RELATIONSHIPS IN
HOLYWELL-CUM-NEEDINGWORTH

Family	Activity Group	Family	Activity Group
FAMILIES INVOLVED WITH ONE FAMILY:			
BAKER	A	RAVEN	C
BATE	A	REYNOLD	C
BOLOYGNE	C	SANDE	A
BRYAN	A	SEMAN	C
COLYERE	C	SEWALE	A
ELYOT	A	SELEDE	C
GEROLD	C	THURKYLL	A
GODALE	C	THURBERNE	C
LANE	A	TAYLLOUR	C
PALFREYMAN	C	TOUSLOND	B
PRONDHELE	C	VALENTYN	B
PYE	C	WEBBESTER	C
FAMILIES INVOLVED WITH TWO FAMILIES:			
BAROUN	A	KYLLENETH	C
BUNDELEG	C	PORTAM	B
CALDECOTE	C	PORTER	A
FISHERE	C	RAULYN	B
GODEMAN	A	REVE	A
HEMYNGTON	A	SCHARP	A
HOUGHTON	A	WRIGHT	A
FAMILIES INVOLVED WITH THREE FAMILIES:			
ATTEWELLE	A	FYCHYEN	C
CAPPE	C	GODFREY	A
CARPENTER	A	MARIOT	C
CRISTEMESSE	A	MERTON	A
FAMILIES INVOLVED WITH FOUR FAMILIES:			
BACOUN	B	RUSSELL	B
MADDE	B	SKY	B
FAMILIES INVOLVED WITH FIVE FAMILIES:			
BERNEWELL	C	CRANFELD	A
BRAYN	A	DEYE	A
CAPUD VILLE	C	HUNNE	A
CLAVIGER	C		

Family	Activity Group	Family	Activity Group
FAMILIES INVOLVED WITH FROM SIX TO TEN FAMILIES:			
ALEYN	B	GRAY	A
ASPLOND	A	LAWEMAN	A
BEAUMEYS	A	MAY	A
BROOK	B	NICHOLAS	A
CARTERE	A	PALMERE	A
COLYN	B	"RADULPHI"	A
CUSSTE	B	RIPTON	A
EYR	A	VENELLE	B
FANNELL	A	SHEPPERD	A
GODRYCH	A		
FAMILIES INVOLVED WITH FROM ELEVEN TO FIFTEEN FAMILIES:			
BRUN	A	GUNNE	A
CURTEYS	A	HAMOND	A
FABER/SMYTH	A	MOKE	A
FAMILIES INVOLVED WITH FROM SIXTEEN TO TWENTY FAMILIES:			
CLERK	A	SCOT	A
FRANKLYN	A	TIFFAYNE	B
GERE	A		

to dealings only with other families of the same station as their own. Indeed, 63 of the 87 families — or 73 % — were involved at least once, but frequently more often, with families of a different activity-orientation or status from their own. In addition, as it has been noted with respect to almost every individual cooperative activity, so too as regards the overall picture, the predominant role in inter-personal relationships in the village belonged to main families, but especially to families of major rank. Fifty of the 87 families, for example — or 57 % — belonged to that category, with 24 families (28 %) of minor rank and 13 (15 %) of main but lesser status. It was the major families who dominated the body of pledges, who were foremost in the employment of contractual relationships and most active in the transferring of properties after 1400. As observed above, their ubiquity probably stemmed in no small measure from their deep involvement in village life in general — as customary tenants, for example, they had a very real stake in the economic life and social stability of the community — but it also serves to reinforce the general impression noted at the end of the previous chapter: that the major families were in fact major families because their members possessed the competence — and sometimes the special competence — to take responsibility and assume leadership in the village. Their prominence in pledging, contracts and other cooperative relationships is but a further example of this competence, and, it may also be suggested, that this may have even further refined their abilities to exercise responsibility in the community.[88] In any event, the evidence of a village society in which many and diverse inter-personal or inter-family relationships played a significant role is undeniable. The ties of dependence hinted at above, at the end of Chapter III — the dependence of main families on minor families for basic services and the dependence of minor families (and the community as a whole) on main families for government and administration — was but a glimpse of deeper and more far-reaching ties of dependence in a local society where individuals relied on their neighbors for surety — indeed, even for membership in the community — as well as for economic assistance. Consequently a picture emerges of a village in which cooperation was both a real and powerful fact of everyday life. Indeed, the picture thus obtained is itself only a fuzzy image of the full extent of the cooperative spirit within the village, since it is limited to a handful of surviving records, in which notice was taken of inter-personal relationships either when they were exploited for legal purposes or when they required legal aid in their enforcement. The ease with which the system of personal pledging operated, for example, points to a tradition of inter-personal guarantees or surety that doubtlessly permeated several facets of village life not concerned with the court — purchases, leases or transfers of property, for example, or debts. The latter, in fact, were obviously not all accounted for in court records, but were only reported when one of the parties to a debt had failed to honour his obligation.[89] As a result, the number of times peasants engaged in contractual relationships with each other, together with the number of times they called upon each other for surety — as well as the full extent of such surety relationships — remains hidden. If an estimate of the number of such relationships that probably received court attention in the years between 1288 and 1339 were to be attempted, the result would most

---

[88] Twenty-eight men from the late thirteenth and early fourteenth centuries, for example, were recorded as serving as personal pledges before they first appeared in the major offices of either taster or juror.

In addition, it should be noted that of 158 men active as pledges or otherwise engaged in contractual relationships or land transfers, 92 — or 58 % — were men who also served specifically as village or manorial officials.

[89] The same applies to joint working arrangements. They were obviously a common village experience, but they entered the records only when the groups involved violated some local ordinance, committed an act of trespass or failed to fulfil their work obligations.

likely be some 150 cases of debt[90] and 1242 cases of personal pledging.[91] But the total number of relationships — those not requiring the official attention of the court — is less readily projected. In the case of debts, for example, if 14 out of 50 villagers between 1288 and 1339 — or 28 % — were involved in two or more contracts coming before the court in single years,[92] then it is not impossible that other villagers noted but once in any given year as well may have been engaged in at least one — if not more — additional contracts that did not require court enforcement. Similarly with pledging relationships. If 41 men out of 141 pledges (or 28 %) could in fact be involved in anywhere from two to seven formal and court-related pledging relationships in any one year, then it is not inconceivable that a villager might be called upon to act as guarantor for a neighbor under more private circumstances some two, three, even more times a year. As a result, it may be possible to double — and perhaps even triple — the number of known and estimated court-related pledging and contractual relationships in the village to arrive at an approximation of the total number of such inter-personal relationships emanating from within the society itself to satisfy a variety of needs — both public and private — from the late thirteenth to the mid-fourteenth century.

But whatever the ultimate solution to the problem of the sheer number of inter-personal relationships in the village, the vital role of such relationships in creating and maintaining social cohesion within the village cannot be denied. Such cohesion — manifesting itself in the general stability of the community, the smooth and peaceful operation of its institutions and even in the continued survival or gradual economic expansion of a large number of its resident families — is best understood as resulting from many and varying ties of mutual dependence between its members, creating a community in which individuals were not set apart in groups isolated from each other along "class" lines, but rather one in which the

---

[90] The estimate is based on averages. Between 1288 and 1339, 54 contractual relationships of a debt nature were recorded in 12 court sessions out of a surviving total of 19. The overall average was three (54 ÷ 19 = 2.8), which produces 96 cases for the 32 years not represented by court rolls. Added to the 54 known cases, the total is 150.

[91] Again the figure is derived from an average of 25 cases a session for the 19 court rolls preserved from 16 years between 1288 and 1339. Assuming one session for each of the remaining unrecorded 35 years, the total is 875 (25 × 35), which, added to a known 367 cases, results in 1242 cases.

[92] Ten persons (Reginald Curpel, Gilbert Faber, Richard Molendinarius, Robert Cusste, Matthew ad Portam, Beatrix Curteys, William Curteys, Nicholas de Ripton, John Brook and Nicholas Scot) were involved in two in one year alone; one (William Moke, 1318) was involved in three; and three (Radulph Venelle, Joan and Ivette Fychyen) were involved in five separate contracts.

vast majority were joined together by networks of cooperation arising from and in service of common needs.

The conditions just described, however, of strong cohesion and a far-reaching and highly-refined cooperative spirit — in short, of a basically inter-dependent community — best apply to Holywell-cum-Needingworth in the years prior to 1350. From the middle of the fourteenth century, changes began to take shape which had profound effects on the overall cohesion and cooperativeness of village experience. As early as the 1350's, conditions began to manifest themselves which ushered in what was to be a century of weakening village cohesiveness in the face of a growing spirit of particularism. Unfortunately, the survival of court rolls from the second half of the fourteenth and first half of the fifteenth centuries has not been extensive enough to permit any deep or thorough examination of the problem, but what records have been preserved at least point to a continuing breaking-down of the older order within the village — especially between 1353 and 1398 — as well as to an increasing disregard of manorial commitments and obligations by the tenant population.

In general, the period from the middle of the fourteenth century to the middle of the fifteenth century was characterized by a turning-away from a strong reliance on inter-personal ties maintaining inter-dependent community experience and was marked instead by an increased exercise of independent actions by peasants and peasant families. If not exactly an "every-man-for-himself" atmosphere, nevertheless Holywell peasants began to display less concern for the rights and privileges of their neighbors than at any time in the late thirteenth or early fourteenth centuries, while there also emerged a tendency for some families — even major families — to adopt a lax attitude towards more formal and public — and court related — institutions for resolving intra-village disputes and conflicts but rather to rely on their own private efforts in maintaining harmonious relationships with their neighbors. In all, the impression given by the records is of a village in which private initiative, interests and responsibility were gradually supplanting the more or less public and inter-dependent activities and relationships so prominent before the middle of the fourteenth century.

The first indication of this change within the village has already been mentioned: the sharp decline in the institution of the court-related personal pledge. For example, in 1353 alone, out of 77 individual violations or cases brought before the court of 24 October — each of which would have required a pledge in earlier years — only six were in fact pledged, and five were cases of violence.[93] In 1356, only 13 out of 73 cases were

---

[93] Specifically, two were cases of hue and cry, three involved assault, and the sixth was a license to marry, outside the manor sought by Joanna Smyth (PRO SC 2-179/25).

pledged, as were five out of 44 in 1359. There were no recorded pledgings in either the court rolls of 1364 or 1369, and only seven out of 108 offenses were pledged in 1372. The number of pledgings dwindled to one in 1378 and two in 1386, while there were only 12 pledgings out of four court rolls from the 1390's. As noted earlier, the reason for the decline of the institution has not yet been adequately examined, but whatever its cause, it resulted in the individual peasant being held personally and solely responsible for his actions and for the execution of any court-imposed obligations. As such, this was not necessarily a catastrophic development for village society, but it did limit the opportunities — and need — for cooperative and shared responsibility within the village.

A more striking example of the change in intra-village cooperation — as well as of the ties of cooperation between the village and the manor — can be found in the truly startling increase in the number of acts of trespass committed in the years after 1350. Trespasses, of course — whether committed against the manor or against individual villagers — had always been a regular item in court rolls from as early as 1288, but although their full number or extent cannot be known due to the sparse court roll survival, they can be said not to have assumed especially alarming proportions prior to the middle of the fourteenth century. Specifically, between 1288 and 1339 record has survived of 170 acts of trespass committed in 15 separate years,[94] for an average of 11 a year, although the number could actually vary anywhere from one (1301) to 27 (1299).[95] An estimate, then, of the probable total number of trespasses between 1288 and 1339 — based on the average 11 multiplied by 36 (the years unrecorded) and the

---

[94] I.e. 1288, 1294, 1299, 1301, 1306, 1307, 1311, 1313, 1318, 1322, 1326, 1332, 1338, 1339.
[95] The number of trespasses recorded in specific years was as follows:

Year	Trespasses
1288	5
1294	12
1299	27
1301	1
1306	12
1307	7
1311	4
1313	5
1318	13
1322	6
1326	18
1328	11
1332	21
1338	16
1339	14

result added to the known 170 acts — is 566. On the other hand, between 1353 and 1398, the court rolls for 14 separate years[96] recorded a total of 305 trespasses. The average was 22 a year, which, if applied to the missing 31 years, results in an overall estimated total of 982 trespasses from 1353 to 1398.[97] But even without pressing overall probable estimates too far, the increase in trespassing in the second half of the fourteenth century from the first half is evident in the figure of known trespasses. In 14 years between 1353 and 1398, the village witnessed almost twice as many trespasses as it had in 15 years between 1288 and 1339. Only after 1400 did a decline in trespassing occur, with 203 known acts recorded in 15 years between 1400 and 1457.[98] In terms of incidence of trespassing,

[96] I.e. 1353, 1356, 1359, 1364, 1369, 1372, 1375, 1378, 1386, 1389, 1391, 1395, 1396 and 1399.

[97] Again the number of trespasses in a year could vary. The actual figures are as follows:

YEAR	TRESPASSES
1353	18
1356	13
1359	12
1364	17
1369	15
1372	51
1375	14
1378	11
1386	42
1389	12
1391	34
1394	33
1396	24
1398	9

[98] I.e.

YEAR	TRESPASSES
1400	17
1402	12
1403	25
1405	24
1409	1
1413	12
1419	5
1423	10
1428	4
1432	17
1437	11
1443	17
1452	15
1455	9
1457	24

The overall average was 14 a year, which, if applied to the 42 missing years, produces an estimated total of 797 trespasses from 1400 to 1457.

more acts were committed in three years of the 1370's (76), two years of the 1380's (54) or four years of the 1390's (100) than were recorded in any decade between 1290 and 1340. (See Table IV). The nature of the trespasses themselves are extremely difficult to discover, since the Holywell court rolls seldom went into great detail,[99] but on the basis of the little information they do supply, it appears that the bulk of the trespassing after the middle of the century was the result of the pastoral involvements

TABLE IV

INCIDENCE OF TRESPASSING IN HOLYWELL-CUM-NEEDINGWORTH, 1288-1457

YEAR	TRESPASSES	YEAR	TRESPASSES
1288	5	1378	11
1294	12	1386	42
1299	27	1389	12
1301	1	1391	34
1306	12	1394	33
1307	7	1396	24
1311	4	1398	9
1313	5	1400	17
1318	13	1402	12
1322	6	1403	25
1326	18	1405	24
1328	11	1409	1
1332	21	1413	12
1338	16	1419	5
1339	14	1423	10
1353	18	1428	4
1356	13	1432	17
1359	12	1437	11
1364	17	1443	17
1369	15	1452	15
1372	51	1455	9
1375	14	1457	24

and needs of the peasants, since in at least 127 instances the rolls spoke of trespasses having been caused by sheep, horses, cows, pigs or simply by "beasts". Indeed, the variety of trespasses found in the earlier fourteenth century — which ranged from fishing infractions to digging up the King's road to trespassing in the woods—was absent after 1350, where the majority

[99] The most frequent expression was the infuriatingly uncommunicative "transgressionem fecit".

of trespasses actually described to any degree invariably concerned the intrusion of animals into the crops of the *nativi*, the demesne or the common. Given the changing tenurial policies of the abbey over the period and the continually declining condition of agriculture throughout England, it is not surprising that Holywell peasants were turning more and more to stock raising — which, in fact, appears to have become predominant by the earlier fifteenth century as evidenced by the quick exploitation of properties and the repeated passing of by-laws to regulate pasturing after 1400[100] — but the evidence of so many trespasses does more than merely point to an increasingly pastorally-oriented peasantry. It points to a peasantry not especially concerning itself with keeping its livestock under control for the sake of its neighbors, the village or the manor. Granted that the wandering proclivities of four-legged creatures are not easy to control, still the fact that penalties continued to be imposed while the village community itself attempted — unsuccessfully — to further regulate such behavior after 1400 indicates that at least some people in Holywell were not completely happy with the continuing damage being done by the seemingly ubiquitous horses, cows and sheep, while the repeated incidence of such trespasses, coupled with the obvious disregard of by-laws in the early fifteenth century, betrays an attitude of indifference to the physical state of the village as well as to any deep sense of communal responsibility.

This may be further illustrated by a consideration of the actual persons responsible for the trespasses in Holywell over the years. Between 1288 and 1339, 170 acts of trespass were committed by a total of 120 men and women. Some 29 — guilty of 35 acts — were transients, outsiders or persons otherwise not identifiable with any local family group, but 91 persons were members of 57 village families. Twenty-seven main families accounted for 53 persons (44%) trespassing some 79 times (46%). Eleven lesser families had 14 members (12%) trespassing 20 times (12%), and 24 persons (20%), representing 19 minor families, trespassed a total of 36 times (21%). In addition, 33 families (58%) were responsible for acts of trespass more than once, with the heaviest concentration — 10 acts — within the major Scot family, followed by the Geres and the Hamonds — at seven acts — and the Lawemans, Colyns and Fannells at five. For 15 years scattered between 1288 and 1339, however, the number of families responsible for the heaviest concentration of trespasses was not remarkably large. After 1350, on the other hand, an altered pattern prevailed. In

---

[100] See *supra*, p. 136 *et seq.*

14 years documented between 1353 and 1398, 305 acts of trespass were committed by 162 persons — over three times the number trespassing prior to 1350. In addition, although 33 of these were transients or outsiders, they were responsible for only 55 acts, or 18 % of the total. The remaining 250 trespasses were committed by 129 local residents, representing 65 village families, and 42 major families were responsible for the overwhelming majority of them — specifically, 102 men trespassing 198 times. Five lesser families had only six persons (4%), trespassing 10 times (3 % of the total), and 21 members (13%) of 18 minor families trespassed 42 times, accounting for only 14% of all the known acts in the 15 years served by court rolls. In addition, 42 families — 31 of major rank — were recorded as being responsible for trespasses more than once, with 24 of them (57 %) committing five acts of trespass or more.[101] Whether explained by their increased pastoral involvements after the middle of the century or not, the fact remains that in 15 years prior to 1350 only 33 families were recorded as trespassing more than once, 18 of which — or 55 % — were major families, while, further, only six families were reported as trespassing five times or more, whereas after 1350, at a time of even a thinning population, 42 families trespassed more than once, of which 31 — or 74% — were of major rank, while 24 families — four times the earlier number — trespassed five times or more.

This heightened tendency of Holywell families to act more according to private interests in the years following the middle of the fourteenth century and, consequently, almost in disregard of the interests of the community at large, was reinforced by the behavior displayed with respect to manorial commitments and obligations. It was evident, for example, in the increased number of trespasses after 1350 that private interests could and did take precedence over those of the manor, since a frequent victim of the roaming livestock was the manorial demesne and the crops being grown there. But there was yet another indication of peasant disregard for the manor's interests, and it was found in the increased incidence of work derelictions — either in failures to work or in poor performance of work — over the second half of the century. Thus, between 1288 and 1339, only 40 derelictions of work had been recorded in surviving court rolls, comprising 23 cases of non-performance of work and 17 cases of

---

[101] With respect to the whole period 1353-1457, the total 508 trespasses recorded by 29 court rolls were committed by 262 persons. Seventy-seven transients accounted for 114 acts, and 185 persons from 75 village families were responsible for the remaning 394 trespasses, with 45 major families accounting for 320 (144 persons), seven lesser families for 16 (10 persons), and 23 minor families for 58 (31 persons).

poor performance of work. In addition, the frequency of such derelictions had been staggered over the period, with only one case in 1288, 1294, 1301 and 1332, and the highest number — 10 cases — occurring but once, in 1313. (See Table V).

The picture was quite different in 1353, however. In that year, 26 derelictions — 25 failures to work and one case of poor performance — were presented. Seven were noted in 1354, 17 in 1356, 10 in 1359, six in 1364, 32 in 1372, seven in 1375, 24 in 1378, 28 in 1386, 10 in 1389, 21 in 1391, 13 in 1394, 12 in 1396, five in 1398, and also in 1400, and four in 1402 and 1403. (See Table V). All told, there were recorded a total of 231 derelictions, consisting of 179 cases of non-performance and 52 cases of poor performance of work in only 17 years between 1353 and 1403:

TABLE V

WORK DERELICTIONS, 1288-1403

YEAR	NON OP'	PERSONS	MALE OP'	PERSONS	TOTAL	PERSONS
1288	1	1			1	1
1294	1	1			1	1
1301	1	1			1	1
1306			4		4	4
1307	3	3	5	5	8	8
1311	2	2			2	2
1313	10	9			10	9
1318	1	1	6	6	7	6
1328	2	2			2	2
1332			1	1	1	1
1339	2	2	1	1	3	3
1353	25	22	1	1	26	22
1354	4	4	3	3	7	7
1356	11	10	6	6	17	16
1359	3	3	7	7	10	10
1364	6	5			6	5
1372	7	6	25	24	32	29
1375	7	7			7	7
1378	24	22			24	22
1386	26	24	2	2	28	26
1389	7	7	3	3	10	10
1391	16	16	5	5	21	21
1394	13	13			13	13
1396	12	10			12	10
1398	5	5			5	5
1400	5	4			5	4
1402	4	4			4	4
1403	4	3			4	3

an almost six-fold increase in derelictions from the period 1288 to 1339.[102]

Although this unprecedented rise in derelictions during the second half of the fourteenth century probably owed something to labour stringencies resulting from the decline in population at the time, it just as likely owed something to a lack of interest by the peasants in demesne cultivation and manorial production. It is significant, for example, that the families most frequently found neglecting their work obligations were also to be found among the more frequent trespassers. Thus, the Beaumeyses, who were responsible for three trespasses at least, were involved in 17 work derelictions, while the Hunnes, with nine derelictions, the Hamonds with five, the Scharps with five, the Brayns with 13, the Scots with 14, the Carteres with seven, the AtteWelles with eight, the Hemyngtons with nine, the Nicholases with 10, the Asplonds with 10 and the Lanes with five were all families involved in five or more trespasses over the same period.

Throughout, the picture presents itself of a large body of peasants — including the bulk of the major families in the village — for whom the pursuit of private interests was assuming a paramount place in their activities, and for whom the preservation of a tightly cohesive village community was becoming more and more a matter of secondary importance. This does not necessarily mean that it was an irresponsible peasantry. A sense of responsibility still remained — as witnessed by the continued service of major peasant families in important village offices — but the sense of responsibility was growing more limited in its application.[103] Nor was it necessarily a rebellious or angry peasantry.[104] Although

[102] It is interesting to note the nature of some of the derelictions. The rolls did not always bother to describe them, normally employing the rather uncommunicative formula "non venit ad opus domini quando summonitus fuit", but in a few cases more precise detail was given. Thus, in 1353 there were eight failures to attend the *precaria*. In 1359, there were four instances of failure to plough and six cases of being late to work ("tarde venit ad opus"). Failures to plough accounted for two derelictions in 1364, while in 1372 there were 21 cases of bad collection of the lord's grain ("male collectavit bladum"). There were 12 failures to attend the *precaria* in 1378, and in 1386 23 derelictions involved failure to mow, one was a failure to plough, and five cases concerned withdrawal of suit to the lord's mill. Finally, in 1396 failure to mow accounted for nine derelictions.

In addition, even though poor performance of work could involve damaging behaviour — such as ploughing up the king's road or neighboring villeins' properties — it could also refer to a half-hearted or only partial fulfilment of an obligation. Thus, John Hamond was fined 40d. in 1359 because he had withdrawn three acres from his ploughing for two years ("De Johanni Haliwell quia subtraxit arrurae iij acras terre per duos annos ..." BM.Add.Roll. 39583.).

[103] An illustration of this is provided by the paradoxical situation wherein major families undertook important offices in the village and manor and yet, at the same time, were themselves the persons most responsible for violating the regulations such offices were designed to enforce.

[104] Cf. R. H. Hilton, "Peasant Movements in England before 1381." *Economic History Review*, 2nd. series, II (No. 2, 1949), pp. 117-36.

its neglect of work obligations was certainly not in the lord's interest, the victims of the numerous trespasses were neighboring villagers as much as the lord Yet, despite such differences, enough confidence still remained in the major families to regularly choose them to hold positions of authority in the community. In short, despite changes in intra-village relationships and the increased devotion of energies to the prosecution of private goals and enterprises to the frequent disregard of village cohesion, the village life and institutions of Holywell-cum-Needingworth did not "fall apart at the seams". This is perhaps best reflected in the fact that no especially highly-charged atmosphere of violence gripped the community — as occurred, for example, in another Ramsey village to the north: Upwood.[105] This is not to say that the village was remarkably peaceful in the years after the middle of the fourteenth century. Between 1353 and 1455, for example, there were recorded (in a total of 18 years) 75 cases of violent conflicts between Holywell peasants. The period of greatest tension was the 1350's, with 31 cases — ranging from the raising of the hue and cry (19), to assaults (five), attacks on officials in the course of "rescuing" distrained properties (five) and breaking and entering (hamsok) (two) — recorded in but three years: 1353, 1356 and 1359. (See Table VI). However, with the exception of the particularly tense 1350's, the overall climate of violence from the middle of the fourteenth to the middle of the fifteenth century was not significantly different from what it had been from the late thirteenth to the mid-fourteenth century,[106] when 77 acts were reported for 15 years between 1288 and 1339. (See Table VI). Indeed, about the only types of acts which had increased from the earlier period were breaking and entering and rescue. Assaults and instances of the hue and cry had apparently even decreased from the middle of the fourteenth century. On the other hand, the most significant change lay both in the persons responsible for the violence and in those who were its victims. In 15 years between 1288 and 1339, 25 members of 16 major families had been responsible for 37 of 77 acts, with 16 transients or outsiders guilty of an additional 23 acts. Thirteen members of lesser and minor families had been responsible for only nine acts. In addition, members of major families had been the victims of 31 acts — 17 of which were committed against them by members of other major families. Minor families had been the object of 27 acts, almost half (13) again committed by major family members. Lesser families and transients, for their part, were subjected to only 14 of the known acts.

---

[105] See Raftis, "Changes in an English Village after the Black Death." *Mediaeval Studies*, **XXIX** (1967), pp. 164-65.

[106] Indeed, the greatest concentration of violence was confined to the fourteenth century. After 1400, the recorded number of such clashes reduced sharply. See Table VI.

TABLE VI

INCIDENCE OF VIOLENCE IN HOLYWELL-CUM-NEEDINGWORTH, 1288-1455

Year	Ofense	Number
1288	insult	4
	assault	1
	hue & cry	2
1292	rescue	1
	hamsok'	1
	assault	2
	hue & cry	1
1294	hue & cry	1
1299	assault	4
	hue & cry	2
1301	assault	4
	hue & cry	1
1306	assault	2
	insult	1
	hue & cry	4
1307	assault	1
	hue & cry	3
1311	hamsok'	1
	assault	1
	hue & cry	4
1313	assault	1
	hue & cry	4
1318	defamation	1
	assault	2
	hue & cry	5
1322	assault	2
	hue & cry	3
1328	assault	1
	hue & cry	4
1332	hamsok'	1
	hue & cry	3
1338	assault	2
	hamsok'	2
	hue & cry	1
1339	hue & cry	4
1353	assault	3
	hue & cry	2
	rescue	1
1356	assault	2
	hue & cry	11

TOTALS: 1288-1339

assault	23
defamation	1
hamsok'	5
hue & cry	42
insult	5
rescue	1
	77

YEAR	OFFENSE	NUMBER			
	rescue	4	TOTALS: 1353-1455		
1359	hamsok'	2		assault	13
	hue & cry	6		insult	2
1372	hue & cry	3		distur'ɔ	
	rescue	4		peace	1
1375	hue & cry	2		contempt	1
	rescue	1		hamsok'	8
1378	hue & cry	1		hue & cry	34
1386	assault	3		rescue	16
	hamsok	1			75
	hue & cry	2			
1391	assault	1			
	hamsok'	1			
	hue & cry	3			
1394	disturb				
	peace	1			
	hamsok'	1			
	hue & cry	2			
1396	hue & cry	1			
	rescue	1			
1400	contempt	1			
1403	hue & cry	1			
1413	rescue	1			
1419	assault	1			
1423	hamsok'	1			
1432	assault	2			
	hamsok'	2			
1452	assault	1			
	insult	2			
1455	rescue	4			

After 1350, however, a new distribution of violence prevailed. Fifty-five of the known 75 acts were committed by 38 members of 22 major families, while transients or outsiders were guilty of only 10. Members of major families were again the victims of most of the acts — 40 — but now 32 were committed by members of other major families, or 80% — as contrasted to 50% in the earlier period. The point to be made is that if the sheer amount of violence in the overall period had not changed radically from the first half of the century, its direction had, becoming all but exclusively characteristic of major village families. It was not, however, an especially purposeful violence — examples of continuing feuds or vendettas between specific families, for example, were not in evidence.[107]

[107] For the incidence of feuds in Upwood, however, see Raftis,"Changes in an English Village ...," *Mediaeval Studies*, XXIX, p. 165.

Rather, it was an almost indiscriminate violence — though predominantly within major families — but it nevertheless reflected an increased degree of tension and conflict of interests between such families as well as indicating a greater readiness on their part to settle conflicts quickly, directly — and forcefully — rather than by more peaceful and more formal, court-related measures. As such, it mirrored — as did the heightened incidence of trespassing and disregard of manorial commitments — the weakening of the cooperative and inter-dependent nature of the village experience, as did, further, the sudden appearance of requests for the court to determine the "metes and bounds" between the properties of individual peasants,[108] as well as — by the 1450's — the increasing failure of persons of the full legal age of 12 to place themselves in tithing groups.[109]

In short, from the middle of the fourteenth century, Holywell-cum-Needingworth was undergoing a profound alteration in the nature of the relationships of its members to the manor, to the institution of the village and to each other. Promoted by the shocks of plague, the steadily decreasing concentration of population in the community, the increased incidence of outsiders wandering in and out of the village for various economic purposes, and the changing nature of the tenurial policies of the manor and the growth of a more distinctly exploitational and pastoral economy among major families, the old cohesiveness and deeply inter-personal and inter-dependent aspect of village life was fading, as private and independent interests and activities took precedence over those of groups. To be sure, the village did not collapse; confusion and anarchy did not prevail. But neither did any special degree of harmony. Something

---

[108] In 11 years between 1356 and 1457, there were 14 such requests made — not a suffocating number, to be sure, but significant when it is realized that there had been no record of such cases in 15 years between 1288 and 1339. Thus, in 1356, there were two (John Hamond and Andrew Godeman, Walter Beaumeys and Letitia Laweman), one in 1359 (John Laweman and Andrew Godeman), two in 1375 (John Fannell and John Porter, John Sande and Elena Shepperd), two in 1391 (Richard Scharp and Thomas Deye, John Newerk and John Deye), one in 1396 (Thomas Scot and John Asplond Sr.), one in 1403 (Richard Sewale and John Hunne), one in 1405 (John Baroun and Henry Kyng), one in 1419 (Thomas Merale), one in 1430 (Thomas Valentyne and Richard Edward), one in 1437 (John Elyot and William Palfreyman), and one in 1457 (John Bry and John Baker). Significantly, perhaps, eight of the requests were between major families, while 20 of the 26 persons involved were members of major families.

[109] In 15 years between 1288 and 1339, there had been a total of only eight cases of persons being *extra decenna*, with no more than two in a year (1288 and 1306). In 1455 and 1457, however, a combined total of 14 persons were described as being 12 years of age or older and not yet in tithing. In 1455, six were so designated, two of them transients but four from resident families (John Shepperd, Thomas Martyn, William Baker and John Cristemesse). BM.Add.Roll. 34322. In 1457, eight men were out of tithing — four transients, and four members of local families (John Kyng, Roger Arnold, John Tayllour, and John Touslond Jr.).

was missing from the picture after the 1350's that had been very much in evidence before. It was a kind of commitment — almost a "family" commitment — to the community as a whole, where the individual members of the society were bound together by several and far-reaching ties of responsibility which they strove to honour. From the middle of the fourteenth century, that commitment steadily weakened — just as the commitment of individual peasants to their own families with regard to tenurial practices weakened. Nor can the coincidence of this social development with the decay and eventual death of the old demesne-oriented manorial economy be disregarded, for as the demesne economy lost its vitality and slipped into its grave, so too did the old village organization. The stagnation and then collapse of the demesne economy brought forth a different economic life for the peasant — dominated by impermanent tenurial commitments and the ready exploitation of properties for quick profit — and the fading away of the old, manor-related village organization brought forth an equally different type of society, where behavior was strikingly particularistic, independent and even impersonal.[110] Again, the peasant of Holywell-cum-Needingworth had displayed his essential pragmatism and skill at the art of survival in abandoning institutions and patterns of behavior no longer practical in the new light of a different day.[111]

---

[110] For an early appreciation of these changes in rural society (especially from the fifteenth century) but associated more strongly with the development of a capitalist spirit, see R. H. Tawney, *The Agrarian Problem in the Sixteenth Century.*

[111] It could be suggested that one possible way of looking at the changes in Holywell society from the late fourteenth century is in terms of, again, the merging yeoman or "proto-yeoman" group, whose interests were so powerfully identified with deriving profit from the exploitation of property that other considerations tended to become secondary. Tawney, for one, hinted at such a situation in his study of sixteenth-century rural conditions (*The Agrarian Problem* ...). In Holywell, perhaps one of the more striking examples of this is afforded by the person of Simon Dallyng, rector of the parish church from 1423 through 1461 and Doctor of Canon Law at Cambridge. At no time during his rectorship did he appear in any known record as an especially ecclesiastical figure. (His Mastership of Trinity Hall, Cambridge, 1441-53, does not necessarily indicate any special spiritual zeal.) Rather, his activities were exclusively land-and-profit dominated, whether in his frequent taking up of properties from the 1430's through the 1450's to his serving as manorial *firmarius* in both 1449 and 1451. In addition, he was one of the more frequent trespassers and violaters of pasturing by-laws in the 1450's. In short, what the student appears to have in Simon Dallyng is an example of a man whose primary concerns were economic, with both his ecclesiastical and community commitments taking a secondary place in his actions. Dallyng was more a yeoman than priest, more a profiteer than villager, and perhaps of equal interest is the fact that when he resigned the rectorship in 1461, he was replaced — through his own recommendation — by another member of his family: William Dallyng, also a Doctor of Canon Law, who in turn served as *firmarius* of the manor as well as rector of the church in the last half of the century.

EPILOGUE

THE foregoing study of the peasant society of Holywell-cum-Needing-worth from the late thirteenth to the middle of the fifteenth century, although revealing various aspects of local patterns of tenure, settlement, the exercise of official responsibility and cooperative and inter-personal relationships among villagers, has wider implications for the student of mediaeval rural England than the simple disclosure of facts about one single midlands community in the late Middle Ages would indicate. As useful as observations on Holywell's peasant behavior are for contributing to the general knowledge and understanding of the mediaeval English peasant and village community, of equal significance is the light this study casts on the very real need — if the nature of mediaeval rural society is to be ever adequately comprehended — for a serious reappraisal of the historiography of that society. The first step in such a reappraisal would involve the recognition of the existence of a peasant society itself as a very real and potent entity in the countryside. This fact has already been stressed, first by Professor Homans and, lately, by Professor Raftis, and it has been reinforced by the present study, where the inadequacy — and even the inapplicability — of such terms as "manorial society" and "manorial economy" to the peasant experience are displayed in the existence in the village of families and individuals having little or no formal connection with the manor and whose economic life centred not on customary tenements or manorial occupations but arose from crafts or services — in short, from the needs of their neighbors. Indeed, if "manorial society" is to have any meaning at all, it is best restricted to a description of but one aspect of the peasant experience: to those persons actually committed and formally related to the manor, and to the nature of those commitments and relationships. Further, by eschewing — or at least severely limiting — the application of such a concept as "manorial society", other aspects of peasant society — indeed, of peasant culture — are given the opportunity to reveal themselves more fully, while other concepts long associated with the peasant begin to lose significance. Among the former is the role exercised by custom within the society. Traditionally associated with the "custom of the manor" (*consuetudo manerii*), as, in effect, emanating from the manor, recent investigations — particularly those of Professor Raftis who continues the exploration of trails blazed open earlier by Homans — have indicated the broad degree to which custom permeated peasant life, from the governing of tenurial practices, familial maintenance rights and even village administration to the regulation of inter-personal relationships within the community,[1] and thereby pointed to the likelihood of the roots of custom being much deeper than the institution of the manor; in short, of custom and customary law as emanating from within the peasant society itself, necessitating the adjustment of the manor to it, rather than as a system imposed from outside. On the other hand, among concepts long associated with peasant life, one that weakens in the face of such a study as the present one is that of the peasantry as being especially dependent on the manor for a livelihood and even for a definite identity. Such a description has become almost classic — it is virtually a textbook commonplace — and yet the Holywell evidence, for one, demands that it be subjected to closer scrutiny, especially in the light again of those villagers living, working and surviving with little or no connection with the manor and whose movements to and from the village were not even kept under surveillance. As for identity, it seems likely that personal importance and even status could arise from within the context of the village — from economic institutions and relationships, the customary law and the identification with official responsibilities within the society — as readily as it could arise from direct relationship with the manor.

Yet another concept frequently used by students that the Holywell evidence indicates is in need of reconsideration is that of the mediaeval village and manor complex as a virtually self-contained and self-sufficient unit.[2] The study of Holywell-cum-Needingworth revealed a regional aspect to peasant life, even to indicating regional dimensions to peasant economy. This can be found, first, in the mobility displayed by local peasants — either permanent or temporary in nature — and in the incessant influx of transients to the village and the presence of outsiders — residents of nearby and distant villages — having economic interests in Holywell or even being "imported" as officials, as in the case of John Bigge, reeve in 1346/47, as well as in those Holywell villagers engaged in occupations or holding land away from home, especially in St. Ives. Faced with such

---

[1] See *Tenure and Mobility*, Part I(Chapters I-III), Part II, Chapter V. For an earlier appreciation of the role of custom in peasant society, see Homans, *English Villagers of the Thirteenth Century*, while an even earlier but nevertheless valuable estimate of the place of custom — or customary law — in the mediaeval English countryside can be found in F. I. Schechter, "Popular Law and Common Law in Medieval England," *Columbia Law Review*, XXVIII (1925), pp. 269-99.

[2] The description of Cuxham by P. D. A. Harvey as a "single and complete economic unit and social community" (p. 9) may be cited, for example.

evidence of a mobile population with economic and even familial connections and interests scattered outside the boundaries of the village,
it becomes increasingly more difficult to view such a community as a
self-contained and self-sufficient unit.

But perhaps the most significant way in which a study of the Holywell
peasant society and experience raises doubts about the adequacy of more
traditional concepts and terms applied to rural life is in the question
of "subsistence" or the conditions normally considered as prerequisites
for a subsistence economy. By current definitions, the Holywell peasantry,
being modestly supplied with land, should have displayed signs of bare
subsistence living. Yet, on close examination, survival patterns and prosperity levels of the majority of individuals and families revealed a population largely living above — and in many cases well above — a subsistence
level, while even close examination of concentrations of personal movables
in the early fourteenth century and patterns of land exploitation from the
end of the fourteenth century further point to a peasantry many of whose
members were operating on liquid capital resources, as distinct from
fixed capital, such as land. It remains to be seen if peasants in other villages
of mediaeval England displayed the same features, or if Holywell was
in some way unique, but nevertheless the question still remains if the
student can readily assume that subsistence or prosperity did in fact strongly
depend on specific acreage quotas and on highly theoretical and speculative
estimates about the annual intake needs of some abstracted "typical"
or "average" peasant's stomach.

To summarize, then: if the student of Holywell approaches the village
as a "manorial society" he quickly finds a large number of people living,
working and contributing to the overall fabric of local life who are but
remotely connected — if at all — with the manor, while he discovers
aspects of peasant culture — of suretyship and contractual relationships,
for example, or private economic practices — that have virtually nothing
to do with the manor. Again, if he approaches the peasantry as especially
dependent on the manor, he finds a large body of locals — as well as
a continuing flow of transients — who function quite independently of
the manor, while even among those peasants definitely committed to
the manor, he is presented with evidence of economic and personal relationships and activities that transcend that manorial commitment. Further,
if he approaches the local community as a self-contained and self-sufficient
economic and social unit, he again is soon faced with contradictory evidence
of frequent outside interests and contacts and regular mobility among
the peasants under investigation, while finally, if he comes to his subject
as exemplifying a subsistent peasantry, he is met with a population a

great number of whom are more than subsisting. Faced with such evidence, the student is forced to admit the inadequacy or inapplicability of several traditional concepts or approaches to the peasant or at least to have second thoughts as to their value. Consequently, he must simply try, as best he can, to set aside his preconceptions and attempt to center his attention around the individual peasant — a process which, as already indicated, is now capable of better realization through the use of local court rolls — and, out of the sometimes overwhelming mass of specific and personal details obtainable for individual peasants, bring some order out of the resulting jumble of facts by searching out common patterns of behavior and experience in an attempt to discover how different institutions entered into the life of the peasant, instead of questioning how the peasant fit into the structure of outside institutions. It is admittedly a fine distinction, for it is often the result of turning older historiographical questions inside-out. Thus, instead of asking: "What place does the peasant occupy in the manor?", the student asks: "What place does the manor occupy in the life and experience of the peasant"? Instead of asking: "What place does the peasant have in the legal system?", he inquires: "What place does the legal system have in the life of the peasant"? He does not ask: "Do these peasants have 15 acres or 30 acres of land so that they are subsisting or prospering?" but rather: "Are these peasants surviving, to what extent, and how are they doing it"? Such, at least, has been the approach directing the present study — to view the local community with the peasant himself as the focal point, and, where possible, to allow the sources to suggest questions and guide research. Hence the large amount of information of land-holding in surviving records dictated an investigation of tenure. The abundance of personal names — and personal details for individual behavior[3] — prompted inquiry into demo-

---

[3] Special note should be made here of the possible difficulties inherent in the mass of personal details to be gleaned from court roll sources. Admittedly, the presentation of all the specific *minutiae* on individual peasants would result in a chaotic and confusing welter of isolated facts. But, despite their magnitude, they are welcomed by the investigator as meaningful parts in the jig-saw puzzle of peasant society, since they are records of individual acts and activities. In reconstructing a view of society — of a human community — they are as necessary as the thousands of isolated notations of prices for corn or inventories of livestock found in account rolls are for the reconstruction of mediaeval economic trends. The challenge to the student is to utilize such details meaningfully — just as the economist. Thus, to simply state that John X was a juror in 1300 and Thomas Y was a juror in 1301 is largely meaningless — just as stating that manor A had four pigs in 1300 and manor B had six pigs in 1301 is without value. But to inquire how often John X and Thomas Y were jurors, how often they held other offices, what their economic background was, what place in village life they regularly assumed and what other persons func-

graphic trends, patterns of office-holding and inter-personal relationships. In the process, there emerged — in addition to the raising of doubts as to the adequacy of the traditional historiographical concepts of rural social life outlined above — evidence of other phenomena that offer avenues for further — and more broadly-based and comparative — research,[4] as well as a growing realization of the possibilities for future study of exploiting the concepts and methods of the social scientist. Thus, study of the village community of Holywell-cum-Needingworth results in a greater awareness of the place and role of groups in the society. In addition, the groups emerging in mediaeval Holywell are not unlike the groups found to be characteristic of contemporary primitive or peasant societies by the social scientist. Thus, there may be seen some indications of what the social scientist calls "corporate groups"[5] in bodies of tenants, tithings and village officials — and even ale-brewers — groups whose place and role in the society remain in clear definition despite a continually-changing personnel. Furthermore, there is an emphasis in the society on the nuclear family[6] — husband, wife and children — and an apparent de-emphasis of the broader kinship group — or extended family — in the absence of distinct clan activities and orientations; itself a point requiring more intensive investigation in other communities, since the stress on the nuclear family

tioned in a similar manner and then to compare and constrast individuals in the context of the governmental and administrative structure of a community is to build up a picture of local re-ponsibility from a foundation of isolated personal details, much as the economist, by tabulating the number of livestock from manor to manor, year to year, and by comparison and contrast of such figures within a bloc of manors, builds up a picture of economic trends and programs.

[4] Specifically, the Holywell study is not an uniquely isolated investigation. The sheer bulk of court rolls on deposit in the Public Record Office, the British Museum and in local English archives makes possible similar — and even deeper — studies into many mediaeval village communities. No attempt can be made here to list the court rolls presently available, but a perusal of the court roll volume of *Lists and Indexes of the Public Record Office* and the catalogue of Additional Charters and Manuscripts of the British Museum will give a rough picture, while Professor J. A. Raftis is currently engaged in a project designed to record the availability of court rolls in local and semi-private collections throughout England. Eventually, the possibility of specific compa-rative studies of village communities will even be realized, as more individual local studies are made. Professor Raftis has recently made advances in this direction in his "Social Structures in Five East Midland Villages" and "The Concentration of Responsibility in Five Villages", while already in progress — or completed — are local investigations of the Ramsey vills of King's Ripton by Anne Reiber DeWindt (Toronto), Burwell and Wistow by Miss M. Patricia Hogan (Toronto) and St. Ives by Miss Ellen Wedemeyer (Toronto).

[5] See Robert Redfield, *The Little Community*, pp. 36-37.

[6] For discussion of the nuclear family concept in terms of contemporary social anthropology, see Eric Wolf, *Peasants* (Engelwood, New Jersey, 1966), pp. 61-73, and Redfield, *The Little Community*, p. 38.

is not normally associated with the mediaeval experience, although, as Eric Wolf has pointed out, the nuclear family tends to assume major importance in societies characterized by an accentuation of the division of labour,[7] and this aspect of division of labour — and even specialization — can be found developed in the Holywell society, as indeed it can be found throughout various mediaeval societal levels. The differentiation in roles is an example of this: in the village official, the day-labourer, the domestic servant, the several craft, trade or service personnel, the *famulus* and the direct cultivator.

Again, within the deeper fabric of the peasant society itself, the presence of an "elite" body of villagers was evidenced in the examples of individuals and families assuming, exercising and maintaining a position of pre-eminence in the economic, governmental and administrative life of the community, while there also emerge networks of relationships — long familiar to the student of contemporary peasant or primitive societies — of what may be called "office-holder and constituency" and "artisan and customer-client"[8] as well as further relationships of sponsorship (pledge and pledged), (lender and borrower). Indeed, Holywell alone provides examples of several categories of inter-personal relationships — or "coalitions", as Eric Wolf has termed them — both horizontal (between locals and outsiders and especially evidenced in land transactions but also in relationships of sponsorship) and vertical (between peasants within the community, whether in terms of land transfers, suretyship, contracts, joint working arrangements, or employment and services).[9]

Indeed, even in the doubts the study of Holywell casts on the adequacy of the notion of peasant dependence on the manor, there arises the possibility of recognizing and investigating — in other villages supplied with fuller records — a more fundamental and intra-societal dependence: of the village community, in short, as a kind of ecological system, comprising several inter-locking or inter-dependent networks of economic, service and personal relationships.[10] Finally, the reality of a peasant and village economy — in contrast to a manorial economy — is equally emphasized

[7] *Peasants*, p. 72.

[8] *The Little Community*, p. 39.

[9] See Wolf, pp. 81-95, for a discussion of the concept of coalitions among peasants in the context of contemporary anthropology.

[10] For example, the ties of dependence between the peasant and land or other economic activities for an income; the dependence of village economy itself on the needs of other peasants; the dependence of villagers on each other for suretyship, and the governmental and service responsibilities of particular groups of peasants creating additional ties of social dependence throughout the community.

through the evidence of local land markets, contractual relationships — especially involving debts — indications of liquid capital resources and the practice of crafts, trades and services, although the Holywell information is not rich enough to permit a close analysis of its component parts. These are all areas of possible future investigation — given the prevalence of court roll sources for mediaeval England and the continuing development and refinement of techniques for exploiting such a source — and it may be advanced that such future investigation requires a more sensitive approach by the historian to the labours of the social scientist, and, especially, of the social anthropologist, since it is the social scientist who has long been intimately engaged with examining — in the context of contemporary peasant and primitive societies — questions and phenomena now beginning to emerge within the context of the mediaeval rural community. Nor is it heresy for the historian to recognize this parallel and be willing to take advantage of the work of the social scientist in attempting to realize the goal of understanding past societies and cultures and apprehending the nature and significance of past human experiences. It does not necessitate the historian's betrayal of his profession; rather it may be the next step in the expansion and refinement of his discipline, another stage of cooperation that has already been preceded by advantageous dialogues between the historian and the lawyer, the economist and the poet. That it is a step that cannot be arbitrarily ignored or rejected is evidenced both by recent studies of mediaeval society — including the present one — and the investigations of social scientists into contemporary societies and communities. If Homans and Raftis were acutely aware of the important place of custom in mediaeval English peasant life and Ruth Benedict disclosed a similar condition in primitive societies;[11] if the present study of Holywell points to close connections between land tenure and social importance in a mediaeval peasant community and G. A. Holmes' examination of the higher nobility in the fourteenth century reveals equally strong ties between land and political power and E. R. Leach demonstrates the importance of land tenure to the peasants of a contemporary village in Ceylon;[12] if Sylvia Thrupp can delineate the behavior patterns of mediaeval London merchants relative to their colleagues and neighbors and their attitudes towards education and religion and Raymond Firth examines the elements of social structures themselves;[13] if F. R. H. DuBoulay can

---

[11] See *Patterns of Culture*.

[12] See *Pul Eliya, A Village in Ceylon: A Study of Land Tenure and Kinship* (Cambridge, 1961).

[13] *The Merchant Class of Medieval London* (Ann Arbor, 1962) and *Elements of Social Organization* (London, 1951).

indicate the regional and many-faceted character of peasant experience on Canterbury estates in the High and Late Middle Ages and Robert Redfield can speak of the contemporary "little community" as an ecological system and a "community within communities";[14] then the time is at hand for a greater willingness on the part of the historian and social scientist to contribute to and learn from each other's disciplines. This does not mean that the day will come when Evans-Pritchard's vision of the metamorphosis of the social anthropologist into the historian, and *vice versa*, will be realized.[15] Indeed, it may be argued that that day need never come, that each discipline still has its own unique function and integrity. But a closer cooperation between the two is at least indicated. It is, in the final analysis, a question of the need of the historian to avail himself of the tools best suited to enable him to comprehend his chosen subject, and, for the student of mediaeval peasant societies the failure of traditional economic and law-oriented historiography to provide concepts and techniques adequate for dealing with the emerging realities of mediaeval peasant life requires that he give closer consideration to the social scientist. What is at stake is the historical understanding of the human dimensions and parts of the peasant experience, and although the mediaeval peasant has been waiting many centuries to be heard, it may be asked: How much longer must he wait?

[14] *The Lordship of Canterbury,* and *The Little Community.*
[15] *Essays in Social Anthropology* (The Free Press of Glencoe, 1963).

BIBLIOGRAPHY

MANUSCRIPT SOURCES

London: British Museum.
Cellarers' Rolls,
Receipt Rolls,
Miscellaneous

Compotus Rolls: Additional Rolls (BM.Add.Roll)
34486 (1358-59)
34487 (1359-60)
34640 (1351)
34641 (1354)
34484 (1351-52)
39592 (1304-5)
34608 (1406)
34609 (1416)
34610 (1424)
34611 (1455)
39736 (1289)

Ramsey Papers Additional Manuscript (BM.Add.Ms)
33445 (Vol. I, 1350-53)
33446 (Vol. II, 1361-62)
33447 (Vol. III, 1389-1508)
33448 (Vol. IV, 1389-1508)

Receipt Rolls: Additional Rolls (BM.Add.Roll)
34353 (1415-16)
34710 (1280)
34711 (1284)
39720 (1362)
39719 (1360)

Charters: Additional Charters (BM.Add.Ch)
33767

Court Rolls: Additional Rolls (BM.Add.Roll)
Broughton: 39471 (1351)
Holywell-cum-
Needingworth: 34337 (1292)
39597 (1294)
39583 (1359)
39860 (1364)
34778 (1386)
34817 (1398)
39480 (1430)
34322 (1455)

Court Book: Harleian Manuscript 445
Public Record Office:
Account Rolls: Series SC-6, Portfolio 877, Nos. 15-30
                                     Portfolio 878, Nos. 1-7
              877/15 (1307-8)
              877/17 (1323-24)
              877/18 (1346-47)
              877/19 (1355-56)
              877/20 (1362-63)
              877/21 (1370-71)
              877/22 (1391-92)
              877/23 (1396-97)
              877/24 (1399-1400)
              877/26 (1400-1401)
              877/27 (1401-1402)
              877/28 (1403-1404)
              877/29 (1404-1405)
              877/30 (1408-1409)
              878/1   (1409)
              878/2   (1412-13)
              878/3   (1413-14)
              878/4   (1415-16)
              878/5   (1417-18)
              878/6   (1449)
              878/7   (1451)

Court Rolls: Series Sc-2, Portfolio, 178, Nos. 94-101
                                     Portfolio 179, Nos. 5-67
      St. Ives: 178/94   (1275)
                      178/95   (1301-56)
                      178/96   (1286)
                      178/97   (1290)
                      178/98   (1292)
                      178/100 (1299)
                      178/101 (1301)

Hemmingford
    Abbots: 179/7   (1291)
Holywell-cum-
    Needingworth: 179/5   (1288)
                      179/10   (1299)
                      179/11   (1301)
                      179/12   (1306)
                      179/15   (1307)
                      179/16   (1311)
                      179/17   (1313)
                      179/18   (1318)
                      179/21   (1322)
                      179/22   (1326)
                      179/25   (1328)
                      179/26   (1332)

179/29 (1338)
179/30 (1339)
179/35 (1353)
179/35 (1354)
179/36 (1356)
179/38 (1369)
179/39 (1372)
179/40 (1375)
179/41 (1378)
179/42 (1389)
179/42 (1386)
179/43 (1391)
179/44 (1394)
179/44 (1396)
179/45 (1400)
179/47 (1402)
179/48 (1403)
179/49 (1405)
179/50 (1405)
179/52 (1409)
179/54 (1413)
179/56 (1419)
179/57 (1423)
179/59 (1428)
179/61 (1432)
179/63 (1437)
179/64 (1443)
179/66 (1452)
179/67 (1457)

Subsidy Rolls: Series E, Portfolio 179, Nos. 122-24
E.179/122 (1327)
179/124 (1332)

Hundred Roll: Series SC-12, Portfolio 8, No. 56
Cambridge:
Cambridge University Library.

Enclosure Map: "Holywell-cum-Needingworth in the County of Huntingdon."
No. 35 (1810)
Huntingdon:
Huntingdonshire County Record Office:

Map of Holywell-cum-Needingworth, 1764
Northampton:
Northamptonshire Record Office.

Leger Book 301 (Le Moigne Papers)
Norwich:
Norwich Public Library.

Ramsey Register

Primary Sources (Edited)

Calender of the Close Rolls preserved in the Public Record Office. London, 1898 *et seq.*

Calender of the Feet of Fines Relating to the County of Huntingdon. Ed. G. J. Turner. Cambridge, 1913.

Calender of the Patent Rolls preserved in the Public Record Office. London 1894 *et seq.*

Carte Nativorum: A Peterborough Abbey Cartulary of the 14th Century. Ed. C. N. L. Brooke and M. M. Postan. Northamptonshire Record Society XX (1950).

Cartularium Monasterii de Rameseia. Ed. W. H. Hart and P. A. Lyons. 3 vols. Rolls Series 79. London, 1893.

Chronicon Abbatiae Rameseiensis a saeculo X. usque ad annum circiter 1200. Ed. W. Dunn Macray. Rolls Series 83. London, 1886.

Court Baron, The. Ed. F. W. Maitland and N. P. Bouldon. Seldon Society IV. London.

Court Rolls of the Abbey of Ramsey and of the Honor of Clare. Ed. W. O. Ault. New Haven, 1928.

Descriptive Catalogue of Ancient Deeds in the Public Record Office, A. 4 vols. London, 1890-1902.

Injunctions and other Documents from the Registers of Richard Flemyng and William Gray, Bishops of Lincoln (1420-36). Ed. A. H. Thompson. London: Canterbury and York Society, XVII, 1915.

Inquisitions and Assessments Relating to Feudal Aids with other analogous documents preserved in the Public Record Office, 1284-1431. 2 vols. London, 1900 *et seq.*

Monasticon Anglicanum. Ed. W. Dugdale. 6 vols. London, 1817-30.

Regesta Regum Anglo-Normannorum, 1066-1154. Ed. H. W. C. Davis, Charles Johnson, H. A. Cronne. 2 vols. Oxford, 1956.

Rotuli Hundredorum tempore Henrici III et Edwardi I. Ed. W. Illingworth and J. Caley. 2 vols. London: Record Commission, 1818.

Monographs and Articles

Ault, W. O. *Open-Field Husbandry and the Village Community*. Transactions of the American Philosophical Society: Philadelphia, 1965.

—. *Private Jurisdiction in England*. New Haven, 1923.

Bean, J. M. W. "Plague, Population and Economic Decline in the later Middle Ages." *Economic History Review*. 2nd series. XV, 1963.

Bennett, H. S. *Life on the English Manor*. Cambridge, 1937.

Beresford, M. W. *The Lost Villages of England*. Lutterworth, 1954.

Beveridge, W. H. "The Yield and Price of Corn in the Middle Ages." *Essays in Economic History*. Ed. E. Carus-Wilson.

Bridbury, A. R. *Economic Growth: England in the Later Middle Ages*. London, 1962.

Cam, Helen M. *Liberties and Communities in Medieval England*. New York, 1963.

—."Studies in the Hundred Rolls." *Oxford Studies in Social and Legal History*. Ed. Paul Vinogradoff. XI. Oxford, 1921.

Cambridge Economic History of Europe. Vol. I: "The Agrarian Life of the Middle Ages." 2nd ed. Ed. M. M. Postan. Cambridge, 1966.

Campbell, Mildred. *The English Yeoman under Elizabeth and the Early Stuarts*. London, 1960.

Chew, Helena M. *The English Ecclesiastical Tenants-in-Chief and Knight Service*. Oxford, 1932.

Darby, H. C. *The Domesday Geography of Eastern England.* Cambridge, 1952.
—. *The Medieval Fenland.* Cambridge, 1940.
Davenport, F. J. *The Economic Development of a Norfolk Manor.* Cambridge, 1906.
Denholm-Young, N. *Seignorial Administration in England.* London, 1937.
DuBoulay, F. R. H. *The Lordship of Canterbury.* New York, 1966.
Duby, Georges. *L'economie rurale et la vie des campagnes dans l'occident medieval: France, Angleterre, Empire IXe-XVe siecles.* 2 vols. Paris, 1962.
Emmett, Isabel. *A North Wales Village.* London, 1964.
Gras, N. S. B. and C. C. *The Economic and Social History of an English Village.* Cambridge, Massachussetts, 1930.
Gray, H. L. *The English Field Systems.* Cambridge, Mass., 1915.
Hallam, H. E. "Population Density in Medieval Fenland." *Economic History Review.* 2nd series. XIV, 1961.
—. "Some Thirteenth-Century Censuses." *Economic History Review.* 2nd. series. X, 1958.
Harvey, P. D. A. *A Medieval Oxforshire Village: Cuxham, 1240 to 1400.* Oxford, 1965.
Helleiner, K. F. "Population Movement and Agrarian Depression in the Later Middle Ages." *Canadian Journal of Economics and Political Science,* XV, 1950.
Hewitt, H. J. *The Organization of War under Edward III, 1338-62.* Manchester, 1966.
Hilton, R. H. *The Economic Development of Some Leicestershire Estates in the Fourteenth and Fifteenth Centuries.* Oxford, 1947.
—. *Medieval Society, A.* London, 1967.
—. "Peasant Movements in England before 1381." *Economic History Review,* 2nd series. II, 1949.
Holmes, G. A. *The Estates of the Higher Nobility in Fourteenth-Century England.* Cambridge, 1957.
Homans, G. C. *English Villagers of the Thirteenth Century.* Boston, 1941.
Hoskins, W. G. *The Midland Peasant.* London, 1957.
—. *Provincial England.* London, 1963.
Huff, Darrell. *How to Lie with Statistics.* New York, 1954.
Hunnisett, R. F. *The Medieval Coroner.* Cambridge, 1961.
Introduction to English Historical Demography, An. Ed. E. A. Wrigley (Cambridge Group for the History of Population and Social Structures, Publication No. 1). London, 1966.
Jacob, E. F. *The Fifteenth Century.* Oxford, 1961.
Kosminsky, E. A. *Studies in the Agrarian History of England.* Oxford, 1956.
Krause, J. "The Medieval Household: Large or Small ?" *Economic History Review.* 2nd series, IX, 1956/57.
Latham, L. C. "The Manor and the Village." *Social Life in Early England.* Ed. G. Barraclough. Oxford, 1960.
Lennard, Reginald. "An Unidentified Twelfth-Century Customal of Lawshall (Suffolk)." *English Historical Review,* LI, 1936.
—. *Rural England, 1086-1135: A Study of Social and Agrarian Conditions.* Oxford, 1959.
Levett, A. E. *The Black Death on the Estates of the Bishopric of Winchester.* Oxford, 1916.
—. *Studies in Manorial History.* Ed. H. Cam, M. Coate, C. S. Sutherland. Oxford, 1938.

Littlejohn, James. *Westrigg: The Sociology of a Cheviot Parish*. London, 1963.

Maitland, F. W. *Domesday Book and Beyond*. Cambridge, 1909.

—. *Select Pleas in Manorial and other Seignorial Courts*. Seldon Society, II. London, 1889.

Mawer, A. and Stenton, F. M. *The Place-Names of Bedfordshire and Huntingdonshire*. English Place-Name Society, Vol. III. Cambridge, 1926.

McKisack, May. *The Fourteenth Century*. Oxford, 1959.

Morris, W. A. *The Frankpledge System*. Cambridge, Mass., 1910.

Myers, A. R. *England in the Late Middle Ages*. Baltimore, Penguin Books, 1961.

Neilson, Nellie. *Customary Rents*. Ofxord, 1910.

—. *Economic Conditions on the Manors of Ramsey Abbey*. Philadelphia, 1898.

Noonan, J. T. *Contraception*. Cambridge, Mass., 1967.

Pearce Higgins, A. G. McL. (Rev.). *A Short History of the Parish Church of Holywell-cum-Needingworth*. Cambridge and St. Ives, 1955.

Pollock, F. and Maitland, F. W. *History of English Law before the Time of Edward I*. 2nd ed. Cambridge, 1898.

Poole, Austin Lane. *Obligations of Society in the XII and XIII Centuries*. Oxford, 1947.

Postan, M. M. "The Famulus: the Estate Labourer in the Twelfth and Thirteenth Centuries." Supplement to the *Economic History Review*, No. 2, Cambridge, 1954.

—. "Some Economic Evidence of Declining Population in the later Middle Ages." *Economic History Review*, 2nd series. II, 1950.

—. and Titow, J. Z. "Heriots and Prices on Winchester Manors." *Economic History Review*, 2nd. series, XI, 1959.

Powicke, Michael R. "Edward II and Military Obligation." *Speculum*. XXXI, 1956.

Raftis, J. Ambrose. "Changes in an English Village after the Black Death." *Mediaeval Studies*, XXIX, 1967.

—. "The Concentration of Responsibility in Five Villages." *Mediaeval Studies*, XXVIII, 1966.

—. *The Estates of Ramsey Abbey: A Study in Economic Growth and Organization*. Toronto, 1957.

—. "Peasant Mobility and Freedom in Mediaeval England." *Report of the Canadian Historical Association*, 1965.

—. "Social Structures in Five East Midland Villages." *Economic History Review*. 2nd. series. XVIII, 1965.

—. *Tenure and Mobility: Studies in the Social History of the Mediaeval English Village*. Toronto, 1964.

—. "The Trend Towards Serfdom in Mediaeval England." *Report of the Canadian Catholic Historical Association*, 1956.

Reaney, P. H. *The Origin of English Surnames*. London, 1967.

Redfield, Robert. *The Little Community and Peasant Society and Culture*. Chicago: Phoenix Books, 1963.

Richardson, H. G. and Sayles, G. O. *The Governance of Mediaeval England from the Conquest to Magna Carta*. Edinburgh, 1963.

Russell, J. C. *British Medieval Population*. Albuquerque, 1948.

—. "Demographic Limitations of the Spalding Serf Lists." *Economic History Review*, 2nd series, XV, 1962/63.

—. "The Preplague Population of England." *The Journal of British Studies*, V, No. 2, 1966.

Schechter, F. I. "Popular Law and Common Law in Medieval England." *Columbia Law Review*. XXVIII, 1928.

Sheehan, Michael M. *The Will in Medieval England*. Toronto, 1963.

Slicher Van-Bath, B. H. *The Agrarian History of Western Europe, A.D. 500-1850*. New York, 1963.

Stacey, Margaret. *Tradition and Change: A Study of Bambury*. Oxford, 1960.

Tawney, R. H. *The Agrarian Problem of the Sixteenth Century*. New York, n.d.

Thirsk, Joan. "The Family". *Past and Present*, No. 27, 1964.

Thrupp, Sylvia L. *The Merchant Class of Medieval London*. Ann Arbor, 1962.

—. "The Problem of Replacement-Rates in Late Medieval English Population." *Economic History Review*. 2nd series. XVIII, 1965.

Titow, J. Z. *English Rural Society*, 1200-1350. London, 1969.

Trevelyan, G. M. *Illustrated English Social History*. Vol. I. London, 1954.

Victoria History of the Counties of England: Huntingdonshire. Ed. W. Page, G. Proby, 3 vols. London, 1926.

Vinogradoff, Paul. *English Society in the Eleventh Century*. Oxford, 1908.

—. *The Growth of the Manor*. 2nd ed., rev. London, 1911.

—. *Villainage in England*. Oxford, 1892.

Wake, Joan. "Communitas Villae." *English Historical Review*. XXXVII, 1922.

Welldon-Finn, R. *Introduction to Domesday Book, An*, London, 1963.

White, Lynn Jr. *Medieval Technology and Social Change*. Oxford, 1962.

Willard, J. F. *Parliamentary Taxes on Personal Property, 1290-1334*. Cambridge, Mass., 1934.

Williams, W. M. *A West Country Village, Ashworthy*. London, 1963.

Wolf, Eric R. *Peasants*. Engelwood Cliffs, New Jersey, 1966.

Wylie, Lawrence. *Village in the Vaucluse*. Cambridge, Mass., 1957.

INDEX *